SMYRNA, SEPTEMBER 1922

Also by Lou Ureneck

Backcast

Cabin

SMYRNA,
SEPTEMBER 1922

*The American Mission
to Rescue Victims of the
20th Century's First Genocide*

LOU URENECK

ecco
An Imprint of HarperCollinsPublishers

For Irene

HarperCollins books may be purchased for educational, business, or sales promotional use. For information please e-mail the Special Markets Department at SPsales@harpercollins.com.

A hardcover edition of this book was published under the title *The Great Fire* in 2015 by Ecco, an imprint of HarperCollins Publishers.

FIRST ECCO PAPERBACK EDITION PUBLISHED 2016.

Designed by Suet Yee Chong

Library of Congress Cataloging-in-Publication Data has been applied for.

ISBN 978-0-06-225989-9

HB 04.19.2024

Put me to doing, put me to suffering.
—*Methodist Prayer*

CONTENTS

—⊱✦ **PART THREE** ✦⊰—

CAST OF CHARACTERS

Rev. Asa K. Jennings
Architect of the rescue

Captain Arthur J. Hepburn
Naval Chief of Staff/
Constantinople

Lieutenant Commander
Halsey Powell
USS Edsall

George Horton
U.S. Consul General/Smyrna

Admiral Mark L. Bristol
U.S. High Commissioner/
Constantinople

Dr. Esther Pohl Lovejoy
Saving lives on the Smyrna Quay

LIEUTENANT COMMANDER
J. B. RHODES
As a young officer

GHAZI MUSTAPHA KEMAL
Supreme Turkish commander

LIEUTENANT AARON S. MERRILL
Navy Intelligence

CAPTAIN IOANNIS THEOPHANIDES
Conspires in rescue

This is a true story. In creating a narrative account of the events at Smyrna, I have drawn on the reports, letters, and diaries of U.S. naval officers, declassified American intelligence reports, and American and British diplomatic cables. I also have employed the first-person accounts of American missionaries and relief workers and British sailors and officers who witnessed the fire and its aftermath. It has been my good fortune to receive access to the personal papers and letters of key figures in the story—Asa Kent Jennings, Halsey Powell, Alexander MacLachlan, Caleb Lawrence, and George and Nancy Horton. Some of this material had not been previously available. The principal contribution of this book is the astonishing story of the American rescue at Smyrna based on the testimony of those who participated in it. For the broader context against which the forward story unfolds, including background on the Paris peace talks and their immediate aftermath, the discovery of oil in the Near East, the life of Mustapha Kemal, and the religious slaughter that swept Turkey in the early twentieth century, I have drawn on the work of numerous eminent scholars and experts including Michael Llewellyn-Smith, Richard Hovannisian, Daniel Yergin, and the late Andrew Mango, who generously responded to my questions in the final year of his life.

Some landscape and seascape descriptions in the book are mine based on numerous visits to key locations in the story. I have relied on contemporaneous newspaper accounts of the catastrophe at Smyrna when those accounts lined up with observations of others who were present.

For the towns and cities of the Ottoman Empire, I have used the names that would have been used by Americans in the story—Smyrna and Constantinople, for example, rather than the Turkish names Izmir and Istanbul. For the names of Turkish figures, I have chosen English spellings that seemed easiest for English speakers to pronounce. I have rendered Turkish words that have letters that do not appear in the English alphabet in ways that create similar sounds. For example the Turkish *paşa* appears as *pasha*. It is pronounced pash-AH.

I use the term "Near East" because it was the term used at the time of these events. The Near East included the Balkan countries and Greece, Asia Minor (meaning the Turkish peninsula between the Black and Mediterranean Seas, and otherwise known as Anatolia), Syria, Lebanon, and Palestine—the so-called Levant, the eastern rim of the Mediterranean down to Egypt. The Near East also embraced Persia and the Arabian Peninsula. The contemporary term "Middle East" came into general use after the events of this story. I use Turkey and the Ottoman Empire interchangeably as was common in the period. The Republic of Turkey came into existence in 1923.

At the time of these events, most Muslims in Turkey had one name; occasionally a second name was added. Names were typically accented on the final syllable: Must-ta-PHA Ke-MAL. Among the Turks, *bey* was an honorific meaning "sir." *Pasha* was a general or high-ranking statesman. *Efendi* was a title of respect for a man of high status or education. *Hanum* meant "lady" or "Madame."

In 1922, the ethnic Greeks of the Ottoman Empire used the Julian calendar; the Turks used the Islamic calendar; and the Europeans and Americans used the Gregorian calendar, which is the calendar used here.

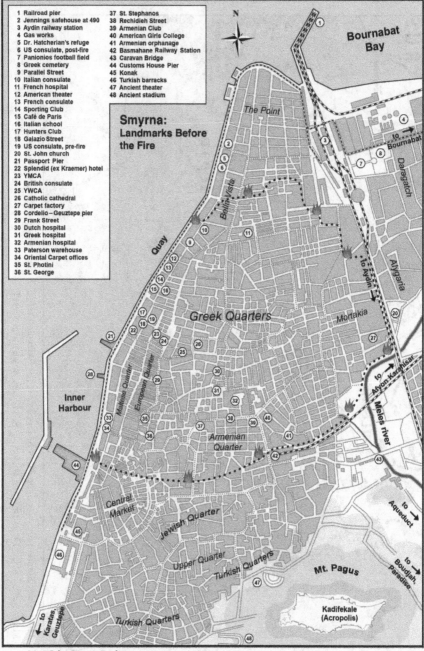

1 Railroad pier
2 Jennings safehouse at 490
3 Aydin railway station
4 Gas works
5 Dr. Hatcherian's refuge
6 US consulate, post-fire
7 Panionios football field
8 Greek cemetery
9 Parallel Street
10 Italian consulate
11 French hospital
12 American theater
13 French consulate
14 Sporting Club
15 Café de Paris
16 Italian school
17 Hunters Club
18 Galazio Street
19 US consulate, pre-fire
20 St. John church
21 Passport Pier
22 Splendid (ex Kraemer) hotel
23 YMCA
24 British consulate
25 YWCA
26 Catholic cathedral
27 Carpet factory
28 Cordelio – Geuztepe pier
29 Frank Street
30 Dutch hospital
31 Greek hospital
32 Armenian hospital
33 Paterson warehouse
34 Oriental Carpet offices
35 St. Photini
36 St. George
37 St. Stephanos
38 Rechidieh Street
39 Armenian Club
40 American Girls College
41 Armenian orphanage
42 Basmahane Railway Station
43 Caravan Bridge
44 Customs House Pier
45 Konak
46 Turkish barracks
47 Ancient theater
48 Ancient stadium

Smyrna:
Landmarks Before the Fire

Bournabat Bay

The Point

Belle Vista

Quay

to Bournabat

Daragatch

Aliyania

to Aydin

Greek Quarters

Mortakia

to Afion-Karahisar

Meles river

Inner Harbour

Maltese Quarter

European Quarter

Armenian Quarter

to Aqueduct

Central Market

Jewish Quarter

Upper Quarter

Turkish Quarters

Mt. Pagus

to Boudjah, Paradise

to Karatas, Geuztepe

Turkish Quarters

Kadifekale (Acropolis)

Map © by George Poulimenos

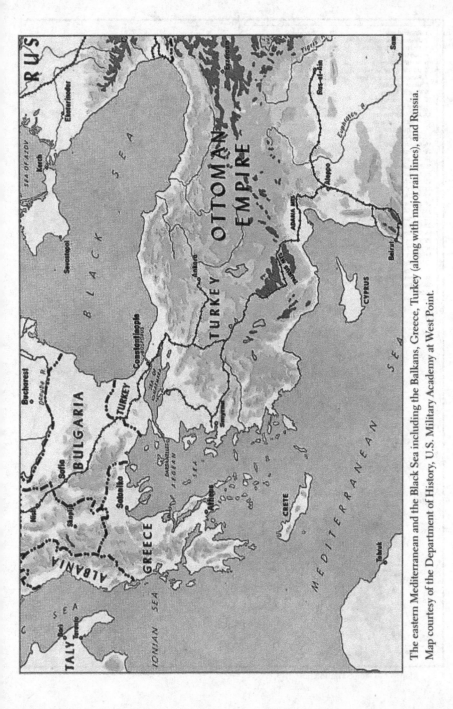

The eastern Mediterranean and the Black Sea including the Balkans, Greece, Turkey (along with major rail lines), and Russia. Map courtesy of the Department of History, U.S. Military Academy at West Point.

> Unreal City
> Under the brown fog of a winter noon
> Mr. Eugenides, the Smyrna merchant
> Unshaven, with a pocket full of currants
> C.i.f. London: documents at sight,
> Asked me in demotic French
> To luncheon at the Cannon Street Hotel
> Followed by a weekend at the Metropole.
> —T. S. Eliot, *The Waste Land* (1922), lines 207–214

These lines follow an evocation of the rape of Philomela; and the speaker is the blind, hermaphroditic seer Teiresias of Thebes, old and barren, once a figure of Sophoclean tragedy, now a degraded male prostitute invited to a sordid assignation with another Greek. But the contempt in which Eliot holds these two Hellenes! His client is a scruffy Levantine merchant (c.i.f., for his pitiful pocketful of raisins, means "carriage and insurance free"). The man can summon only pidgin French, and his Greek surname, Eugenides, literally "of noble birth," is viciously sardonic. The poet T. S. Eliot, a Harvard grad with Boston Brahmin roots, newly transplanted to Britain, generally reserved his unfathomably venomous hatred for my own tribe, whose name even after the Holocaust he refused to capitalize in new printings: ". . . the jew squats on the window sill, the owner, / Spawned in some estaminet of Antwerp, / Blistered in Brussels, patched and peeled in London." (*Gerontion*, 1920) "The rats are underneath the piles. / The jew is underneath the lot." (*Burbank with a Baedecker: Bleistein with a Cigar,* 1920). But in the surreal, postwar landscape of the Waste Land, a Greek of Asia Minor is made to bear the multiple stigmata of degeneracy: homosexuality, bodily ugliness, base material greed, and the linguistic inarticulacy of an uprooted alien. One reads a work in the context of its time, and an anachronistic judgment of its prejudices, one based on the standards of a more liberal age, is to a degree unfair. The Roaring Twenties: flappers, the Charleston, the speakeasy, John Dos Passos's *Manhattan Transfer.* But also Harvard's notorious "secret courts" that persecuted and destroyed gay students, Harvard president Lowell's infamous *numerus clausus* that shut the gates of learning to Jews, lynchings of young black men, eugenics, nativist hysteria about *Untermenschen*— subhuman immigrants mobbing the gates. It is almost an unfamiliar world. Almost.

But look at the date, the date. 1922. In the late summer of that year the armies of Mustafa Kemal, the later Atatürk, "Father of the Turks," broke the Greek lines in western Anatolia and smashed through to the Ionian coast on the Aegean. Smyrna—the Izmir of today—was a vast, rich, modern, cosmopolitan city with up-to-date movie theaters, newspapers, schools, motorcars, cafés. It has ancient roots: it faces the Greek island of Chios, Homer's home, across the harbor. The climate is pleasant; people are cultivated, courteous. Outside town are the lush orchards where half-European, half-Greek, or Armenian businessmen and women called the Levantines—people like Mr. Eugenides—grow figs for the table of the king of England. They speak perfect Turkish, Greek, Armenian, English, Italian, and, yes, French. But now the Greek army is retreating in long, weary columns, followed by fleeing farming families with terror in their eyes. The population swells. The Kemalists conquer the town and drive the Christian population onto the quay, and begin to sever limbs with their cavalry sabers and to push screaming human beings into the water. They flail helplessly and drown. Muslim mobs torture the Greek archbishop to death, gouging out his eyes. Then the Turkish army, working according to plan, empties jerry cans of kerosene into buildings and roundabout the Greek and Armenian quarters of the town. On September 13, an easy day to remember—think of two days before, three generations on—the entire city goes up in flames. Nothing like it has ever been seen before, not even in the Great War just ended.

And what is the response of the West? Newspapers duly report the horror, but the great powers refuse to act. An Allied destroyer in the harbor turns up gramophones on deck to drown out the screams, and sailors are forced to turn away swimmers trying to clamber on board. Some of the latter are sucked into the ship's propellers. The harbor is choked with floating corpses. The American plenipotentiary in Constantinople, a naval officer named Mark Bristol—may God blot out his name and memory—derides Greeks and Armenians as mongrel races quite as inferior as the Jews, and attempts to frustrate all attempts at rescue. As I write these lines in 2015, refugees from Syria are drowning in those same waters. His Holiness Pope Francis is right to speak of the globalization of indifference, but perhaps the Holy Father errs slightly in implying that the phenomenon is new. And, considering the poison lines of Mr. Eliot, one might add that at the edge of the vast black tarry ocean of indifference to the sufferings of the innocent flicker the hellish little flames of derision and contempt. America is interested, not in Greek and Armenian lives—has it ever been?—but in its new postwar geopolitical position as the world's creditor. It needs a foothold in the Near East, and France and Britain have already appropriated Syria, Iraq, Egypt, Lebanon, and the Land of Israel to themselves. The US does not wish to offend Turkey.

As always, the conscience of the world rests on the frail shoulders of an individual. A newly arrived official of the YMCA, Asa Jennings, manages the impossible: pretending authority, he marshals a fleet of merchant vessels and passenger steamers—the fleet of Agamemnon and Menelaus on a mission of mercy, or Dunkerque *avant la lettre*. Hundreds of thousands are lost; but nearly as many are saved, and to this day you may see their descendants in the neighborhood of Nea Smyrni, New Smyrna, which began as a refugee shantytown in central Athens. Marjorie Housepian Dobkin, professor of English and dean of students at Barnard College, was the daughter of one of the refugees from Smyrna. She assaulted the archives and wrote the first book, *The Smyrna Affair* (or *Smyrna 1922* in other editions), about a great crime whose very memory the United States, in its indecent eagerness to placate its Turkish ally, attempted for decades to suppress. I read it as a young man in one sitting, through the night, looking up baffled and chilled at the dawn light seeping through the windows of the library at Wadham College, Oxford. Some years later came Milton's ironically named *Paradise Lost,* whose particular virtue is its vivid evocation of the lives of the "Levantines."

But now we have the all-embracing work on the Smyrna disaster of a professional historian. Lou Ureneck's authoritative book is a masterpiece of scholarly precision unlikely ever to be superseded. It draws on new scholarship, additional sources, and more archival material. One comes to know better Asa Kent Jennings, the YMCA hero, and learns more about the despicable Bristol. Ureneck has discovered the extraordinary contribution of Lt. Commander Halsey Powell, who risked his career to support the evacuation. The book details the communication between Jennings, Powell, and a third important character, the Greek battleship commander Ioannis Theophanides, who supported Jennings as the latter called the bluff of the Greek government in Athens so he could assemble his rescue fleet. The book shows that the rescue was arranged without the knowledge of Bristol—when its full dimensions were revealed to him, he sought in vain to block it. Most of this material comes from a close reading of State Department cables and reports, while other key elements emerge from the personal papers of Jennings and others.

The dark tides of the Smyrna disaster spin and eddy very close to home. One of the Smyrna refugees was an Armenian priest literally plucked from the water, Fr. Ghevond Tourian, a relative of Bedros Tourian, whose lyrics are in many ways the foundation of modern Western Armenian poetry.[*] After the Smyrna disaster Fr. Ghevond studied in Britain, and went on to become the archbishop of the Armenian Church in America: he was brutally assassinated on Christmas Day 1933 in a political struggle between Armenian factions as he celebrated mass at

---

[*]   See James R. Russell, *Bosphorus Nights: The Complete Lyric Poems of Bedros Tou-rian,* Armenian Heritage Press and Harvard Armenian Texts and Studies 10, Cambridge, MA, 2005.

the Holy Cross Church of Armenia in Washington Heights, New York City. As he lay dying the parishioners rang the nearest doctor, who lived a block away on Wadsworth Avenue, and little Marjorie Housepian, the physician's daughter, was the one who picked up the phone. The horror of the killing of a man himself saved from an unimaginable massacre made the front page of the *New York Times* for weeks and strangely sparked the mainstream American imagination: ten years after the killing the father of the Beat poets, William S. Burroughs, was to name a character Tourian in his first novel, *And the Hippos Were Boiled in Their Tanks*—the story of another murder.*

Washington Heights is where I grew up, a leafy, middle-class neighborhood where Jews, Armenians, Greeks, Irishmen, Dominicans, Italians, and many others live together in harmony and eat each other's pizza, bagels, and rice and beans. An Armenian American friend, Gladys Pratt, lived next door to me and made delicious stuffed grape leaves. One of her relatives had been a lawyer who defended one of Archbishop Tourian's killers: she recalled the convict, released after decades from prison, crying as he cradled a little child of his family. And on the wall of her dining room was a little painting of a pleasant side street with overhanging balconies and shade trees in another country— I learned that it was her ancestors' hometown, Smyrna. The political passions of the old country had reached these shores. But it is not all bad. Some years later as a professor at Harvard I had the honor to teach Armenian to a Turkish student named Murat, who loves Woody Allen's *Manhattan* and whose hometown is Izmir. There is a new generation of Turkish scholars, humanists, and activists who refuse the enforced oblivion of the system: they and people like them everywhere are our brothers and sisters and our hope.

We must think carefully, says my Turkish colleague and dear friend, Himmet Tashkomur, about the kind of world we want to live in. Surely it is not a world of indifference, still less of hatred; and for it to be free

---

* See James R. Russell, "The Black Dervish of Armenian Futurism," *Journal of Armenian Studies*, Belmont, MA, 2015. The murder in the Beat circle, and the beginning of the literary careers of Allen Ginsberg, Jack Kerouac, and William S. Burroughs, is the subject of Gus Van Sant's recent film, *Kill Your Darlings*.

of those evils, it must not be one of globalized oblivion, either. Lou Ureneck's Smyrna, like the Salonica of my Sephardic grandmother Margue-
rite Saltiel, may her memory be for a blessing, is a city of ghosts. But not
all of them are bloody spectres: in his book we find also heroes, great
souls whose light of individual conscience and courage may yet show us
all a way, all of us Near Easterners with a pocketful of currants.

James R. Russell
Mashtots Professor of Armenian Studies
Harvard University
Cambridge, Massachusetts
November 2015

Wednesday, September 13, 1922

Smyrna was burning, and U.S. Navy captain Arthur J. Hepburn prepared to evacuate the one hundred twenty-five Americans under his protection. A destroyer dispatched from Constantinople stood by in the harbor ready to take the Americans aboard.

In his navy whites, which seemed to gather the dying light of the Mediterranean dusk, Hepburn was a smudged and sweating emblem of American prestige. He stood on the waterfront only a few blocks from the massive fire that was consuming the city and allowed his sailors a few moments to take their positions before he gave the command to begin the evacuation. The American citizens waited in a movie theater on the city's Quay, a two-mile promenade that traced the sweeping edge of the harbor.

This was no ordinary city fire. Huge even by the standards of history's giant fires, it would reduce to ashes the richest and most sophisticated city in the Ottoman Empire. The fire would ultimately claim an even more infamous distinction. It was the last violent episode in a ten-year holocaust that had killed three million people—Armenians, Greeks, and Assyrians, all Christian minorities—on the Turkish subcontinent between 1912 and 1922. It would also serve as a marker of the end of the Ottoman Empire.

Hepburn was a practical officer, and as the fire raced toward him and his men he had no time to consider the fall of empires or the ways in which history pivots to crush old orders and create new nations. He had a job to do—and he already had made a mess of it by beginning the evacuation late.

He had directed two navy whaleboats and a motor sailer to stand ready at the Quay's mossy seawall to ferry the Americans to the destroyer, but he faced another big obstacle. It was as dangerous as the giant of wall of flame that was racing toward the waterfront.

The fire had trapped a huge and surging mass of people on the Quay. The crowd was packed tight for a half mile or more in either direction—nearly an entire city of people was caught on the narrow strip of cobbled pavement between the wall of flames and the sea. Hepburn had to some-how move the Americans through the dense crowd to the waiting boats. The transfer would be dangerous, maybe impossible. The people on the Quay were desperate—they could see the flames and feel the intense heat just as Hepburn and his men could—and they too wanted to escape the fire, hoping that the American officer would take some of them on board. Surely the Americans would not leave them behind. America was the one country everyone in the Near East trusted—Arabs, Muslim Turks, Christians, and Jews—and at this moment Hepburn was standing in for America.

Hepburn had decided to form a detachment of American sailors into a double line as a tunnel through the crowd. Twenty young sailors, dressed in swabby whites and landing-force leggings and armed with pistols and police batons, had taken their positions, elbow to elbow, and created a pas-sageway from the movie-theater door to the seawall through the frantic horde. Most of people in the crowd were women with small children. Wild and fighting for their lives, they tried to break through the sailors' lines to board the navy boats, which they saw as their only deliverance from certain immolation. The sailors had orders to beat them back, which they were forced to do by the sheer weight of the frenzied mass. It leaned and pressed against them as a single relentless body. Women were wailing, holding their babies over their heads. "Take my child with you. In the name of God, take him." It was a frightful chaos of smoke, heat, screams, wild eyes, black kerchiefs, and military batons. The young American sailors held their ground against the refugees' desperation and constant shoving and pulling, and their two parallel lines—the sides of the tunnel—held.

Hepburn gave the order to go, and the evacuating Americans passed quickly in single file out of the theater and safely between the sailors to the whaleboats bobbing at the splashing seawall. Some of the Americans were the wives and children of missionaries; some were agents for American tobacco companies; others were naturalized Americans of Greek and Armenian descent who owned farms and shops in and around Smyrna and faced possible execution if they remained ashore. Hepburn had orders to protect all of them. The destroyer, the USS *Simpson*, whose long gray hull, tall bridge, and deck guns came in and out of view through the thick smoke, was anchored less than one hundred yards from the Quay, and it had lowered its gangway to the waterline to take the Americans on board.

As the Americans dashed between the sailors, a desperate man in the crowd jumped from the seawall into one of the half-full whaleboats, nearly capsizing it. The sailors immediately tossed him overboard. Other refugees leaped into the water and tried to swim to the *Simpson* and a second American destroyer, the USS *Litchfield*. None succeeded. Some were clutching children when they drowned, weighted down by their clothes and pulled below the surface by mushrooming heavy skirts. There were other warships in the harbor, British, French, and Italian, and the people tried to swim to them too. Those who had managed to reach the ships by stripping off their clothes before jumping into the water found that the ships' hulls loomed over them like tall and unscalable metal cliffs. In the choppy water, they gasped, shouted, and begged to be taken aboard, all the time trying to stay afloat. They banged on the ships' steel plate and grasped anchor chains. Bodies floated on the surface, some of them mangled by the propellers of the warships.

There is no good time for a fire to break out in a city whose backstreets are narrow and congested and whose neighborhoods are packed with wood-and-masonry houses. But this was a particularly bad moment for Smyrna to have been torched. During the previous two weeks, three hundred thousand refugees, nearly all homeless and destitute, had flooded into the city seeking its safety—a grim and deadly miscalculation. The refugees had crammed into the city's streets, railroad stations, cemeteries, and school and church yards; and then the Turkish nationalist army, from which they had been fleeing, had also entered the city and occupied it with thousands of poorly paid, hungry, and battle-hard troops. A nightmare of slaughter, rape, and robbery had ensued.

As the fire spread across the city, residents were flushed from their homes, and the heat and flames pushed them and the mass of refugees to the Quay.

Some few minutes before 7 P.M., by which time the fire had claimed nearly half the city, and the blaze was more than a mile wide and a half mile deep, Hepburn and his men had managed to transfer almost all the Americans to the destroyer. But two important evacuees were still missing—the American consul general, George Horton, and his wife, Catherine. They were nowhere to be found, and the flames drove closer to the waterfront. It was getting dark, though the fire cast a dome of rosy light into the night sky, and the wind was lifting and gusting with the force of a gale. The fire had created its own howling storm, sucking in air and blasting geysers of cinders and flames into the sky. Hepburn could feel the searing heat on his arms and face, and his lungs burned with the acrid smoke blowing over the Quay.

Hepburn, a veteran officer with a reputation for thoroughness, already was angry with the consul general, and now there was this damnable delay that endangered the captain and his men.

Hepburn looked again at his watch. It was now 7.30 P.M. The fire soon would reach the American consulate, then the movie theater. Leaving the consul general behind was out of the question. The captain had to assume that Horton was waiting until the last possible minute to board the ship, possibly supervising the loading of his personal collection of books, rugs, and antiquities, and that if he were to delay much longer, the sailors Hepburn had dispatched to get him would simply carry him and his wife to the Quay.

Hepburn estimated that the fire soon would breach the long line of waterfront mansions, hotels, and warehouses. He doubted that any of the crowd would survive if the fire came to the Quay. It was too big and too hot, and the people had no barricade or shelter to protect them. The heat was so intense that the hemp hawser lines on some of the ships in the harbor had already ignited. Horses and donkeys were crazed and running up and down the Quay and kicking madly to free themselves of the bundles on their backs that had burst into flame. "The practical destruction of the entire wretched horde either by fire or drowning," Hepburn would later note in his official report, "seemed inevitable."

At 8.30 P.M., the consul general was still missing. Hepburn had no choice but to make his way back to the consulate. Finding Horton there, he ordered him to the Quay for evacuation. Hepburn returned to the waterfront and again waited for Horton to arrive.

Hepburn looked in every direction, his weak eyes straining. Then, coming up the street toward him, ahead of the fire, was the truck he had sent hours earlier to retrieve Horton and his luggage. It inched through the crowd, plowing through the people. Hepburn felt a wave of relief.

As far as he knew, all the Americans he intended to evacuate were now accounted for—at least all those from the movie theater and the consulate. But there had been a lot of confusion, and he had begun the evacuation late and without an appreciation of the speed of the fire, Hepburn knew it was possible that he might be leaving ashore some of the American missionary workers who had refused the evacuation order earlier in the day, before the fire had reached its full fury. He had sent sailors in search of them, but the search parties themselves had gotten lost in the fire.

There was also one American who had chosen to remain in the burning city, working furiously to cope with the nightmare around him. Asa Kent Jennings, a former itinerant minister in the small towns of upstate New York, found himself in a tumult of panicked refugees at the far end of the city's Quay, a few hundred yards from Turkish soldiers who were blocking retreat from the fire. Jennings had only just arrived in Smyrna a month earlier as an employee of the YMCA, and the violence and confusion around him were terrifying new experiences. He was a small and mild-mannered man in poor health whose work in the previous few years had been to provide Bible study and hot coffee to decommissioning American and Allied soldiers in Europe. In the last week, confronted by intense suffering in the city, he had on his own initiative taken several Quay-side mansions that had been abandoned by wealthy Greek and Armenian owners when the Turkish army had been drawing close to the city and turned them into makeshift safe houses for refugee women. Many of the women were pregnant; others had been raped and badly injured by soldiers. Now he was intent on staying with them despite the fire.

Several hours earlier, Jennings had put his family aboard one of Captain Hepburn's whaleboats for evacuation. Though his wife would have had trouble seeing him through the masses of people on the Quay, Jennings had been able to watch the destroyer his family had been loaded onto depart through the smoke.

Jennings's safe houses were about a half mile north of the movie theater where Hepburn had loaded the Americans onto the destroyer. The young American sailors who had been watching over the houses were now gone. Jennings could see the *Litchfield* through the smoke from the front of one of the houses, and of course he could see the enormous fire. Its flames towered over the city and were reflected in the harbor.

As he hobbled among the refugees, Jennings was absorbed with the work of caring for the people who had come to him for safety. In addition to the women, he had also collected hundreds of orphaned children, many of whom had watched their parents killed by Turkish soldiers. The children as well as the women looked to him for deliverance from the giant fire and the army.

Before it burned itself out, the fire would destroy 13,100 buildings—homes, hospitals, school, warehouses, businesses, churches, and factories—and cause 250 million dollars in damage, billions of dollars in today's terms. Only the Turkish and small Jewish quarters of the city and a few patches at the perimeter would remain unburned. The number of dead would never be firmly established, though some would place it on this night in the tens of thousands.

Hungry, tired, and suffering terrible pain in his crooked back, Jennings retreated into one of the safe houses and made his rounds of the women spread on its marble and parquet floors, some clutching newborn babies and others frightened into a permanent speechlessness. He prayed for their deliverance, as well as his own.

PART
ONE

End of an Empire

Decades after the burning of Smyrna, a Jewish legal scholar would introduce the term "genocide" to describe the terrible events in Turkey in the slaughterhouse years between 1912 and 1922.

In its intent and methods, the genocide carried out in Turkey was a portent of even more terrible events in the fearsome century ahead. It was on the lips of Adolf Hitler weeks before his invasion of Poland. "The aim of war is not to reach definite lines but to annihilate the enemy physically," he told his generals. "It is by this means that we shall obtain the vital living space that we need. Who today still speaks of the Armenians?"

Often known as the Armenian Genocide, the slaughter actually extended to all the indigenous Christians in Asia Minor. The Armenians, an ancient people who had inhabited eastern and central Anatolia since the sixth century BC, suffered the most deaths, about 1.5 million people. They were taken from their towns and villages, segregated by sex and age, and summarily executed (the men) or forced to march (the women and children) long distances to their deaths from starvation and exhaustion. The death trails, which led from Armenian settlements throughout Anatolia to the deserts of Syria or Iraq, were littered with the bones of hundreds of thousands of Armenian women and children. The deportations and executions of Greek and Assyrian Christians, which mostly came later, added about another 1.5 million deaths. The decade of mass killing, engineered by two successive Turkish governments, was the first religious and ethnic cleansing of modern times—and the end of Christianity, for all intents and purposes, in the place where it had first taken root, Asia Minor. It was there, in western Anatolia, that the first Christian churches had been established and St. Paul had journeyed to spread the message of Christianity.

The story of Smyrna today is mostly forgotten. It seems to have left no strong impression on the world's collective memory. This is strange. Smyrna (with the attendant events that led to it and those that immediately followed) contains lessons about current-day conflicts between the West and Islam; about oil diplomacy; about the uneasy balance between national strategic interests and advocacy of human rights. Smyrna, for all that it represents, ought to appear in the same list of place-names that carry the burdens of history: Sarajevo and Yalta, for their failures of diplomacy; and Treblinka, Bosnia, and Rwanda for the scale of the killing. Each is a place, and each a history lesson waiting to be unpacked.

The story of Smyrna also is a surprising tale of individual men and women—of ambition and brutality, bumbling statecraft, extraordinary military and political leadership, and unlikely heroism. In all of this, including the heroism, and perhaps most especially the heroism, the United States played a crucial role.

UP UNTIL THE EARLY twentieth century, the Ottoman Empire embraced a vast swath of territory from the Arabian Peninsula to the border of Austria in southeastern Europe. Its perimeter more or less included most of what was called the Near East, and the empire's hereditary leader, the sultan, was regarded by his Sunni Muslim subjects as the caliph of Islam, the successor to Mohammed on earth.

But by 1900, the once-great and feared empire was at the tail end of a centuries-long decline, fraught with inept leadership, corruption, and revolts by the peoples it had subjugated, including the Christian peoples of the Balkans. At the turn of the century, the Ottoman Empire was a creaky machine ruled by a paranoid and ruthless leader, Sultan Abdul Hamid II. He was known in the West as Bloody Abdul for vicious attacks on his Christian subjects.

In 1914, at the beginning of World War I, the Ottoman Empire allied itself with Germany in a secret treaty, and a new sultan, Mehmed V, Abdul Hamid's witless brother, declared a jihad against the European Allies. Counting on the might of German militarism to prevail in the great contest, the Ottoman leaders hoped to revive the empire, restore its old glory, and regain lost territory in Europe.

As the Great War raged, the Allied powers looked ahead to the eventual defeat of Germany and its partners and the dismantling of the Ottoman Empire, which they (and the United States) regarded as a cruel and despotic anachronism. In secret, and beginning with the Treaty of London in 1915 and then the Sykes-Picot Agreement in 1916, Britain, France, Russia, and Italy had decided that the Ottoman capital, Constantinople, would go to Turkey's old rival, Tsarist Russia, and, based on further agreements and the shifting contingencies of a war whose victory was not assured, other sections of the empire would go to Britain, France, Italy, and Greece. The Allies intended to preserve a small central section of Anatolia as the Turkish nation. They were applying the old formula of war—to the victor go the spoils. Britain and France thirsted especially for the empire's immense reserves of oil.

After the war ended, the victors gathered in Paris in January 1919 to settle the terms of the defeat of Germany and its war partners, Austria-Hungary, Bulgaria, and the Ottoman Empire. Each would require a separate treaty. But America's entrance into World War I had shifted the terms of the future peace terms and the division of Turkey. On the Ottoman treaty, President Wilson refused to accept the colonial land grab laid down in secret by the Allies during the war years. Instead, Wilson proposed a system of mandates, which would amount to temporary supervision by the victors of new nations carved out of the Ottoman Empire. The mandate territories (in Wilson's vision) would eventually become independent democratic countries.

Wilson wanted to maintain the territorial integrity of the Turkish homeland by assigning to postwar Turkey all of Anatolia. Yet, at the same time, he wanted to provide the persecuted Christian minorities of Anatolia "an absolutely unmolested opportunity of autonomous development." The president's idealism hardly suited the complexity and violence in the religiously torn Ottoman Empire. In their effort to make a purely Muslim nation, the Turks had uprooted and killed millions of Christians before and during the war, and they would continue to do so after the war as the Allies sought to settle the terms of the Ottoman defeat. It was unclear how Wilson's vision of both security and democracy could be made real unless some powerful Western nation—nearly everybody looked to the United States—accepted a mandate over all Anatolia and occupied it with tens of thousands of troops to protect the lives of Christian minorities as democracy took hold and a civil society emerged.

Four months into the Paris talks, in April 1919, a new crisis erupted that created a fiendish complication for the Allies in Turkey and changed the course of Turkish history. It began with Italy's demand that it get Fiume, a Slavic-majority city on the Adriatic Sea that had been part of Austria-Hungary. Wilson objected. The Italian demand violated his principle of drawing national lines based on national identity. The Italian delegation was outraged. It walked out, and, sensing that Italy might also be denied western Anatolia, which Britain had secretly promised it during the war, the Italians took unilateral military action to gain Turkish territory. Italy had lost six hundred thousand soldiers in World War I, and it had resolved not to be cheated of its share of the war's spoils. It landed troops on the southern coast of Turkey and sent warships to Smyrna. It would seize what it believed it had earned.

The Italian action infuriated Wilson and Lloyd George, the British prime minister. To prevent Italian seizure of Smyrna, but without any intention of committing their own nations' troops, the two leaders invited Greece to occupy Smyrna ahead of the Italians. The Greeks, in the person of the charismatic and forceful Greek representative, Eleftherios Venizelos, had made a persuasive claim in Paris that it should get Smyrna based on an ethnic Greek majority in the region. He also argued that Ottoman Christians in western Anatolia (mostly ethnic Greek) needed protection against Turkish harassment and killing. Greece was prepared to provide the protection. Venizelos, a former guerrilla fighter against the Turks on Crete, was a sophisticated and formidable diplomat, and he captivated Wilson and Lloyd George. In arguing for the Greek claim to Smyrna, Venizelos also pointed to the British promise that Greece should get the city as recompense for joining the Allies in the war against Germany. He prevailed. The Paris negotiators laid down terms for a Greek occupation of Smyrna: it would be limited and provisional, and a plebiscite would be held in five years to determine the city's future. It remained technically under Ottoman sovereignty.

The decision to send in the Greeks was a disaster, and it accelerated the slaughter of Ottoman Christians. The Greeks and the Turks were old enemies. Their animosity had been so cultivated, nurtured, and refined over hundreds of years that the word "enemy" seemed hardly sufficient to capture the mutual loathing.

The Greeks hated the Turks for their four-hundred-year occupation of Greece and saw the millions of ethnic Greeks who lived inside the Ottoman Empire as their natural countrymen, oppressed and unredeemed citizens of a greater Greece. In the Greek mind, Constantinople, not Athens, was the center of the Hellenistic firmament, and the Turks were Asiatic barbarians whose sacking of Greek Constantinople in 1453, ending the thousand-year Byzantine Empire, remained a fresh wound. A symbolic artifact of the Turkish occupation of Greece was punishment by impalement: the insertion of a stake into a man's anus, then running it through his body to exit between his shoulder and neck. It had been an Ottoman weapon of terror. Sometimes the impaled man was roasted over a fire. (The Greek word for such a stake is *souvla*, hence the mocking name for the skewered lamb dish, souvlaki.)

The Turks, for their part, saw the Greeks as disloyal and untrustworthy Ottoman subjects who had achieved national independence from the Ottoman Empire in 1832 through treachery and interference from the West. The European nations that had helped Greece revolt were the same troublesome "Franks" that had sent armies to wrest Jerusalem from the Muslims a thousand years earlier. (The Crusades remained lodged in Muslim consciousness; memories were long in this part of the world.) Greeks, in the Turkish view, wore their Hellenism with an air of superiority as if they had invented civilization, and making matters worse, they were Christians, a lesser people—*raya*, or sheep. In daily conversation, they were *givaours*, infidel dogs.

Sent to Smyrna by Britain and the United States, the Greeks bungled the landing. Poorly disciplined and led by a fiery local bishop carrying an Orthodox cross, Greek soldiers overreacted to shots fired from a Turkish army barracks, a provocation that most likely had been planned well in advance. There was mayhem on the city's waterfront, and Turkish soldiers taken as prisoners were beaten in plain sight. So hostile was the local ethnic Greek population to the Turkish soldiers, after years of Turkish mistreatment, that a British officer recounted watching a Greek woman squat over a bayoneted Turkish soldier and piss in his mouth when he had begged for water.

The stiff Allied-imposed armistice ending World War I had already triggered a Turkish resistance. The Greek landing further insulted Turkish pride and inflamed the resistance. Soon a full-scale war broke out between Greece and the army of a revolutionary movement of Turkish nationalists inside the country led by a former Ottoman army officer named Mustapha Kemal. Turks throughout Anatolia flocked to his side to fight the Greeks and oppose the Allies. "Remember Smyrna in your heart," read Turkish armbands. "Weep until it is avenged."

The Greek army occupied Smyrna, but progress on drafting an Ottoman treaty stalled when Wilson, back home, failed to persuade the U.S. Senate to approve the German treaty package he had negotiated in Paris, which included establishment of a League of Nations. The country, and especially the Republicans in the Senate, wanted no part of Wilson's League and internationalism. Quietly, the United States, which had not declared war on Turkey despite its being an ally of Germany, removed itself from discussions of an Ottoman treaty and left the task to Britain, France, and Italy.

The Europeans went ahead and drafted a treaty in Sevres, France, in 1920 that accommodated their colonial designs. The Sevres Treaty established mandates and zones of influence over Ottoman territories, and its logic was midwife to many elements of the Mideast that we know today. It created three nation-states out of the non-Turkish sections of the Ottoman Empire: Iraq and Palestine under British mandate but Syria (including Lebanon) under French mandate. France also got a zone of influence in southeastern Anatolia. Italy got a zone of influence in southwestern Anatolia. The Palestine mandate incorporated Britain's Balfour Declaration, which prepared the ground for a Jewish homeland though not necessarily a Jewish state.

The treaty also affirmed an independent Armenia, intended to be a secure homeland for the beleaguered Armenian people, and created a Kingdom of Hejaz, which later merged with a neighboring sultanate to form Saudi Arabia. The Sevres Treaty slashed the Ottoman military, declared the Dardanelles an international neutral zone, and demanded guarantees for the protections of Christian minorities, which had been among the Allies' published goals of the war.

The Turkish nationalist movement rejected the Sevres Treaty, and Kemal declared a new jihad against the Allies. By then, Kemal was in open rebellion against the sultan's government. It was as if a German general had rejected Berlin's acceptance of the Treaty of Versailles, formed a populist army in Bavaria, and marched against French forces occupying the Rhineland. It was an astonishing turn of events brought on by the failure of France and Britain to back the Sevres Treaty with the resolve needed to enforce it. It was also a demonstration of Kemal's stunning leadership and a fierce Turkish will not to give an inch of Anatolia to the infidels, the Greeks and Armenians.

The absence of an Allied force in Anatolia to support the Greek army or enforce the Sevres Treaty led to a resurgence of Turkish brutality against the Christian minorities. Executions and deportations of Greek and Armenian Christians resumed with new ferocity throughout Anatolia. "Two thirds of the Greek deportees are women and children," reported an American aid officer who witnessed the marches. "All along the route where these deportees have travelled Turks are permitted to visit refugee groups and select women and girls whom they desire for any purpose." The routes of the deported population, the aid worker observed, were "strewn with bodies of their dead, which are consumed by dogs, wolves, vultures. The Turks make no effort to bury these dead and the deportees are not permitted to do so. The chief causes of death are starvation, dysentery, typhus. Turkish authorities frankly state that is their deliberate intention to exterminate the Greeks, and all their actions support this statements."

The army of Greece plunged deeper into Anatolia to defeat the nationalists, but it was soon mired in a grueling and brutal fight east of Smyrna on the high plains of the Anatolian interior. It won battles, but proved unable to finish off the nationalists. The country was too vast, and popular support for the nationalists among Anatolia's Muslims was too deep. Soon, Greece's only real ally in the war, Britain, walked away from its support of Greece, assuring its eventual defeat.

Emboldened by Allied indecision and infighting, the nationalists attacked the French, who had occupied the zone in southern Anatolia assigned to them in the Sevres Treaty. Lacking the stomach for a war against the nationalists, the French departed, leaving the Armenians who had returned to the region to the nationalists. Thousands of Armenians were slaughtered. Satisfied with their possession of Syria, the French split from the British and essentially negotiated a separate peace with the nationalists. The nationalists also attacked Armenia, the new nation in the northeast corner of Anatolia. The Allies and the United States, which had encouraged the Armenian nation, failed to respond, and an independent Armenia disappeared.

Meanwhile, the Greek army had successfully fought its way east, but nationalist forces stopped it nearly within artillery-firing distance of Ankara in the summer of 1921. The Greek army retreated to a line near the Sakaria River on the Anatolian plateau. It was exhausted, and the nation of Greece was broke and isolated. Greece prepared for a unilateral withdrawal, but Britain counseled delay until an armistice was arranged. Desperate to improve its position, Greece concocted a plan in the summer of 1922 to seize Constantinople, which would have altered the military situation in its favor, but the British and French objected. It was checkmate for the Greek army.

And there matters stood until the hot late summer of 1922—the Greek army was spent and out of options and allies; the Turkish nationalists, who had resumed the slaughter of Greek and Armenian civilians, were rested and amply supplied with guns, artillery, and planes by their recently acquired friends, Italy, France, and a new troublemaker on the scene, Soviet Russia. The stage was set for triumph of the nationalists and a final bloody act. It would occur in a matter of weeks.

CHAPTER 2

An Innocent Arrives

In mid-August 1922, Asa Kent Jennings, a forty-four-year-old minister from upstate New York, was traveling with his wife and three children to a new job as the boys' work secretary of the Young Men's Christian Association in Smyrna. Standing together on the deck of the steamer, they could have been mistaken for a mission family dispensing religious leaflets on a street corner of an American city—Chicago, New York, or Kansas City.

Jennings was a small man in wire-rimmed glasses, barely over five feet tall. He stood not quite straight: his back was hunched, an artifact of tuberculosis, which had struck him in his twenties. To conceal his deformity, he always wore a suit with a loose jacket, two sizes too big, that covered the bump on his back. He wore it even now in the Mediterranean summer heat. He was slightly jowly, the thick lenses of his spectacles gave his eyes a strange magnification, and he seemed always to be smiling. "The YMCA smile," some said mockingly. There was something elfin about him—the enforced miniaturization from his disease, the cock of his head when he turned to look up at a taller man to show his smile, and his pleasant appeal to the spirit. He seemed not quite of this world. Jennings had grown up in a religious family on a farm in upstate New York on the south shore of Lake Ontario.

Jennings's wife, Amy, forty-two years old, was the picture of a proper church wife: hair parted in the middle, then up and gathered in two buns on each side of her head in the convention of the Gibson girl, but with a Sunday-school decency, a modest dress tight at the neck, and glasses. The children were two boys, Asa Will and Wilbur, also in glasses and jackets, though tighter fitting, and a girl, Bertha, with a bow atop her head.

Leaving Constantinople, their steamer had slipped out of the Bosporus and plied westward across the Sea of Marmara, squeezed through the Dardanelles, and churned down the Aegean coast of Anatolia, that long rhinoceros head of subcontinent whose foreshortened horn is the isthmus that connects Asia to Europe. Jennings's assignment in Smyrna would be to engage boys of different faiths and ethnicities—Greeks, Turks, Armenians, and Jews—in sports and healthy outdoor activities to teach tolerance, responsibility, and Christian virtue. Jennings didn't know it, but he was headed to a job where the boss didn't want him. The YMCA director in Smyrna had asked headquarters to send someone else—a person he knew to be smart, athletic, and handsome; his preferred candidate had been a member of the Syracuse crew team and president of the student body. He had the robust physical presence that would make a strong positive impression on potential donors in Smyrna. Instead, Smyrna's YMCA was getting a funny-looking, crooked, and pious little man sent by higher-ups who had been impressed with the work he had done in Czechoslovakia, managing a YMCA hut for decommissioning Czech soldiers and starting an athletic program for boys. "Jennings has a most attractive personality," his boss had written to Smyrna's YMCA director in consolation. Jennings liked to sing and laugh, and this had made him a hit with the soldiers.

Even if he had known about the behind-the-scenes opposition, Jennings was not a person who worried much about the condescending views of others. For a little man, he had a big spirit. As he would later write to his son about his impairments, "I do not despair of handicaps. Unless one has a weak desire to master them, they may be able to contribute to our success and the development of a stronger character." The bigger problem was Jennings's ignorance of the violent forces that were converging on his destination. For this he could be excused: even at this late moment, Smyrna itself was not fully aware of the danger it faced. As usual, Smyrna was busy having fun.

On that sweltering August day, as his ship plied southward, passing the island of Lesbos on the right, Jennings approached Smyrna with a proud missionary history, but with an indifference to his safety that was nothing short of breathtaking. Smyrna was a city occupied by a foreign army (Greece) engaged in a brutish war with an indigenous enemy (Turkish nationalists). Here was a man of uncertain health with a wife of uncertain nerves (she soon would suffer a nervous breakdown) and three young children traveling to a city that was only two hundred miles from a rugged plateau where two armies—with a combined strength of 450,000 men—faced each other across a field of arid and rugged ground with blood in their eyes. Both armies had been conditioned by five hundred years of conquest, revolt, and religious hatred.

Some of Jennings's lack of caution may have been his American can-do spirit and faith in a beneficent God. Some of it may also have been due to Smyrna's reputation—it was widely known as a place unlike anywhere else in the Ottoman Empire, well governed during World War I by a liberal and pro-Western Turkish *vali* named Rahmi Bey and now by a stern and even-handed Greek governor, Aristides Stergiades. Even during the deportations of 1915 and 1916, Armenians in Smyrna had lived mostly free of intimidation and death.

The Greek army and civil administration were firmly in control; Allied warships were present in the harbor. There were also Americans in Smyrna—an American consulate, missionary schools and an orphanage, the staffs of the YMCA and the YWCA, and American businessmen, buying tobacco leaf and selling kerosene, sewing machines, farm tractors, cars, and even ice from a factory owned by an Armenian American. Ice was in big demand in Smyrna during this torrid summer.

Jennings seemed not at all worried about what lay ahead. He was eager to encounter it, and he enjoyed the cucumber smell of the sea. Like his Protestant countrymen back home, he was obsessed with the geography of the Bible, and now, as the tawny hills of Anatolia slipped by the left side of the ship, he was entering that holy land as if in a Sunday-school storybook.

Jennings had grown up in a family of ministers and faithful Methodist churchgoers. The family farm was in New York's "burned-over district," so-called because it had been so Bible thumped and evangelized decades earlier that there was no more fuel for human conversion.

In his late teens as a student at Syracuse University, Jennings had been swept up in the Protestant enthusiasm that was running strong on American college campuses in the late 1800s. Already a devout Methodist, Jennings was further inflamed by the religious fervor at Syracuse that was stirred and channeled into missionary service by the YMCA's Student Volunteer Movement. Forced to drop out of college by lack of money, Jennings went to nearby Utica, where he got a job as an assistant secretary for boys' athletics at the local YMCA. The following year, he married Amy, also a devout upstate Methodist. Jennings moved to a better job with the YMCA in Carthage, New York, and that same year Amy had a child, a girl named Ortha, who died in infancy.

Jennings, then twenty-seven years old, contracted typhoid fever, recovered, then relapsed, and, in poor health, returned to Utica. He suffered through a long and difficult period of convalescence. At about the time he turned thirty years old, he had tried and failed to make a living as a minister. He had served as the traveling pastor at Methodist churches in the small farm hamlets of Barneveld, Cleveland, Trenton, Forestport, Panama, and Chateauguay. Asa and Amy's next three children were born in the years that Jennings was moving from one white wood-framed church to the next, never quite making a living, and in 1911 he returned to the steady pay of the YMCA in Utica, which always seemed to take him back, then he went to another pastorate in Richfield Springs, New York. It was an itinerant and insecure life, and it further preyed on Amy's nerves, but she accepted that Asa was cut out for a life of religious service.

In each of his assignments, Jennings had applied the earnest manner and simple Christianity that were the products of his upbringing, and while he remained a confirmed Methodist, he was irreverent enough, by Utica (and current Prohibitionist) standards, to risk Amy's ire by drinking the occasional glass of sherry. Hadn't Christ (he reminded her mischievously) taken wine at dinner? America in 1920 was still very much a

rural Protestant nation, and Jennings reflected the American Protestantism of the day—a practical religion drained of mystery, animated by a
spirit of social reform, and defined by a personal relationship with God,
good works, and a clean white shirt.

SMYRNA WAS ONE OF THE SEVEN churches of the Book of Revelation,
and the thought of its past thrilled Jennings. Smyrna had been home to
St. Polycarp, who had preached with St. John, the last of Jesus's twelve
apostles. Jennings could recite the words John had written from the
nearby island of Patmos about Smyrna. "Be thou faithful until death
and I will give thee a crown of life." Not far to the south of Smyrna was
Ephesus, another one of the seven founding churches and the ancient
city where Mary, the mother of Jesus, had lived out her life, St. Paul
had disputed with its residents over their worship of Artemis, and some
years earlier Antony had spent a lively summer with his Greek queen
of Egypt, Cleopatra. For Jennings, the assignment to Smyrna was an
answered prayer—it was getting him closer to his dream, a chance to see
Jerusalem.

As Jennings's steamer approached Pelican Point at the entrance to
Smyrna's harbor and churned its way through the blue-green water, he
saw Smyrna bustling and gleaming along its two-mile waterfront, its
Quay lined with mansions, hotels, cafés, theaters, and private clubs.
Many of the buildings along the Quay were constructed of white mar-
ble, and from the water they shimmered like sugar cubes in the intense
light of the summer sun. The names along the Quay, as Jennings would
soon find, read like a lyric to the city's *joie de vivre*: Café de Paris, Club
Hellenique, Club de Chasseurs, Théatre de Smyrne, Hotel Splendid,
Sporting Club, and Pathé Cinema.

IN THE NINETEENTH AND early twentieth centuries, Smyrna was the richest and most cosmopolitan city of the eastern Mediterranean, a busy
trading center of a half-million people—Turks, Greeks, Armenians,
Jews, and Levantines, the long-settled and fabulously wealthy Euro-

pean merchant families that had come seeking their fortunes in the 1700s. It was mostly a Greek city—it had more Greeks than Athens, and its principal languages were Greek and French—fused with a dash of Turkish to create a Smyrniot argot not always understandable to the Greeks of old Greece. A Smyrniot might begin a joke in Greek and finish it in Turkish.

Situated midway down the westward prominence of Asia Minor where the Turkish peninsula splinters into a confetti burst of Aegean islands, Smyrna was a multicultural aggregation of merchants and entrepreneurial adventurers. Blessed with sunshine in summer and rain in winter, Smyrna had a deep harbor and an industrious population that possessed a genius for commerce. The business of Smyrna was business. At the western end of one of history's most famous trade routes, the Silk Road, it provided a gateway to the wider world for farmers whose expert and intensive cultivation yielded an enormous variety of fruits, vegetables, tobacco, and fiber along a fertile coastal plain drained by rivers with echoes of classical mythology, Meles, Hermus, and Meander.

Those who lived in Smyrna in its best years remembered it as a dream of lavender-scented breezes, garden parties, dancing, and parasols along the harborfront. Smyrna was an emporium and a seaport and a kind of polyglot city-state inside the Ottoman Empire; it was marble mansions, tobacco leaf and opium cake; it was a long table set with grapes, lamb, eggplants, artichokes, red fishes, caviar, oysters, pomegranate, and cheeses; it was rows of busy cafés and coffeehouses; it was folded carpets on the backs of sleepy-eyed camels; it was the sound of the Anatolian lute, the smell of jasmine, and the taste of anise from its favorite liquor, *raki*; it was Italian opera and Greek operetta and the call to prayer of the muezzin and the ringing of the Russian-cast bells of Agia Photini. For the Greeks, Smyrna was wealth; for the Armenians, it was wealth; for the Levantine Europeans, it was even greater wealth; for the Ladino-speaking Sephardic Jews, expelled from their Iberian homes by Ferdinand and Isabella, it was the safety of not Spain; and for the Turks, it was *"Giavour Izmir,"* Infidel Smyrna. Smyrna was an enchantment, an emotion, and an idea that in the end could not close the circle of its own aspiration toward religious tolerance.

Smyrna grew rich from its carpets, silk, tobacco, opium, raisins, fragrant oils, and figs, considered the best in the world. When Americans in California wanted to develop a fig industry in the late nineteenth century, they traveled to Smyrna to learn its secrets. They discovered growing a fig was a complicated business, requiring the husbandry of wasps.

The city was also a principal source of Turkish tobacco—the region grew a small and aromatic leaf that commanded high prices. The American cigarette industry would not have been possible without Turkish tobacco. Virginia burley had a harsh taste so the industry, just getting started in the early twentieth century, blended Turkish tobacco with homegrown burley, and cigarette sales soared. R.J. Reynolds created a new cigarette blended with Turkish tobacco and called it Camel. It became the first national cigarette brand in America—one of the first national brands for any consumer product.

Smyrna was home to the Oriental Carpet Manufacturing Co., the world's biggest purveyor of oriental carpets. The company was a cartel, created by Levantine and Armenian merchants, and it controlled 90 percent of the Ottoman Empire's carpet trade. The company brought Turkish carpet production to astonishing heights, employing more than a hundred thousand women as piece workers weaving carpets on home looms. It took four weavers six weeks to make a single eight-by-twelve-foot rug, which would sell in the United States for 275 dollars, which was about half of the annual wage of an American industrial worker in 1910. The company sold its carpets by the thousands in London, Paris, and New York. It had a showroom at 160 Fifth Avenue in New York, and many a Turkish carpet graced the best town houses of Manhattan.

A center of cultivated leisure, Smyrna published dozens of newspapers—eleven in Greek, five in Armenian, seven in Turkish, five in Hebrew, and four in French. Book publishing houses prospered. The city had concert halls, seventeen movie theaters, playhouses, grand hotels, private clubs with extensive menus, yacht races, hunting estates, a racetrack, and the first golf course in the Near East. It also had 226 saloons, 24 distillers, and 465 coffeehouses, which often were small gambling parlors. There was nothing a Smyrniot liked more than a wager. It had first-class steamship service to London and New York, a French department store, and a football league and stadium. It sent athletes to the early modern Olympics.

Divided by religion and ethnicity, Smyrna was a city of districts—there was the Armenian Quarter, the Greek Quarter, the Turkish Quarter, the Jewish Quarter, and the Frankish or European Quarter, though by the end of the nineteenth century the truly wealthy Levantines had moved to one of the city's nearby towns, the richest of which was Bournabat, with homes on the scale of the Newport robber barons. The servant staffs of some of the Levantines could populate small villages. A good deal of the Levantine treasure had come as a consequence of the so-called capitulations, special privileges foreign governments had negotiated with the sultan to encourage trade. One of the privileges was exemption from taxes. One sultan, his treasury depleted, took out a loan from a Levantine family at Smyrna.

The people of Smyrna could listen to opera from Italy, waltzes from Vienna, intricately sung Asian-modal melodies in the seaside cabarets, or Anatolian folk tunes in the city's hashish dens and brothels. Ever sensual, Smyrna loved its lemon sherbet and short dresses. Its penchant for frivolity outshone even its celebrated neighbors of the Levant. Compared to Smyrna, Athens was a dusty village, Beirut a backwater, and Salonika an aging slum. Even Alexandria—also founded by the insatiable Macedonian boy-king Alexander the Great—was a lesser flower of cosmopolitanism. Chateaubriand said Smyrna was another Paris; a Greek soldier, evoking the city's ancient Greek past as he approached it from the sea, called it "the bride of Ionia, the city of a thousand songs."

Smyrna had one more distinction—it was the first city in the Holy Land to receive American missionaries.

The first two missionaries assigned to the Near East departed Boston in 1819 to make New England Congregationalists of the region's inhabitants—Jews, Muslims, and Orthodox Greeks. The two young men, Levi Parsons and Pliny Fisk, in whose hearts the missionary spirit of America burned bright, stopped first at Smyrna on their way to Jerusalem. They intended to reclaim Jerusalem for the Jews by converting them to Christianity, a necessary precondition (as they understood the

Bible) for the second coming of Christ and a reordering of the world according to God's plan.

Their pilgrimage gripped America's religious imagination. From its
beginnings, America had seen itself as a New Jerusalem. (The wilderness
of the New World had sprouted innumerable Canaans, Salems, Gosh-
ens, Jerichos, and Bethels. Maine even had a Land of Nod, Indiana a
Nineveh, and New York a Babylon.) Pliny and Fisk sent letters home for
publication, and they were read in small towns all over America. Every
rock, spring, cave, and dry riverbed of the Holy Land held a fascination
for Americans. A powerful bond was conjured between America and the
Near East. The Pliny-and-Fisk journey shaped American attitudes toward the Near East for a century—and it played an important part in
forming American foreign policy. No American president—not even the
personification of isolationism, Warren G. Harding—could ignore it.

Pliny and Fisk were the vanguard, though in time the mission altered
from conversion to service through schools, orphanages, and hospitals.
Many men, and eventually many women, some of them single and traveling with other women, would follow, at great risk and personal sacrifice. Jennings was planted firmly in that tradition.

AS JENNINGS DREW CLOSER to the city, his eyes swept along the Quay,
from north to south, taking in the grand homes, hotels, and theaters
down to the big Custom House Pier and its swarm of small boats and
barges. There, he saw a long row of redbrick warehouses, trading de-
pots, and banks and export offices. Behind these buildings, and slightly
south, minarets appeared like white candles climbing a steep slope. They
marked the city's Turkish Quarter, a dense neighborhood of narrow half-
pipe streets and alleys, a bazaar shaded from the sun by cloths stretched
between poles and buildings, and stacked stucco homes with second-
story bow windows.

Jennings and his family came ashore at the Passport Pier, about the
midpoint on the long Quay.

The new arrivals found themselves pressed among Turkish porters,
piles of shipping crates, and hundreds of other passengers, some, like

the Jennings family, just arriving, and others departing for Constantinople, Salonika, Alexandria, or Beirut. The Turkish stevedores—*hamals*, in Turkish—carried enormous loads on their backs, pianos or a dozen chairs. The waterfront was busy with men pushing, lifting, loading, or just loitering, and all about them there were animals—cats, donkeys, horses, and camels. The camels, seeming a little drunk in the loose-jointed swing of their legs, regularly came into the city, threaded nose to tail, led by a tiny donkey and loaded with cargo, from carpets to spices, from the high arid interior of Anatolia.

Greek soldiers stood guard at the pier and important buildings. Other soldiers were walking along the waterfront or sitting in chairs around tin-topped tables outside the numerous cafés. Despite the military presence, the atmosphere was casual, genial, and seemingly carefree. The city sparkled in Jennings's eyes, and it seemed both secure and calm.

Ernest Otto Jacob, who was running the Smyrna YMCA, met Jennings at the pier. (The Smyrna Y's nominal director was in Constantinople on vacation.) Jacob was thirty-six years old; he had a serious look and close-set eyes, and his receding hairline gave him a high smooth brow. His career was on a fast track at the Y, though recently one of its leaders had spotted in him a tendency toward being difficult to work with—maybe through a worrisome streak of narcissism. The YMCA had sent Jacob to Smyrna to inject energy into the three-year-old chapter and get it moving, and it was Jacob who had opposed Jennings's appointment to Smyrna. Jacob was very much a YMCA type of the period—well educated, committed to reform through Christian values, modern in his outlook, and full of aspiration and vigor. There's no record of the expression Jacob wore when the little man with the hunched back came ashore as the new boys' work secretary. Jennings twisted his neck sideways to look up through his thick glasses at the much taller Jacob. He shook his hand and smiled.

The YMCA had arranged for Jennings and his family to stay at a home near the campus of International College, a preparatory school for boys in the nearby suburb of Paradise, a name chosen because of the town's profusion of flowers. The family's belongings, contained mostly in one big trunk, were loaded for the five-mile trip, which would take the family along the Quay and then (with a right turn, heading east) through the Greek and Armenian neighborhoods of Smyrna before turning south through the dry hills, spiked with cypress trees, to the American enclave at Paradise. Looking around at his new surroundings, Jennings was eager to get his family settled and begin his work. Wilted in the heat but wide-eyed about the exotic scene around them, Jennings and his family rode off to Paradise.

CHAPTER 3

The Great Offensive

On the morning of August 26, 1922, two hundred miles east of Smyrna, Mustapha Kemal, supreme commander of the Turkish nationalist army, put field glasses to his eyes and scanned the hills to the north and west of the stone bunker in which he was crouched.

He was at the summit of Kocatepe, a 6,100-foot peak overlooking the ancient Hittite town of Afyon Karahisar, the junction point of two major rail lines and the forward salient of the Greek army. The day's first light was only beginning to seep from the eastern horizon, making visible the bare hills and valleys of Anatolia's western plateau, which rolled like yellow-brown combers to the west. It remained mostly dark, but the field glasses gathered the scarce predawn light and Kemal could make out the slopes, rocks, and dug-in Greek positions. Everything was still except for the slow push and scratch of a tortoise somewhere on the mountain, the song of a bird at the approach of the day. The Greek soldiers were mostly asleep in their tents and redoubts, though a few were returning from a dance in Afyon, which was inside their line.

With Kemal were the pashas Fevzi, Ismet, and Noureddin, the core command of his army. Fevzi, the nationalist minister of defense, was the army's steady keel: senior, conservative, broad chested with a thick mustache, and a devout Muslim. He recited the Koran to his soldiers on the battlefield. Ismet was chief of the general staff and closest to Kemal, a boyish-looking tactician and latecomer to the nationalist cause, always worried but well prepared; and Noureddin, commander of the First Army, the bearded and bloody scourge of Greeks, Armenians, and Kurds.

In the half-light, spread below Kemal on the downward slopes to the right and left, was the Turkish First Army, coiled for an attack. Secretly, Kemal had left his headquarters in Ankara nine days earlier and, traveling at night, made his way to Kocatepe. Kemal was forty-one years old and already he had been given the exalted title "Ghazi," Muslim warrior. He wore a miniature Koran around his neck even though he was not in the least religious. He thought religion was for old women, mere superstition. He had assembled his idiosyncratic worldview from the ideals of the French Revolution, the militarism of Prussia, the poetry of Turkey, and the cafés and brothels of Salonika.

Among the poets he had absorbed as a young man was Namik Kemal, the Ottoman patriot.

> We are Ottomans,
> Noble lineage,
> Noble race.
> Leavened throughout
> By the blood
> Of zealotry.

Kemal was small, wiry, and blue-eyed with high cheekbones and a light complexion. Always attentive to his appearance, he wore knee-high black boots, jodhpurs, a khaki tunic, and the Turkish officer's kalpak, a black lambswool hat. Robert S. Dunn, an American intelligence officer who had met him in Ankara in 1920, said Kemal first struck him as a "well-trained superior waiter." In that meeting Kemal was dressed nattily in a slate-blue lounge suit, white pique shirt, and black bow tie, and his blond hair was combed straight back in the style of college men of the day. As Kemal spoke, Dunn's impression changed. "The whole face was sensitive rather than cerebral, subtle and mercuric rather than domineering. I felt his power of concentration, ruthlessness with an instant grasp." As a battlefield commander, Kemal dressed without adornment. His kalpak, the rough hat of the martial Anatolian male, was a powerful symbol of his identification with the people. He won battles by fusing his will to the Islamic faith and endurance of his peasant soldiers.

Kemal had decided to concentrate his forces for an overwhelming assault at Afyon Karahisar, a strategy that would (if successful) separate the Greek army from the rail line back to its base in Smyrna, cut off its supplies, and impede its retreat. It was risky, and his generals had argued against it. If it failed, they had told Kemal, the army might be finished. Kemal trusted his intuition, which so far had been flawless. He was striking at the strongest point of the Greek line, counting on surprise and ferocity to prevail. The Greek line was terribly long, a three-hundred-mile spinnaker of tired but battle-tested troops that reached from the Sea of Marmara in the north to the port of Ephesus on the Aegean coast on the south.

Only weeks earlier, British officers had visited the Greek line and reported it to be strong and battle worthy. An intelligence report said (prophetically) that the Greeks were excellent offensive fighters "strong, active and enduring, and impetuous to close with the enemy. Their impetuosity, however, makes coordination with them difficult."

The forces along the entire front were evenly matched: The Greeks had 225,000 men and an advantage in machine guns, field guns, and motorized transport. The Turks had 208,000 men and an advantage in cavalry and heavy artillery. The Greeks had the Evzones, elite mountain fighters dressed in the traditional uniform of woolen leggings, pleated kilts (400 pleats for each year of the Turkish occupation of Greece, beginning in the fifteenth century), baggy-sleeved shirts, and laceless decorated shoes. They were armed with bolt-action Mauser rifles and daggers.*

---

* The writer in Ernest Hemingway's short story "The Snows of Kilimanjaro" said it was the first time he had seen "dead men wearing white ballet skirts and upturned shoes with pompons on them." The work of Hemingway is dotted with references to the Greek-Turkish War though he did not arrive in Turkey until after the war was over in late September 1922, and even then he spent most of his time in a hotel room suffering from malaria. The aftermath of the Greek-Turkish War made Hemingway's career as a newspaper correspondent and informed his work for the rest of his life.

The Turkish army had a cavalry of skilled horsemen that attacked with long curved swords and sharpened lances, and foot soldiers armed with a bastard mix of German, French, Italian, and Russian rifles.

The Turks had the advantage in command; they had Kemal.

Kemal's soldiers, faithful Muslims, revered him; some thought he could not be killed on the battlefield. He may have believed it himself. Nowhere had his courage, brilliance, and ruthlessness been more vividly demonstrated than at Gallipoli, where he had contributed to the devastating defeat of British forces early in World War I. Gallipoli had made his reputation. Seeking in that first year of the Great War to seize Constantinople and divert Turkish troops that were threatening their ally, Imperial Russia, the British had attempted to storm and hold the westward peninsula that flanked the Dardanelles. The fighting had lasted for nine months, an Allied disaster that had cost 120,000 lives. Winston Churchill, author of the campaign, had lost his job as first lord of the Admiralty over it.

At the start of battle in April 1915, Britain had landed troops at two Gallipoli beaches. Turkish forces, under the command of German general Limon Von Sanders, were dispersed on the fifty-mile-long mountainous peninsula in anticipation of an assault, though without a clear sense of where it would occur. Kemal had commanded a division that was being held in reserve so that it could be moved rapidly to reinforce the Turkish forces that would engage the British landing force. Kemal had learned the location of the British landing soon after it occurred and quickly, and on his own initiative, marched his troops to confront the enemy force. Moving through the rugged and thorny terrain toward the landing, Kemal, traveling ahead with a small advance party for speed, encountered a regiment of Turkish soldiers in flight from the British. "What are you doing?" he asked. They were out of ammunition, they said, and they were retreating from the advancing British. Kemal ordered them to drop to the ground and remain in place. He told them they could fight with bayonets. "I don't order you to attack. I order you to die. In the time it takes us to die, other troops and commanders can come and take our places." Seeing the halt of the Turkish retreat over the rocks and low bushes of the hillside, the British force—soldiers from

Australia and New Zealand—also stopped and inexplicably lay down. The pause gave Kemal time to bring up the rest of his division. In the end, very few of the Turkish regiment had survived, but Kemal's orders halting the fleeing regiment had saved Gallipoli for the Turks.

Now seven years later in the interior of Anatolia, Kemal had given the order to prepare for an early-morning attack. This time, it was his army that would make the uphill assault. Turkish soldiers sharpened their bayonets, filled their cartridge belts, and prayed to Allah. Kemal had ordered the infantry of the Turkish First Army to slip quietly in the darkness to within a few hundred yards of the Greek line.

Over the preceding weeks, Kemal had covertly brought forces down from the north, to this point, moving them at night and hiding them under trees to avoid exposing them to Greek air surveillance. At this moment, in the region around Afyon Karahisar, the Greeks were unaware that they were outnumbered three to one. Based on private British intelligence, the Greeks had expected an attack in the north, near Eskishehir, where Kemal had ordered numerous campfires lit each night to create the illusion of a concentration of Turkish troops.

The Turkish attack was going to be a bone-breaking and bloody charge. The Greeks were dug into the mountaintops to the north and west, giving them command of the steep slopes, valley, and town below. Kemal's plan called for Turkish infantry to fight uphill toward the Greek machine guns and rifles, then overwhelm the Greek trenches, where the fighting would require bayonets, daggers, and bare hands.

Kemal had been preparing for this moment for three years. Almost single-handedly he had built a nationalist movement, begun a revolution, created an army, opposed the sultan, rebuffed the victorious Allies who had attempted to impose a treaty on Turkey, and engaged the Greek army in a series of brutal battles that despite many Greek victories had ended in stalemate. Exactly a year earlier, the Greek army had crossed the Sakaria River and come within sixteen miles of Ankara, the nationalist capital, and a Turkish defeat seemed imminent. The Sakaria battle had raged along a line sixty miles long and twelve miles deep for twenty-one days, one of the longest continuous battles in history. The deep-seated hatreds of the two armies had brought a terrible fury to the battlefield.

On both sides, the urge to war was fanned by nostalgia for old empires, Byzantine and Ottoman, and for what each side thought was rightfully its own.

"Greeks and Turks alike fought with reckless courage, threw themselves into the storms of lead in a white madness to get at each other with cold steel," wrote a British agent in Turkey at the time. "A Greek regiment refused to take cover or use trenches: the divisional staff came up into the line with it, and both were wiped out by machine-gun fire. A Turkish battalion wavered: the brigade general ran forward over the open, pulled up the colonel, blew his brains out with his revolver, steadied the battalion, and was himself blown to pieces by Greek riflemen. One division lost three-quarters of its men, another was blotted right out. Seven divisional generals were killed in close fighting."

The Battle at Sakaria had ended without a clear victor. Both sides celebrated their successes. For the year that followed, the contest had remained static as diplomacy favored the Turkish cause. In the eyes of the Allies, everything short of a complete victory was taken to be a Greek defeat; for the Turks, everything short of annihilation of their army was viewed a victory.

Kemal had put the quiet year that followed to good use: obtaining arms and supplies from Italy and Soviet Russia, playing the Allies against one another, and drilling his army. In the meantime, the Greek soldiers, many of whom had been fighting in one war or another for ten years, had waited, suffering summer heat, winter cold, lack of food, political discord in the ranks, and abandonment by the British. The Greeks had one friend—Lloyd George, who encouraged them forward with speeches in Parliament but sent neither arms nor aid.

Just before dawn, the battle began with a furious artillery assault. The Turkish guns coughed enormous exploding shells and caught the Greek troops by surprise. The Turkish foot soldiers attacked. Kemal had ordered his generals to fight with their troops. Nothing was to be held back. The Greek machine guns rattled, and the Turkish bodies piled high, but the soldiers continued to swarm uphill, and by 9:30 A.M. all but two of the mountains held by the Greeks had been taken. At one, Chigiltepe, on the Turkish left flank, a young Turkish officer in command, shamed at his failure to achieve the summit, committed suicide. Kemal scorned the useless sacrifice. At the second point of stubborn Greek resistance, to the right, Kemal appeared among his troops, cursed and insulted their fighting spirit, and told them they were inadequate to their women. Roused to anger, the Turks charged up the hill to the stuttering guns of the dug-in Greeks. Wave upon wave of Turkish assaults overcame the Greek positions, and soon, the Turks stood atop both hills. In the meantime, the Turkish cavalry, charging with guns and sabers, had swung behind the Greek line, attacking it from the rear. Kemal won the day.

The Greek troops fell back to a broad high meadow between the mountains thirty miles to the west at a village called Dumlupinar. Here, it became clear to the Greeks that they had retreated into a trap formed by quickly moving Turkish troops. Elements of the First and Second Turkish armies closed the line of escape, a narrow pass that carried the single rail line westward to Smyrna. An attempt was made to retreat over the hills to the north, but without success. Half of the Greek army in the Afyon sector was killed or captured; the other half, those who had managed to exit the valley before the escape door had been shut or had avoided it altogether, retreated back toward Smyrna. Mostly leaderless, pursued by Turkish horsemen, and harried by armed and vengeful Turkish civilians intent on killing Greek soldiers, the Greek troops left a scorched trail of burned villages on the way back to the sea. Meanwhile, the Greek army to the north of the main point of Turkish assault had maintained a semblance of command and coherence and was fighting its way back to the Sea of Marmara in the hope of reaching Mudania and Panderma, from which ports it could be evacuated back to Greece.

It was a complete and humiliating rout, and the Greek Southern Army's retreat back to Smyrna was a chaotic rush to the sea. News of the Greek disaster would take days to reach Smyrna and Constantinople. Communication lines had been cut, the frontier closed. Kemal issued terse daily communiqués, and in the cities away from the battlefields, people were unsure who the victor was—or who it would turn out to be.

CHAPTER 4

George Horton, Poet-Consul

At the end of August, American consul general George Horton and his wife, Catherine, visited Sevdikuey,* a small town of wealthy Greek and Dutch merchants about forty minutes southeast of Smyrna by way of the British-owned Smyrna–Aydin Railroad. They had friends in the town, and August was the month when people of means closed their stuffy offices to escape the city for the countryside or nearby islands. Under the Anatolian sun, faraway objects shimmered in waves of liquid heat and even lizards sought the shade of rocks. Smyrniots treated August as a long afternoon nap.

At sixty-three years old, Horton was an experienced hand in Turkey, and not easily rattled. He had pulled men out of Ottoman jails, saved others from imminent hangings, and interceded with government officials against religious killings. He had served in the Near East through two Balkan wars and World War I, and three decades of consular service, beginning in 1893, had hardened him to religious strife and massacre. But now, as he stepped back on to the train at Sevdikuey at the end of his holiday, he was deeply worried. He sensed serious trouble, possibly a catastrophe.

Sevdikeuy lay at the southern end of the Greek army's long defen-

---

* Pronounced Sev-dee-kyu-ee.

sive line, and Horton had picked up rumors that the army of Greece had suffered serious losses near Afyon Karahisar. The nationalist army was moving west, he was told, and it was pressing the Greek army along the French-operated Casaba rail line toward Smyrna. Telegraph lines had been cut, leaving the Greek command in Smyrna unable to determine the army's fate or position, and what little news there was came from Ottoman-Greek farmers who were fleeing ahead of the shifting battlefront.

If any American, or European for that matter, knew what was happening in and around Smyrna, it was Horton. In Smyrna as well as the hinterlands to the south and east, Horton's friends and network of discreet sources kept him informed. Horton's web included the Onassis brothers, successful tobacco traders in the city, but there were many others—Greek, Armenian, Levantine, and Turkish eyes and ears—upon which he relied for intelligence.

Tall and leaning on a long cane, and typically dressed in jacket and tie, Horton made a formal first impression, but he was actually a sociable old gentleman, a little florid in his language, and he relished his contact with people high and low. He spoke impeccable Greek and French and passable Italian and Turkish, and he had made it his business to parley with local officials, clergy, shopkeepers, foreign consuls, shepherds, fig traders, farmers, waterfront men, and soldiers. Based on the little he had picked up already, Horton was growing more certain that the Greek occupation of western Anatolia was drawing to an end. He had predicted a disaster from the start—comparing Greece's armed entry into Turkey to ancient Athens's calamitous invasion of Syracuse two thousand years earlier. (Horton, who had a degree in Greek and Latin from the University of Michigan, was capable of a touch of classical bombast.) He returned to Smyrna convinced that the Greek army's setbacks portended serious trouble for Smyrna's Christian population.

From the vantage of his consular postings over thirty years, Horton had watched the religious strife of the Near East evolve from isolated incidents of persecution and cynical retribution to outright government-sponsored genocide. Decaying empires, like decaying isotopes, throw off powerful amounts of dangerous energy. Turkey was a decaying em-

pire, and Horton was one of a small group of American consular officials and missionaries spread through the Near East who had witnessed
the terrible consequences of radical religious nationalism.

AFTER ARRIVING BACK at the consulate in Smyrna on August 30, Horton
began sending agitated cables to Washington with news of the Greek
debacle in the east, near Afyon Karahisar, and his fear that the nationalist
army might soon approach Smyrna.

He swept up as much unofficial information as he could about the
Greek army, which, he was told, was in rapid retreat and burning towns
and villages in its path back to the sea. Most people in Smyrna were
unaware of the scope of the Greek losses and remained calm and even
festive in the final days of August. "The three big kinema theatres on the
north Quay were doing a good business," observed an Englishman in
the city, "and the smart uniforms of the Greek officers were everywhere
prominent, and one's thoughts went back to the amusements of Paris and
London during our Great War." Even as the Greek army was falling back
toward Smyrna, an Italian opera company performed *Aida* in the big
theater at the Quayside Sporting Club.

Horton knew better than to assume the city was safe. His cables to
Washington grew more anxious. The first, on August 30, reported the
break in the Greek lines at Afyon Karahisar. "Turks have advanced along
the Casaba Railroad seventy kilometers," he wrote. By September 2, the
Greek army's setbacks had become public knowledge in Smyrna, though
most people thought the Greek command would reconstitute its line
to hold the city based on the dispatch of reinforcements by sea. Greek
troops were arriving from Thrace, the easternmost province of Greece.
On September 2, Horton cabled the State Department with a careful
description of the positions of the Greek forces between Smyrna and the
collapsing front and wrote:

"My opinion is that the situation is so serious that it can not now be
saved. Panic is spreading among the Christian population, foreigners as
well as Greek, and many are trying to leave. . . . I respectfully request that

a cruiser be dispatched to Smyrna to protect consulate and (American) nationals."

Anticipating an indifferent response from his antagonistic boss, Admiral Mark L. Bristol, in Constantinople, and possibly from Washington too, he added a postscript: "Urgently request your support." It would take four days for Horton to get an answer to his plea, and when it finally came, it would leave him disappointed. But disappointment was something he had learned to live with in Smyrna. It had hollowed out his natural idealism and left him bilious and frustrated. He already had made it clear to Washington that he wanted a transfer out of Smyrna. Even those entreaties had gone unanswered.

HORTON HAD BEEN A CONSUL for twenty-nine years. Consul positions at the time were patronage appointments and often went (as Horton candidly put it) to saloonkeepers, broken-down preachers, and political henchmen. Horton had fitted himself into that disreputable list as a former newspaperman. Consuls weren't diplomats: they were the hod carriers of the foreign service, stamping visas, intervening on behalf of American businesses, and sending commodity prices back to Washington. The pay was low, and a consul could be pulled at any moment to reward someone else with a political favor, but a consul who was a skilled party hack could make the job a sinecure if he chose, and many did. One American consul in the Near East ran a tavern across the street from the consulate. In contrast, Horton took the job seriously.

Horton's first aspiration had been to become a poet. He had graduated from the University Michigan in 1878 with honors and a passion for Greek poetry. He headed west to Nevada and California, where he had knocked about in odd jobs including, when he was fully broke, teaching school in a frontier town. He wrote verse, married young, and scraped by. It was an adventure that he had relished and, being a natural raconteur, would draw on for years as he told stories about the Wild West. After his young wife died, he traveled to Chicago and snagged a job at the *Chicago Herald* by writing about a carriage horse that wore a

summer hat with holes cut from the brim for its ears. He earned a reputation as reporter with an eye for sentimental human-interest stories,
and he was surely the only reporter in Chicago translating the poems
of Sappho while waiting around the old Des Plaines police station for
a murder that he could bang into a story. He published a volume of
his own poetry, climbed higher at the *Herald*, a Democratic newspaper, and wrote editorials praising Grover Cleveland. The president was
pleased and surprised Horton with an offer of a Foreign Service job—a
plum position in Berlin. Horton asked instead for a posting that was
open in Athens. The president gave it to him.

In 1893, Horton had traveled to Athens with his second wife, whom he
had married in Chicago. He served there happily, feasting on its sights,
collecting stories, and enjoying the parade of characters—archaeologists,
artists, and politicians from throughout the world, including the Greek
royal family. He befriended Stephen Crane, "a slender earnest young
man who was drinking himself to death." Then, in 1898, the newly
elected McKinley administration, exercising its own patronage rights,
recalled him and sent a hard-money Republican in his place. Horton
returned to Chicago and wrote even more seriously. He published two
best-selling novels with Greek settings and moved among a group of
rising literary stars of the Midwest. His friends included Edgar Lee
Masters and Theodore Dreiser. Walt Whitman praised his poetry, and
William Dean Howells his prose. He seemed to have a brilliant literary
career ahead, but in 1903, his second wife left him for a wealthy Chicago
businessman, and he sank into a paralyzing depression. An anonymous
letter from a jealous lover had disclosed the affair to Horton. Unable to
concentrate or write, Horton resigned his newspaper job, traveled aim-
lessly around the country with his young daughter, Dorothy, and her
nurse, and eventually ended up in the small upstate New York town
where he had grown up. In today's language, he was most likely clini-
cally depressed.

He was rescued by an assassination. In September 1901, an anar-
chist shot President McKinley, and he died eight days later. Horton's
friends lobbied the new president, Theodore Roosevelt, to return Horton to the consulship in Athens. Roosevelt was willing to help a prom-

ising American writer. Horton reluctantly sent Dorothy to her mother in Chicago, and he returned to Athens, exploring again his beloved ancient ruins, reciting Attic verse, and handling his old consular duties with pleasure.

Horton had liked the irreverence of Chicago newsrooms, and he had a Chicago journalist's instinct for the common man, but he also was a romantic. Walking through Chicago's Greektown, Horton had enjoyed the greetings of Greek American lunch-counter cooks who called him "*Kyrie Georgios*," "Mr. George." He responded to their peasant vernacular in ancient Greek, the language of Pericles, which only further endeared him to them as an eccentric. Horton loved Greece, the idea of it as well as the reality of it. He was a sentimentalist, and he wore his sentiment proudly. It was a characteristic that would hurt him with the diplomatic professionals in the State Department, where a cool indifference to the inhabitants of foreign countries was held in high regard. As events would demonstrate, Horton was anything but detached.

In 1910, the State Department posted him to Salonika. The next twelve years of his career would give him an education in religious conflict and ethnic cleansing.

He had arrived in Salonika, then still an Ottoman city, at a time of political tumult in the Ottoman Empire. Two years earlier, a group of young Ottoman army officers, embittered by the empire's decline and its territorial losses, had forced Sultan Abdul Hamid II to reinstate Turkey's constitution. Abdul Hamid, ruthless, paranoid, and reclusive, had suspended it three decades earlier, and there was a sense among the army officers, the "Young Turks," that a return to constitutional government would revive the empire's fortunes by wresting it from the backwardness of the aging sultan. The return of constitutional government created a brief moment of celebration among the peoples of the multicultural and multireligious Ottoman Empire—Muslims, Greeks, Armenians, and Jews. There was a surge of Ottomanism—the idea that the empire's many different people could live together as equals and in peace in a Muslim state. The goodwill was brief. Conservative Muslims led a countercoup on behalf of the sultan; the Young Turks put it down, and this time the military leaders forced Abdul Hamid's abdication. The Young Turks replaced him with his brother, Mehmet V, a puppet.

The doctrine of a liberal and tolerant Ottomanism rapidly evaporated, and soon it became clear that the Young Turks saw the expulsion of Christian minorities and creation of a homogeneous Muslim nation as the way to rescue the empire. They enforced their vision with brutality. Horton watched as Turkish authorities executed a terror campaign against Christians around Salonika and the backcountry of Macedonia. Christians began to disappear without explanation or were found dead in their fields. Horton put his reporting skills to work, documented the terror, and sent numerous descriptions of the harassment and killing back to Washington. Nor was the killing limited to the Balkans. Nearly thirty thousand Armenian and Assyrian Christians were slaughtered in pogroms in Adana, a region in southern Anatolia. These episodes of religious cleansing, however, were mere preliminaries to the slaughter that would follow.

In 1911, the State Department transferred Horton again, this time to Smyrna. He swooned at his good fortune. Smyrna was the legendary birthplace of Homer, and the Aegean coast of Asia Minor once had been home to the Ionian Greeks who counted among their citizens the philosophers Thales, Pythagoras, Anaximander. His favorite poet, Sappho, had written her love lyrics on the island of Lesbos, near Smyrna, and classical allusions everywhere scored the landscape—Phocaea, the Greek city-state celebrated by Herodotus for its resistance to the Persians in 500 BC, still stood at the tip of Smyrna's harbor. Herodotus himself, the father of history, was born in nearby Halicarnassus.

Horton moved into the America consulate at Smyrna, a mansion at 17-23 Galazio Street with his third wife, Catherine, a beautiful and cultivated Greek woman twenty-five years his junior whom he had met in Athens. His energy, eccentricity, and friendly personality won favor with Turks and Greeks of the city, and he pursued his interests—he played golf at the club in Paradise, went woodcock shooting on nearby estates, and occasionally joined the archaeological dig at Sardis, the ancient capital of the Lydian Empire and its famously rich king, Croesus. Within the year, at age fifty-one, he was a father again. Nancy, his second daughter, grew into a bright blond girl, and the Hortons sent her to the French convent school in the city.*

IN THE FIRST FEW DAYS of September, the Turkish nationalist army had continued to draw closer to Smyrna, bringing its cavalry, infantry, and artillery forward in a rapidly moving line. By September 3, it had taken the city of Ushak, only one hundred and twenty miles distant by way of the Casaba Railroad, and General Nikolaos Trikoupis, the senior Greek commander in the field, had been taken prisoner.

By September 3, Smyrna's newspapers stopped publishing the reassuring false reports planted by the Greek authorities and plainly reported news of the Greek army's retreat. A tremor went through the Christian and expatriate residents of the city. The Asia Minor Defense League, a local organization of Greeks, distributed guns and ammunition to its members. The League was a political (and quickly becoming quasi-military) organization formed months earlier by Smyrna Ottoman Greeks when the Greek government in Athens had signaled that its army would pull out of Turkey. Unwilling to accept the return of Turkish rule and the harsh consequences that would follow, the Defense League had hoped to create a force of local Greeks and supportive elements of the Greek army to resist a Turkish takeover of Smyrna. It was a desperate idea, given the strength of the nationalist army, but for Greeks and Armenians whose home was Smyrna, desperation seemed the only response.

It was becoming clear there was no ready escape for most of the Christian residents of Smyrna, and most assumed that the Turkish army would retaliate against the Christian population. Horton had already begun planning for the worst. He encouraged his wife to depart, but she insisted on staying with him.

He also encouraged his friend Socrates Onassis to leave. Onassis was one of the richest Greeks in the city, president of the tobacco exporters association, and the eldest of five brothers who operated a trading company

---

* Nancy Horton, at 102 years old, was living today in Athens as this book was written. She was interviewed several times.

in the city. On being tipped early by Horton to the possibility of a nationalist occupation, Socrates had sent his wife and three daughters to Lesbos
but kept his eighteen-year-old son, Aristotle, with him at their home in
Karatas, a seaside neighborhood just south of Smyrna. Aristotle was a
small, muscular, and clever young man who liked to have a good time,
and a good time often included women who wanted to be paid for their
companionship. (It was a trait he took into adult life when he became the
world's richest man.) Aristo, as he was called, was often in conflict with
his father, a strict, serious, and observant Orthodox Christian. One of the
Onassis brothers had departed for Athens, and two others went to towns
east of Smyrna, where they had tobacco connections and where they
thought they would be safe. A fourth was already in the countryside. As
prominent members of the Asia Minor Defense League, they all were in
danger. On Horton's advice, Socrates, the family's leader, had also hurried away two ships with cargoes of tobacco and cotton for Britain.

The Greeks in Smyrna recognized Horton's philhellenism and
counted him as a friend. On September 4, the Greek governor Stergiades asked Horton to request American mediation for a peaceful tran-
sition from Greek to Turkish occupation. Horton sent the request, along
with a recommendation of approval, to Constantinople and Washington.
As the Turkish army drew nearer to the city, the Greek metropolitan,
Chrysostomos, came to Horton and pleaded for American protection of
Smyrna's Christians.

A stream of Greeks and Armenians—some Ottoman subjects, some
naturalized Americans—also showed up at the American consulate and
filled its first-floor reception room. Agitated and panicky, they wanted
Horton's help to leave the country. He told them he would do what he
could, and he tried especially to assist the naturalized Americans and
those he knew would be in danger because they had collaborated with
the Greek administration. The people needed papers and transportation.
He wrote letters on consulate stationery that might pass as substitutes for
authorization to travel and went in search of ships that could be chartered
to carry people away. He tried without success to put some of the people
who had come to him on British ships. In the meantime, he waited for
an answer from Washington.

CHAPTER 5

Garabed Hatcherian*

G arabed Hatcherian lived in the Smyrna Armenian neighborhood
at 109 Tchakildji Bashi Street, near the Basmahane train station.
He and his wife, Elisa, had two daughters and three sons. Their
youngest child, a girl named Vartouhi, was one year old. Their oldest,
a boy named Hatcheres, was thirteen. Garabed Hatcherian was a doctor whose patients were mostly from prominent Armenian families. He
was a general practitioner with special training in gynecology. He had
lived alone for most of the summer seeing patients and living frugally
while his wife and children had been visiting his wife's family in Akhisar,
about fifty miles northeast of Smyrna. With news of the Turkish army
advances, they returned to Smyrna on Saturday, September 2.

Dr. Hatcherian was forty-six years old. He had deep-set eyes, a narrow sensitive face, and hair that was parted high on the right and closely
cropped near his ears. He conveyed an impression of intelligence, caution, and skill. He looked like a doctor.

---

* This summary of the life and experiences of Dr. Hatcherian, and those that follow,
are taken from *An Armenian Doctor in Turkey—Garabed Hatcherian: My Smyrna
Ordeal of 1922.* Dr. Hatcherian's diary was a family heirloom, discovered by his
granddaughter Dora Sakayan in 1991. Professor Sakayan, a scholar of applied lin-
guistics, first published it in Armenian and subsequently in English (Arod Books,
1997). It is a rare and astonishing document.

He had been born in an Armenian village on the Sea of Marmara, studied medicine in Constantinople, and served four years as a captain and medical officer in the Ottoman army during World War I. While he had been away at war, in the Dardanelles and Romania, Armenians in his home village had been deported or massacred, and the village destroyed. After the war, he had moved to Smyrna, which had put him and Elisa not far from Elisa's family. Dr. Hatcherian was not rich as were some of the Armenian doctors in the city, but he had methodically built his practice and reputation; the National Armenian Hospital in the city had taken him on the staff, a matter of distinction.

Dr. Hatcherian was not an excitable person or prone to exaggerated fears but the nationalist army's advance toward Smyrna weighed heavily on him. Like nearly every other Armenian family, his had suffered during the deportations of 1915–16. Many of the most prominent Armenians in Smyrna, including other doctors, had already chosen to leave Smyrna. They had packed their belongings and departed with their families on steamships for Constantinople. Now Dr. Hatcherian had to make a decision about leaving or staying. It was not an easy choice. He had forebodings of what might happen if the nationalist army occupied the city, but he also had begun to assemble a practice that promised to give him and his family a comfortable life in Smyrna in the years ahead. He consulted with others about what to do, including a friend at the French consulate who, as a personal friend of the French consul, reassured him that all would be well despite the disorder and anxiety prevalent in the city. This trouble would pass, the man had said. Dr. Hatcherian was cheered by the advice. Nonetheless, evidence of the war's brutality, moving ever closer to Smyrna, was obvious to him.

"The streets of the city have become completely impassable," he wrote in his diary. "Along with the refugees, wounded soldiers are filling the city as hundreds arrive at the hospital in trucks. The situation has seriously worsened."

Dr. Hatcherian continued to see his patients and carried on as normally as possible, calming his wife and children even as he encouraged the family to take precautions.

"Bread and food supplies have diminished. We start to store food and, at the same time, to pack our valuables into boxes and sacks. Despite these preparations, thousands like me are firmly convinced that the Turks cannot enter Smyrna."

Despite the confidence displayed in the diary entry, Dr. Hatcherian had not fully persuaded himself that he and his family were safe. He wrestled with the doubt, and at the same time feared an overreaction that would upset the progress he had made in his life and career.

He turned the matter over in his mind during several sleepless nights. Unwilling to make his wife anxious, he recorded his thinking in the diary: "I held the position of a municipal doctor for almost ten years; I have completed four full years in the military and I have official documents at hand confirming my impeccable service. Therefore, I do not wish to lose my enviable position, achieved after three years of steady work in Smyrna, when the danger seems so remote."

He decided to stay in Smyrna.

CHAPTER 6

Admiral Bristol,
American Potentate

In Constantinople, Rear Admiral Mark Bristol often scheduled his work at the U.S. embassy in the Italian villa Palazzo Corpi in the mornings so he could escape to his naval yacht, the USS *Scorpion*, in the afternoons.

The city was crowded, noisy, and unbearably hot, and the streets smelled of a nauseating stew of garbage, sewage, and grilled meat. Even in the fashionable embassy district along the Grand Rue de Pera, street vendors shouted, wood carts clanged over the narrow side streets that cascaded down cobbled steps, beggars harangued tourists, and men with tiny uniformed monkeys and tin cups banged their tambourines.

Bristol's routine, when he could manage it, was to finish his meetings and written reports in the early afternoon, then ride in his admiral's barge to the *Scorpion*, a sleek two-masted motor vessel moored six miles up the Bosporus at Therapia, an old Greek resort town of blue and pink mansions where he kept his yacht as a summer residence. There was often a cool breeze at Therapia that lifted off the Black Sea, and it was a pleasant place to sit on the deck with an iced drink or play tennis in the dappled shade of the giant plane and eucalyptus trees.

Constantinople in 1922 was a heaving and rotting city of a million and a half people—Turks, Greeks, Armenians, Jews, Bulgarians, Circassians, Arabs, Persians, Albanians, Russians, Georgians, Ukrainians, Tartars, and Kalmucks—among others. It was also the temporary home of a hundred thousand Russian refugees, poor soldiers as well as Russian officers and aristocrats, men and women, who had fled Soviet Russia in 1919 and 1920 after the defeat of White Russians in the civil war that had followed the Bolshevik revolution. The Russian refugees were packed into wooden barracks, cheap boardinghouses, and hotels. Russian soldiers, wearing their tsar's army medals on their tunics, sold paper flowers along the streets to get coins for food, and elegant Russian women whose families had owned country estates waited on tables and sang Russian folk songs for tips in restaurants—the Muscovite and Maxim's were two American favorites. Maxim's was owned by a black American who had left his restaurant in Moscow and come to Constantinople with his White Russian wife.

The Bosporus, a thirty-mile natural canal of southward-rushing water, divides Constantinople between Asia and Europe. The Bosporus connects the Black Sea to the turquoise basin called the Sea of Marmara, which in turn flows into the Mediterranean by way of a thirty-eight-mile slim passage called the Dardanelles. The Bosporus is a maritime anomaly of two flows—fresh water on the surface moving from the Black Sea into the Mediterranean, and salt water at the bottom moving from the Mediterranean to the Black Sea. Gorged by the great rivers of Europe (Danube, Dniester, Dnieper), the Black Sea is twenty inches higher than the Mediterranean; the Bosporus is the geological pipe that connects the two, swollen by swift water and swirling currents.

Constantinople sits at the terminus of the Bosporus. Bisected by the river, the city is fissured yet again by a deep inlet on the European side—the Golden Horn. So it is a metropolis of three parts—on the European side, Pera, which in 1922 was the redoubt of Europeans, embassies, including the Palazzo Corpi, hotels, cafés, and brothels; and Stamboul—the site of the old walled city of Christian Byzantium and location of the St. Sophia Mosque. In 1922, the two parts of the city were connected by the floating Galata Bridge, a span first erected in the sixth century by Byzantine Emperor Justinian the Great. On the Asiatic side of the

Bosporus lay Scutari—in 1922, the dense urban aggregation of oriental Anatolia. After World War I, Constantinople was a whispering city of down-market intrigue: "The Bosporus," wrote a navy intelligence officer, "was a dumping of all Europe's war crooks and spies."

Punctilious and ordered, Bristol maintained a crisp military demeanor even in Constantinople's torpor, which was particularly thick and uncomfortable on this day. At his desk in his spacious office on the second floor of the embassy, the Italianate mansion atop Pera Hill, he wore a double-breasted blue jacket with gold admiral's stripes and a star on each arm, a stiff white shirt, and a tie pulled tight to his thick neck. His blue serge trousers touched his polished black shoes when he rose to greet a guest. A British tailor custom-made his uniforms, and they showed an impeccable fit. Hardly an American of any standing passed through Constantinople without climbing the eleven marble steps of the embassy and traversing its high-ceilinged and frescoed halls to call on the admiral. Built by a Genoese trader in the nineteenth century, the mansion with its grand staircase and parquet floors was a fitting address for Bristol. He was the center of American commerce and diplomacy in the region—he gave speeches to the Chamber of Commerce, arranged transportation on his destroyers for American oil executives, and put himself at the center of the city's network of American relief agencies.

His first caller on Saturday September 2, 1922, was the manager of the local branch of the Guaranty Trust Co., one of America's largest banks. It was closing its Constantinople office and selling its business to the Anglo-Ionian Bank, a British company with close ties to Greece.

On hearing the news, Bristol exploded. He had worked for two years to bring an American bank to Constantinople, even leaning on a close friend, Lucian Irving Thomas, a director of the Standard Oil Co. of New York, to open an account and deposit company funds to give the bank a good start, and now he was hearing that it was being sold to the British and Greeks. Bristol was perpetually suspicious of the British, and he despised the Greeks. In Bristol's mind, Greeks were worse even than Jews and Armenians; they were a race of clever and dishonest merchants.

American businesses, he huffed at the young and apologetic bank manager, were always quick to ask for the help of the U.S. government, but when the government (in this instance, Bristol) wanted their help, they shrugged their shoulders and showed indifference. Bristol was sure that the British were intent on squeezing the Americans out of commerce in the Near East, and making matters worse, the Ionian Bank had connections to Basil Zaharoff, the notorious Ottoman-Greek arms dealer who had helped finance Greece's army in Turkey and maintained close relationships with both Lloyd George, the British prime minister, and Eleftherios Venizelos, architect of the Greek presence in Anatolia— both detested by Bristol. The bank was probably a subterfuge for British and Greek imperialism or Zaharoff's personal designs.

As Bristol talked, he frequently raised his chin in the manner of a boxer taunting his opponent. An American bank was necessary for American business, he insisted, though the manager was offering no opposition to the admiral's argument. His temper let loose, Bristol raged on: there was opportunity here in Turkey, and there was money to be made—money for Americans. The young manager lowered his eyes and agreed with the admiral but there was nothing he could do. He had his orders from New York. The bank had not been profitable and it would be closed. He handed Bristol the papers outlining the sale terms, which included a pledge from the Guaranty Trust Co. to promote the Ionian Bank. Bristol was disgusted. Simply disgusted.

Stern-looking and jowly at fifty-four, with receding hair parted in the middle, Bristol projected military discipline and authority. His barrel chest, dark eyebrows, one of which formed an upside-down V like a proofreader's caret, and a mouth turned down on either side when at rest—all these physical characteristics combined with his piercing dark eyes to give him the aspect of a firm but (in his own way) fair prison warden. He liked to think of himself that way—firm, but fair, a proponent of the "square deal." He also liked to think of himself as man who dealt in facts. He kept voluminous records, adhered to protocol, and forcefully advocated the interests of his country as he construed them. Sometimes, his construction of those interests was at odds with his superiors' views back in Washington, but Washington was a long way from Constantinople, and Washington often had other things on its mind besides this bluff old salt.

Bristol's official title was U.S. High Commissioner to the Ottoman Empire. Since the two countries did not have diplomatic relations, Bristol did not carry the title of ambassador, but that essentially was his job—representing America and looking out for the interests of Americans in the Near East. So broad was his authority that its eastward boundary had never been established. Bristol also was the chief naval officer in the Eastern Mediterranean, officially the Commander of the U.S. Naval Detachment in Turkish Waters. STANAV, in naval jargon. He had two staffs, one diplomatic and the other military, and the broad authority and workload that came with the double assignment suited his industriousness. He had eight destroyers under his command, and on that day in September, six of them were in the Black Sea—two of them at Russian ports and four along Turkey's northerly coast. The other two were at Constantinople, moored in the Bosporus, within view of the terrace of the American embassy and off Dolmabache Palace—a "wedding cake gone moldy." Bristol had repeatedly asked the navy for a battleship to add heft and prestige to his naval force, but it had been repeatedly denied.

THE NAVY HAD SENT Bristol to Turkey in 1919 with the title "Senior United States Naval Officer in Turkish Waters." It was a modest title for what appeared to be a modest job. At the time, the United States already had a commissioner in Constantinople, Lewis Heck, a thirty-two-year-old graduate of Lehigh University who had worked as a secretary under the former ambassador, Henry Morgenthau.

The State Department had directed Bristol to cultivate cordial relations with the Allies in Turkey and safeguard Americans and their interests in the Near East. Even before arriving at his new duty station, he had chafed at his title and the limits of his authority. He had construed the job as more like a high commissioner—an ambassador. He sought the help of his wife, Helen, and his friend Irving Thomas at Standard Oil to aright this injustice. He encouraged Helen to discuss his situation with Thomas in Washington and use her contacts to help him. "Anyway Irving is the one to fix things," he wrote to her. "Wait until you see Irving then use your head and you can help me." Then in a subsequent letter: "By the way be careful in regard to anything you do there not to go against the (Navy) Department especially so they know it. . . . I know what a 'long head' you have when it comes to doing things—you love to do—this is only a hint."

The letters between them show a determined couple working assiduously on his ascent. The young Heck was no match for Bristol, a tough inside politician with a well-connected wife. Heck was gone by the summer, and Gabriel Bie Ravndal, a Norwegian American and former newspaper publisher from North Dakota with long service in the Near East, replaced him. Ravndal and Bristol battled, and Bristol prevailed over him as well. In less than a year, by working his connections, assuming powers not explicitly denied him, moving uninvited into the former ambassador's residence, and sending a torrent of correspondence to his naval superiors and the State Department about his need for a grander title, he was named U.S. high commissioner. Bristol had called in chits in all directions, but his promotion to high commissioner actually had come because of the Greek landing at Smyrna. (Ironical, that it was the Greeks who helped him get the job he craved.) The crisis that followed called for the United States to have a person with broad authority in Constantinople. Bristol was standing by. President Wilson accepted the recommendation of Secretary of State Robert Lansing, who had been helped along in his thinking by Bristol's superior officer, Admiral William S. Benson, chief of Naval Operations. Benson would be remembered for his inability to conceive of any use the navy could make of aviation.

Bristol claimed authority over the entire region inside the prewar borders of the Ottoman Empire. His headquarters were in Constantinople, but there were also posts in Jerusalem, Damascus, Aleppo, Beirut, Baghdad, Samsun, and Smyrna. His staff consisted of consuls, military and commercial attachés, counselors, secretaries, and translators. He consolidated his authority rapidly and set up an extensive system for collecting intelligence employing his ships' commanders as well as a staff of intelligence officers. For Bristol no detail seemed too trivial for the files he kept on the missionaries. One of his officers provided him with personality sketches of the missionaries in Mersina, a port in southern Anatolia: "Rev. Mr. Willson: About 40 to 45 years old, of the Reformed Presbyterian denomination; is very much of a 'stay at home' does not go out and mingle the people: this may be on account of his not speaking Turkish. He speaks Arabic. His denomination is one of the strictest. Is a fair conversationalist and is fairly broad-minded. Does not think any great results can be obtained by the missionaries in a short time, but hopes for results after a long time by absorption. . . . His wife is a typical missionary type."

A lot of Bristol's intelligence was questionable. He once reported that a British general was on his way to Turkey with an important Turkish political prisoner—only to have the State Department wire back that the general was in New York. The British considered him naive in dealing with the Turks, and the State Department suggested removing his principal intelligence officer, Robert Steed Dunn. Dunn had a reputation for dealing in barroom gossip, and the intemperate prose in his reports drew a rebuke from Admiral Harry Knapp, vice admiral of the navy.

Mrs. Bristol had joined her husband in Constantinople in the summer of 1920. He was devoted to her, and she to him. She accompanied him on his sea trips, including one to Smyrna when she had apparently made a remark that was construed as impolitic by Armenian residents. On learning that a Smyrna newspaper had made a reference to it, Bristol wanted George Horton to correct the record. Horton, responding diplomatically to his boss, suggested that it was better not to stir up more attention. There was one other incident, Horton said, that he had struggled about mentioning to the admiral, but felt that he should. He told Bristol of a tea he had attended following Bristol's stay in Smyrna. "The Armenians present were discussing your party in the most friendly—even enthusiastic way, speaking in English. One young lady remarked that it was a pity that Mrs. Bristol was doing some indiscreet talking." It seemed that Mrs. Bristol's opinions about the "races" in the Near East were every bit as strong as her husband's. Horton offered to interview the lady if Bristol wanted him to, but he advised against it. Bristol agreed that it would not be helpful, but the subsequent correspondence between Horton and Bristol afterward was cool. Sometimes Bristol didn't respond at all.

The Bristols ran the American naval and diplomatic apparatus in Constantinople like a mom-and-pop business. Helen Bristol threw herself into creating a busy and useful social life for them in Constantinople that included charity and relief work on behalf of Russian refugees. She arranged parties and dances to raise money for the displaced and homeless Russians and was not above twisting the arms of acquaintances with the means to make donations. She spoke to tourists aboard visiting cruise ships and then asked for donations. She held events inside the Palazzo Corpi, knowing that guests would be willing to pay to view the frescoes, grand hall, and elaborate rooms. Not everyone found the Bristols charming, or even good company. "A nasty pair," said a British officer who was part of the set in Constantinople.

Helen Bristol was the daughter of a prominent family from Mobile, Alabama, and even as a young woman she had put her energy and social status to work in a society newsletter, "Social Season," which reported on the debutantes, cotillions, Confederate balls, and important marriages in the South. Helen's marriage to Bristol, in June 1908, was her second and his first. He was forty; she was thirty-nine. Helen had been married previously to a railroad executive, William Bailey Thomas, who had died in 1901 but not before she had aggressively intervened with personal connections that led directly to President McKinley to advance her first husband's army career. She had worked through the U.S. postmaster general, a family friend, who after much pressing from Mrs. Thomas spoke to McKinley. "I went to the White House this afternoon expressly to see the President on your matter. . . ." She had been a widow for seven years when she met Bristol—her family was involved in the harbor-dredging business, run by her father and brother, Rittenhouse Moore and Rittenhouse Moore Jr. Helen (Moore) Bristol was a practical, capable, and imposing woman, and the ambitions of her and her husband fused in his career. It sometimes needed a little help from a woman who knew her way around polite society and military politics.

Bristol's career was not without blemish. In 1912, the destroyer USS *Albany* ran aground under his command in the fog off the south coast of China. A naval panel found him at fault and recommended a reprimand. The rocks struck by the ship had been well marked on maritime charts, and he should have known the ship was headed directly toward them. Most revealing about the inquest that followed the accident was not the person who had misread the compass or erroneously taken down the ship's course, both of which were points of dispute in the case. The memorable point was Bristol's hectoring of the young navigation officer who had been on the bridge. At the naval inquiry, Bristol placed blame for the grounding on the man and brushed away any suggestion that he, despite being the commanding officer on the bridge, bore any fault. In response to Bristol's request for a review of the navy's decision that went against him, he received firm affirmation that the navigational error was his. The review also said this: "The Captain (Bristol) subjected the officer-of-the-deck to a set of series of cross-questioning which savored very much of 'bullying,' with insinuations as to the O.D.'s (Officer of the Deck's) age, rank and experience." It is not difficult to see the future blustering Admiral Bristol in the bullying of the younger Captain Bristol.

Soon after the Albany incident, in July 1914, Admiral Bradley A. Fiske, the great naval inventor (telescopic gun sights, aerial torpedoes, the artillery rangefinder), picked Bristol to head up the Office of Naval Aeronautics—at the very beginning of the military's interest in aircraft as a weapon. Bristol's expertise was naval ordnance. At the time, the navy had seven pilots and decided to place its flight-training center at Pensacola, Florida, instead of Annapolis (based on better weather). Bristol threw himself into the job with his trademark energy. He also got into a dispute with the pilots over aircraft design. The pilots favored the so-called tractor approach, which places the propeller ahead of the engine so that the plane is pulled ahead by its prop. Bristol favored propellers behind the engines so the propellers pushed the plane forward. The tractor approach was safer—when a plane crashed, which was not uncommon in the early years, the engine absorbed the impact, helping the pilot to survive. "I hope you will not use up too much time on arguments in regard to tractors and pushers," Bristol lectured a pilot, "because arguments not based on facts and evidence will waste your time and mine. . . . The tractor is doomed for military purposes." Of course, the pilot-favored approach eventually prevailed, but not before several pilots were killed. The rancor he stirred at Pensacola had eventually stalled his promotion to rear admiral.

In 1916, after working behind a desk in Washington, Bristol returned to sea duty but continued to experiment with naval aircraft, including launching planes from battleships and cruisers. He commanded the battle cruiser USS *North Carolina* and the battleship *Oklahoma*, and in 1918 he took command of the U.S. Navy base at Plymouth, England. From there, he went to Belgium, then to Turkey. He brought with him no knowledge of the country and no background in diplomacy. He considered himself a quick study.

ON THIS MORNING of September 2, Bristol had a lot on his mind besides the American bank that was closing. The military situation in Turkey was rapidly deteriorating. It was conceivable that the embers of the world war would burst back into flame in Asia Minor, and the British might soon find themselves in a hot war again with the Turks. In 1922, the military forces of Britain, France, and Italy, ostensible allies who were actually at one another's throats, lightly occupied Constantinople. The sultan was hiding in his waterfront palace.

Only days before, Bristol had received a report from his chief of staff that a force of the Turkish nationalists had fortified its position within fifty miles of Constantinople. The British, along with the French and Italians, were moving a thin contingent of troops out of Constantinople along the intervening railway to block a nationalist sweep into the city. The Allies had continued to officially recognize the government in Constantinople with the sultan as its titular head of state. His imperial majesty, the sultan Mehmed VI, emperor of the Ottomans and caliph to the Faithful throughout the world, now sixty-one years of age, had become a prisoner in his waterside palace with his courtiers, eunuchs, and five wives. By September 1922, he lacked even the power of a symbolic ruler. If the nationalists decided to move their army into Constantinople, the British would have difficulty stopping them. The French and Italians were fully unreliable. At the same time, Bristol had learned, nationalist forces had begun an offensive against the army of Greece in the country's interior, with apparent success.

In London, the government's war cabinet was meeting to consider its military options. Bristol judged the entire situation in the region a diplomatic hash. Yes, he thought, all of this was an inept and sorry jumble, especially for the British and the Greeks, but it was shaping up as a win for the Americans if he could continue to steer United States policy in the right direction—toward a friendly partnership with the nationalists. It was clear that a new order was beginning to emerge, and Bristol intended to continue guiding it for the benefit of the United States. This had been his self-imposed mission almost from the day he had arrived in Turkey three years earlier. He consoled himself with the thought that he was giving his government good counsel and doing what Washington had asked of him when he had come to Constantinople—to watch over American interests. Bristol had worked to open a door for American commercial interests, including the oil companies in the Near East, and now events were turning in the direction in which he had pushed.

He cheered the successes of the nationalists and gloated over the failures of the British and Greeks. All in all, despite disappointment with the Guaranty Trust Co., his mood was brighter than it had been in days. The day was Saturday and he planned to take the afternoon off. A long holiday weekend lay ahead—Labor Day. A little huffing and puffing over the bank had probably improved his disposition. The Bosporus sparkled outside the office windows of his office.

Bristol left the Palazzo around noon, bound for Therapia. His mind was on his yacht with its two raked masts and his tennis game. He played tennis every day and golf at least twice a week. Later, he made a note in his diary: "The afternoon was a half holiday, which was spent on board the *Scorpion* at Therapia. We had as guests for luncheon Dr. C. N. Ratcliff and Lieut. Commander L. C. Evans-Thomas, both of the Royal Navy. I took them up in my barge and had them to luncheon so that they could complete the Tennis tournament before their ship sailed."

In the evening, the admiral wrote, he and Mrs. Bristol (he always referred to his wife, Helen, as Mrs. Bristol) joined guests at the Summer Palace Hotel in Therapia for dinner and attended a dance. The Summer Palace Hotel was the grandest of Therapia's destinations, and Therapia, like Constantinople, was a whirlwind of legation dinners, dances, and lavish entertainments. The world might be headed for a second war in Turkey or the Balkans, but the fun continued in Constantinople. The Bristols were often present as a couple of senior chaperones—the military's Victorian parents of a smart young set of officers and their wives swaying to jazz bands, dancing the foxtrot, and drinking the whiskey-and-sodas that were banned back home.

On that pleasant afternoon of September 2, when Consul General Horton had sent his urgent cable from Smyrna, four hundred miles to the south, pleading for a ship to provide protection, Bristol was playing tennis with the British officers in white shorts on the lawn at Therapia.

CHAPTER 7

Washington Responds

A t about midnight on Saturday, September 2, George Horton's cable reached the Near East desk of the State Department in the south wing of the State, War, and Navy Building, one block from the White House on Pennsylvania Avenue.*

A telegraph operator at the Eastern Telegraph Co. on the Smyrna waterfront had tapped out dots and dashes of letters and numbers that contained Horton's message ciphered into the State Department's Gray Code. The message had moved over the British-owned system of undersea cables, and when it had reached the United States, a Western Union operator had routed it to the State Department. It typically took a message an hour or two to travel from Smyrna to Washington on the network, and there was a seven-hour time difference between the two cities.

It was the first day of the long Labor Day weekend, the last holiday of summer, and an excuse for the city's residents to depart muggy Washington for the seaside resorts of Delaware or Maryland. It had rained furiously late Friday and early Saturday, sending Rock Creek over its banks, flooding streets and stalling trolley cars along Connecticut Avenue, but

---

* The building is now called the Eisenhower Executive Office Building.

by the end of the workweek most everyone who had planned a holiday at the Atlantic shore had already left, and the sun had come out in time for the last-place Boston Red Sox to trounce the Washington Nationals at Griffith Park. It was a double-header, and the Red Sox won both games. The State Department was thinly staffed, and eventually the cable reached the chief of the Near East desk, Allen Dulles, a promising twenty-nine-year-old Princeton graduate who had only recently returned from Constantinople. He had served there as Mark Bristol's diplomatic assistant, smoothing relations between the admiral and the British and gathering information that would help Washington formulate a strategy to secure oil supplies in the Near East. Dulles and Bristol remained in friendly contact, and Dulles had become a kind of buffer and interpreter on behalf of the outspoken admiral in Washington

On Tuesday, September 5, Dulles sent Horton's cable to William Phillips, who had just returned from his family's estate in Massachusetts, where his wife had just given birth to their first child. Phillips was the acting secretary of state, while the secretary of state, the formidable Charles Evans Hughes, former governor of New York and justice of the U.S. Supreme Court, was on a passenger ship with an American delegation traveling to Rio de Janeiro for Brazil's centennial. Phillips was in charge while Hughes was away and out of radio contact.

Phillips was a lean, starchy, and well-bred Bostonian, forty-four years old, who had entered service at the State Department in 1903 through a family friend, the U.S. ambassador to Great Britain. Phillips was prodigiously patrician. His family traced its beginnings in America to the Massachusetts Bay Colony, and Phillips had degrees from Harvard College and Harvard Law School. His family had homes in Boston's highbrow Back Bay and on Massachusetts's North Shore, an oceanfront escape of farms and polo ponies. Phillips was the sort of man who had often dropped in for lunch with the aging eminence Henry Adams at his home on H Street. Phillips had served as undersecretary of state for President Wilson, an intellectual whom he admired, and briefly as the American minister to the Netherlands. He now served a president he did not admire, or even respect—Warren G. Harding. "Too many of his evenings," Phillips wrote, "were spent playing poker with his cronies, of which I was not one, and imbibing more than was good for him in spite of national prohibition."

The State Department's attention was mostly focused on Europe and the debate over German reparations—France wanted them paid in full, Britain was for relaxing them. Runaway inflation was ravaging the Weimar Republic, which was printing Deutschmarks by the billions to pay its bills. The department was also keeping an eye on Turkey, and Phillips had been tipped to serious trouble well before he read Horton's cable on Tuesday. The U.S. embassy in Paris had picked up word from the British nine days earlier that the Turkish nationalist army had resumed hostilities, and Phillips had also seen Horton's earlier cable, sent August 30, reporting the nationalist attack on the Greek line. Sitting in his office on the building's second floor, Phillips could just as easily have looked at the front page of the *Washington Post*. The lead headline reported: TURKS NEAR SMYRNA; CROWDS AT SMYRNA, SEEKING TO EMBARK FOR U.S., BESIEGE AMERICAN CONSULATE.

Nonetheless, the warning in Horton's cable concerned Phillips. It said Americans needed protection. Horton had a reputation for the rhetorical flourish, but the situation appeared genuinely dangerous. ". . . I respectfully request," Horton had written, "that a cruiser be dispatched to Smyrna to protect consulate and nationals." Another aspect of the cable caught Phillips's careful attention. It requested naval protection but Horton had addressed it to the secretary of state, not to Admiral Bristol. From the copy Phillips had in hand, it appeared that Horton had not even copied the admiral on his request for a ship. Everyone who knew Bristol understood he was sensitive to slights, and jumping over him to appeal directly to Washington for naval protection was no mere oversight. Horton's reporting relationship as a consul was sufficiently ambiguous to allow him direct communication with the secreatry of state, but the end run around Bristol suggested that the trouble between the two men had opened into a serious breach at a bad time.

The snub, if that's what it was, was a stupid move. Bristol had a long memory. Even Phillips knew it.

The State Department understood Bristol's pro-Turkish reputation and Horton's admiration of the Greeks. The two men stood poles apart in opinions and temperament, but Bristol had the more commanding position in Washington. He outranked Horton in the State Department hierarchy, held a rear admiral's commission, and possessed Dulles as his advocate. The department in the last two years had been repeatedly forced to defend Bristol against his critics, especially among American missionary organizations. Ironically, on the same day Horton had sent his request for help to Washington, Phillips had sent a cable to Constantinople informing Bristol that Senator William King of Utah, a Democrat, had introduced a resolution asking for an investigation into Bristol's pro-Turkish attitudes. The resolution had been diverted to a Senate committee, where Phillips hoped it would die, and in his cable to Bristol, he had assured the admiral that he had the department's support.

Phillips understood that Horton's cable presented a political dilemma for President Harding. The conflict in the Near East and the plight of the region's Christians were highly charged domestic issues. For years, newspapers and church organizations had made the American public keenly aware of Turkish atrocities against Christians, and religious leaders had agitated for a more forceful American role in defense of Turkey's Christian minorities. In May, a public debate had broken out between Secretary Hughes and the leader of one of the country's biggest Protestant denominations over the American government's unwillingness to stand up for persecuted Christians, and ultimately the president was dragged into the dispute.

Also, in June, the British had asked the United States to join an Allied investigation of Turkish deportations of Christians along the Black Sea. The press had carried sensational (and accurate) reports of Christians being sent on long death marches. Secretary Hughes had sent the British request to Harding, and Harding responded with a note containing his thinking but no decision on whether the United States should participate in the investigation. Harding had little interest in foreign affairs and left the decision to Hughes. He was happy to defer to his secretary of state, but Harding's note to Hughes offered a concise description of America's dilemma:

> *Mr. Dear Secretary Hughes: I have your note of this morning relating to our participation in the proposed inquiry into the*

atrocities in Armenia. [Actually, the atrocities were not in
Armenia—they were in Turkey. Armenia had ceased to exist as an
independent country. Harding was weak on geography.— Author]
Frankly, I very much hesitate to hold aloof from a participation
which makes such a strong appeal to a very large portion of our
American citizenship. At the same time I can not escape the
feeling that we will be utterly helpless to do anything effective in
case an investigation proves the statements concerning atrocities
are substantiated. I am very sure that there will be no American
support for a proposal to send an armed force there to correct
any abuses, which are proven. I am wondering if the possible
manifestations of our impotence would not be more humiliating
than our non-participation is distressing.

Hughes ultimately chose to participate, but the matter had dragged out
and by now, in September of 1922 with the Turkish military victories, the
matter was moot. In making his decision, Hughes had weighed the matter
as the judge he had been and sent Harding a note fleshing out the pros and
cons of not participating—he had phrased the question in the negative,
Should the United States not participate in the investigation of atrocities?
Pro: Not responding would prevent a finding of atrocities, so there could
be no demand for military action. Problem solved. Con: Not participating
would be politically damaging to Harding. "We should offend a large body
of Americans who have deep interest in the Christians of Anatolia. . . . It
would be naturally said that we were far more solicitous about American
interest in oil than about Christian lives."

Indeed, many of America's religious leaders already viewed American
policy as favoring acquisition of oil over protecting Christians, and their
argument would grow louder in the coming weeks and months.

IN 1922, AMERICA WAS HAVING its first bout of oil anxiety. Getting and
holding foreign oil supplies was by then already a central concern of the
nation's foreign policy.

The country feared that its domestic petroleum supply would last only another ten years—twenty years at best. The worry permeated the country: petroleum experts, the president, the Congress, the military, and the public. "The position of the United States in regard to oil can best be characterized as precarious," said George Otis Smith, director of the U.S. Geological Survey.

In 1900, there were hardly more than 3,000 cars in the United States. By 1914, there were 1.8 million, and by 1920, 9.2 million. The most ubiquitous was Ford's Model T, which could be bought for $260, the price of a horse. By 1920, 4,698,419 Model Ts had come off Ford's production lines. A car for the people, it packed a ten-gallon gas tank and burned ten miles per gallon—a hundred miles to a fill-up. Models Ts rolled from Ford's Highland Park plant at the rate of more than a million a year, and other auto companies' factories turned out fleets of their own brands: Buicks, Studebakers, Chevrolets, Coles, Columbias, Dusenbergs, Durants, Hudsons, Overlands, Stutzes, Packards, and many many others.

Each year Americans drove their Model Ts and Model As and Chevy 490s longer distances. Between 1900 and 1920, the nation built 225,000 miles of hard-surfaced roads, enough to circle the earth about ten times. The road-building created a voracious demand for asphalt, a petroleum product. The new roads encouraged the sale of new cars, which created demand for additional new roads. And so it went: more cars, more roads, and more cars—an ever-widening spiral of oil consumption.

There were also the needs of the military, which by the 1920s ran on prodigious volumes of oil, and a rapidly expanding merchant fleet, which required oil to carry the nation's burgeoning flow of manufactured products to foreign markets. The mechanization of agriculture demanded petroleum, and there was also the less visible but equally compelling need for industrial lubricants. U.S. oil consumption was rising at the rate of 9 percent per year in 1920. Already, America was "gasoline alley"—both the world's leading producer and consumer of oil.*

In the first decade of the 1900s, U.S oil production moved west from its birthplace in Pennsylvania and the Alleghenies to Oklahoma, Texas,

---

* *Gasoline Alley,* the popular comic strip, began in the *Chicago Tribune* in 1918 and featured a group of guys talking about cars.

and California. The great gusher at Spindletop, in Beaumont, Texas, threw its first oil into the sky in 1901; other wells sent more oil skyward. But the years immediately following World War I had failed to produce major new discoveries—a worrisome problem for an oil-addicted nation. America's top geologist said the country had two choices—conserve oil at home or find it abroad. The national consensus was to keep guzzling and put new holes in the ground, and it didn't much matter whether those new holes were in Midland, Texas, or Mesopotamia. The likely places: South America, the Dutch East Indies, and the Near East.

Supply worries were immediately followed by price worries. In 1920, gas peaked at thirty cents per gallon, a price that would not be reached again in real terms until 1981. By the time of the Harding administration, Americans already had decided that they had a God-given right to cheap gas.

IT WAS AGAINST this political background, fraught with conflicting issues of morality and economic self-interest, that William Phillips, sitting in his office, the windows open to admit some air into the stuffy building, considered George Horton's request and judged it important enough to bring to the president's attention. He sent it along to the White House with a cover note that was deferential yet decisive, acutely aware that Harding would accept the department's guidance. Phillips recommended that Admiral Bristol be directed to send one or more destroyers to Smyrna for the protection of American life and property.

At the time, President Harding was dealing with simultaneous national coal and railroad strikes, which threatened the country's industrial production—Ford Motor Co. had said it would stop its assembly lines because of the strikes. Harding's wife also was seriously ill with kidney disease and bedridden in the White House. In the best of times, the president was more likely to engage in issues at home rather than crises abroad, and this was not the best of times. The country was emerging from a deep recession, and the Roaring Twenties were only just beginning to roar. Mostly, Harding's attention was turned to the labor strikes and his wife, Florence. Phillips awaited a response, fully aware of the president's proclivities, interests, and habits.

BEFORE BECOMING PRESIDENT, Warren Gamaliel Harding had sold insurance, taught high school, and worked as a reporter for his father's small-town newspaper in Ohio. Harding was handsome, affable, and loyal to his friends—a natural politician. As a young man, he had pulled together a stake to buy his own newspaper, the *Marion Star*, in Marion, Ohio. The paper made him more friends and lots of money. The newspaper avoided controversy, and Harding married a wealthy divorced woman who had a good eye for business, and together they prospered. He was the ultimate small-town American businessman: he joined lodges, sat on the porch, counted his money, and reminisced about the old swimming hole. (He also had a secret affair with a neighbor, the wife of the owner of a local dry goods store.) In 1914, he was elected to the U.S. Senate. He missed more sessions than he attended, but he was well liked and served as a genial bridge between Republicans and Democrats. In 1920, after being picked by Republican Party leaders in Suite 408-10 at Chicago's Blackstone Hotel, the original "smoke-filled room," Harding was elected president in a landslide. His platform rejected internationalism and promised a return to "normalcy." Some said he was elected because he looked like a president, and indeed he did—tall, lionesque head, graying hair, black eyebrows. He loved to give a speech.

Harding's response to Phillips's note came later the same day—first as a phone call from the president's executive secretary, who said the president concurred with Phillips's recommendation—Send ships to protect Americans and American property. Later in the day, Phillips got a note from the president's personal secretary confirming approval of the instructions to Bristol.

As these White House messages were sent and received, Phillips received a second and more urgent cable from Horton expressing his fear that Smyrna might be destroyed by the Greek army as it exited the city. Some Greek officers, talking loosely, had threatened to burn the city rather than leave it and the munitions it contained to the Turks. Horton said the situation was worsening, and he asked that Bristol, who was known to have good relations with the nationalist Turks, mediate between the nationalist forces and the Greek government to save Smyrna. Horton made it clear that the request had come from the Greek governor of the city: "In the interest of humanity and for safety of American interests beg you to mediate with Angora (Ankara) government for amnesty sufficient to allow Greek forces to evacuate. Amnesty would avoid possible destruction of Smyrna, which may result from blowing up ammunition dumps. . . . I repeat my request for one or more naval units."

The heading on the second cable indicated it had been sent to Bristol as well. Phillips sent it to Harding and advised against American mediation. "It seems to me it would be wiser for us to confine our acts to caring for the lives of Americans and protection of American property." Harding was content to follow the advice, and he sent Phillips a note of agreement.

Yet another cable came in from Horton during the day reporting that Americans in Smyrna had formed a relief committee to help the refugees flooding the city. It asked the State Department to intervene on Smyrna's behalf with Herbert Hoover of the American Relief Administration. Hoover was secretary of commerce and head of the ARA, which was feeding victims of a famine that had swept Russia in the wake of the Russian civil war. Hoover had tons of supplies stored in warehouses in Constantinople. Horton said food, medicine, and blankets were needed for 150,000 refugees in Smyrna.

Amid this flurry of cables, Phillips sent a note to Theodore Roosevelt Jr., son of the former president and acting secretary of the navy. Roosevelt's office was down the long marble hall and around the corner from Phillips's office. (The twenty-foot-wide hallways were so long that messengers rode through the building on bicycles.) Phillips's note explained the situation and "respectfully" asked him to direct Bristol to send destroyers to Smyrna for the protection of American lives and property. He did not mention his communication with the president. There was no need to invoke the president's authority between gentlemen. (Roosevelt was also a Harvard man.) In the note to Roosevelt, Phillips had tactfully added the sentence "I assume Mr. Horton is in communication with Admiral Bristol and is keeping him fully informed." (As it turned out, he was: Horton's first request for protection had been addressed to the State Department without a "cc" to Bristol, but Horton had indeed sent a copy to Bristol—making it clear he was asking Washington for a ship. This would have served the clever purpose of letting Bristol know to whom he was appealing while covering Horton against criticism that he had failed to inform Bristol. The relationship between the two feuding men had fallen that low.)

Phillips followed up with a call to Roosevelt, who agreed to the request for ships and said he would leave the decision about landing U.S. sailors in Smyrna to the naval officer on the scene. Phillips concurred. Roosevelt immediately cabled Bristol: "Direct one or more destroyers as necessary proceed Smyrna/protect American interests/employment confined to American lives and property and not as naval or political demonstration." America had serious interests in Smyrna, but there would be no saber-rattling as there had been in the previous administration when Wilson had sent the navy and marines to protect American oil interests at Vera Cruz during the Mexican revolution. In this instance, the absence of American action was more likely in the long run to help American oil interests than a show of force on behalf of Christian refugees.

Finally, Phillips responded to Horton. The message arrived at the Eastern Telegraph office and was delivered to Horton at the consulate early on September 6. Horton decoded it in his private office upstairs, which was part of his family's living quarters. "Department is not inclined to do more than send destroyers to Smyrna to assist in protection of American lives and property," it said. "The situation would not appear to justify this Government assuming the role of voluntary mediator."

CHAPTER 8

Jennings's Suggestion

T he Jenningses had been settled into their new home at Paradise for only two weeks when they saw a troubling scene outside their door. Paradise was a stop on the Smyrna–Aydin Railroad, and the hard-packed dirt road, which traced the rail line through the fig-and-grape country to the south, ran past the college's wrought-iron front gate and the porch of their house.

Beginning on Friday, September 1, Asa and Amy saw knots of people, four or five at a time and sometimes more, passing along the road in the direction of Smyrna. They carried sacks on their backs and small children in their arms, and some were leading oxen or riding on wooden carts. Most were women, children, or old men. They walked quietly, seeming to occupy some timeless private space of patient suffering. Like others in Paradise, Jennings had heard rumors of a Greek setback at Afyon Karahisar, and there was speculation that a shift in the position of forces at the front had uprooted farmers on the frontier. It all seemed the inevitable dislocation of distant people by the armies that were ranging and fighting around them, but there was no immediate sense that something seismic had occurred. These people, it appeared, had wisely and probably temporarily cleared out of an area where new fighting had broken out along the front.

As the hours passed, and the number of people on the road increased,

Jennings could not escape the conclusion that the flow of people represented more than a minor shift in the battlefield—there must have been some major disruption in the Meander Valley to the south or the high plateau beyond the mountains to the east, and most certainly the flight of these people from their farms and villages was tied to the war between the Greek army and the nationalists. But beyond that general surmise, Jennings did not comprehend the scope of what was unfolding. Most of his neighbors, and this included nearly all the faculty at International College, were away on vacation during the last week of August and the first week of September. The town and school grounds were mostly empty of Americans, and he didn't have anyone to turn to immediately to get an explanation. His boss, Ernest Jacob, was among those on vacation. Jacob and his wife and young daughter were at Phocaea, a seaside town about twenty miles northwest of Smyrna that was a favorite escape for the American missionaries. The only means of communication with Phocaea was a ferry that departed daily from Smyrna.

When Jennings had arrived in Paradise, he had been told that the war was a long way off, and he had absorbed the general impression that the Greek army would maintain its strong position along its line in the east and the stalemate would continue from there until the Allies worked out a diplomatic solution. Jennings simply had not given the military situation much thought. He had come to Smyrna to organize activities for boys, and his thinking had been along the lines of teams and leagues and lessons to impart about sportsmanship and character. Political and diplomatic events swam outside his daily considerations. Family and work bounded his thinking.

In the meantime, the people kept passing along the road in bigger numbers, trudging under their burdens. There was no letup on Saturday and Sunday, September 2 and 3; they kept coming and coming, passing by the porch of the Jenningses' cottage. The sheer number of them by Sunday night was unnerving. It was as if the few people he had seen on Friday were the small advance flocks of a great migration of birds that was now filling the trees and blackening the sky. The road was a long and congested parade of families and farm animals reaching far to the south and east.

Monday, September 4, was Labor Day but Jennings decided to drive into Smyrna.

THE HOUSE THAT JENNINGS and his family had settled into—the one from which they watched the passing refugees—was one of the comfortable stone-and-masonry cottages near the campus of the International College in Paradise.

The town was in a pleasant valley between tall and often snow-capped mountains to the east and a low line of undulating coastal hills to the west. It was a quiet suburb of big and small houses with wood-rail porches, English flower gardens, and lavender hedges. There were shops, a bakery, and a tiny stone and slate-roof train station that looked like it had been lifted from a commuter stop along the New Haven Line. The Meles River flowed through the valley, and two aqueducts from Roman times crossed it, still bringing water down from the mountains to Smyrna.

International College was a boys' high school founded twenty-five years earlier in Smyrna by a Scots-Canadian missionary, Alexander Mac-Lachlan, an ecumenical-minded minister who had graduated from the Union Theological Institute in New York in 1887. Under the auspices of the Missions Board back in Boston, MacLachlan had built the school into the best college preparatory school in the Ottoman Empire. The school offered a rigorous curriculum in the humanities, physics, and mathematics taught by a bright group of American missionary teachers and scholars: Ralph S. Harlow of Harvard, J. Kingsley Birge of Yale, Cass Arthur Reed of Pomona College, and Samuel L. Caldwell of Carleton College—all of whom were ordained ministers.

The Jennings family found the school's atmosphere of Protestant religious purpose friendly and familiar—music in the evenings in the family parlor, the missionary sensibility, Protestant hymns sung at chapel,

> *Rock of Ages, cleft for me,*
> *Let me hide myself in Thee . . .*

For Asa, there was also the college's farm. Jennings had grown up with the rhythms of family, farm, and church, and while the fruits and vegetables of Asia Minor (figs, lemons, olives, pomegranates, and trees that grew pods of carob) were exotic, the texture of life was not so different from the Finger Lakes country. He had spent his boyhood picking raspberries and taking cartons of them by wagon to sell in the nearby boomtown of Rochester.

Asa Jennings had brought something else to Turkey—his illness. Barely a day passed that he didn't have a low-grade fever, and he sometimes broke into coughing fits that could not be quelled. He was frequently racked by pain along his spine, though he never spoke of it to his colleagues. It was a private matter, and his suffering was an intimacy he shared only with Amy.

Asa was victim of a tubercular infection that had ravaged his body sixteen years earlier. When he was twenty-eight and working at the YMCA in Utica, he had developed a high temperature, night sweats, and nearly continuous pain that doctors had diagnosed as typhoid fever. He had seemed to get better, but twice relapsed. Amy had taken him to a succession of doctors, and they eventually diagnosed his illness as acute tuberculosis. (Tuberculosis can follow typhoid fever, which weakens the immune system.) The doctors at the General Hospital in Utica told Amy to make Asa comfortable in his final days; the disease was far too advanced to save his life. She might take him to a warm climate, they said, to help him breathe with less effort, but there was no chance he would survive. His condition was hopeless.

Amy had been distraught at the prospect of Asa's death. She had lost her firstborn child, Ortha, only two years before, and she had come close to losing her second. Now she was told she would lose her husband. Frightened and unwilling to deliver the news to Asa, she sought guidance from her Bible. She opened it at random, hoping to find a message that would tell her what to do. She looked down at the page, and her eyes fell on the eleventh verse of the Gospel of St. John, which tells the story of Lazarus, whom Jesus had raised from the dead. She read and reread the passage and grew calm with its repetition, seeing in it a message of hope: "This sickness is not unto death, but for the glory of God, that the Son of God might be glorified thereby." She read it over and over and over again.

At the hospital the next morning, Amy told Asa first of her fated encounter with the passage from John's Gospel and her interpretation of its message, which was that he would overcome his sickness and his recovery would be a sign from God of work that he would do in the future. Only later did she tell him of the doctors' consensus about his disease and impending death. Asa took the prognosis stoically. They talked, with Amy returning again and again to the meaning of the biblical passage, and reading it aloud in tears. Together, they resolved not to accept the doctors' conclusion. A long and difficult period commenced in which Amy threw herself into saving her husband's life. It was a period of setbacks, anguish, pain, and home therapies, but it seemed only to deepen their faith in God. Another two years would pass before Asa showed signs that he was likely to survive.

Jennings did survive—and he seemed determined to accomplish Amy's prediction of important work ahead. Early in 1918, while he was working for the YMCA in upstate New York, Jennings answered some inner call of mission or adventure. He took a job as a YMCA army chaplain, and he traveled, without his family, to bases in Virginia and New Jersey where he ministered to soldiers departing for the war in Europe. The little man with the big smile and the hunched back was a success with the men—he gave them songs, quips, Bible verses, and reminders to write home to mother. A year later, with the war ended and Amy and the children still back in her hometown of Cleveland, Jennings had asked the YMCA to send him to France, and off he went with a group of forty-eight other YMCA men across the Atlantic.

Jennings's job in France had been to direct the YMCA's "huts" at the military forwarding camp at Lemans, the main staging area for American troops' return to the United States. Jennings and his YMCA colleagues served hot coffee and little cakes to the soldiers, held Sunday-school classes, entertained the men with silent movies and vaudeville skits, and arranged sports events. Sports were embedded in the Y's culture—a healthy body being one of three points of the "Y." (The other two were a healthy mind and healthy spirit.) By the war's end, the Y had shipped a half-million baseballs to France for the soldiers.

By the start of the 1919 season, the soldiers were back home in the United States and sportswriters had picked the Chicago White Sox, with slugger Shoeless Joe Jackson in left field, as the team to beat in the American League. Jennings had departed France too. He traveled by train across middle Europe to Czechoslovakia, where he continued to minister to demobilizing soldiers with the Y's mix of books, Bible passages, hot coffee, films, and sports including the new game of basketball, invented just a few years earlier at the Y's training center in Springfield, Massachusetts. Balls were bouncing in the gymnasiums of Silesia, and Jennings was still reminding soldiers to write home to mother when he had gotten orders to pack for Smyrna.

IN PARADISE, Jennings had use of his boss's Chevrolet—a small four-seat touring car with a soft top. He decided to use it for his trip into Smyrna. Driving it required double clutching to change the gears, and the brakes needed heavy pressure to bring the car to a stop, but Jennings found that he could handle it. The continuing passage of so many people through Paradise on their way to Smyrna was mystifying to Jennings, but he did not see it yet as dangerous. He decided not to call Jacob back from his holiday and drove off to get an explanation at the American consulate.

The trickle of people he had seen on the road the previous three days had turned into a river, and the trains passing by the Paradise station were full of people and baggage, and the human cargo included soldiers. People were hanging on to the sides of train cars and riding on top of them, and the trains were passing more frequently than usual, not any regular schedule.

He took Amy with him in the car to Smyrna. The children were safe at home; the college was right there if they became frightened or needed an adult. On the way into the city, Jennings and Amy passed refugees trudging along the road, stepping aside to make room for them to pass, and they saw that many people were camped at the outer edge of the city where the ancient Caravan Bridge spanned the Meles River, not much more than a sluggish creek in late summer.

Once in the city, they saw many thousands more people—all more or less in the same condition as the people on the Paradise Road. They were coming in from the north and east as well as the south, on foot and by train. Jennings drove through the Armenian Quarter and by the Basmahane station, which was the terminus of the Casaba line that reached to Afyon Karahisar and was serving as the main path of retreat for the Greek army. The train station was across the street from the American Girls' College, but Asa decided against stopping there. Jennings saw soldiers, unshaven, tattered, and dirty, leaving the station and walking toward the Quay. There were also many people sitting and standing in the public spaces around the station and gradually sifting into the city's streets as the area around the station became too crowded to accommodate all the people who wanted to linger there. Most of the people were obviously country dwellers, in simple clothes—women in long skirts, aprons, headscarves, and rough homemade shoes, and men in cotton work shirts and vests, loose trousers, boots. The faces were brown, deeply wrinkled, and strangely passive. They were setting down their bags and luggage wherever they could find space: churchyards, small public spaces, cemeteries, or just in the streets. Many had already gathered along the Quay.

Jennings and Amy were shocked at their physical condition—they looked like they had walked a long way and were covered with a thin layer of white dust from the backcountry roads and apparently without much food or water. Women were nursing babies. Old women were carrying sickly men on their backs, their big work-roughened hands hanging from their sleeves. Families found small polygons of shade in which to sit and spread their household possessions, all the time holding the ropes of their goats or donkeys. It was terribly hot in the sun—in the high nineties, and it was not yet noon.

Asa and Amy clattered in the Chevy through the city and reached the YMCA, which was in a building it rented at 28 Frank Street, the city's main shopping street, two blocks back from the Quay and a block south of the American consulate. It was an attractive building with a series of floor-to-ceiling windows at street level that offered a view inside to a sitting area arranged for reading and conversation. Inside there were classrooms where young men took classes in English and French, a bigger room for amateur plays and movies, and a thousand-volume library with current magazines and newspapers.

Alarmed but unsure how to interpret the presence of so many people—refugees, really, they were in flight and homeless—Jennings decided it was time to suggest to Jacob that he return, and he sent a message by way of the ferry to Phocaea. The YMCA building was next to the Grand Bretagne Restaurant, about two hundred yards from the American consulate on Galazio Street, and in a neighborhood of brasseries, dress shops, and the offices of tobacco brokers. The refugees were there too, shuffling along, looking for shelter. Amy was horrified by what she saw. "Women with nursing babies and nowhere to go," she noted in a diary. "Streets packed with people of all ages sleeping on the pavements." Leaving Amy at the YMCA, Jennings walked up Frank Street to the American consulate to find out what was happening. On the way, he stopped a man who looked to him like he spoke English and asked what was going on.

Don't you know? They are running from the Turks, he said.

The American consulate was an established gathering place for Americans, one block back from the Quay and the fashionable Hunters Club. Americans were used to dropping by the consulate to chat with Horton, who was informal and gregarious and liked to tell a story. There were several good cafés, restaurants, and private clubs on the surrounding blocks, including the Boston Cafe, which American businessmen could retire to after getting the morning's chatter and news at the consulate from Horton or other Americans doing business in the city.

Entering the consulate, Jennings found the receiving area full, and Horton and his two young vice consuls, Maynard Barnes and A. Wallace Treat, besieged with people, mostly naturalized Greek and Armenian Americans who were seeking the papers and means necessary to leave the city. There was barely room to squeeze in. The talk inside added to what Asa had heard on the street. The Greek army had suffered a serious setback, and the Christian population in the backcountry, fearing the advance of the Turkish army, had abandoned their farms and villages for the safety of Smyrna. The talk was fraught with rumor and speculation. No one seemed to know for sure what was happening. The Greek losses had come quickly and unexpectedly—and it seemed improbable that there had been a complete collapse of the Greek line. People were attempting to understand the situation by exchanging information about what they had seen, rumors they had heard, and conflicting reports they read in the city's newspapers. The reports included a forceful published assertion by the Greek commander that Greek troops would hold the city against a Turkish assault and a statement by the Italian consul that thousands of Italian troops were standing by at Rhodes to be transported to Smyrna if needed to bring order.

Two British battleships, the *Iron Duke* and *King George V,* had arrived the day before, on Sunday, and the city's oldest and most respected Greek newspaper, *Amalthea,* quoted the senior British officer in Smyrna, Admiral Osmond de Brock, as saying that he was confident of the city's safety, but the paper then suggested, inaccurately, that he was also promising Allied intervention on behalf of the Greeks if it became necessary for their protection. More than a few Greek and Armenian civilians had armed themselves in anticipation of a battle for the city, and the Asia Minor Defense League was secretly distributing guns and bandoliers of ammunition. Many had judged the appearance of the British ships, along with this day's arrival of a French battleship, *Waldeck Rousseau,* as evidence of Allied intentions to land troops on their behalf. Eleven warships were anchored in Smyrna harbor—British, French, Italian, and Greek. The warships were the spear points of Allied diplomacy, except that there wasn't a unified Allied diplomacy. Each of the Allies—Britain, France, and Italy—was pursuing its own interests. All remained technically at war with Turkey, but the French and the Italians had found their own private accommodations with the Turkish nationalists, and the Italians had been arming them against the Greeks. The British stood alone as a serious potential belligerent. This was not apparent to the people onshore. Given the importance of Smyrna as a trading and banking center, residents took the Allied naval presence in the harbor as reassurance against disorder and a Turkish occupation. Still, there was also a lot of loose talk about the Greek army burning the city if it was forced to abandon it. Greeks and Armenians intent on resisting a Turkish takeover had hidden stockpiles of ammunition throughout the city, and the prospect of arson was frightening. There was also the troubling awareness that the British had brought a hospital ship, HMHS *Maine,* into the harbor and had requisitioned three merchant ships, *Bavarian, Antioch,* and *Magira,* to evacuate British nationals.

Jennings heard speculation and rumor that was ominous, confused, anxious, and mostly uninformed. He grew alarmed. What about his family and neighbors in Paradise, he wondered; were they in danger? Should the foreigners in the city be doing something to protect themselves? He, like everyone else in the consulate, knew there was no American military in Smyrna, and Paradise was even more exposed than the city itself. Jennings could see that Horton already had begun arranging for the naturalized American citizens with Greek and Armenian backgrounds to leave the city, and the situation's gravity was further evident from Horton's anxious demeanor and the feverish pace at which he was working. The diplomatic capitulations on which the foreign consuls relied in Smyrna allowed the consuls to designate "protégés," local people who worked for the consulate and received limited diplomatic protection as representatives of foreign governments. In an unorthodox attempt to save people, Horton was writing letters that associated the naturalized Americans (and some others) as American protégés in the hope that the letters would be accepted as visas for travel or a means of protection.

Working his way through the crowded office, Jennings talked with other Americans at the consulate about the need for Americans to understand the situation as a group. Together they asked Horton to call a meeting of the American community so it could understand what was happening and take precautions for its safety—if indeed precautions were necessary. Horton agreed and said he would call the meeting later in the day. He wrote a note announcing the meeting and sent a courier to American institutions and businesses around the city to spread the message and went back to work.

HORTON HAD SLEPT HARDLY at all in the five days since his return from Sevdikuey. He had met the night before, on Sunday, September 3, with Governor Stergiades, who already had concluded that the Greek army would evacuate Smyrna. Stergiades worried that disaffected soldiers might set fire to the city. Horton had met that morning with the British consul, Sir Harry Lamb, and Admiral de Brock, and de Brock had informed him of British plans to evacuate its nationals. Horton and Lamb were friends as well as colleagues, and they would frequently collaborate over the next several days. They shared similar views about Smyrna, and both were married to foreign women whose fathers were diplomats, in Lamb's case, an Italian woman. Only a few years younger than Horton, Lamb cut a familiar figure in Smyrna, his easily recognizable hat a racing trilby. He carried a walking stick and wore a Marlborough collar and tie.

Horton sent cables to Bristol and Washington about the British evacuation, and, still not having heard back from Washington by the end of the day Monday, September 4, he repeated his request for an American ship. In addition to the State Department cable appealing for supplies from the American Relief Administration, Horton appealed directly to the Near East Relief in Constantinople for aid.

At about 3:00 P.M., leaders of the American community gathered at the American consulate in response to Horton's message. They were either missionaries or businessmen, and although there was often tension between the two groups, they were now bound by common concern for their safety and the safety of the organizations they represented. The missionaries were mostly aligned with the Greeks and Armenians; the businessmen with the Turks, in part because Greek and Armenian merchants and traders were formidable competitors and not so easily handled as the Turks. Among the missionary group were Alexander MacLachlan, the president of International College; Dana K. Getchell, a fifty-two-year-old Missions Board missionary from Northfield, Minnesota, attached to the American Girls' School in the city; Jean Christie, thirty-nine years old and a Wellesley graduate, director of the YWCA; and Asa Jennings for the YMCA. The businessmen included Stanley W. Smith, director of Standard Oil of New York in Smyrna; representatives from the four

American tobacco companies in the city, Gary, Standard, Glen, and American; and Chester Griswold, an agent for MacAndrews & Forbes, the licorice company in Camden, New Jersey. American tobacco companies used licorice to sweeten their cigarettes, and the herb grew profusely around Smyrna.

George Horton appeared strained and tired as he leaned on his cane and called the group to order. He reported much of what he knew, which was that the Greek army had suffered a serious defeat, and, in disarray, it was burning villages as it retreated toward the sea. It was less a Shermanesque strategy to deny the Turkish army provisions and more the result of a leaderless army, which, feeling betrayed by its government and hunted by Turkish civilians, had turned into a destructive rabble. There was discussion about rumors of the Greek army's total collapse and the possibility of it being pulled back together for the city's defense. It was hard for the Americans to believe that the Greek defeat had come so quickly and completely, but the Americans had seen, on the way to the meeting, Greek soldiers entering the city, and their ragged and disconsolate condition suggested the worst. Some of the soldiers were ditching their uniforms for civilian clothes and selling or giving away their guns. Getchell, who had just returned to Smyrna from a trip to towns east of Smyrna on the Casaba rail line, reported that he had seen Greek soldiers rounding up Greek civilians for transport to Smyrna on train cars ahead of the Turkish army. Turkish civilians, he said, had begun firing on Greek soldiers and departing Greek civilians, and a battle had broken out at the train station of the hinterland town where he had spent the night.

Horton told the group that he already had cabled a request for naval protection but had not yet received a response. Stunned at the suddenness of events, the Americans were unclear about their next steps. Horton was not advising them to leave the city, but neither would he give them assurances that all would be well as the Italian and French consuls were advising their nationals. He did not want to alarm the assembled Americans, but neither did he want to suggest that the situation was safe. Privately, he expected the worst, and his posture and demeanor more likely spoke more forcefully than his words. Horton asked the group to meet

again the next day at the YMCA, where there was more room; he would
schedule daily meetings, he told them, so he could provide updates.

After the meeting, Jennings took Horton aside and offered another
idea—again as a question. Would it be possible for the Americans, Jennings asked, to organize help for the refugees? At the moment, Horton
said, his hands were full trying to find all the Americans in Smyrna and
secure passage out of the city for those who seemed most immediately
in danger. Horton suggested that Jennings talk with the other Americans who had been at the meeting and raise the idea for discussion the
next day. Later in the day, Jennings took the idea to his neighbors at
International College, and Caleb Lawrence, a professor at the school,
agreed to make the proposal when the group met again, the next day,
Tuesday.

HORTON HAD COME TO SMYRNA in 1911 expecting to deepen his learning and savor the classical ruins of ancient Ionia. His actual experience
had been far different. The year after he arrived, in 1912, the religious
strife in the Balkans erupted into the First Balkan War, pitting Greece,
Serbia, and Bulgaria against their old oppressor, the Ottoman Turks.
To the astonishment of Europe, the Ottomans lost the war, and the city
of Salonika and the Aegean islands passed to Greece. It was a humiliation the Young Turks would not soon forget, and ethnic Greeks
throughout the Ottoman Empire would pay a heavy price in property
and blood for the victory of the Hellenic state in the Balkans.

In the region outside Smyrna, in the villages along the coast and inland toward the Meander Valley, Horton witnessed a Turkish campaign
of terror against Christians every bit as brutal as it had been around
Salonika—perhaps even worse. Its goal was to drive the ethnic Greeks,
who were Ottoman subjects, out of the country.

The sultan and his Islamic government had always considered
the ethnic Greeks—like all Christians in the empire, including the
Armenians—second-class citizens. But they had been allowed to practice their religion, live in peace (mostly), and run their own affairs as
long as they respected the sultan's authority, paid their taxes, and ac-

knowledged their lower status. Christians could not bring testimony against a Muslim in court, and Turks harassed Christians on the street with impunity. "*Giavour!*" they shouted, laughing and tossing rocks, "Infidel dog!" In American terms, it was a kind of Jim Crow system in which religion rather than color was the dividing line. But it had been tolerable to the Christians, who had little choice but to accept it. They kept to themselves, inside their church-dominated communities, which were governed by a council of elders; and in cities such as Smyrna and Constantinople, many Greeks and Armenians had managed to become rich through skill and determination. Ultimately, they formed the commercial ligaments of the empire.

The age-old Muslim tolerance of Christians (a "people of the Book") ended with the Balkan wars—a second war had quickly followed the first—along with the emergence of a rising Hellenic consciousness among Ottoman ethnic Greeks, similar to the rising national consciousness among the Armenians. A Hellenic consciousness, like an Armenian consciousness, presented a serious threat to the established order, which was grounded on second-class citizenship for Christians in a unified empire governed by Muslims and ruled by Sharia law.

By 1913, as a consequence of the First Balkan War and intensifying anxiety among the Young Turks, it was no longer safe to be a Christian in many parts of Anatolia, especially along the Aegean coast. Homes were burned or torn down; men, women, and children were slain in the fields.

The Ottoman government unleashed a propaganda campaign against Christians in the schools and mosques. In all this, Germany played an important part—encouraging the propaganda and ejection of Greeks from western Anatolia. Germany had cultivated a close military and commercial relationship with Turkey, coveted its natural resources, and viewed it as a potential client-state. The kaiser had declared himself protector of the Muslims, and there was a persistent rumor (untrue) through the Near East that he had converted to Islam. Ultimately, the German-Ottoman relationship would fuse in August 1914 in a secret agreement allying the two empires in the war against Britain and France.

As in Salonika, Horton witnessed the Christian persecutions in the coastal towns north and south of Smyrna and filed detailed reports to

Washington, inventorying destroyed villages and conveying the brutality in journalistic detail. In one report, he described the frontal decapitations of Greek men working as woodcutters. "The unfortunate men had been tied, and their faces and shins were slashed as they had tried to bend down their faces to protect their throats." A massacre against Ottoman Greeks in nearby Phocaea left fifty dead, their bodies thrown into the sea or down wells.

The killing escalated with the outbreak of World War I. At the urging of Germany, the Ottoman government stepped up its campaign to remove ethnic Greeks from western Anatolia. Turkish terror drove nearly two hundred thousand Greeks out of the country to the Aegean islands or mainland Greece. Muslims, mostly rough mountain people who had fled the Balkans during the Balkan wars, flooded into Anatolia and took the homes the Greeks left behind.

The Greeks were not the only targets of Turkish terror. Horton became aware of a separate and even bigger terror campaign—the one being waged against the Armenians. Because foreigners traveling to the Anatolian interior often passed through Smyrna, Horton received copious first-person accounts from Americans and others about the killing field inside the country. In a report to the State Department, he wrote: "From what all these trustworthy people of the highest credence tell me, from 800,000 to 1,000,000 human beings are going through this process of slow and hideous torture, and the movement instead of waning is increasing in ferocity, so that before it is finally over, in the neighborhood of 2,000,000 will be affected, a very large proportion of whom will certainly perish as they are driven along for weeks or months without food or shelter and without means of procuring these."

The accounts of Armenians being rounded up, brutalized, raped, and marched to their deaths flowed into the State Department from Horton's consular colleagues in Aleppo, Trebizond, Harput, and Samsun. The Protestant missionaries in these places added their own first-person accounts of the horrors. Three thousand women and children made up the first convoy that deported from Harput in July 1915. They were marched southward toward the Syrian desert, and on the seventieth day of the trek, after having covered a thousand miles, thirty-five survivors reached

Aleppo. The experience was repeated throughout Anatolia. The paths southward were lined with corpses.

Somehow, Smyrna, the city itself, had remained an exception to the violence. It was generally a liberal city with a tradition of religious tolerance, a lily in a stagnant pond. Smyrna's prosperity helped cover the conflicts. Its Ottoman governor, or *vali*, was deliberately slow to follow orders that came from the Young Turk government in Constantinople, and he protected British and French nationals and local Christians when it was possible to do so without endangering himself. Occasionally, he had to sacrifice a few Armenians to quiet the Turkish leaders in the capital.

In 1917, when the United States entered the war against Germany, the Ottoman government severed diplomatic relations with Washington, forcing Horton to leave Smyrna. (The United States did not declare war on Turkey, principally because President Wilson did not want to endanger missionary property in the country.) Horton returned to America and made a speaking tour and received an honorary degree from Georgetown University. A year later, the war had shifted decisively in favor of the Allies—American troops had joined the war on the western front in Europe, the British had defeated Ottoman forces in Palestine and Syria, and French, Greek, and Serbian forces had broken the Bulgarian army on the Macedonian front, opening a path to Vienna. Germany and its war partners sued for peace. The Great War was over, and Horton returned to Smyrna.

He arrived shortly after the Greek landing. He went back to work at Galazio Street and built a relationship with the new Greek administration, and especially its governor, Aristides Stergiades, whom he admired for his learning and religious tolerance. Horton also maintained friendly connections with the Turkish community. Tens of thousands of Greeks who had fled Turkey during the period of prewar depredations were returning to their farms and businesses, reassured by the Allied victory. Some of the Greeks returned from America, where, as naturalized citizens, they had opened candy and flower shops and restaurants in Boston, New York, Newark, and Philadelphia. The Greek lunch counter had become a fixture of urban America.

By 1922, Horton had aged into a respected figure in Smyrna, and the city's ethnic groups held him in high regard. He was sixty-three and no longer the scholarly young poet on holiday who also happened to be doing his country's work as a consul; he had merged his love of the past with a fatherly relationship to Smyrna and its people. Horton more or less appointed himself their protector. The religious hatred in the city had grown acute, and the likelihood of a calamity seemed to him inevitable. As a young man, Horton had not been religious—in fact, he had rebelled against his father's fundamentalism as a boy—but his attitude changed with time, and he chose to be baptized into the Anglican Church in Smyrna. He moved ever closer in outlook to the American missionaries of Anatolia. He had a flock to care for—Ottoman Christians in and around Smyrna. His paternalism put him in direct conflict with his superiors. It was the old problem of detachment. Horton had no gift for it.

Consul Horton once had loved Smyrna, and probably he still loved it deep in his heart, but he had been worn down by his duties—by the way in which Admiral Bristol had ignored his reports and disrespected his views. Horton was also discouraged about the lack of a redeeming American policy for postwar Turkey that acknowledged the dangers to its Christian population. Like many others, he had advocated an American mandate over all Anatolia to protect the Christian minorities, pull Turkey out of its cruel past, and create a modern democratic state. Horton had tried to make the Christian cause in Turkey an American cause. But he learned, as many others were learning, that American sympathy extended to generous financial support of the Christians; it did not extend to armed intervention or governance, even temporarily, of the Ottoman Empire. It had taken unrestricted German submarine warfare to drag America into war with Germany; America was not prepared to send troops to Turkey to settle matters between its Muslims and Christians.

Saddened by these events, Horton carried on at Galazio Street: he stamped visas and responded to the daily minor requests of American citizens traveling through the Levant, often on their way to Ephesus and the Holy Land. In the evenings, he listened to his wife, Catherine (he called her "Kittens"), play the piano and read aloud to his daughter Nancy. He was only two years short of the enforced age of retirement.

Horton knew the city was living with a false sense of security. At the beginning of the summer of 1922, he and Catherine had sent Nancy to Catherine's parents in Greece. It was safer there.

BACK IN PARADISE, the roads were clogged and the rail line busy. Long trains carrying refugees passed through town on the way to Smyrna, each train pulling as many as fifty cars. The boxcars were filled with baggage and household goods; the cattle cars were packed with people. They peeped through the small square holes that were intended to bring air into the cars for livestock, sometimes two or three faces looking out the rough openings. At one point, one of Jennings's neighbors saw a woman pass a dead child out of the rail car's window. It had been smothered in the crush aboard the train. Those who could not fit inside the train cars rode on top or hung off the sides. The roads too were full of shuffling crowds of people, some with their arabas, rough wood-wheeled carts, and others with flocks of sheep or a few goats. Some were leading cows or oxen. The boys at International College set up a water brigade for the refugees as they passed on the road by the gate.

The next day, Tuesday, September 5, Horton called the second meeting of the American community to order at the YMCA. By now, Smyrna harbor contained even more warships: in addition to the *Iron Duke* and *King George*, the British had brought two destroyers, *Sparrow Hawk* and *Senator*; the French had two more battleships, the *Ernest Renan* and *Edgar Quintet*, and two destroyers; the Italians had the battleship *Venezia* and two destroyers; and the Greeks had two battleships and two heavy cruisers. The American navy remained absent. Bristol had not yet sent a ship, nor had he even sent a message to the consulate in Smyrna. Given the likelihood of a crisis in the city, Bristol's lack of a request for information on conditions in the city ahead of the Turkish advance suggests a strange lack of curiosity or a willful isolation of Horton and indifference to Smyrna's fate.

Horton reported to the Americans that he still had not heard from Washington or Constantinople. The group decided to send a telegram to Admiral Bristol supporting Horton's request for naval support: "We the undersigned fully endorse the requests previously made by the American Consul for the sending to this port of sufficient ships of war and marines for the adequate protection of American citizens and property and furthermore we believe the present situation to be of such gravity and danger as to warrant the immediate granting of such requests."

Neither Bristol nor Washington would ever respond to the cable. It was forwarded by an administrative employee to Phillips and Robert Woods Bliss, the third assistant secretary of state, with a note: "This telegram from Smyrna does not seem to me of particular importance—though it mentions marines, for the first time. It reflects the natural state of mind of persons in a beleaguered city. Its chief interest is that it gives an idea of the variety of American interests in Smyrna."

Then at the meeting, as Jennings and Lawrence had rehearsed, Professor Lawrence suggested the formation of a committee to organize relief for the refugees. Rufus Lane, a businessman and former consul in the city, spoke in favor: "We did not come here," he said, "solely to save our skins." Lawrence made a motion to form the committee, and Jennings rapidly seconded it. The group approved the motion. Jennings offered to collect subscriptions to pay for the effort. Stanley Smith of Standard Oil pledged $350. Francis Blackley, a tobacco broker, offered $150. The group elected Caleb Lawrence as the relief committee's chairman. It split the other positions between the missionary group and the businessmen, electing another teacher at the school, Samuel Caldwell, as treasurer, and the export agent, Roger Griswold, as secretary.

The group operated under Robert's Rules of Order with a respect for authority and process that was second nature to them. The scene could have been mistaken for a New England town meeting. (A motion has been made. Now, do I have second? Okay, I have a second. All in favor say, "Aye." Okay, the Ayes have it. Motion passed.) Lawrence was from rural Maine, where the town meeting was the principal form of governance and a way of life.

Professor Lawrence was a natural choice to lead the group. Lean and resolute at fifty-four years old, Lawrence was a missionary teacher who had been in Smyrna since 1896 with only two interruptions—one to complete his master's degree at Queen's College in Kingston, Ontario, and the second required by America's entry into World War I. He had taken advantage of the second interruption to seek a Ph.D. at Harvard but within weeks of arriving in the United States, the YMCA called on him to serve in Europe. He dropped his studies and went to France, where he cared for wounded soldiers and drove an ambulance, at one point distinguishing himself during a German gas and artillery attack on a retreating column of French soldiers by bringing his wounded passengers to safety. A taciturn Mainer with a calm demeanor that inspired confidence, Lawrence was a minister's son raised by relatives after the death of his mother in childbirth. He taught English and philosophy at International College—a gentle but steady man whose hobbies were weather and astronomy. On many evenings, he invited his children and others to join him at the school's observatory to view the planets under the dazzling Anatolian sky. He wrote poetry and served as the college librarian, but with his size and build he could have passed for a Maine lumberjack.

As chairman of the Smyrna Relief Committee, Lawrence took responsibility for the city's numerous orphanages. If there was a commodity that Smyrna had in excess, it was orphans. Missionaries had brought them there from throughout Anatolia because the city was considered a safe location. Lawrence gave Jennings the job of finding flour and bakeries to bake bread, a seemingly impossible job given the numbers of hungry people already in the city. Most had come with only a little bit of food to sustain them on their journey. Others on the committee were charged with setting up food stations, mainly at churches, and distributing whatever bread could be baked. Edward M. Yantis, an agent for the Gary Tobacco Co., a subsidiary of Liggett & Myers Co., was in charge of transportation.

The group pooled their cars and trucks, and soon each was affixed with a small American flag for protection in the event of the Turkish army's entry into the city. (Horton seemed to have an inexhaustible supply of flags.) In the meantime, Horton had arranged for the Smyrna Theater, which was on the Quay and close to the consulate, as a meeting place for Americans and a sanctuary if they needed it. (Nearly everyone called it the "American Theater" because an American had built it—the same man who had erected the ice factory.) Horton said he would brief them there twice a day. The theater had a stage and orchestra seating plus three tiers of balconies. The opera *Rigoletto* had been performed the previous week, and at the moment the theater was advertising, in electric lights out front, a French silent movie, *El Dorado*, by the famous French director Marcel L'Herbier.

Later in the day, still not having heard back from Washington or Bristol and operating without instructions or protection, Horton asked the commander of a French ship in Smyrna harbor, the *Edgar Quintet*, to send a cable to another French ship, in Constantinople, for relay to the American embassy. The ship's captain agreed: *"Consul General Estas Unis a Smyrne vous prie demander Admiral Bristol si celui ci a bien recu ses telegramme."* ("The consul general of the United States in Smyrna asks Admiral Bristol if he has received his telegram.")

JENNINGS, AS CHAIRMAN of the Kitchen and Feeding Committee, went to work procuring flour and ovens. By now, there were tens of thousands of homeless and hungry people in the city. They were arriving each day by the thousands. Those who had the money—and there were very few from the countryside who had money—were attempting to depart on steamers and coastal ferries. The ticket offices were jammed with prosperous residents, and the lines stretched into the streets. Others— the great mass of others—found a piece of pavement on which to wait, hoping that providence would provide for them. The calamity could not have come at a worse time for those who had left their farms, and that was most of them, this being the time when the fig, raisin, and tobacco crops would be brought down into the city for sale. The greater part of their crop had already been gathered but much of it was undelivered, which meant no payment for the season's work. The wheat crop also was in harvest. Kemal, in fact, had timed his attack for late August because granaries would be full, providing food for his army. The people on the streets didn't know what would come next: Would the Greek army hold the city? Would the British and Americans protect them? Would they eventually return to their farms? There were no answers. The women brushed the flies from their children in the heat and waited.

The flow of people from the backcountry continued into the night, and families attempted to claim small spaces in which to sit and pull some bread or cheese from a wrapped cloth to distribute among their children. A British observer offered this description for a London newspaper: "Those who were still left on the Quay at night camped on the water's edge, and one saw the remarkable spectacle of mothers preparing their children's beds for the night within three or four feet of the water so that they would be in a good position next morning to get on board some vessel. Those who could not get on the Quay had to make their beds on the footwalks of the side streets leading to the Quay, and it was pathetic to see how they had endeavored to arrange their little furniture to give their three or four square yards of footwalk some appearance of a home. One very frequent article of furniture was the sewing-machine, neatly packed in its wooden cover bearing a well-known name."*

By the night of September 5, there were more than a hundred and fifty thousand refugees in the city. At Paradise, the Jenningses continued to watch columns of people and animals pass on the road to Smyrna. The ragged parade continued into the night, wood wheels creaking, sheep bleating, pots and pans clanging. It was as if the entire Anatolian landscape for hundreds of miles back from the coast was disgorging itself of frightened Christians.

---

* Singer Sewing Machine Co.

Theodora*

The Gravos family gathered outside their home in Gritzalia, a village in the high country east of Smyrna. The elder Gravos had one last look before beginning the trek to Smyrna with his wife, children, including fourteen-year-old Theodora, and extended family. Maybe they would return; maybe this trouble was temporary. The figs hung black, purple, and pendulous among the big green leaves of the trees, ready for picking; the grape harvest had already begun on the vines that ranged on the hillsides outside the village; the olives would be ripe in another month.

The family group was nine—mother and father, three sons, and Theodora and her two younger sisters and Theodora's aunt. Theodora was a brave and curious child, and she observed her mother and father and three older brothers making ready for the trip. There were food and blankets to pack; possessions to worry over. In the meantime, Theodora watched her two younger sisters, two and a half and three and a half years old.

The day was hot, and the women covered their heads with cloths against the sun. The cicadas beat their little drums in the eucalyptus

---

* The substance of this narrative comes from an interview with Theodora Kontou in the collection of the Asian Minor Research Center in Athens.

trees, speeding the rhythm with the increase in heat until the sound was simply one long buzz.

It was a terrible decision to abandon one's home, but the Gravos family no longer felt safe. The anger of their Muslim neighbors had simmered for three years—the Turkish residents had been powerless against the Greek soldiers, and they had suffered the dominance of Gritzalia's Christians, but Mustapha Kemal and the nationalist army were routing the Greeks, and it was their turn now, and the Greek villagers understood that they must remove themselves from the fury that soon would be unleashed. A Greek already had been hanged from a tree for firing at a hodja from a minaret as he had called Gritzalia's Muslims to prayer. Accounts were being settled. The Turks came out of their homes to watch the Greeks pass by. Occasionally, they threw stones at them or uttered curses.

Gritzalia was Theodora's world—her universe. She knew her small home and the dirt street that passed in front of it, the church with its red-and-gold iconostasis and the sight of the *papas* with his black robe and toadstool hat, and her aunt, *thea*, and the shops in the village that she visited with her mother and the orderly lines of the hillside grapevines and the red grasses that waved on mountains, and the flat shaded place above the village where Greek families gathered on religious holidays for picnics. She knew the taste of blackberries—Gritzalia was famous throughout the mountains for its blackberries—and the scent of the pine trees that made the mountains green.

Gritzalia was a village in three parts—the upper village was Greek and Turkish; the middle village was Turkish; the lower village was Greek. Situated at the crossroads of five trails that wended their way to the main road to the east toward Casaba, it had been a prosperous place for its two thousand inhabitants, split evenly between Ottoman Greeks and Ottoman Turks. Caravans often stopped there for final provisioning before making the long march into the depths of Anatolia, and beyond.

By the first week of September, all the Greeks were leaving Gryzvalia, and many were already on the road that led north down the mountain to the main road that cut west through the pass and descended to the coastal plain and Smyrna.

The Gravos family soon fell into a long line of people moving along the main road. These other people had come from villages and farms farther east, Casaba, and even Ushak, and they already had been walking for days. The road down from the mountain was a series of switchbacks among the cutbanks, and it was only the weight of the big animals in harness that kept the carts from careening down the steep pass. Out of the mountains, the landscape was mostly a treeless rolling plain of grass, low bushes, and rocks broken by cultivated fields, orchards, vineyards, and villages. They passed through the town of Boudjah with its Levantine villas. The road wound visibly into the distance in both directions, east and west, and the line of people, animals, and carts could be seen for miles. It was as if there was some gigantic and medieval agricultural procession under way, and it was moving inexorably westward toward the sea but at the slow speed of the heavy-hipped oxen.

Theodora was in that big and pitiful parade of black-garmented women and farmers and priests and barefoot children and shopkeepers with hats and vests and leather shoes. Strangely, there would appear a woman with a parasol. The old people, bent or crippled, had the most trouble. Sometimes they had to be carried on litters or on the backs of family members. The heat and the exertion were too much for others. They died along the way.

Young Theodora saw that some of the people on the road were soldiers, and they seemed very tired, and those that seemed to have been hurt were being helped by other soldiers. Their uniforms were torn, and some were bloody, and they were dirty. Sometimes, soldiers would pass on the backs of camels or donkeys. The Gravos family, in this winding serpent of tattered humanity, crossed the Meles River and entered Smyrna from the north. They found a Greek church, St. John's, and rested there on its floor and benches. It was a small church, built with green stone, but it was crammed with people who were frightened and a long way from home like the Gravos family. Theodora looked after the small children. Her father found a friend, a resident of Smyrna, and he took them all to his house for safety. They slept there that night.

CHAPTER 10

An American Destroyer Arrives

Admiral Bristol spent Sunday of the Labor Day weekend aboard the *Scorpion* hosting a lunch for eighteen guests, including British naval officers, some of his ships' commanders and their wives, the Japanese high commissioner, and prominent Americans in Constantinople, including Nataline Dulles, Allen Dulles's younger sister who was a Red Cross nurse in Athens. They dined on the ship's deck under a canvas canopy and within view of the Summer Palace Hotel at Therapia.

Big luncheons aboard the *Scorpion* were common occurrences, and the yacht was well furnished for fancy dining. One of Bristol's early acts as high commissioner had been to order china for entertaining, down to finger bowls and oyster forks. After lunch, Bristol and his guests went ashore at Therapia for a tennis tournament.

On Monday, Labor Day, he led a group, mostly Americans, on a picnic to the Sweet Waters of Asia, a pleasant retreat of brooks, wooden bridges, and greenery along the Bosporus and once favored by sultans for their royal outings. The picnic lasted into the evening. Bristol dressed for these excursions in civilian clothes—blue sport coat and tie, white trousers and white bucks, and a summer homburg. He enjoyed taking snapshots of the gatherings. He and Helen were childless, but the outings put them at the center of an admiring family of naval officers and their wives, many of whom dressed casually in the latest fashion: cloche hats and dresses at the knee and revealing bathing suits (by 1920s standards) for swimming in the Bosporus.

Bristol had grown up on a small farm in southern New Jersey and muscled his way up in the navy. More than once his ascent had nearly faltered, but he had been saved by the intervention of friends and his own indefatigable nature. (A family friend who went to elementary school with Bristol in Glassboro, New Jersey, remembered that Bristol's favorite poem was "Invictus": "In the fell clutch of circumstance / I have not winced nor cried aloud. / Under the bludgeonings of chance / My head is bloody, but unbowed.") Glassboro, during Bristol's boyhood in the second half of the nineteenth century, was a company town that manufactured glass, and his family lived in nearby rural Clayton Township. He attended Glassboro Academy, the local public school, and received an appointment to the Naval Academy from U.S. Rep. Thomas Ferrell, a one-term Democratic congressman from Glassboro.

Ferrell had been a labor leader at the glassworks, and as a congressman he had sought to ban companies from recruiting foreign labor, which competed with native-born Americans. Immigrants from eastern and southern Europe were flooding into the country at the time, creating a backlash in some quarters because of fears that the Italians, Greeks, Serbians, and other foreigners took American jobs and depressed wages. With Ferrell's letter of appointment, Bristol went off to Annapolis at age fifteen, only slightly younger than most of the entering cadets. He graduated four years later in the middle of his class.

One possible explanation—though remote—in Bristol's background that may account for his animus toward Greeks and Armenians could be the nativism that motivated Ferrell. Perhaps the dislike of Europe's poor and darker-skinned immigrants had floated in the air that Bristol had breathed as a boy in Glassboro.

While he was definitely not from a patrician family, and he seemed to lack the air of irony and ease that was often a gift of the upper class, Bristol, as the American potentate in Constantinople, was surrounded by young men of privilege of the sort that had populated the Naval Academy in the late nineteenth and early twentieth centuries. These young men often worshipped the strong-minded and up-from-the-farm admiral. One such man, though not so young as the others, was Robert Steed Dunn, a Harvard graduate from a prominent Newport family, who served as one of Bristol's intelligence officers. An extraordinary man by any measure, Dunn would ultimately shape and encourage Bristol's contempt for the Armenians in Turkey.

Dunn came to the navy late in life—he was forty-one years old when he joined in 1918—commissioned as a junior-grade lieutenant. By then, he had already worked as a reporter in New York for the great muckraking editor Lincoln Steffens, joined the first expedition to attempt the summit of Alaska's Mount McKinley, made the first ascent of Mount Wrangle, explored Siberia and the Aleutian Islands, covered the war in Europe with John Reed (from inside Germany and Romania), and ridden with General Pershing in Mexico in search of Pancho Villa. Dunn brought his adventurous spirit to Bristol's naval staff, sometimes disappearing with only a sidearm into the Anatolian interior on self-appointed intelligence missions. Dunn was with Bristol when Bristol made a trip to Tbilisi to meet with the premier of the new Armenian republic, created by Sevres, and he made two long trips himself, mostly on horseback, through the Caucasus and eastern Anatolia, befriending some of the Turkish nationalists' highest leaders. He interviewed Mustapha Kemal in 1920. In the end, he may have turned out to be a better journalist than intelligence officer and contributed to skepticism in Washington about Bristol's judgment. Dunn showed astute powers of observation (landscapes and faces were a specialty), and his writing was superb, but the State Department was not happy with his methods or results. The problem with Dunn— and the same could be said about Bristol—was that, in summing up the religious conflicts in Turkey, he judged the Armenians to be as brutal as the Turks, arguing from a position that assumed Armenian history began at about 1919. The mass slaughter and deportations of Armenians during World War I seemed to not have made a strong impression on either of them. Bristol was an early form of a type that would emerge later in the century—the holocaust denier. Dunn left Constantinople in 1922, but he remained close to Bristol, who always referred to him as Bobby. In his letters to the admiral, Dunn called him Mark.

AFTER THE LABOR DAY WEEKEND, Bristol returned to Constantinople. His first order of business on Tuesday, September 5, was a routine inspection of the USS *Simpson*, a destroyer moored in Bosporus. (This was the day of the second meeting of the American community in Smyrna.) Afterward, he had several meetings at the embassy including a long conversation with Miller Joblin, the regional general manager of Standard Oil of New York. Bristol lectured him on the importance of controlling costs and the danger of hiring local people. ("He quite surprised me," Bristol noted in his diary, "by stating that he intended to develop an organization with local employees. I told him I didn't think he had sufficient experience and knowledge . . .") It's hard to know what the oil executive made of Bristol's confident assumption that he knew more about operating an oil depot than his guest but the performance was typical Bristol—full of strongly held opinions delivered with the utmost confidence.

By Tuesday, September 5, Bristol had already received three cables from Horton—the first, addressed to the State Department, requesting naval protection; the second reporting that the British were evacuating their nationals; and the third asking for his mediation to save Smyrna from possible arson and again asking for naval protection. Bristol got around to answering these messages late in the day Tuesday. He cabled Horton that a destroyer would arrive in Smyrna Wednesday morning, and he warned Horton not to take any action that could be construed as favoring one side. (It was obvious to both men that this meant Horton should not favor Greeks over Turks.) By the time Bristol's cable arrived in Smyrna, Phillips had already cabled Horton that the navy was directing Bristol to send a destroyer to Smyrna.

For the trip to Smyrna, Bristol chose to send the USS *Litchfield*, whose skipper, Lieutenant Commander John B. Rhodes, had been at the big lunch aboard the *Scorpion* on Sunday. Bristol directed his chief of staff, Captain Arthur J. Hepburn, to prepare the orders and have the ship under way that night. Bristol also ordered one of his intelligence officers, Aaron S. Merrill, a young lieutenant commander from Natchez, Mississippi, to make the trip with Rhodes. Bristol wanted his own eyes and ears in Smyrna: he didn't trust Horton, and Rhodes might also prove unreliable, though for different reasons. Bristol had complete confidence in Merrill, and Merrill, in turn, revered Bristol.

Small and light, young Merrill had been the Naval Academy's bantam boxing champion. He was bright and sociable with curly brown hair and brown eyes and popular among the other cadets for his athleticism and patrician yet irreverent ways. He enjoyed a good laugh—especially at someone else's expense. While on a trip to Bulgaria with Bristol, he had found it amusing that their car frightened the animals of the local peasants, causing them to upend the peasants' carts. Merrill had joined Bristol's staff in 1919, and he relished the work and pursued it with zest. His admiration of Bristol's leadership made its way into the letters he sent home to his mother in Mississippi. The letters also showed that Merrill had absorbed Bristol's point of view: the Greeks were unlikable, and to know a greasy Armenian was "to dislike his lying, thieving ways." In praising the light-skinned Russian refugees in Constantinople, he wrote to his mother that they "would make far more desirable (American) citizens than the weekly thirty thousand Polish Jews and Italian bootblacks that are pouring in." Merrill and Robert Dunn also were close friends, having met stateside in Newport in 1918; in fact, Merrill had originally recommended Dunn to Bristol as an intelligence officer.

In January, Merrill had married Louise Witherbee, the daughter of Walter C. Witherbee, a mining magnate and one of the richest men in America. Louise had grown up with Japanese servants, Thoroughbred horses, and a palatial floating summer home on Lake Champlain so big that it had a first-floor ballroom. Merrill had returned to New York for the wedding at St. Thomas Episcopal Church on Fifth Avenue, then Louise had joined him in Constantinople, where she added sparkle and prestige to Admiral and Mrs. Bristol's social circle.

When Merrill got his orders on Tuesday to board the destroyer for Smyrna, no doubt he was eager to get into the action. By September 5, word had reached Constantinople that the Greek-Turkish stalemate was broken. Everyone by then knew something very big was unfolding to the south, and Merrill was particularly well informed since staying abreast of the military situation was his job. The Smyrna trip was a chance for him to please the boss and enjoy an adventure—the frequent letters home to his mother read like a boy having a great time at summer camp.

Two hours before the *Litchfield* was scheduled to depart, two reporters—John Clayton of the *Chicago Tribune* and Constantine Brown of the *Chicago Daily News*—sniffing a big story, bounded up the ten marble steps of the U.S. embassy and called on Bristol. They wanted to hop a ride to Smyrna aboard the destroyer. The American and British press were well represented in Constantinople, and Bristol often met with reporters and other writers to propound his views on background. John Dos Passos was among those who had passed through the city and interviewed the admiral. (Ernest Hemingway would be a regular at his press briefings later in the month.) Bristol knew Brown and Clayton well and was particularly close to Brown, a British citizen in his twenties who had grown up in the United States and married an American girl from Iowa. Brown had replaced the previous *Chicago Daily News* reporter, who had been transferred after mixing it up with Bristol. Dapper with a pencil-thin mustache, Brown was a regular at Bristol's parties aboard the *Scorpion*. Something of a scamp, he had outfitted a houseboat as his living quarters in Constantinople, and during Bristol's evening parties at Therapia, he would bring his boat alongside the *Scorpion*, providing a non-naval deck for an ample bar. Prohibition was in force back in the United States, and navy rules forbade alcohol aboard its ships. A plank was laid between the *Scorpion* and Brown's houseboat, and partygoers could move back and forth to get cocktails from a bartender who was detailed to serve drinks as navy musicians serenaded guests on the *Scorpion*'s deck.

Both Brown and Clayton had covered the war in Europe, and both were prepared to go anywhere for a good story. Clayton had gained notoriety after the war by sneaking into the Soviet Union, via Finland, on skis to report about starvation in Petrograd and the dissatisfaction of Emma Goldman, the American communist, with the Soviet system. She had been a guest of the Soviets at the time, and Clayton scored a major scoop. In Turkey, Clayton had shown some annoying independence earlier in the year when he had filed long and vivid stories back to Chicago about the Turkish massacres of thousands of Ottoman-Greek civilians along the Black Sea. Bristol had worked hard to keep the stories out of the newspapers, and ultimately, to his satisfaction, the stories were never published. Clayton remained in Bristol's good graces.

Bristol was a student of the new field of public relations. He controlled the press by staying on message and using his authority to provide transportation to news hotspots and allowing reporters to use the naval radio system for transmitting stories at no charge. He agreed to let them board the *Litchfield* but, as he noted in his diary, he made it clear that he wanted them to "uphold my interests." By the summer of 1922, Bristol's interests were widely known to anyone who had come in contact with him. They were the primacy of American commerce in shaping an American policy toward the Ottoman Empire and rehabilitation of the image of the Turks as brutal oppressors of Christian minorities. The two reporters, having more than once been on the receiving end of Bristol's tirades, got the point and agreed to the conditions of travel.

The *Litchfield* departed Constantinople at 7 P.M., Tuesday, September 5. Like all American destroyers of the day, it was a small warship, 314 feet long and 31 feet wide, giving it a narrow profile, easily distinguishable by its array of four aft-leaning smokestacks. It was armed with four .50-caliber guns, a smaller antiaircraft gun, torpedoes, and depth charges. It had been built to find and destroy submarines. The ship carried eight officers and a crew of about 115 men. It could travel as fast as 35 knots (40 mph) under full steam, but a typical cruising speed would be about 14 knots (16 mph). The *Litchfield* was ordered to steam at the slower "economical" speed; Bristol was in no hurry to get the destroyer to Smyrna.

Lieutenant Commander Rhodes had taken command of the *Litchfield* three months earlier in Norfolk and had brought it to Turkey. He was thirty-six years old, an Annapolis graduate, and son of a successful merchant from a small town near Philadelphia. Rhodes was a capable and at times brilliant officer—when he was sober. His quick wit and navigation and gunnery skills had won him the respect of superior officers, and his knowledge of metallurgy and shell design—self-taught—was so extraordinary that the navy had selected him in 1918 to design and build a modern armor and projectile plant in Charleston, West Virginia. His commanding officer had objected to the transfer, but the top brass concluded that Rhodes, only thirty-two at the time, was the only officer in the navy capable of handling the complicated project. After the plant's completion, the Bureau of Ordnance took the unusual step of nominating him for a Navy Cross, the second-highest military award (after the Medal of Honor), but navy secretary Josephus Daniels, a teetotaler, reduced his recognition to a Silver Star. By then, Rhodes's weakness for alcohol was well established. It was a flaw that may have played a fortuitous part in later events at Smyrna.

Rhodes had a soft and aristocratic face with an expression so supremely placid that it seemed to mock the world for its unnecessary exertions. In his navy photo as a young officer, he wears a look just this side of playful. As an ensign, following his graduation, Rhodes had been cited more than once for being drunk on duty, and he had avoided a court-martial for early-morning intoxication aboard ship in San Francisco only because the squadron was sailing that morning. One of his superiors had recorded that Rhodes was "intemperate" and another reported that he "lacked self-control," predicting that Ensign Rhodes would have a life-long problem with alcohol. It was an accurate look into the future.

Several months before being transferred to Turkey, Rhodes had been declared unfit for duty while serving as the executive officer aboard the USS *Huron*, an armored cruiser that was patrolling Asian waters. "There are indications," a navy doctor in the Philippines wrote, "of mental derangement evident by egotistical and erratic conversation, vague ideas of persecution and grandiosity, inconstancy of purpose and religious enthusiasm." Rhodes was escorted from the Philippines to the Naval Hospital in Washington for treatment. Adding to his alcohol problem was Rhodes's wife, Katherine—she was constantly running up debts that he couldn't pay, and the debtors turned to the navy with their complaints. She also had begun an affair the previous year, and Rhodes, fabulously drunk, had challenged the man to a duel. No shots were fired, but Rhodes had taken a bad fall off a porch and damaged his eye—the second drunken fall in two months. The doctor who examined him in Washington wrote, "This officer has a rather brilliant mind and has for many years had the reputation of being queer and eccentric. He's also a hard drinker."

THE *LITCHFIELD* DEPARTED as the setting sun threw its orange light on the minarets and towers of Constantinople. Rhodes had been briefed on the situation and shown the cables from Horton. Along the way, on the Marmara coast, he and the other men on board saw fires blazing on the Turkish mainland—villages set ablaze by the retreating Greek army or the advancing Turkish army. It was hard to know which. By September 5, the northern detachment of the Greek army, which had largely escaped the Turkish assault, had arrived at Mudania, where it was embarking on Greek ships to reach Thrace, the province of Greece on Marmara's opposite shore. Rhodes saw troop transports making their way across the inland sea.

The long and narrow design of the *Litchfield*—like other Clemson-class destroyers built immediately after the war—could make for an uncomfortable ride in heavy seas. Its bow rose high and fell hard and the ship seesawed from side to side with twists and shudders. Some sailors could never get used to it and required transfer to less nausea-inducing vessels. Fortunately, on its run to Smyrna, the sea was mostly calm and the wind light. A full moon rose and threw a pale column of light over the dark sea. It was about a thirteen-hour trip to Smyrna from Constantinople at the slow speed.

The *Litchfield* came into the mouth of the Gulf of Smyrna soon after daybreak, Wednesday, September 6, and at 8:30 A.M. it passed through the narrows at Pelican Point buoy. The sun had already risen over the eastward hills and was beating down on the city's red roofs and reflecting in sparkling shards off the harbor's calm surface. As it approached the city, the *Litchfield* passed numerous small steamers and boats under sail heading out to sea, all of them overflowing with people and luggage. The exodus from Smyrna was under way.

The *Litchfield* cleared the harbor's net defenses and dropped its anchor off the Quay at 9 A.M. The harbor flashed with Allied warships. There were also numerous Greek merchant vessels employed as troop and cargo carriers as well as British, American, and Japanese freighters. Already, an Italian battleship had landed forty sailors to guard the Italian school and Italian consulate, both one block from the Quay on Rue Parallele, and the French had landed fourteen sailors who stood outside the

French consulate on the Quay. The British navy had put a small force of royal marines ashore, but kept them at the pier. British officers, working with the British consulate, had gone ashore to plan an evacuation of British nationals. Two British merchants ships—the *Magira* and the *Antioch*—would leave later in the day for Malta with British evacuees.

The *Litchfield*'s launch was lowered to the water, and Rhodes and Merrill got in it to go ashore. Both in their thirties, and neither a spit-and-polish officer, the two officers, wearing their summer whites, were getting along well, and Merrill, with typical irreverence, was calling his fellow lieutenant commander "Dusty"—Dusty Rhodes. Merrill was "Tip"—nicknamed for his grandfather who had fought the Shawnee at Tippecanoe. Merrill went about his intelligence work like a boy fitting himself into an adventure story. The prospect of a little danger and derring-do appealed to him, and he handled his duties with bantam swagger and a ready quip. He was confident, funny, and not averse to a little luxury when he could manage it, and he soon would manage it in Smyrna. His diary entries, recorded in a hardbound accounts book he had picked up in France, were vivid and detailed and read like notes for a novel that might one day get written. The title might be, *My Lark in Turkey*. Merrill also had a less endearing quality—he seemed devoid of empathy. His observations on the refugees he would encounter over the next several weeks were often heartless; they revealed a man whose sense of personal superiority disconnected him from the omnipresent suffering. Rhodes, on the other hand, would react with compassion though sometimes-questionable judgment.

From the destroyer's launch, Merrill and Rhodes could see that people were crowded along the waterfront, but on reaching the Quay, they discovered that the mass of people with their bags, trunks, and household possessions was nearly impenetrable. The streets nearest the waterfront were chaotic and congested with soldiers, refugees, cars, carriages, and animals. Having just arrived from the disintegrating battlefront, the Greek soldiers in the streets appeared exhausted and dirty, with torn uniforms and the darkened eyes of chimney sweeps. They were lying in groups awaiting embarkation on troopships and requisitioned steamers anchored in the harbor and tied alongside the northerly end of the Quay. The wounded were on litters or in carts.

The Passport Pier (where Jennings had landed with his family three weeks earlier) was nearly unapproachable for three hundred yards in either direction due to boxes, crates, and throngs of people seeking to depart. Furniture, rugs, bedding were piled in heaps. Children slept on boxes. The refugees were standing in clots with their bundles and animals (goats, chickens, donkeys) while others from their group madly sought places for them on the small fishing boats along the seawall that were taking aboard passengers who could pay outrageous prices. Others—the commercial class in the city, men in straw boaters and white summer suits and women in big sunhats and calf-length summer dresses—waited in long lines at the steamship agencies. Their carriages and cars stood by on the Quay with servants prepared to load their luggage on the passenger boats alongside the pier.

Merrill and Rhodes threaded their way through the people toward the American consulate. With the harbor on their right, they walked south along the Quay past the French consulate, the Sporting Club, Café de Paris, and the Boston Bar, turning left on Galazio Street. At the consulate, they found George Horton busy arranging for the departure of naturalized Greek and Armenian Americans. Horton pulled himself away from the people and briefed the officers on the military situation and Greek administration of the city.

By Wednesday, September 6, the line of Greek resistance had fallen back to Salihli, less than sixty miles from the city. The rear of the Greek Southern Army, to the extent that it was still a cohesive force, was marching westward at night (under the light of the same full moon that Rhodes and Merrill had seen from the bridge of the *Litchfield*) and fighting rearguard defensive actions during the day.

Horton described his meetings the previous day with the Greek military commander general Georgios Hadjianestis and the Greek governor Stergiades. They had offered opposite views on the prospect of the Greek army holding the city against the Turks. Stergiades had told Horton the Greek soldiers were unwilling to fight any longer, but Hadjianestis asserted that a fresh division of Greek troops had arrived that morning from Thrace and he planned to put a defensive line between the city and the advancing Turks. Horton also reported that he had gathered together Greek and Armenian naturalized Americans in a place near the waterfront to prepare for their embarkation on a small steamer he had leased with their money, a notion that Merrill found fanciful. "We will be glad to see them go tomorrow morning," he noted in his diary, "as they would very likely swear at the Turks in Greek behind American flags were they staying on for the big show." His view was typically insolent, and it seemed to draw on the reservoir of animus that he had brought with him to Smyrna. He had been in the city less than an hour, and already he was condemning its Greek residents for cowardice.

After the meeting with Horton, Rhodes and Merrill returned to the harbor and got back in the naval launch to call on the flagships of the other Allied navies. Merrill was gathering information, and Rhodes was tagging along. They were both more or less enjoying themselves; so far it was light duty and the scene was interesting to behold. They went first to the *Iron Duke* and found that Admiral de Brock was ashore. They went next to the *Kilkis* to talk with the Greek admiral. The *Kilkis* was one of two *Mississippi*-class battleships in the Greek navy, both of which had been purchased from United States just before the outbreak of the world war. The Greek admiral also was ashore. Rhodes and Merrill then went to the *Edgar Quintet*, the French battleship where they found Rear Admiral Henri Dumesnil, the fifty-five-year-old commander of the French fleet in the eastern Mediterranean. The admiral, a cheerful but odd-looking man who had small dark eyes, a large nose that turned left, and full lips, welcomed them. He was friendly and talkative.

Merrill spoke to him in French. Dumesnil told them that he had met with Governor Stergiades and General Hadjianestis and (similar to Horton's experience) had received conflicting messages about defense of the city. Enjoying the company of the two American officers and bringing them into his confidence, the French admiral went on to criticize Admiral de Brock, who had said he would only protect British nationals.

Merrill asked the French admiral if he thought it was feasible for the Allies to take control of the city between the departure of the Greek army and arrival of the Turks. Responding forcefully, Dumesnil said he had considered the possibility and added that he would not stand by and let the population be massacred or the city burned. He threatened to block Greek military transports if he did not get a Greek guaranty of its intentions to enforce order in the city. (It was bluff talk; the Greeks refused to guaranty order, and the French did nothing.) Then, relaxing a bit, the admiral introduced his wife and daughter, who were aboard, and Merrill, practicing his southern charm as well as his French, pronounced them "delightful."

Merrill was proud of his command of the language—one line of his family had been French. He had been born in Natchez, Mississippi, at his family's home, Brandon Hall, once the largest slaveholding plantation in the rich delta country of Adams County. Among his ancestors were the Surgets, the enormously land-rich French planters in Mississippi, some of whom returned to France after the American Civil War. His grandfather and great-grandfather had been Mississippi governors and another grandfather had been a Confederate army officer.

Merrill and Madame and Mademoiselle Dumesnil passed pleasantries, and the women asked after Admiral and Mrs. Bristol and sent their regards. The admiral's wife invited Merrill for tea later in the day. Merrill was clearly enjoying himself and buoyed by the meeting with the ladies, and after he and Rhodes said their good-byes, they returned to the *Litchfield* for lunch with the Chicago reporters, Vice Consuls Maynard Barnes and James Park, and two American businessmen.

Always seeking some excitement along with intelligence work, Merrill went back ashore after lunch and hired a Studebaker to drive to the front. He took Clayton and Brown with him. (Rhodes remained with the ship.) Merrill and the two newspapermen took the road out of the city that followed the Casaba rail line, cutting first to the north toward Magnesia and then east to the interior.

On the narrow road, they made slow progress against the tide of refugees and soldiers moving toward the city. They encountered a flood of people walking quietly, steadily. They had with them cows, sheep, goats, and even dogs and cats, and some were leading water buffalo that pulled rickety two-wheeled carts loaded with carpets, kitchen utensils, furniture.

The unshaven footsore soldiers, pants torn at the knees, walked among the refugees. Some soldiers rode on donkeys and a few on camels. Merrill estimated the number of soldiers at about five thousand. At one point, a mounted Greek officer fired a shot to stop their car, but when he saw Merrill's uniform, he continued on his way. After about two and a half hours, the three Americans had made only about fifteen miles—their Studebaker was moving not much faster than a walk. With the numbers of people on the road seeming to increase as they pushed farther east, Merrill decided it would be impossible to reach Magnesia and turned back to Smyrna.

Back in the city, Merrill resumed his adventure. He had gotten back too late for tea with Madame Dumesnil so instead he called on the director of the Aydin Railroad, a retired British military officer. The British officer and his wife, an American, invited him to stay for dinner and the three of them talked into the evening. Merrill accepted an invitation to return the next day for lunch. By day's end, he had sent two cables to Bristol describing the scene in the city and asserting that the Greek army was devastating the countryside on orders from Athens. "Greek troops in panic and pouring into Smyrna. No fight in them." For sure, the Greeks were furiously loading military supplies and men aboard ships at Smyrna for a rapid evacuation, but there was no panic, just exhaustion, and Merrill did not indicate how he had established that Athens was directing devastation of the countryside. The Greek military command had been out of communication with its forces for almost twelve days since the offensive had begun. But it was a message that would surely please the admiral.

Meanwhile, Constantine Brown, who had obtained a letter of introduction from the Greek high commissioner in Constantinople, had gone to interview General Hadjianestis. The government in Athens had already sacked the general for his failure to anticipate the Turkish attack, but the field commander who had been named as his successor was out of communication with headquarters and unaware of his promotion. So Hadjianestis had continued to serve. Unknown to him and the government in Athens, his successor had been captured at Dumlupinar and was a prisoner of war in Magnesia. The second replacement for Hadjianestis was on his way from Athens and would take command later in the day.

Hadjianestis had been an odd choice to lead the Greek forces in a military campaign that by any measure would have been extremely difficult. He was fifty-eight and reputed to be mentally unstable, possibly insane. A ladies' man, "he was tall and thin, straight as a ramrod, and extremely well groomed, with a pointed gray beard and the air of an aristocrat." He looked like Don Quixote. Years earlier, as a young officer fighting in the Balkans, he had faced a mutiny of his troops, an event attributed to his strange manner and maniacal discipline, habits that he displayed in Turkey. At an inspection of battle-weary troops at the front, he paid close attention to their haircuts. As commander in chief of the Greek forces in Asia Minor, he had directed the land war against the Turkish nationalists from his flagship in the harbor while he was having a Quayside mansion fitted out with expensive furniture and Turkish carpets.

Brown met Hadjianestis at Hotel Splendid on the Quay, seated at a big table inlaid with mother-of-pearl. The general assured him that the Greeks had won "smashing victories" in the last two days. Then, anticipating a question from the reporter about why he was in Smyrna and not with the troops, the general said, "You know, my legs are made of glass, and I can not take the chance of breaking them." (In two months, the general, showing increasing signs of mental deterioration, would be executed by a firing squad in Athens for high treason.)

At 8:30 P.M., a second U.S. destroyer, the USS *Simpson*, arrived in the harbor. The *Simpson* came alongside the *Litchfield*, and the ship's commander, Lieutenant Commander Harrison Knauss, went aboard for a briefing by Rhodes. Knauss, a fellow Pennsylvanian and classmate at Annapolis, was a serious, even pensive officer. Knauss had skippered President Wilson's yacht, *Sylph*, and during the war he had served as the executive officer aboard a destroyer, USS *Jacob Jones*, that lost sixty-six men when a German U-boat sank it in the North Sea. Once ashore at Smyrna, he would write some of the most sympathetic and moving accounts of the refugees.

THE CITY'S POPULATION WAS swelling, its food stores diminishing, and, with a hostile army fast approaching, Smyrna's defense was growing more doubtful. There was no serious indication that the powers represented by the warships in the harbor would intervene.

The Smyrna Relief Committee, monitoring the arrival of refugees by train and on foot, estimated that thirty thousand people were arriving each day. Dispersed and wandering in search of shelter and food, the refugees had become impossible to accurately count but they were everywhere except for in the Turkish Quarter.

Like the Gravos family, many of the refugees looked to the churches for a resting place. Armenians jammed the courtyard of the city's biggest Armenian church, St. Stephanos. Many of the Greeks gravitated toward St. George or St. Photini, the Orthodox cathedral, which was on Frank Street, several blocks south of the YMCA. The entrance to St. Photini's stone-paved courtyard was reached through a narrow passageway of homes and shops under its tall belfry, one of the city's principal landmarks. A British officer making a walking tour of the city went into the courtyard and offered this description: "Old wrinkled women, lying on the pavement in rags, or propped up against a wall, asleep. Babies in mother's arms, or sometimes two or three on an old sack, in a row, looking like waxen images. Will they ever awaken again, one wonders? The mothers in many cases sit staring blankly in front of them but ready to spring at the first person who would dare harm their child. Women with hair all over the place, and wild eyes."

By the time the *Litchfield* had arrived on Wednesday morning, the Americans' relief committee had already formed itself into an effective working group and was using the YMCA building as its headquarters.

Jennings was out seeking flour to buy and ovens where it could be baked into loaves of bread. Searching the city in Jacob's Chevrolet and on foot, Jennings identified bakeries, both big and small, and negotiated payments for their production of the big round loaves that could be distributed by the hundreds to refugees. The city had nearly fifty small bakeries, nearly all of them owned by Greeks, and two big steam bakeries, also owned by Greeks. The two big bakeries were in the European Quarter, not far from the YMCA. The other bakeries, though, were scattered throughout the city, with each small neighborhood containing at least one bakery. Most of the ovens were fired by wood or charcoal, now-scarce commodities that Muslims from the countryside typically brought into the city. Jennings went up and down the streets, opening doors and seeking to communicate with bakery owners. He had local assistants at the YMCA who spoke Greek, and they could help him arrange prices and payments. The money was coming from the donations of other relief committee members, principally the American businessmen. There were other foreign nationals in the city—Italians, French, and British—but only the Americans had organized a relief effort. Jennings's assignment required him to walk long distances, and exertion was difficult for him. His lung capacity had been reduced by more than half as result of his bout with tuberculosis, and he suffered an ongoing case of cardiac asthma. The heat worsened his discomfort, but he kept on, wearing his loose jacket and tie and straw boater, up one cobbled street and down another, making deals despite his almost-constant low-grade fever.

Back in Utica, on the day the doctors had informed Amy that Asa soon would die, they said their collective diagnosis was acute tuberculosis, a bacterial infection of the lungs. In the days and weeks that followed, his condition had steadily worsened. His weight fell to eighty-five pounds. He gasped for breath; the pain in his chest and back had grown worse. To Amy, he seemed barely alive in the hospital bed: a thin and fragile creature in bedclothes. Among the torments that Amy experienced as she watched him waste away was her awareness of her husband's ambition. He had often told her that he wanted to do something important with his life. Now, Amy saw, the prospect of some future achievement was slipping away as his life was slipping away. But she kept up her belief, at least for him, that he would recover, and Asa had continued to fight for his life.

In the eighth week of his hospitalization, he announced to Amy that he wanted to leave the hospital. He needed air, he told her, and he wanted her to take him to the Adirondack Mountains, where the air was clean and he could bring it into his diseased lungs. He was sure clean air was the thing he needed. Reluctantly, the hospital released him into Amy's care, and she put him in a car and took him to a lodge and set of cabins at Seventh Lake, a pristine surface of blue among the Adirondacks' tall spruce and pine trees. There was a breeze, and the air carried the scent of the conifers around their cabin. The setting was peaceful, the air cool and pleasant, but Asa's condition only worsened. There was no magic in the mountain air. Amy took him to another doctor, and this time Asa received a new diagnosis, actually an additional diagnosis: He had developed Pott's disease, a condition in which a tubercular infection travels from the lungs to the spine. The new infection had inflamed his vertebrae and eroded the cartilage discs between several of them. His spine had begun to curve and collapse. The pain was awful. Losing the support of his spine, his body folded like a cloth puppet. There was no choice but to put him in a full-body plaster cast, which allowed him to move only his head and arms and parts of his legs. He insisted on a re-turn to Seventh Lake, and Amy complied. She set his bed near the cabin window, where he could catch the mountain air, and she read the Bible to him, especially the story of Job's unjust punishment and test of faith. So much of Job's suffering mirrored Asa's. "And the Lord said unto Satan, Behold, he is in thine hand; but save his life. So went Satan forth from the presence of the Lord, and smote Job with sore boils from the sole of his foot unto his crown."

Amy was nearly out of hope, and possibly because he saw the direc-tion of her thoughts, Asa said to her, "Amy, I can't die. I have great work to do and I must go to see Jerusalem." His words only left Amy more con-fused and upset. Jerusalem? What had Jerusalem to do with his battle? She wanted him only to live. "I could not understand," Amy later wrote, "how he would be able to do either (work or travel) for I was not asking more than that his life be spared, which seemed so much." Thereafter, he often returned to the theme of Jerusalem—the place to which he must travel. The word itself became a talisman.

One night at Seventh Lake, he could hardly breathe. He struggled, but the gasps could not bring enough air into his lungs. He was suffo-cating. Amy summoned the local doctor, who said Asa required surgery to understand and remove whatever it was that impeded his breath-ing. As Amy prepared to drive him to the hospital in Utica, Asa began coughing up pus. At first, he and Amy thought he was expelling the whitish tissue of his lung. His death seemed at hand. The coughing lasted through the night, but in the morning it ceased, and the pus stopped coming up. He breathed more easily; his temperature returned to normal.

The doctor explained what had happened: a cold abscess had formed in his thorax and broke open in the night. Its contents had come up through his larynx. The development was an important turn, but he was not healed, and Amy decided on a new next step. She took him to Clifton Springs, a Christian sulfur-springs resort in the Finger Lakes region of New York. She learned massage, and for an hour and a half each morning and each night, massaged Asa's back and chest. In between, she placed him in the healing waters. Slowly, he returned to health, or at least turned away from a sure slope toward death.

By 1907, he was back to his pastoral duties at the Barneveld Methodist Church. Their second child, Asa Wilbur, was born that year, and he lived. Asa was working again, but the damage from the illnesses he had endured was permanent. The collapse and curvature of his spine had reduced his height by five inches and left him with a hump on his back. It had also displaced and enlarged his heart. He would suffer near-constant pain, fevers, and shortness of breath his entire life, and they were with him as he searched for flour and ovens in the backstreets of Smyrna on September 6, 7, and 8, 1922.

With his perpetual smile, but with the odd gait forced on him by his misshapen back, Jennings worked his way through the crowds, searching out the means for feeding the refugees. Finding surplus food of any sort was difficult. Because of the war, there had been spot shortages of food in Smyrna even before the Greek army's retreat. Jennings realized that there would be only one adequate source of flour before emergency supplies arrived—the departing Greek army, which had been feeding more than two hundred thousand men. So that's where Jennings went—to the commander of the Greek forces, General Hadjianestis, who had already rejected the relief committee's requests for supplies. The Greek army's warehouses contained more than a million pounds of flour. The greater part of it was kept in a warehouse at the Point. The Greek general yielded to the persuasions of the little motor of a man in front of him. Unfortunately, for the committee and the refugees, the gift came too late. As the

Greek troops departed the city, looting soon broke out, including at the warehouse, and in a very short time the Turkish army would seize the warehouse and everything in it to feed its troops.

Despite his effectiveness with the bakeries, Jennings was removed from his Feeding Committee assignment. His boss, Jacob, now back from vacation, took Jennings's place and assignment as the ranking YMCA member on the relief committee. Pushed aside, Jennings fell into the role of courier—everyone else's assistant. He became the committee's errand boy. It appeared that Jacob was unwilling to let loose of the judgment he had formed about Jennings before his arrival at Smyrna—that he was not the man for the job.

Jennings was unperturbed. As a Methodist minister, he was familiar the Methodist pledge:

> I am but one, but I am one.
> I cannot do much, but I can do something.
> What I can do, I ought to do.
> What I ought to do, I will do.

And so he did, finding ways to be useful. Providentially, while making his rounds of the city, Jennings had come in contact with a prominent Greek doctor, Demetrius Marsellos, who was preparing to leave the city with his family. He had a mansion on the north end of the Quay, at No. 490, in the neighborhood of grand residences called Bella Vista. He offered it to Jennings for the relief committee's use. After consulting with Horton, Jennings accepted the house and rapidly turned it into a first-aid station and shelter for injured and pregnant women. The city's hospitals were overwhelmed with patients, many of them refugees with serious wounds they had suffered in flight from their villages. In many villages, Muslim civilians had turned to violence against their Christian neighbors. Jennings's aid station and safe house became the only available source of medical help and sanctuary for women who were unable to enter—or get themselves to—one of the city's hospitals. He set off one large room as a maternity ward.

Jennings's new routine in the job he had assigned to himself was to move through the city finding women, either far along in their pregnancies or suffering with serious injuries, and take them to his shelter. Again, his odd form with its strange up-and-down gait was seen making its way through the city's backstreets. He identified the neediest cases and took them to his house on the Quay, where he used what primitive supplies he had to treat their injuries. At night he returned to Amy and the children at Paradise.

ON THURSDAY, SEPTEMBER 7, the British landed marines to guard the British consulate, a British bank, and the British-managed gasworks, which turned coal into gas to illuminate the city. It was just north of the Point and near the Standard Oil pier. The senior British naval officer also sent a train to Boudjah to bring British nationals into the city for evacuation on British merchant ships.

The defense minister of Greece and a new general arrived from Athens, and Hadjianestis was relieved of his command. The new general announced that the evacuation of the Greek army would cease and the city would be defended. He said the fresh troops that had arrived on ships from Thrace would form a perimeter around the city to prevent the Turkish army from entering. Martial law was declared.

Merrill's job was to keep Bristol informed, but he was finding it difficult to send his cables from the radio room of the *Litchfield* because of radio interference from the other ships.[*] In that first week, there were few ports in the world with as much aggregated armor and naval firepower as Smyrna. Five navies were present, four of them with capital ships, and every ship had its own telegraph transmitter. A ship's telegraph at that time employed high-voltage sparks to form the dots and dashes that were sent into the atmosphere as radio waves that oscillated indistinctly over a wide range of frequencies. Two ships transmitting

---

[*] Arthur Godfrey, the future radio and television star, was a radioman on the *Litchfield*. (Levantine, memoir, Mrs. Lawrence)

simultaneously were like two conversations over the same phone line; eleven ships was a telegraphic babble. Few or no messages were getting out from the ships' telegraphs.

On Thursday morning, Rhodes sent Knauss and the *Simpson* out to sea to escape the radio interference. The *Simpson* steamed fifty miles from the city and still it encountered interference. Knauss judged the situation in Smyrna too dangerous for him to put more running time between him and the city. In the meantime, Merrill used the Eastern Telegraph Office on the Smyrna waterfront to send his coded messages back to Bristol. He also returned to the French flagship and got Mme. Dumesnil's consent to hand-carry his written messages back to Bristol in Constantinople. The ship had moved its day of departure from Smyrna up to the next day, and she was happy to help the pleasing young American officer who spoke excellent French.

Merrill continued to stroll the city, absorbing the scene and filtering it through his skewed perspective for messages back to Bristol. In the morning he inspected the American Theater and later had lunch with the retired British officer and railroad director, who, he learned, was operating as an intelligence agent for the British. With a tobacco agent from the Standard American Trading Co., he went to the railroad pier at the end of the Quay and watched Greek soldiers embarking on transports. Despite the assertions of the new Greek commander about a halt to the evacuations and protection of the city, the transports were leaving at the rate of one every hour. At the pier, Merrill also met a French intelligence officer named Lafont, with whom he struck up a friendship and budding alliance.

In his rounds, and in his inimitable way, Merrill had found lodgings in the city far more comfortable than the bunk he had been assigned on the *Litchfield*. A departing Greek merchant had turned his elegant house over to Everett Washburn, the local agent for the U.S. Shipping Board, reasoning that there was no better way to protect his property than to leave it with the Americans. Washburn invited Merrill to stay in the house, which was only a short distance from Jennings's shelter on the Quay. Soon, the reporters Clayton and Brown joined in, which made five of them, including Washburn's local mistress. Knauss and Rhodes also made occasional use of the mansion. It was comfortably furnished and well stocked with wines in the basement, which Washburn put to use entertaining his growing list of guests.

The relief work continued: Greek civil authorities turned over an orphanage at Boudjah to Professor Lawrence along with enough money to support it. Lawrence put a young instructor from International College, Raymond Moreman, a graduate of Pomona College, in charge of the orphanage, and children from other institutions around the city joined the two hundred fifty already there. Moreman's first act was to raise an American flag over the building.

The relief committee also took possession of a warehouse near the Custom House Pier owned by the Patersons—a wealthy Levantine family that had left its property in the care of their American agent Roger Griswold, the committee's secretary. Griswold was tightly connected in Smyrna—he owned and operated his own export business with the nominal Turkish mayor of the city as a partner, as well as being an agent for the American licorice company MacAndrews & Forbes. (He would later be accused of pilfering relief committee funds.) The Paterson warehouse contained foodstuffs that had been intended for export, and the committee created a record of items it withdrew for the refugees so that it could eventually reimburse the absent owners. Behind the warehouse there was a big aboveground water pipe that the relief committee opened and let run as a source of water for the refugees, who eagerly cupped it in their hands, drinking it and washing with it.

The Greek reinforcements that had arrived from Thrace saw the sorry condition and morale of the soldiers on the Quay, and many refused to disembark. By Thursday, September 7, it was clear that there would be no attempt by the Greeks to hold the city. The army was departing, and with the army would go the civil administration as well. Stergiades made an unsuccessful effort to charter ships to evacuate the ethnic Greeks who were Ottoman subjects—traitors in the eyes of the Turkish nationalists. Nothing else would be done. The Greeks and the Armenians were on their own, unprotected.

By late Thursday, the rear guard of the Greek forces, maintaining its cohesion and ability to fight, held a line less than fifty miles from

Smyrna. The Turkish cavalry was now only a day's ride from Smyrna, and what had been the prospect of a possible Turkish occupation became certain and imminent.

Around midnight, George Horton boarded the *Litchfield* and requested that Rhodes land American sailors as guards in the city. The situation, he said, was too dangerous and unstable to leave Americans unprotected. Rhodes consented. He sent twelve sailors with rifles and two machine guns ashore and split them between the consulate and the American Theater. Further prodded by Horton, he summoned the *Simpson* back to Smyrna so that its crew could provide a bigger landing force. The *Simpson* received the recall message at 4 A.M. and was back at 7 A.M. Rhodes put sixty-four men ashore: in addition to the consulate and theater, he put sailors at the American Girls' School, the YMCA, International College, the Standard Oil property, and the homes and businesses of Americans in Smyrna and nearby Bournabat. None were assigned to Jennings's safe house since the house belonged to a Greek and the people inside were Ottoman subjects. The guards were limited to guarding Americans and American property.

The sailors were armed with rifles and three additional machine guns and given five days' rations to allow them to remain at their posts onshore. Unsure that this was a sufficient force, Rhodes, in a quirky move, distributed U.S. Navy uniforms to some of the American civilians. He also detailed four sailors to watch the Washburn house, where Merrill was staying, and he detailed an orderly to assist him in his work. He positioned the *Simpson* to keep a close watch on the Standard Oil dock and tanks.

BY THE MORNING, FRIDAY, September 8, the Turkish army was twenty-five miles east of Smyrna, and the Greek army continued to load men and material onto ships in the harbor.

Merrill called on the Greek governor a final time and found him tired and defeated. Afterward, he had lunch with his new friend Lafont at the Union Française, where he learned from him of Allied plans to arrange a meeting between Mustapha Kemal and the Allied admirals and consuls general in Smyrna. The objective was to broker a peaceful handover of the city. The French officer said he would be at the meeting, and Merrill eagerly sought to be included. The meeting was to take place the next day, at a secret location just east of the city. The French officer agreed to let Merrill join in, and he told the intelligence officer to meet him early the next day, before sunrise, at the Italian consulate. Merrill was elated at the prospect. He would be in the same room with Kemal. It would make a stirring report to Bristol.

Merrill returned to the *Litchfield*, where he read the daily roundup of press reports compiled by Bristol's staff in Constantinople and routinely transmitted to his ships' commanders. When Merrill saw that the British press was inaccurately reporting that the Turkish army was seeking armistice talks because it had been stopped by the Greeks outside Smyrna, he went to the reporters on board and laughed at the inability of press to get the story right. Nonetheless, being the good fellow that he was, he invited them along on another trip he planned to take that afternoon to the approaching battle line east of the city, and off they went, this time taking along Lieutenant Knauss. Merrill's French friend also came along for the spectacle.

They passed through Bournabat on the road to Magnesia, and about twenty miles out of Smyrna they found themselves in a valley between the Greek and Turkish armies with both sides firing artillery, machine guns, and small arms. The Turks were advancing slowly on the Greeks. Knauss recorded the scene:

> The Greek troops passed to the rear singly, in couples and even in sections. All faces appeared weary, tired and beaten. The refugees were employing every conceivable method of conveyance and were a pitable [*sic*] sight. They collected in herds outside of the town. While the troops have thrown away every kind of equipment, they all keep their rifles. All along the road was strewn articles of all descriptions from sewing machines to baby carriages while dead horses added zest to the scene. However, the Greeks have evidently great confidence in their rear guard as they passed along the road in a leisurely manner.

The group returned to the city, and Clayton filed a story for the next day's paper.

I have just returned from the improvised Greek front about fifteen miles from Smyrna, on the Magnesia road. The Turkish irregulars were advancing slowly, while the Greeks were retreating in good order, defending the road as they retired.

We were on the front before we became aware that the Turkish advance was so close. As we rounded a bend in the road we heard the Turkish rifles, machine-guns, and one field gun open fire. I left my motor-car and climbed a ridge, from which I could see actually the advancing Turkish lines.

Merrill still had plenty of energy. He fit in two social calls—the first to the wife of the British consul, Harry Lamb, whose daughter had recently died, and he offered his condolences. His second call was to the family of the Danish consul, Henri Van der Zee, who welcomed him and asked for American protection. Merrill sent a navy orderly with a note to Rhodes and Horton, requesting that the family be included on the protection list at the American Theater. These trips through the city took Merrill past Jennings's safe house, but Merrill took no notice of it. The refugees seemed invisible to him. His cables to Bristol were filled mostly with critical accounts of the Greek army and administration. Merrill went back to the house he shared with the shipping agent and reporters, enjoyed a big dinner with his friends, and stepped out for a late-night stroll before going to bed.

By then, the British had taken Stergiades aboard a British launch, which took him to the *Iron Duke*. A Turkish crowd had gathered at the waterfront as he departed and beat tin pots in celebration. He was the last Greek official to leave the city.

At 4 A.M., Saturday, September 9, an orderly woke Merrill for his appointment with the French officer to go see Mustapha Kemal. He went to the Italian consulate, where he expected to meet his friend and the Italian colonel. The French officer had told him that the three of them would then proceed from the Italian consulate by car to the secret location to meet Kemal. It was still dark at 4 A.M. and the city was eerily quiet despite the number of people who were sleeping in the streets. The moon still appeared full, and it was low in the southern sky. "As I walked down the narrow paved streets," Merrill noted in his diary, "the hollow sounds of my footfalls could easily have been heard in Constantinople."

At the Italian consulate, Merrill had trouble getting in—doors were locked and no one seemed awake. Finally, after banging on the door, he was let in, and the Italian colonel told him that he was still waiting to hear from Kemal. When word was received, he told Merrill, the French officer would come to pick him up. Merrill returned to his house. At 7 A.M., the French officer came by and said he was going to the French consulate to get updated directions for their mission and that he would return to pick up Merrill. As the French officer departed, an orderly from the *Litchfield* came into the house and reported that a third U.S. destroyer, the USS *Lawrence*, had arrived in the harbor and Captain Hepburn was aboard. He wanted to see Merrill immediately. Merrill had no choice—he would have to go to the *Lawrence* and possibly miss the adventure of meeting Kemal. "I left with fear and trembling," he wrote in his journal. "I feared Lafont (the French officer) would return and not finding me at the mission would leave without me." He would miss the adventure of a lifetime.

CHAPTER 11

The View from Nif

On September 9, Mustapha Kemal stood at a mountain pass eighteen miles directly east of Smyrna and looked down on his prize. Spread below him were the farms and villages of the Aydin coastal plain; the minarets, domes, and steeples of Smyrna; and the sickle-shaped harbor that bristled with Allied and American warships.

It had been seventeen years since he had visited Smyrna, and he had been a newly commissioned officer in the Ottoman army. Twenty-two years old and fresh out of the War College in Constantinople, Kemal had been making his way, in 1905, to Syria, his first military posting. The ship on which he was traveling had stopped briefly in Smyrna en route to Beirut, and when it reached Beirut, he had traveled by train to Damascus. Kemal took up his duties there, rounding up Druze brigands in the countryside. It had been tedious duty for an officer determined to make his mark for the empire. Ali Fuat, a young fellow officer and friend from the War College, had made the trip with him. Ali Fuat was now one of Kemal's most important aides in the fight against the Greeks and the British.

Kemal and Ali Fuat had come through much together since those early days—they had caroused in the cafés of Constantinople, made careers in the Ottoman army, faced arrest for plotting against the Ottoman government, and fought, successively, the Serbs, Bulgarians, British, Russians, and Greeks—this latest fight begun in defiance of the Ottoman government in Constantinople. Now the Greeks were finished in Anatolia, and Smyrna was within his grasp, and with it the prospect of making real the vision that had propelled him to take up arms against the Allied powers—a Turkish nation.

Mustapha Kemal had been born in Salonika, the same place George Horton had been posted to before World War I. Kemal's father, a clerk, died when he was a boy; his mother and aunt raised him. Proud, bright, and strong-willed, Kemal had enrolled in a military preparatory school at age eleven, drawn by the cadets' uniforms. He had felt himself transformed when dressed as an officer, even when he was a boy, and uniforms and appearances would remain important to him for the rest of his life. He had excelled in his studies, especially in math, and later transferred to a military high school in Monastir (now Bitola, in the Republic of Macedonia), where he also had shown exceptional ability. Then he went on to the Ottoman War College in Constantinople. In his last year, he ranked at the top of his class.

By then, Kemal already owned a reputation for being high-strung and difficult—and for drinking, gambling, and whoring. He drank raki and talked politics through the night with his fellow cadets and turned out fresh for duty in the morning. (Ali Fuat had introduced him to raki, the liquor that eased his racing mind.) Kemal was not a big man—though he was careful to be photographed to seem tall—but his proportions were perfect and lithesome, projecting a refined masculinity, like a male leopard, and those who noticed his hands (and his feet) remarked on their delicacy. (He liked to show off his feet, removing his shoes to bathe them.) He was fastidious in presentation—even to that which could not be seen. He favored French crepe de chine underwear with its silk nap. He loved clothes. When he was the Ottoman military attaché to Sofia in 1913 he gained the attention of the king of Bulgaria at a costume ball by wearing the elaborate and high hat and blue-and-red uniform of the Janissary Corps, the elite bodyguards of medieval sultans. Out of uniform, he liked to dress as a country gentleman: riding breeches and hacking jacket.

LIKE SO MANY OFFICERS of his generation, Kemal had been obsessed as a young man with the decline of the empire and the backwardness of the sultan and his government. The inheritors of a fierce martial culture, the cadets who had come of age just before World War I had watched with shame and horror as their imperial inheritance slowly slipped away. They looked back longingly on the Ottoman horsemen and religious warriors who had created a vast Islamic empire in Asia, Africa, and Europe beginning in the fourteenth century. They carried within them the collective memory of a glorious past—fierce, conquering horsemen of an expanding Islamic empire that reached back to Osman, a fourteenth-century Seljuk chieftain and the empire's founder whose son, Orhan, wrested Constantinople from the Byzantine Greeks.

The empire had reached its apex under Suleiman the Magnificent, whose armies reached but failed to conquer Vienna in 1529. The empire required expansion to maintain its wealth, and it drew energy from its religious mission, which was to bring Islam to the infidels. Without expansion, it began a slow decline. Without new lands to conquer, the empire slid into indolence, intrigue, and inefficiency. By the nineteenth century, the empire was regarded as the "sick man of Europe," deeply in debt and backward.

The Young Turks of Salonika had cast their gaze on the proud Ottoman past; an unbroken dynasty of thirty-four sultans connected them to the tradition of Islamic conquest. In their present, they saw something quite different—a sclerotic state, territorial loss, and humiliation by their former Christian subjects—Greeks, Serbs, and Bulgarians.

The Greeks and Serbs had broken free of the empire in the early nineteenth century; in the late nineteenth century, at about the time of Mustapha Kemal's birth, the British seized Cyprus and Egypt. In 1908, Bulgaria gained its independence and in 1909 Austria seized Bosnia-Herzegovina, also Ottoman territory. Soon, Albania would break away. The empire's borders were shrinking, and the Grand Porte—the sultan's government—appeared helpless to stop the disintegration. The anxiety was acute among Kemal's generation of military leadership, and they sought, often in secret cells, a path toward a renewal of the Ottoman state.

AFTER SYRIA, MUSTAPHA KEMAL had returned to Salonika, where the Young Turks were plotting against Sultan Abdul Hamid. In 1908, Kemal participated in the coup that forced the sultan to reinstate the constitution, and after the unsuccessful, conservative countercoup, the Young Turks deposed Abdul Hamid and installed his brother as a puppet. (This happened at the time of Horton's posting in Salonika.) But the Young Turks' revolution did not stop the empire's decline, and their anxiety only worsened as more pieces of the empire broke off: Italy seized Libya in 1912, the same year Albania gained its independence; Crete joined Greece in 1913. Finally, like a cannon shot, Montenegro, Serbia, Greece, and Bulgaria formed a military alliance and pushed the Ottomans out of Macedonia. Salonika fell to the Greeks. Three men of the Young Turks movement had emerged as the principal leaders; each was fiercely nationalistic. Their names were Ismail Enver, Mehmet Talat, and Ahmed Djemal. They held absolute power. History would remember them as architects of the Armenian genocide during World War I.

The new nationalist phrase was "Turkey for the Turks," and the Three Pashas, as they were called, brutally executed the new ideology. Ambassador Henry Morgenthau put it this way:

Their passion for Turkifying the nation seemed to demand logically the extermination of all Christians—Greeks, Syrians, and Armenians. Much as they admired the Mohammedan conquerors of the fifteenth and sixteenth centuries, they stupidly believed that these great warriors had made one fatal mistake, for they had had it in their power completely to obliterate the Christian populations and had neglected to do so. This policy in their opinion was a fatal error of statesmanship and explained all the woes from which Turkey has suffered in modern times.

Enver in particular admired the Germans and brought them to Turkey to train the army. On August 2, 1914, five days after the start of World War I in Europe, the Ottoman government signed a secret treaty of alliance with Germany. The Turks mined the Dardanelles, and its ships fired on Russian ports. The Allies responded with declarations of war, and on November 13, Sultan Mehmet V, pressured by the governing pashas, signed a fatwa, declaring a holy war against Britain, France, and Russia.

During the war, Kemal distinguished himself at Gallipoli, then in the east against Russia, and later in Syria and Palestine against the British. He was a winning general in a losing cause. The war ended for Turkey in September 1918 when Allied forces broke through the Bulgarian front. "We've eaten shit," the Bulgarians told their ally Talat in Turkey. The Bulgarian defeat convinced Ludendorff, general of the German army, that there was no prospect of a German victory.

The Turks sued for peace in October, and the sultan's representatives signed an armistice aboard a British ship named, ironically, *Agamemnon*—for the Greek king who, legend says, had brought his army to Anatolia to defeat the Trojans three thousand years earlier. The Three Pashas fled Turkey for Germany, and Kemal's resistance to the armistice began almost the moment it was signed. He was in Syria when the end came, and he began shipping arms to the interior of Anatolia to preserve a Turkish fighting force. The new government in Constantinople ordered him back to the capital, which was occupied by the victorious British, French, and Italians.

What happened next was astonishing: the Allies demanded demobilization of Ottoman forces and prosecution of the Young Turk leaders for their war crimes against Armenians. The Allies (the British, in particular) also insisted on an end to Turkish harassment of Christians. The Ottoman government promised to send an officer to supervise the seizure of weapons and investigate the treatment of Christians along the Black Sea. It picked Mustapha Kemal for the job. He departed Constantinople, and on May 19, 1919, he landed at Samsun—a city on Turkey's Black Sea coast—and soon made contact with like-minded military men in the Anatolian interior who wanted to resist the armistice. The Ottoman government and the British, who had rounded up other Ottoman leaders whom they suspected of trouble, almost immediately realized the giant mistake and tried in vain to recall him. It was too late. The tiger was loose.

IN THE THREE YEARS after landing at Samsun, Kemal had done the impossible: He had taken Turkey from a defeated nation, prostrate before victors, and transformed it into an assertive power that was intent on dictating its peace terms to the Allies. He had organized an army, a government, and a set of demands—the Turkish National Pact.

Now, Kemal was on the edge of success. The mountain pass, called Nif by the Turks and Nymphaion by the Greeks, a place where the nymphs were said to inhabit mountain springs, was a notch between the peaks through which the downward running road switchbacked steeply to Smyrna. (It was this pass through which Theodora and her family had passed after Gritzalia days earlier.) Mustapha Kemal's army was camped around him. It waited on his command.

The Allies had proposed to mediate an armistice at the Greeks' request, but Kemal rejected the offer. He said it was pointless; the Greeks had been defeated. He had given the Greek army forty-eight hours to evacuate Anatolia, and Greek units were still hurriedly boarding ships at Chesme, a small port at the end of the long peninsula southwest of Smyrna. The deadline had already passed.

The day before, at Salihli, he had received a message from the Allied high commissioners in Constantinople, sent by way of the French ship *Edgar Quinet* at Smyrna, proposing a meeting to arrange the peaceful handover of the city. (This was the meeting that Merrill had hoped to attend with the French lieutenant Lafont.) Kemal was contemptuous of the proposal. The city was his to take; there was nothing to negotiate. Nonetheless, he agreed to meet them here, at this mountain parapet, in the headquarters abandoned days earlier by the Greek army and still displaying a portrait of Venizelos. He had sent a message to the Allies but it had been received late, and by now an advance contingent of his cavalry was already entering Smyrna.

CHAPTER 12

Back in Constantinople

On Wednesday, September 6, by which time there were at least two hundred thousand refugees in Smyrna and many tens of thousands more on the beaches along the Aegean and Marmara coasts, Admiral Bristol summoned leaders of the principal American relief and service organizations in Constantinople to the American embassy.

The American relief community in Constantinople was small and tight, and its members knew one another well. They had been meeting weekly at the embassy for almost two years to coordinate relief for the Russian refugees in Constantinople and Armenian orphans in the country's interior. The group was bound by work, not affection. Both the Missions Board and Near East Relief had attempted to persuade the State Department to remove Bristol as high commissioner.

Among the people in the room were William W. Peet, the senior missionary administrator in Constantinople, and Harold C. Jaquith, managing director of Near East Relief in the Near East. Peet had instigated the campaign to remove Bristol, and Jaquith had banged heads with Bristol over his unsuccessful attempt to suppress reports of the Turkish slaughter of Ottoman Greeks. Jaquith, with his bland face and spectacles, was precisely the sort of "missionary type" that annoyed Bristol—earnest and dedicated to Armenians.

Bristol was openly hostile to the Missions Board for what he called its conversion mentality and the Near East Relief for what he considered its anti-Turkish attitudes and fund-raising propaganda in America.

BOTH THE MISSIONS BOARD and Near East Relief were formidable foes, and Bristol's ability to survive their campaign demonstrated the strength of his personal determination and Washington connections. The Missions Board had been sending missionaries to Turkey for nearly a century.

The Near East Relief organization had begun with the former American ambassador to the Ottoman Empire, Henry Morgenthau. A Jewish American businessman born in Germany and a big fund-raiser for Woodrow Wilson, Morgenthau had come to know the Ottoman leaders personally while serving in Constantinople and was in the country when the worst of the killing took place. His vivid testimony led to American outrage and a hugely successful fund-raising campaign to save the Armenian people. Organized in 1915 under the auspices of the American Committee for Syrian and Armenian Relief, the campaign to save the Armenians was the first broadly based public fund-raising campaign of its type, and it has never been surpassed in its outpouring of public philanthropy.

In 1916, Near East Relief, as it came to be called, raised $2.4 million in the United States through public donations; the amount doubled in 1917; and doubled again in 1918. In 1919, when America was in a postwar recession, Near East Relief raised $19,885,000—$3 million in one month. These were enormous figures for the period. By the end of 1921, it had raised about $40 million. With many businessmen and religious leaders on its board, Near East Relief was a fund-raising machine of astonishing success. In 1921, Near East Relief enlisted 48,364 churches and 7,877 fraternal organizations in its appeal. The Brotherhood of Railroad Train Men, the Masons, the Eagles, the Veterans of Foreign Wars, and B'nai B'rith participated, as did many others. Twenty Masonic Lodges in Wisconsin adopted fifty orphans. In St. Claire County, Michigan, the Daughters of the American Revolution, the Elks, the Ladies Library Association, the Knights of Columbus, and the Christmas Carolers Association donated to a campaign run by the *Port Huron Times Herald* that adopted thirty-two orphans. The Central Presbyterian Church in Denver donated $5,000; North Reformed Church in Newark, $4,000; First Presbyterian Church, Evanston, Illinois, $3,500; and on and on throughout the country. Yale, Williams, Vassar, Mount Holyoke, Smith, Johns Hopkins, the universities of Delaware, Wyoming, and Michigan, and many other colleges and universities organized appeals. One hundred factories in New York State donated $1,000 each. The American Federation of Labor solicited its members and sent money. Fourteen state governors were chairmen. Movie celebrities joined the effort. There was a Jackie Coogan chapter in Brooklyn. Children set up lemonade and flower stands on street corners and sent their earnings to feed Armenians. The world had never seen anything like the American response to Armenian suffering. It made America's reputation for generosity.

THERE WERE STRONG PERSONALITIES in Bristol's spacious parquet-floored office on that hot and humid September morning but not a lot of trust. The talk was civil, but lines were drawn and well understood.

Nonetheless, cooperation was essential. Bristol had ships and government authority; the relief organizations had food, supplies, and manpower. Bristol knew also that the State Department and millions of Americans were watching. America was anxious about the consequences of the Turkish victories. It was no time for Bristol to make a show of his anti-Greek and -Armenian sentiments or publicly display a callous attitude toward the country's Christians. (Former ambassador Morgenthau had been quoted in the previous day's *New York Times* as favoring a swift Allied and American evacuation of Christian refugees from Anatolia to avoid a massacre.) Bristol would express his concern publicly but had already decided privately on a go-slow strategy—his plan was to gather information at Smyrna and decide on a response later. Only he knew how much later. His real concern was protection of Americans and American property and cultivating Turkish favor. He was not in the business of rescuing and feeding Greek and Armenian refugees.

Bristol saw responsibility for the refugee problem at Smyrna as a problem for the British and Greek governments, and (as the coming weeks would show) he would use every opportunity to deflect the cost and blame in their direction. His plan was to take small steps and allow the situation to unfold without significant American engagement. He was reluctant to commit American resources, public or private, to the job. If the situation worsened, a disaster at Smyrna (he reasoned) would only reflect badly on Britain and Greece, not an unwelcome result from his perspective. ("The Greek is about the worst race in the Near East," Bristol had written.)

At the meeting in his office, Bristol produced a note he had received the previous day from the British high commissioner in Constantinople, Sir Horace Rumbold. Bristol's scorn for the note set the meeting's tone. Marked "urgent," it urged Bristol to use the American Relief Administration to help the refugees in Smyrna. (It was essentially the same request Horton had sent to the State Department.) The note infuriated Bristol—as almost anything would if it came from Rumbold. Bristol said he considered Rumbold's note impertinent and he would give it the answer it deserved. (The answer would be sent the next day, and it would drip with sarcasm.) The two men despised each other. Bristol refused to allow U.S. Navy ships to acknowledge the passage of the British high commissioner's yacht with the traditional manning of the ship's rails and sailors' salutes, and he would decline a dinner invitation if Rumbold was seated more prominently than he at the table. Rumbold, for his part, had written to the British foreign secretary that Bristol had "limited intelligence and outlook." Foreign Secretary Lord Curzon concurred: "We have had abundant proof for nearly two years that he is suspicious, anti-British, stupid and at times malignant." A British admiral would call him a "snake in the grass."

The British ambassador in Washington, Auckland Campbell-Geddes, had taken the British complaints to Secretary of State Hughes and requested Bristol's removal. Hughes, with some urging from Dulles, had rejected the complaints. The episode ended with a note to Bristol that made it clear that the secretary of state was aware of Bristol's truculent nature. Hughes said it would be "a gratification" if Bristol would establish cordial relations with the British. "I desire you, there, on receipt of my letter to make renewed effort to establish that informal contact with your Allied colleagues which may facilitate the settlement of questions which arise between you and the Allied mission without allowing them to reach an acute issue."

Stiff by State Department standards, the note brought absolutely no change in Bristol. He knew that he had prevailed in the dustup, and the British were unlikely to appeal for his removal a second time. He continued on his unpleasant way.

Bristol's position as chairman and titular head of the Red Cross in Constantinople strengthened his ability to ration American engagement at Smyrna. He formed the American Relief Committee for Smyrna in his office under the auspices of the Constantinople branch of the American Red Cross, and specifically the Constantinople Relief Committee, a subcommittee of the local Red Cross, which he also led. He engineered relief-effort hierarchy to give him full control at every juncture. He cabled the Red Cross in Washington for $50,000 and made it clear that he was sending the message in code so that the British (as he said) would not learn of it and conclude that they could rely on the Americans to pay the cost of the refugee relief.

He told the group in his office that he planned to send a relief team to Smyrna by destroyer the next day, Thursday, or after he had received word from Lieutenant Merrill about conditions in the city. This gave him room for further delay. He actually waited until Friday to send the ship. They discussed who should go, and the meeting broke up.

THE NEXT DAY, THURSDAY, September 7, Bristol met with Hamid Bey, the nationalist representative in Constantinople and one of Bristol's two key nationalist contacts since Bristol had arrived in Turkey. The other was Halide Edib, the nationalists' chief propagandist. A corporal in the nationalist army, she was, at this moment, moving with Kemal toward Smyrna. Hamid Bey struck Ernest Hemingway, who interviewed him some weeks later for the *Toronto Star,* as a crook. He was, Hemingway wrote, "big and bulky," with wing collars, a gray mustache, and a porcupine haircut. Hamid Bey operated as Kemal's foreign minister in Constantinople, and he and Bristol often met at the embassy. Always exceedingly polite to the admiral, Hamid Bey had begun the meeting with copious apologies for his tardiness. On this occasion, Bristol instructed his guest, one of the most sly and powerful men in intrigue-filled Constantinople, on the importance of Turkish good conduct. The nationalists, Bristol told him, had an opportunity "to reassure the world generally that they desired to properly protect minorities in the country." Hamid Bey was his usual agreeable self to the admiral.

Satisfied that his advice was welcomed, Bristol had an additional suggestion for Hamid Bey. Bristol said he had learned from a nationalist leader in Ankara of the Greek army's atrocities. Why not let a newspaper correspondent travel to those towns and villages destroyed by the Greek army in its retreat? It would be a public-relations masterstroke. Stories of Greek atrocities would improve the Turkish image and help Bristol undermine support for the Armenians and Greeks and their advocates in the United States. Hamid Bey listened carefully, obviously interested. Bristol said he just happened to have a correspondent in mind—Charles Sweeny of the *New York World*.

Sweeny was a fascinating figure, an original of the sort that eventually becomes a caricature: a journalist and soldier of fortune with a charismatic personality that appealed especially to those who liked their heroes mysterious and a little dangerous. As a young man, he had been booted from West Point and fought as a mercenary in the Mexican and Venezuelan revolutions. In 1914, to get into the big war, he had enlisted in the French Foreign Legion, and he won France's Legion of Honor for wounds received at Champagne. He had joined the American Expeditionary Force when the United States entered the war. Afterward, he worked as a reporter in the Paris bureau of the *New York World*. Tall, hawk nosed, and ruddy faced, Sweeny had traveled to Constantinople to cover the Greek-Turkish war. Young Hemingway was an admirer in Paris, and the two became lifelong friends; Sweeny served as a model and mentor for Hemingway in his life and fiction. Many years later, Sweeny, in his eighties, would walk as a pallbearer at Hemingway's funeral. Bristol also fell under Sweeny's spell and invited him on the outings he often arranged on weekends with navy officers and their wives.

In Constantinople, Sweeny, then forty years old, was working not only for Joseph Pulitzer, owner of the *New York World*—he was employed as a spy for the French government, and he had been busy collecting information on Basil Zaharoff, whom the French wished to disparage both for his support of the Greeks in the current war and for his connections to the Germans in the last. Sweeny probably had been the source of Bristol's information about Zaharoff, which had found its way back to Washington as an intelligence report. The British, Turks, and French all had a good bead on Sweeny. He lived in a way that drew attention; he switched hotels several times a week, and he could be found wandering in the most dangerous sections of Constantinople, where (as the British observed) he would meet French intelligence officers. The only people who seemed unaware of the full range of Sweeny's activities were the Americans, namely Bristol and his intelligence staff. Sweeny's pro-Turkish reporting and his military background endeared him to Bristol, and while Bristol may have thought he was using Sweeny, it was more like the reverse. A newspaper reporter who doubles as a spy can do worse than to have an American admiral interceding on his behalf.

After proposing stories about Greek atrocities to Hamid Bey, Bristol met the same day with Sweeny and told him of the arrangements he was seeking to make for him with the nationalists, to which Sweeny gave his enthusiastic approval.

Finally on Friday, two days after the relief meeting in Bristol's office, the people selected to travel to Smyrna assembled on the destroyer USS *Lawrence*. They were Harold Jaquith of Near East Relief; Charles Claflin Davis of the American Red Cross; and Dr. Wilfred Post and two nurses, Sara Corning and Agnes Evon. Davis, a tall, stout, and gentle man, was a prominent Bostonian who had left his law practice to drive a Red Cross ambulance in France and had remained with the Red Cross to manage relief for the Russian refugees in Constantinople. As the group was departing, Bristol told Davis not to make any commitments in Smyrna without checking with him first and to keep matters in Smyrna in perspective, warning him "that under such circumstances people were a bit hysterical and the situation always seemed worse than it would turn out to be." Bristol recorded in his diary, "I told him that he thoroughly understood my policy and therefore I would leave it in his hands to carry out that policy and to keep me informed in every way."

A sixth member joined the group aboard the USS *Lawrence*—Mark O. Prentiss, who had attached himself to Near East Relief but whose real career had been as a publicist in New York. Prentiss was a peculiar character, a kind of gray-flannel flimflam man with a talent for inventing and inflating his résumé and insinuating himself into situations where he saw personal gain. He had been an early member of the Council on Foreign Relations but had been pushed out of the organization, apparently for questionable bills he had submitted. He had shown up in Constantinople in August and introduced himself to Bristol as an efficiency expert who had come to Turkey to observe the operations of Near East Relief. Prentiss, incredibly, would end up filing stories to the *New York Times* and other prominent publications that provided Americans with some of the most influential and ultimately distorted coverage of the Smyrna catastrophe. Before the year was out, he even would be implicated in a murder involving a jealous lover in Italy.

Bristol added one more person to the trip—his naval chief of staff, Captain Hepburn. It was an unusual step that did not bring any additional aid or expertise to the mission but was a public demonstration of Bristol's concern for the refugees. It was empty symbolism but good PR. He emphasized the point time and again in the press coverage—he took the situation in Smyrna so seriously that he had sent his naval chief of staff. The ship slipped its mooring in the swift Bosporus current in the late afternoon of Friday, September 8, and steamed toward Smyrna "at an economical speed."

CHAPTER 13

Captain Hepburn's Dilemma

The USS *Lawrence* entered the Gulf of Smyrna early Saturday morning, September 9, its upward-sweeping bow slicing through the blue-green water. Hepburn noted the numerous small sailboats and shabby coastal steamers that were overburdened with passengers and headed toward the sea. Some of the steamers pulled lines of small barges piled high with ragged pyramids of people and luggage. There were also numerous caiques, the small boats without keels, pointed at both ends and rigged with lateen sails, that were common to ports of the eastern Mediterranean. They skimmed on the sea's surface like dry leaves with upturned edges, and the big bow waves of the *Lawrence* set them rolling.

Ahead was the city and the dense dark mass of refugees lining the waterfront, and to the south, along the coastal road, Hepburn, squinting into the bright morning sun that was rising behind the city, discerned a long thin line of Greek cavalry moving like a scraggly centipede over the green-and-brown stubbled landscape. The men, mounted on horses and camels, were headed toward Chesme, where Greek merchant ships were picking up remnants of the Greek army. The Greek line was two and a half miles long, and the boom of Greek naval artillery reverberated over the water as a Greek battleship several miles distant covered the army's retreat.

Hepburn was arriving with little current information—few of Merrill's cables had gotten through to Constantinople. He had only just learned from a cable received at sea that the Greek governor had departed the previous day, and he was unaware of the extent of the Greek army's collapse and evacuation. As the *Lawrence* approached the inner harbor, passing Pelican Point, the four stacks of the *Litchfield* came into view. The *Litchfield* was anchored near the Quay not far from the terminus of Galazio Street. The *Simpson* was moored off the Standard Oil dock, to the left and about a half mile farther north.

Captain Hepburn's eyes swept over the city's waterfront as he evaluated the situation ashore and his approach for the *Lawrence*'s anchorage. There were numerous other men-of-war in the harbor, and Hepburn strained to make out their flags and names. Twenty-five years earlier, he had nearly washed out of the navy because of his poor eyesight. A routine vision test after graduation revealed astigmatisms in both eyes and low visual acuity. The navy doctor declared him unfit for duty. His discharge papers were prepared, but an appeal up the chain of command kept him in the service, and as a newly minted ensign, he was sent to the USS *Iowa*, which soon engaged the Spanish navy off Santiago, Cuba, in the Spanish-American War. As subsequent eye tests showed, his vision had only worsened since then.

Hepburn was from Carlisle, Pennsylvania, the son of a prominent attorney and his second wife, a Frenchwoman, Marie Japy Hepburn. "Japy" became Hepburn's middle name as well as his nickname. Pronounced with a long "a," it followed him through Dickinson College, the Naval Academy, and into the navy. Five feet, nine inches tall with thin hair parted at the middle and round rimless glasses, the captain had the long, loose, and kindly face of an English vicar. It would have been easy to imagine him in vestments instead of a naval uniform. At the Academy he had been a good student, and his superiors knew they could rely on his judgment and attention to detail. He had passed the war mostly in administrative jobs, superintending the refitting of a captured German vessel into a troopship and serving as a detachment commander at a naval base in Queenstown, Ireland. It was hardly heroic duty, but it was necessary and he had done the work well. In June, he had joined Bristol's staff, and a less efficient officer would not have sur-

vived the demanding and ambitious admiral. Hepburn was not without
his own ambition, and while he lacked Bristol's sharp elbows and commanding presence, he had demonstrated his own upward persistence
through diligence and hard work. Ultimately, he would go further than
Bristol—far further, to the highest rungs of the navy. Along with poor
eyesight, Hepburn's service had been dogged by poor health, with bouts
of bronchitis, arthritis, appendicitis, fevers, foot pain, eczema, and an
especially bad case of hemorrhoids that required surgery. Maybe it was
these chronic minor ills and physical humiliations that softened his demeanor and gave him a sympathetic disposition.*

The *Lawrence* anchored to the left side of the *Litchfield* very near the
Quay. Lieutenant Commander Rhodes came aboard and sketched the
situation for Hepburn, and then together, they and Merrill, who had also
come aboard the *Lawrence* after being summoned from his house that
morning, climbed into the destroyer's motor launch to go ashore. Davis
of the Red Cross brought his portly frame into the launch, rocking it with
his considerable weight.

Ashore, they worked their way through the crowd on the Quay and
went first to the American Theater, where twenty-five naturalized Americans had sought shelter in the cavernous interior, and afterward they
walked through the nearby neighborhood. Hepburn saw refugees on the
streets and squatting in tiny public spaces among their bags, boxes, and
small collections of household goods—sewing machines, pots, blankets,
and rugs. He also saw Greek soldiers in scattered groups of four or six
or eight moving silently and sullenly southward along the waterfront,
sometimes carrying wounded comrades on litters or even their shoulders.
They were mostly unarmed and ragged, and they seemed to pay no atten-

---

* Like Rhodes, Hepburn may also have had trouble holding his alcohol. Much later
in his career, the widow of Van Clear Black, the wealthy former owner of the *Baltimore Sun* and close friend of FDR, accused Hepburn of insulting her with a proposition while he was drunk at the Mayflower Hotel in Washington. Mrs. Black wrote
several letters to Roosevelt about the incident, and the correspondence indicates
that Roosevelt asked the secretary of the navy to get involved. Hepburn had also
been a friend of the late Mr. Black. (President Franklin Roosevelt's Office Files,
1933–45; Jessie Gary Black correspondence)

tion to their surroundings. A few were riding on donkeys, moving southward along the Quay. The men were exhausted but orderly and showed no panic. These were the last of the Greeks who had come in from the front, and they were among the last of the last to pass through the city. The troop transports had departed from the Smyrna railroad pier the previous day. The Greek rearguard cavalry, which had attempted, mostly with success, to provide time for the retreat, already had passed them by on the way to Chesme. These detritus soldiers were stranded in Smyrna. They would have to either rouse themselves for the fifty-mile walk to Chesme or lose their uniforms and blend into the Smyrna population. They did both.

Hepburn found the city tense but quiet and the stores and cafés open. With Rhodes, Merrill, and Davis, he went to the American consulate—only a block from the Quayside theater. He wanted to get right to work. Consul General Horton was absent so the captain asked Horton's vice consul to summon the local American relief committee for a meeting within the hour.

Hepburn was troubled that American sailors had been put ashore as guards—Bristol had specifically ruled out any demonstration of naval force, and these men were armed, some with machine guns—but given the lack of local police or any civil authority, as well as his inability to know when the Turkish army would arrive in the city, he assented to keeping them ashore for now. He saw that their presence was a reassurance to the Americans in the consulate.

While he waited for the local relief committee to arrive, Hepburn looked over a big map of the city brought out by one of the vice consuls, and with Rhodes, Merrill, and now Knauss present, he changed the distribution of the guards to reduce their exposure by eliminating protection of the private homes of American businessmen. He also relieved Rhodes of command of the shore force and installed Knauss. Rhodes got the task of making regular rounds of the guarded locations several times a day and reporting back to Hepburn. The naval uniforms that had been distributed to civilians by Rhodes were recalled, and Hepburn ordered the display of American flags at locations where he had decided to keep navy guards. He put fifteen men with two machine guns at the Smyrna theater; four men at a nearby bakery that Jennings had arranged to bake bread for the refugees; twelve men at the American Girls' School, which was inside a walled-in square block with a courtyard about a mile from the consulate in the Armenian district; twelve men at the YWCA compound, which was in the middle of the city midway between the consulate and the girls' school; two men at the YMCA; four at the consulate; and sixteen at International College in Paradise. The postings remained a wide and thin distribution of the men, but Hepburn made the judgment that they were unlikely to encounter serious trouble of the sort that required a more substantial defense. The sailors, mostly in their twenties, were dressed in their working whites, flared trousers tucked into white-canvas gaiters, long-sleeved blouses with blue neckerchiefs, and white sailor's caps pushed back on their heads. They went about the work eagerly, laughing and smoking cigarettes, astonished at the scene in which they found themselves.

The men had enlisted from every corner of the country, and their names read like the roster of an All-American baseball team: Toney Bello (Newark, New Jersey); John Brown (Nashville, Tennessee); John Bugdonvich (Springfield, Massachusetts); John Ciepiewicz (Chicago, Illinois); Friola Domingo (Boston, Massachusetts); Birchall Hamilton (Philadelphia, Pennsylvania); Harry Friedman (Kansas City, Missouri); Sam Honeycutt (Raleigh, North Carolina); John Kilinski (Milwaukee, Wisconsin); Sigrid Landgrun (Buffalo, New York); Freddie Stewart (St. Louis, Missouri).

As Captain Hepburn worked with his officers at the consulate, they could hear the concussion of Turkish artillery shells, which were falling on the plain between Smyrna and nearby Bournabat. In the harbor, men on the ships could see the Turkish cavalry on the bare slope behind the city entering Bournabat. Some of the Turkish cavalry, coming down from the high pass at Nif, split from the main column and moved south in the direction of nearby Koukloudja, a Greek farming village, and soon it was in flames.

Within an hour, by about 10 A.M., members of the relief committee, including Professor Lawrence, President MacLachlan, Jacob, Jennings, and many of the city's businessmen, gathered at the consulate, and

Hepburn introduced the Constantinople delegation—Davis, Jaquith, Prentiss, and the medical team. Hepburn explained Bristol's orders—to gather information and protect American property—and asked for the formation of a single committee that would work under the direction of the Constantinople American Relief Committee. Charles Davis would take charge of it, he said. There were no objections. Hepburn said he wanted their help in gathering the facts that would allow Admiral Bristol to direct the resources that would be needed in Smyrna. He said he was keeping the YMCA as the relief committee's headquarters, despite his concerns that the word *Christian* in its name might antagonize the Turkish army. He also designated the waterfront theater as the military headquarters onshore. He would work between the theater and quarters on the *Litchfield*.

The local committee members hung on his words and accepted his directions. They were grateful for his presence, but they made it clear that they were worried about their safety once the Turkish army entered the city. Horton had returned to the consulate by then, and he too said he was concerned, especially for the ethnic Greeks and Armenians in the city who were naturalized American citizens. Most of them were indistinguishable from the refugees, and as Ottoman subjects who had left the country and taken a new citizenship or expressed sympathy with the departed Greek administration, it was likely the Turkish authorities would single them out for retribution. They needed protection, he said, and the only way to ensure it was their evacuation. Hepburn was skeptical. The problem, from what little he had already seen and heard, was not the Turks but the refugees themselves—there were enormous numbers of them, and they were panicky and gathering in large groups outside the consulate. The challenge, he surmised, would be controlling the crowd.

In response to the committee's fears, Hepburn said he would maintain the guards, then he proceeded to do what he was trained do—bring order and planning to the task that he had been assigned, which was to protect Americans and American property and evaluate the situation for Bristol, who would decide on next steps. But after two hours ashore, the captain was already feeling the tension between his orders from Bristol—restraint and surveillance—and the local Americans' strong sentiment for a forceful American presence ashore and evacuation of their community. Until he was directed otherwise, he planned to stick to his original orders—and given that the Greek administration had dismantled the city's telegraph office before departing and radio transmission remained spotty, he realized there would be limited, or nonexistent, opportunities for consultation with Bristol unless he sent a ship back to Constantinople. He was on his own. The conflict between Bristol's orders and the sentiment of the Americans (as well as what he would observe) would only grow more intense over the next three days. It would grow into a personal struggle that tested his judgment and conscience. As the situation in Smyrna worsened, Hepburn would become a fulcrum of American action, which tilted between indifference and engagement.

With his talk to the committee ended, Hepburn sent the relief volunteers back into the honeycomb of neighborhoods to identify places where they could collect and concentrate refugees, distribute food and supplies, and (most important) establish the scope of the problem. He wanted numbers and other information he could take back to Bristol. He set a second meeting for the afternoon. If there was trouble, he told them, they should retreat to the theater for protection. It was agreed that a signal flag would be raised over the theater if danger were imminent.

The medical team of Dr. Post and nurses Agnes Evon and Sara Corning, present at the meeting and mostly silent, needed no guidance from Hepburn. Deeply experienced in relief work, they had seen more death and suffering than Hepburn or any of his officers. Post, a forty-seven-year-old Princeton graduate with a thick mustache, heavy black eyebrows, and a horseshoe of hair around his otherwise bald head, had been in the Near East since 1911. He had started a hospital in Konya, in central Anatolia, which had served mostly Muslims in a region as big as the state of New York. The hospital's location, situated along one of the trails used during the Armenian deportations, had exposed him to the Armenian suffering and death during the war. He had gone back to the United States on a speaking tour as an articulate advocate for Armenian relief, then returned to continue his medical work.

Miss Evon, born in Detroit, was the director of nursing for Near East

Relief—she was easily recognized by her broad-brimmed black sunhat and round, black thick-framed glasses. In her mid-forties, she had served in the navy and worked for the Red Cross in Paris during the war and in Czechoslovakia afterward, before making her way to Turkey. Sara Corning, thirty-seven years old and from a small town in Nova Scotia, had cared for sick and wounded orphans in Marsovan and Samsun, on Turkey's Black Sea coast, where she had witnessed the deportations and killings of ethnic Greeks in 1920. The three—the doctor and two nurses—plunged into the city to find a hospital where they could receive and treat sick and wounded people from the streets. Like battlefield surgeons, this was work with which they were familiar and skilled.

AFTER THE MEETING, at about 10:45 A.M., Hepburn retreated with George Horton to the consul general's office on the consulate's first floor to the right of the entranceway. It was a simple space: rolltop desk, swivel chair, two armless wooden chairs, and a typewriter table. As the two talked, Horton's obvious exhaustion made an impression on Captain Hepburn. His fatigue was written on his face and showed in his posture. His eyes were dull; he had gotten little sleep. He moved stiffly. For the past nine days, Horton had been besieged by pleas for help—some coming even from other consuls in the city who feared for the safety of their nationals and themselves—and he had tried to respond to all of them. He was no longer young; the heat, the long hours, the demands of getting about the city—and especially the looming prospect of a Turkish occupation and what he felt in his stomach would be its inevitable and gruesome outcome—had worn him down physically and mentally. Hepburn had already absorbed the animus toward Horton at the embassy in Constantinople, but he felt a brief moment of sympathy for him.

As they talked, they heard a commotion outside the consulate, the sound of a human stampede, then they heard shots from the direction of the waterfront. Horton left the office, went to the front door, and saw the crush of people outside. He led Hepburn to the consulate's rooftop terrace for a look at what was happening. Below them, hundreds of people surged up Galazio Street toward the consulate. Looking toward the har-

bor, the two men saw a column of Turkish cavalry moving slowly southward and in good order along the Quay.

The soldiers were dressed in dusty, brown khaki uniforms, and their
heads were wrapped in rags that lay back on their necks against the sun.
Their faces were brown, their bodies lean, and most had their rifles
slung across the croppers of their saddles. They rode quietly except for
the sound of the horses' hooves on the cobbled street. The morning sun
glinted off their swords, stirrups, and rifle barrels. Their horses, small and
delicate Turkish mountain ponies, walked with a prance despite their
evident exhaustion. A steamer in the harbor sounded a single horn in
salute. The Quay, lined with thousands of refugees only minutes earlier,
was vacant except for the trunks, furniture, and personal goods they had
abandoned in their rush to the city's backstreets. There on the Quay, sitting straight in their saddles and looking directly forward through tired
Asiatic eyes, was the embodiment of the fear that had gripped the refugees and triggered them to flee their villages.

From the ships, terraces, and other vantages along the street, the foreign military officers who watched the procession could not help but be
a little thrilled by the display of martial discipline and the battle hard-
ness of the Turkish soldiers. "Swarthy hard-bitten men, with growth on
their faces," a British officer said, "they showed evidence of their long
advance of over one hundred miles during the week, but despite a lack
of smartness they impressed one with the discipline displayed, and there
was little arrogance in their manner as they entered the town."

The cavalry had entered the city from the north, come down around
the Point, past the mansions of Bella Vista, past Jennings's safe house,
where he stood out front watching them go by, past the clubs, restaurants,
hotels, and movie houses, and past the consulates, and at the moment
they were nearly abreast of the American Theater. Some carried loot:
brass jugs, trays, electro-plated goods, guitars, rugs, china ornaments,
and one even had a garden table balanced across his saddle. Some had
no saddles—they had ditched them to lighten their loads and ride faster
in pursuit of the retreating Greek army.

Their entry into the city had been marked a few minutes earlier by an
event that could have been lifted out of a Gilbert and Sullivan operetta.

At a place behind the Point, a British officer, Captain Bertram Thesiger, commander of the HMS *King George* V, was ashore inspecting the British guard at the gasworks when he saw the column of Turkish cavalry moving toward him. He stepped into the road in front of them and raised his hand to signal a halt.

"Who are you?" asked the diminutive Turkish officer at the head of the column. He was Cherefeddine Bey, a major of the Turkish Fourth Regiment. He spoke in French.

Thesiger, responding in French, introduced himself as an officer of the British navy. (It would later come out that Cherefeddine misunderstood and thought he was the commander of all British forces in the Mediterranean.) Thesiger summarized the situation in the city—the Greek army had departed and the British and others were holding the city until the arrival of the Turkish army. There was no need for aggressive action; the city was calm.

"Thank you," responded the Turkish captain. "What do you want me to do?"

Thesiger suggested that the cavalry proceed into the city along the Quay instead of the backstreets, which was the direction in which it was headed. He said it would be safer for them, and they would avoid getting lost in the welter of unfamiliar streets.

As this polite conversation went on between the officers, some of the soldiers in the column pointed revolvers at the heads of Greek men on the street, demanding money. One man refused and was shot and killed. Thesiger protested.

"But it is only one man," the Turkish officer responded, "and he is dead."

The Turkish officer gave the order to advance, and he followed the British officer's directions and turned right to the Quay. The cavalrymen drew swords and some fired their revolvers into the air.

Now, on the Quay, silent but alert and erect in their saddles, the soldiers might as well have been moving through defiles of the Anatolian plateau in anticipation of an ambush. Theirs was the order of men who had ridden long and hard over a hot dry landscape. Someone threw a bomb, and Cherefeddine suffered a shrapnel cut to his face, but he remained mounted. The soldiers cleared the street with a whiff of rifle fire. Several people in the street were killed. The soldiers continued on their horses without breaking formation. As they moved along the seaside, with the harbor on their right, past Galazio Street, and approaching the Turkish Quarter and the Konak, the city's main administration building, Turkish crowds gathered and cheered them, bringing them glasses of water. The air was full of red fezzes thrown skyward.

Inshallah, Izmir was back in Turkish hands.

MacLachlan and Merrill, who had been in the consulate when Hepburn and Horton had been meeting in Horton's office, fought their way through the Turkish crowd to the Quay. (Davis was at one of the city's better restaurants enjoying lunch. It was mostly empty except for him and the waiters.) Greek soldiers were still departing the city when the Turkish cavalry came on to the Quay, and a group of them was caught near the Konak as the Turkish cavalry arrived. There was a brief firefight, and the Greeks were captured and some were killed. Merrill, wanting to be near the action, had followed the Turkish cavalry to the Konak. He wiggled and squeezed his way through the crowd like a boy at a crowded parade route and entered the building, producing a document that Horton had prepared for him in French the previous night identifying him as a naval representative of the United States. There, among the gathering Turkish officers, he recognized Major Cherefeddine, the small, slight officer who had led the cavalry into the city. Exhilarated and never shy, Merrill introduced himself, and the two officers chatted in French. Other Turkish officers arrived at the second-floor reception room outside an office occupied by the ranking general in the city, Murcelle Pasha, commander of the First Cavalry. Merrill offered his congratulations and shook their hands. The Turkish major, whose shrapnel showed under his eye, told Merrill the story of the bomb that had been thrown and a second that failed to explode. The two had a good laugh about it. Merrill had made another friend.

NOW THAT THE TURKISH ARMY had entered the city, it was necessary for Captain Hepburn to make official contact with the Turkish command, but the jubilant Turkish crowds made it impossible for him to get near the Konak. He decided to wait until the Turkish celebrations calmed down and the crowds dispersed.

The appearance of Turkish troops had created panic among the refugees, and they attempted to enter any building that showed a French, British, or American flag, often crowding the entryways and trying to force their way past the guards. Using a relief-committee car with a small American flag flying from the grill, Hepburn, Knauss, and Davis made a round of the buildings guarded by American sailors and directed them to lock the doors and remain inside. At the American Girls' School, the refugees, frightened by a Turkish civilian who was leveling his rifle at them in the street, broke through the doors and entered the building while Hepburn was inside talking to his men. By midafternoon, Hepburn saw that the Turkish army had posted sentries on most of the main street corners, sometimes accompanied by Italian reservists in the city. The captain returned to the theater. At 4 P.M., he finally was able to make his way to the Konak, bringing Davis, Jaquith, and Dr. Post with him. Merrill, who had returned to the consulate after meeting with the Turkish officers, also came along. Hepburn entered the general's office and, with Dr. Post serving as his Turkish interpreter, congratulated him on the good appearance of his troops. Their arrival, he said, was a great relief to the city.

Murcelle listened with polite formality. A broad-chested veteran of World War I, Murcelle had fought the British and Russians at the Battle of Baku, and after the war, he had been arrested by the British as a nationalist threat in Constantinople and then released, allowing him to join Mustapha Kemal's army in the interior of the country. His cavalry had fought hard from the initial assault at Afyon Karahisar fourteen days earlier and formed the vanguard of the Turkish force in the final push toward Smyrna. Hepburn told the Turkish general that he had positioned sailors as guards at the consulate and other locations. Murcelle in turn said the guards could remain. Hepburn then introduced Davis and Jaquith, at which point Murcelle realized he was speaking with Americans, not the British. He brightened and ordered his aides to offer his American guests cigarettes. More relaxed and cordial, Murcelle promised to send a liaison officer to the American consulate in the morning to coordinate refugee relief. All of this pleased Hepburn; it's what he had expected.

As Hepburn left Murcelle's office, he was satisfied that he would get the general's cooperation and the relief committee would be able to do its work. As the group was departing, Merrill recognized three faces in an anteroom. They were Clayton and Brown, and a third showing its familiar ruddy complexion. It was Sweeny, whom he knew from Constantinople. With Bristol's encouragement, Sweeny had come to Smyrna on the *Lawrence*. His goal was to take a trip on the road that led east from Smyrna to the towns and villages burned in the Greek army's retreat so he could write an account of the Greek atrocities that Bristol had told him about. Merrill peeled away from Hepburn and joined the reporters who said they were waiting for an interview with Murcelle. Merrill admired Sweeny's reputation for military adventure—he had heard from Bristol of Sweeny's many exploits—and decided to stay with the reporters, where there was likely to be some action. Hepburn returned to the consulate.

General Murcelle gave the reporters an interview, and then Sweeny, who was armed with letters of introduction he had brought with him from Constantinople, presumably from Bristol and Hamid Bey, persuaded Murcelle to give them a pass to travel to Magnesia. Sweeny wanted to meet with Mustapha Kemal for an interview about his victory and the Greek retreat. Apparently, Bristol's suggestion to Hamid Bey about the utility of the Greek atrocities had fallen on receptive ears. Sweeny was in Smyrna to show the Greeks for the dishonorable race that they were, but to do that he needed access to the villages burned by the Greek army and an interview with the supreme Turkish leader. Murcelle provided the pass and assigned him a Turkish lieutenant as a driver and interpreter, and off the reporters and Merrill went on their sanctioned errand toward Magnesia. It would be Merrill's third attempt to get there since arriving on the *Litchfield* three days ago.

Just outside of the city, near Bournabat, the four encountered a crowd blocking the way. There were several bodies lying in the road, and an Italian army officer stood between a group of Turkish civilians and a group of Italian residents of Bournabat. The two sides were in a deep dispute, shouting and threatening each other. The Italian officer appealed to the Americans to intervene with the Turks, though the root of the dispute was unclear, and the Turkish lieutenant who was their driver joined the argument against the Italians, making matters worse. The dispute was moving toward a violent climax when a contingent of Turkish cavalry came up the road in full gallop followed by a big touring car. The crowd quieted, and the car skidded to a stop next to the Americans. The Turkish lieutenant, looking frightened, stiffened and clicked his heels. It was obvious he recognized the imposing man in the rear seat. Merrill and the reporters would soon learn from the driver that the man was Noureddin Pasha, commander of the Turkish First Army and a hero of the recent campaign.

A big man with closely cropped hair and beard, Noureddin struck Merrill as having the bearing of a Prussian officer. ("The only man I had ever seen who could strut sitting down.") He barked at them in German, and his car pulled away. Now, with Sweeny snapping orders to the Turkish driver, the Americans followed and pulled up alongside the pasha's car. Sweeny thrust his bundle of letters at him, the ones he had brought from Constantinople. After shuffling through them, the general motioned for the Americans to follow him back to Smyrna. At the Konak, Noureddin told Sweeny that his cavalry clogged the roads to the east and he would not allow the reporters passage farther inland until the army had passed. Sweeny argued with him, asserting the importance of propaganda and publicity to the Turkish cause. Noureddin said he didn't give a damn for either and dismissed him. The Americans returned to the house that served as home base for Brown, Clayton, Merrill, Washburn, and his mistress and now for Sweeny.

What the Americans didn't know was that command of the city had passed to Noureddin. It was a fateful step.

IN THE FIRST FEW HOURS after the arrival of the Turkish cavalry, the city was quiet except for Turkish celebrations. Hepburn had radioed Bristol that the city was orderly and conditions favored a peaceful occupation. "Large supplies will undoubtedly be needed, but approximate data not yet obtained." Hepburn was confident of Turkish cooperation. "There is no question as to the intention of the authorities to preserve order; and they are taking efficient measures," he cabled his boss. He added this final note: "Special troops are detailed to protect refugees." This is what Bristol had foreseen—or at least had hoped for—a smooth and peaceful occupation by the Turkish army. It would affirm the argument he had been making to Washington—that Turkish atrocities in the past had been exaggerated. It was the Greeks and Armenians who were instigators of trouble.

But by midafternoon, Hepburn's assessment proved wildly inaccurate: Looting and violence had begun, and it would take Hepburn at least two more days to accept the extent of his misjudgment and alter his view of the Turkish command's intentions. In the meantime, many thousands would die. Almost immediately after the arrival of the cavalry, Turkish residents had begun leaving the Turkish Quarter and roved the Armenian Quarter with clubs, rifles, and shotguns. In increasing numbers as the afternoon wore on, they swarmed the backstreets, the Armenian Quarter in particular, and were harassing, robbing, and killing Christians they encountered outside their homes. The Turkish sentries posted throughout the city looked the other way. Sometimes, the Turkish soldiers joined the civilian mob as perpetrators.

Knauss witnessed the violence firsthand on his late-afternoon rounds. On nearly every street that he passed in the Greek and Armenian neighborhoods, there were bodies lying about, shot from close range in the face or the back. The victims were young and old, and mostly men, though there were also the bodies of old women on the street. Often the man's shirt or pants had been removed, and in every case his shoes had been taken. The method was the same: Several Turks would stop a Christian they found on the street, and with two men holding him, another would search his pockets. He would be ordered to hand over his clothes, then shot in the head or back at point-blank range. Knauss had brought Horton with him on the late-afternoon circuit, and together they witnessed three killings. As Knauss drove through the Armenian Quarter in the car, which was flying the small American flag, residents dashed from their homes, put their hands and faces to the windows of the car, and pleaded for the Americans to save them. In one instance, an Armenian dashed from his home, and Turks on the street who could not see the American flag on Knauss's car began firing at him, barely missing the car. Knauss was under orders not to interfere to save refugees. He drove on, leaving them behind. The shooting increased with each passing hour, and Knauss counted twenty-five bodies in the streets between the YMCA and the Girls' School.

At the consulate Hepburn grew worried. There seemed to be no end to the number of refugees coming into the city, based on reports he was getting from the relief committee. The Greeks and Armenians who lived in the city were staying inside their homes behind locked doors and shuttered windows, but the refugees from the countryside were crowding ever more tightly near the Quay, and the two or three streets parallel to it—Rue Parallele, the first street back; Quay Inglise, the second street back; and Frank Street, the third street back, which formed the heart of the shopping district. The city's forty-six Christian churches—Greek Orthodox, Armenian, Roman Catholic, and Anglican—were packed with refugees, and those who had not been able to gain entrance collected in the cemeteries and other public spaces where they could gather their goods and animals and spread a blanket. An American officer whose car tires had been shot out while traveling back to the theater from Paradise reported to Hepburn that Turkish snipers with long-range rifles had begun picking off refugees who had sought refuge at International College. There would be a muffled shot heard far in the distance, the elapse of a second or two, and then a refugee would drop to the ground, struck in the chest or head by a bullet. Each shot turned the refugees into a panicked herd.

Late in the afternoon, the congregations of several of the city's Greek churches, led by priests in their black robes and toadstool hats, appeared in front of the American consulate and begged for protection inside the building or its courtyard. Hepburn declined, and fearing the people would storm the building, he sent an aide to the Konak to request Turkish guards for both ends of Galazio Street to keep it clear. By now more naturalized Americans and their families gathered at the American Theater. Hepburn ordered the exit of everyone in the theater who did not have proof of American citizenship, which meant pulling apart extended families and sending those without passports or legitimate claims to American naturalization into the street. There were sobs and shrieks as family members were ejected. Horton was increasingly disconsolate. Pleading didn't help. Hepburn's orders were to offer protection only to American citizens. Protecting Ottoman subjects might be an affront to the Turkish military. As it grew dark, the crowd of refugees outside the consulate continued to swell until the Turkish guards arrived from the Konak. At their appearance, the refugees melted into the side streets or joined the tens of thousands on the Quay, where families camped in small groups and prepared small spaces for the night.

The Turkish cavalry that had entered the city in the morning had been about three thousand strong, but by evening many thousands of foot soldiers began appearing, some along the route traveled by the cavalry, others seeping into the city from the rear and entering the backstreets of the Greek, Armenian, and European neighborhoods, where they took what they wanted from shops and homes, including young women.

Hepburn returned to the *Litchfield* to get some sleep. He could hear gunfire on the backstreets from the ship's deck. There was no fusillade as would be the case with the encounter of two armies. Rather there was the intermittent sound of a single shot, or two or three shots at a time, indicating killings of individuals or people in small groups. It was the sound of fatal muggings and executions. Hepburn lost count. It went on through the night.

BRISTOL HAD INSTRUCTED HEPBURN not to coordinate a relief effort with the Allies, and consequently Hepburn did not meet with the British, French, or Italian officers at Smyrna. The ill will between Bristol and the British in Constantinople was spilling over into Smyrna.

Like the Americans, the British had no intention of evacuating Ottoman Christians, but they were faster to decide on an evacuation of their nationals and more sympathetic to the plight of the city's Greek governor. The British admiral de Brock, commanding the *Iron Duke*, had steamed immediately to Smyrna on learning of the Greek setbacks from British consul Harry Lamb on September 2. He also ordered the *King George V*, another capital ship, to head to Smyrna. Both ships had arrived the next day. De Brock had gone ashore, and after meeting with Lamb and Governor Stergiades, he had decided to evacuate British nationals. De Brock and his officers had spent Monday, September 4, preparing for the evacuation, and on Tuesday he had landed British marines before sunrise to supervise the embarkation of the British onto the hospital ship, HMHS *Maine*, and British merchant ships that he had requisitioned from the Levant Steamship Co. And on Friday, he had taken Governor Stergiades aboard. On Saturday morning, the day that Hepburn had arrived, de Brock had put ashore a strong force of additional marines to protect the British consulate and property. He established British headquarters at the Oriental Carpet Manufacturing Co., which because of its height offered a good vantage for British signalmen. As he did all of this, de Brock kept close tabs via radio on the situation at Chanak, the eastward flank of the Dardanelles where the British expected a Turkish incursion into a neutral zone established by the Sevres Treaty. If the Turks were going to pursue the Greeks into Europe, or if they intended to take eastern Thrace, their prewar possession in Europe, they would have to cross the Dardanelles at Chanak. Britain had decided its response would be to engage them with naval artillery and a small force of infantry and sink any vessels that attempted to make the crossing. In other words, de Brock, while evacuating British nationals at Smyrna, was also preparing for war with the nationalists.

HEPBURN WAS NOT PREPARING for war. The U.S. Navy was in Smyrna to protect Americans and American property, and the captain's assignment was to collect information for Bristol. The necessity of protecting Americans would continue, but it's hard to see what additional information Hepburn needed to gather. The situation was clear, and it was alarming. Hundreds of thousands of people lacked food and shelter. Nonetheless, Hepburn appeared in no hurry to steam back to Constantinople with his assessment or a list of necessary relief supplies.

On Sunday morning, September 10, his second morning in the city, he drove with Lieutenant Knauss to Paradise to evaluate the danger at

International College. The road passed through the Armenian Quarter, and the two officers saw streets littered with bodies. Hepburn counted thirty-five, including two old women, one of whom was still kneeling, though lifeless. They saw a man lying on the ground who had been shot in the back but was still alive. They did not stop. Turkish civilians and soldiers were looting Armenian homes and shops, often with the body of the shop owner lying across the doorsill or on the pavement just outside the shop. There was no attempt to hide the looting as the American officers drove by—it was being conducted casually and out in the open. Carts were being loaded with rugs, furniture, pots and pans, and bolts of cloth.

As the two American officers passed over the Caravan Bridge at the back of the city and entered the countryside, they saw empty carts tipped over without animals, unwanted goods scattered on the road, and the bodies, presumably of the owners, lying nearby. There was the body of a man who had been shot while trying to climb out of a steep ditch beside the road, and in a farm enclosure, they saw several Turkish boys throwing stones at a refugee man who had been shot in the head but had not yet died. And through all of this, the refugees continued moving along the road toward Smyrna.

At Paradise, about a thousand refugees had gathered inside the college grounds. Many more refugees were camped in a field adjacent to the college. Hepburn and Knauss passed through the college gate, where American sailors were posted with a machine gun, and entered the college grounds as a church service was ending. Hepburn spoke to MacLachlan and the school's staff and many of the town's residents, including the Jennings family, in the central courtyard as gunfire popped in the nearby fields and hills. Turkish troops had passed by the college all night, and in the morning, Hepburn learned, the college's staff had awakened to looting of some of the empty houses and closed shops in town. MacLachlan praised the American guards and assured Hepburn that the situation at the school was tense, but there was no need to evacuate. The American guard consisted of twelve men, eight from the *Lawrence* and four from the *Litchfield*. A twenty-nine-year-old chief gunnery mate named Louis Crocker, from Everett, Massachusetts, was the lead guard. Crocker had been particularly reassuring to the American wives and daughters at Paradise. "His name," Hepburn noted, "seemed to be on the lips of every woman."

The situation at the college soon would turn more dangerous, and MacLachlan's confidence would prove misplaced.

On their return to Smyrna, Hepburn and Knauss heard more frequent rifle fire coming from the hills and fields between Paradise and the city and saw fresh bodies on the way back. They lay in groups of three or four along the roadside and in the adjacent fields. Knauss had been keeping count, reached forty, and then for the purpose of his ship's diary gave up counting and concluded only that "great numbers" had been killed. The man whom they had seen on the way out—shot in the back but still alive—had been shot in the head and now lay dead along the roadside. They returned to Smyrna over the Caravan Bridge and upon entering the city managed to get lost in the maze of narrow streets. As they blindly navigated the Armenian district trying to find their way back, they heard more rapid shooting and saw that Armenians were no longer just being robbed and shot in the street. Turkish civilians and soldiers were breaking down doors, killing people inside their homes, and pulling out household goods. The bodies of families—victims of all ages, men, women, and children—had been dragged out of the houses and were strewn about the streets. Every shop had been broken into and where steel shades had been drawn against looters, the shops showed signs of battering and forced entry. Bales of rugs, dry goods, and store merchandise were lying along the street and sometimes blocked the officers' car until a smiling looter pushed some of it aside for their passage. Hepburn and Knauss finally wended their way back to the Quay through the Turkish Quarter and the bazaar.

AT THE THEATER, Hepburn found relief committee members anxious about the brazen street killings, lootings, and disorder. The captain received reports of killings throughout the city. One officer reported eight bodies at the two railroad stations, at either end of the city, and another officer, in a different neighborhood, had counted fifteen bodies. Altogether, his officers had seen fifty-eight bodies in the streets on Sunday. Hepburn did not realize that these body counts were low. The Reverend Dobson of the Anglican parish near the Point had been removing bodies of refugees from the streets for burial—some of them children and naked women with bloodied genitals. Many of the dead were also left inside the houses, and Dobson had pulled them out of hedges and abandoned carts. Working with an Orthodox priest who administered rites, Dobson (with the help of others) saw that the slain refugees received decent burials.

Despite the Turkish occupation of the city, the cascade of refugees into Smyrna showed no sign of abating. The people arriving did not know of the brutality that was occurring within the city limits, and most were still reassured by the presence of the Allied and American warships. Thousands had converged on the YMCA and YWCA and attempted to force their way into the buildings. About two hundred were admitted to the YMCA and twelve hundred at the YWCA, where there was a gated courtyard. Hepburn, meanwhile, was puzzled and annoyed that the Turkish liaison officer that General Murcelle had promised at the previous day's meeting had never appeared. He soon would learn why. Murcelle was out, and a different man was now in charge.

The relief committee was making modest progress, but its resources were hardly sufficient to the magnitude of the problem. Jennings continued to bring injured and pregnant women to his safe house, and he had begun to investigate other abandoned mansions along the Quay that he might put to use as shelters. The spread of the killings was also creating yet more orphans, and Jennings had begun to collect children too.

Charles Davis, the Red Cross chief of the relief committee, sent the YMCA's Ernest Jacob and others on an inspection tour of the city. They left the YMCA building near the American consulate and drove to the northern end of the city at the Point, where they counted about two thousand refugees who had congregated near the American Tobacco Warehouse, one of their feeding stations. They then turned inland to the Panonios Football Field, which the committee had designated as a collection point for refugees. Collection points, they had reasoned, would provide safer locations for the refugees and make it easier to feed them. The committee members arrived at the football field to find that the two thousand refugees who had been there the previous day were gone, but their baggage remained. It was an eerie sight of rifled trunks and scattered belongings. The relief workers knew the tenacity with which the refugees had held on to their possessions, and they knew also that the refugees could not have been separated from their belongings except by force, or the threat of it. Turning south on their inspection tour, they encountered the looting of stores and homes in the Greek Quarter, and farther south, toward the Basmahane train station in the Armenian district, there was more looting and bodies were lying in the streets. Jacob and the group then moved back in the direction of the consulate, crossing Frank Street, where they saw more looting and bodies. They turned toward the Quay and traveled south to the Turkish and Jewish sections, where excited crowds gathered in the streets but there was no looting or trouble. Jacob and the others then traveled inland to a refugee camp that had been established at Balchova, not far from the base of the pass at Nif, but it also was empty. They turned back toward the city and stopped at the Greek hospital to deliver medical supplies and found that the Turks had taken over the hospital and put its patients in the street.

In the meantime, Davis had gone to the Quay to evaluate the condition of the refugees who had boarded the harbor's lighters—barges used to load and unload larger ships in the harbor. People had fled to the lighters when Turkish patrols of the city had begun the previous day. Most of them were inside the breakwater of the Passport Pier, taken there two days earlier by the British, who wanted to give its destroyer, HMS *Tribune*, a clear field to fire its deck guns toward the city if necessary. The Turks had initially given the British permission to bring food (boiled potatoes) and water to the people on the lighters, after men between eighteen and forty-five years old had been weeded out, but the order had been later rescinded and the British were not allowed to deliver food or water. One lighter had capsized from the weight of the refugees, resulting in several drownings. Another lighter had become untethered from the pier and floated haphazardly in the harbor with people and luggage aboard. The British offered to take the refugees ashore from the barge, but they refused—preferring hunger and thirst to the brutality onshore. From time to time, refugees would leap into the water from one of the lighters and try to swim to an Allied or American navy ship, hoping to be picked up. Turkish soldiers shot them in the water, bracketing their gunfire by observing the splashes until a bullet struck its swimming target.

The relief committee had been able to provide bread only to ten thousand people per day, less than 5 percent of the refugees. On Sunday, the Turks had inexplicably closed the bakeries, and Davis was working furiously to get the order countermanded. Also by Sunday, Jacob had taken responsibility for the orphanages, and Jennings was walking the city in the places where refugees congregated. He was shaken by what he saw. "No one can ever describe the sensations of those days," he later wrote. "I have seen men, women and children whipped, robbed, shot, stabbed and drowned in the sea."

Concentrating his energy on the worst cases, Jennings (his pain ever present, his peculiar gait, jacket, and straw boater a now-common sight in the city's backstreets) picked up wounded children and pregnant and injured women in the Chevrolet and took them to the Quay. He and the American sailors who, without authorization, helped in these rounds, did their best to provide medical care with the scant supplies that had arrived on the *Lawrence*. The house at No. 490, despite its many big rooms, soon was full, so Jennings collected the orphan children on the apron of cobblestones out front. He asked the American sailors at the American Theater—about a quarter mile distant in the direction of the Passport Pier—to keep an eye on them, and they eagerly agreed. The sailors soon began bringing to Jennings women and children they found on the streets.

Greek and Armenian girls from the American Girls' College, fearful of remaining in the district where the killings were most flagrant, also began showing up at 490, seeking protection. Soon five hundred people were crammed into his house. Faced with these numbers, and the extent of their injuries and illnesses, Jennings had taken several nearby mansions along the Quay that had been abandoned by their wealthy owners and turned them into safe houses. The people were spread on the floors, in the rooms and hallways. There was hardly space to pass among them.

Jennings had to step over them as he moved through the houses. The American sailors continued to bring him more.

Jaquith reported back to the Near East Relief office in Constantinople: "Thousands of exhausted refugees, the majority of whom are women and children, are blocking all the roads leading into Smyrna. The city is terribly crowded, and the refugees who fled with only what they could carry on their backs are exposed to famine. The lack of shelter is causing intense suffering and misery. Many deaths have been caused by starvation, and the local hospitals, which are overflowing, need doctors, nurses and medicines."

The *Times* of London, which published his cable, reported: "All accounts, nevertheless, agree that Smyrna has been turned into a charnelhouse. Several streets were so littered with mutilated bodies that it was impossible to pass for the sickening stench."

Less than two full days had passed since the Turkish cavalry had entered the city, and already Jennings and other relief committee members were beginning to sense that the worsening situation would require more than the arrival of food and medical assistance. The growing ruthlessness that was being visited on the Armenian Quarter and the impunity with which stores and homes were being looted and Christians were robbed, beaten, and shot suggested that there was no safe place for the refugees in Smyrna. There was an emerging sense that the only way to save lives was an evacuation. It was a realization that was both inescapable and inconceivable. Smyrna was far too dangerous for Christians to remain there, and a return to their farms and villages was impossible. Yet, a decision to evacuate meant removing hundreds of thousands of people from the place that was their home and taking them somewhere else—and that somewhere else was unclear. There was no alternative to departure. Yet there also appeared no way to take them away. The numbers of people were too big; the means of escape unavailable.

THE SITUATION WAS SEVERE all along the western coast of Anatolia and the Sea of Marmara. Refugees—Ottoman subjects but Christians—had abandoned their farms and villages with the retreat of the Greek army and were gathering on the beaches hoping to find passage on Greek or Allied ships to Greece. (Most were people who had never been to Greece, and most would be accounted as strangers when they arrived. Many would not be understood when they spoke.) Villages from Vourla, just south of Smyrna, to the tip of Chesme peninsula were emptying out. People were attempting the crossing to Chios or other islands in their small fishing boats even as the Greek navy continued its artillery fire to cover retreating soldiers. Sixty thousand people waited for rescue on the southern shore of the Sea of Marmara, and twenty-five thousand people huddled on the beach at Mudania. The *Morning Post* in London reported: "Five hundred thousand starving Christian refugees are awaiting shipment at Smyrna, Aivaly [Ayvalik], Mudania, Dikili, and Ghemlek [Gemlik], and the Greek Government is without available money or ships." The paper's correspondent added, "The scenes on the roads from Brussa to the coast are reminiscent of those in France and Belgium during August, 1914." The *London Daily News* called for the intervention of the League of Nations to rescue the refugees.

Greek merchant ships serving as troop transports carried some of the refugees across the Sea of Marmara to Thrace, and the Greek patriarch in Constantinople was attempting to charter ships to evacuate Christians at Smyrna and other Aegean ports, but he lacked the money even if he could find the ships. He appealed to the British government and American relief organizations, and he issued an encyclical to the Greek community, enjoining prayer, calm, and abstinence from all provocative conduct and language.

CAPTAIN HEPBURN MET through the day on Sunday with Davis and Jaquith, who were pessimistic about Turkish intentions. The looting and intimidation on the streets had created an ominous feeling of a looming massacre—on a greater scale than what was already occurring in small family-sized groups. The relief committee was painfully aware that Turkish command showed no interest in stopping the disorder. It was as if the nationalist generals—in the old Ottoman tradition of warfare—were giving poorly paid soldiers and camp followers three days to sack a conquered city. Turkish soldiers, initially respectful of the Americans, were growing belligerent, and it was dangerous for a British citizen to be on the street. A Turkish guard was posted outside the British consulate, preventing British citizens without papers from getting near the building.

Then Hepburn received additional unsettling news: military executions had commenced. Ottoman Greeks and Armenians who had cooperated with the now-departed Greek administration of the city were being shot or hanged near the Konak. A hanging was accomplished with a makeshift gallows: three long poles fastened together at the top, teepee style, and a rope dropped with a loop to fit around the neck of the victim. Hepburn saw Turkish soldiers marching Greeks and Armenians in groups of twelve to fifty along the Quay, with two abreast bound together at their wrists. Pulled from their homes, or other places of hiding, they were being taken toward the Konak and the military prison. The Turkish army also had obtained a list of the names of the members of the Asia Minor Defense League, and its members were being rounded up. Executions were swift, bodies often mutilated. The Turkish commander of the city also called on Turkish civilians to come forward with grievances about individual Greeks and Armenians, who were then brought before tribunals for swift judgment. Reporter John Clayton saw the execution of sixteen men who had been rounded up. Accounts were being settled with murderous speed.

"We watched our soldiers pass with bayonets," a Muslim woman later recalled, "leading desperate Greek men with their hair on end, their beards grown. They took them in a column, their hands tied behind, and then shot them in the mountains. Every evening."

In the afternoon, Hepburn, troubled but strangely conflicted about how to evaluate what was happening around him, sent a reassuring radio message to Bristol. There had been scattered killings, he reported, but the victims were "all Armenians and Greeks of the peasant class." As for the relief work, he wrote, "Government control not sufficiently established to make much progress." The message contained no request for additional food or supplies, but he included this important bit of news: "Mustapha Kemal expected to arrive hourly."

AT ABOUT 5 P.M., Mustapha Kemal rode into the city in the backseat of a 1911 Mercedes-Knight 1640. It was sixteen feet long with deep leather seats, and the top was down. A detachment of cavalry carrying flags and lances marched ahead of the car. With Kemal were Fevzi Pasha and Salih Bozok, his aide-de-camp. Salih's loyalty was so deep to Kemal that years later, on learning of Kemal's death, he shot himself out of grief.

The army had advertised Kemal's entrance, and his route was decorated with red Turkish flags hung from windows. Like the cavalry the day before, he came into the city from the northwest, turned onto the Quay, and traveled along the harborfront, passing (among the clubs, cafés, and other mansions) Jennings's safe houses. He stopped at the Hotel Splendid, which would serve temporarily as his headquarters, then continued to the Konak, where he met with Noureddin and discussed the military situation. Afterward, he returned to the hotel and still later descended to the hotel's bar, where the waiter did not recognize him and apologized for not having an open table. But there were patrons in the bar who knew the face and the uniform. They were astonished at the man now among them. Kemal joined them at their table. He ordered a drink and threw it down, the first since the great offensive had begun on August 26. There were Greeks in the bar, nervously watching him, and he turned to them and said, "Did King Constantine ever come here to drink a glass of raki?" They said no he had not. "Then," Kemal responded, "why did he bother to take Smyrna?"

BY SUNDAY AFTERNOON, the situation at International College had deteriorated despite MacLachlan's hardheaded Scots optimism, which had been on display the previous day. The long-distance potting by Turkish snipers of refugees inside the college's walls was more frequent, and Turkish soldiers stepped up the looting of homes and stores in Paradise. Refugees continued to move along the road coming up from the south, and they were easy prey for soldiers and bandits. The Turks picked them off like blackbirds sitting on a telephone wire.

Both the Jennings and Jacob families had Greek and Armenian

household help, as did nearly all of the American and European families in Paradise, and they brought the servants and their servants' families and others into their homes for safety. Ernest and Sarah Jacob had forty people in their home.

The American sailors patrolled inside the college's walls, but many of the Americans' homes (including Jennings's and Jacob's) were outside the gate. A guard was posted in the clock tower of MacLachlan Hall to keep watch and communicate with the *Litchfield*, three miles distant, by semaphore. From the tower, the sailor on guard saw homes and vineyards set afire throughout the Meles valley. The British consul came out to the college and removed a British subject who was married to a Greek-born woman and their children. Unlike Captain Hepburn, he had judged it too dangerous for the young family to remain out of the city. The Turkish command in Smyrna had also sent guards to the college, but they were a rough lot. On arriving, they demanded liquor from the women in the American homes and paid no attention to the looting that was going on in the abandoned homes of the Americans despite the presence of American flags.

Amy Jennings, at home with three children, watched from her window the burials of Greeks who had been shot outside the college yard and of a child who had died at its starving mother's breast. Amy was at the end of her wits. At one point, bandits attempted to enter the Jenningses' home, coming over a wall at the back of the house, and the older son, Asa, fifteen years old, fired at them with a pistol his father had left with him. He killed two and wounded a third. Amy was coming unglued.

The violence at Paradise was even more severe in the other expatriate communities of Bournabat and Boudjah.

In Bournabat that day, Turkish cavalry had passed through the town, terrorizing the Levantine residents and looting their homes and busting up furniture and killing refugees in the streets. In one instance, Turkish soldiers fired on a group of Greek women and children, killing forty-eight. A British officer described a scene in which a boy of about three years old played around the body of his dead mother, still holding a baby, who was alive: "A Turkish soldier appeared in the street, came up and saw the little boy, raised his rifle and fired point blank at the child. The little fellow fell dead. The noise evidently startled the baby, who commenced to cry. Shooting the smaller child as well, the Turk proceeded on his way." Later, in another instance, the British officer reported, "One of the superior Turks collared a girl of nineteen-twenty, who was with a sister of twelve and her mother, and took her round the corner of the road. The mother and sister were forced to proceed, the mother crying, shrieking, and protesting for her other daughter, without avail . . . the girl was seen to be embraced by the Turk, who stripped her of all her clothing, and then raped her. Having finished, he pulled his revolver and shot her."

British subjects were also victims. A retired colonel, a doctor, lived in Bournabat. Turkish soldiers broke into his home, then stripped and raped his Greek servant girls in front of him and his wife. The doctor fought them and was shot through the lung and he died the next day. Another resident of Bournabat reported the rape and killing of two large groups of women servants in the town.

In Paradise, a contingent of Greek troops that had become lost wandered into the Meles valley as they tried to find their way to Chesme. The Turkish army became aware of their presence and opened a barrage of artillery fire from the hilltop behind Smyrna. The American guards rapidly collected the families who were in houses outside the college gates and brought them into the college as the fighting intensified nearby. Artillery shells whizzed overhead, and several landed near the college. Amy Jennings watched the battle from an upper window of the college's main building. After the artillery had decimated the ranks of the Greeks, the Turkish cavalry attacked. She saw the slaughter through a pair of binoculars.

At around dusk, Jennings and Jacob returned to Paradise to spend the night with their families, who by then had gone back to their homes outside the college gates. The Greek soldiers who had survived the battle had been marched into Smyrna and paraded along the waterfront. Through the night, families in Paradise heard occasional shooting and the screams of women on the road in the direction of Boudjah. The sounds carried far over the treeless hills.

IN THE CITY, Hepburn once again returned to the *Litchfield* for the night, his second since arriving. Reports of bodies lying in the streets continued to reach him, and he was aware that the body count he was keeping based on the actual sightings of corpses by his officers was far below the number of shots being fired day and night. He was reluctant to concede that the bodies of murdered Armenians were being left inside their homes or that he was underestimating the extent of the killings. He stuck to his belief that the Turks would drag the bodies of their victims into the streets to increase terror and that his count was accurate. Why he believed this is a mystery—possibly he wanted to find ways to keep his estimate of the killing conservative for Bristol's approval.

In his message to Bristol, the captain stopped short of calling the bloodbath in the Armenian Quarter a massacre and put the number of dead at two hundred. Hepburn compared the number of killings to that which "might have occurred in certain sections of a large American city, should all police protection have been withdrawn . . ."* As seemed to be the case with Merrill, Hepburn was selecting and interpreting information to provide a picture of events that would most likely conform to Bristol's expectations—or his wishes. (Serving up intelligence to confirm the views of higher-ups is not a new phenomenon.) Hepburn again fell asleep that night to the sound of scattered gunfire. There was no fighting—it was the *crack-crack-crack* of executions.

Ashore, and about a half mile away, in the backstreets of the city, nurses Agnes Evon and Sara Corning were taking turns watching over the women and children who had sought shelter at the YWCA. This is where they and Dr. Post had slept on their first night in the city after they had found a hospital in which to treat refugees, and they would sleep there again on this night.

After their arrival the previous day, the medical team had left the meeting at the consulate and taken a relief-committee car with a three-inch American flag stuck on the grille and gone in search of a suitable medical base. Almost immediately they had run into the column of

---

* It's hard to know what American city Hepburn was thinking of. In 1920, Prohibition's first year, Chicago was America's most dangerous city. There were 229 killings for the year. That number was likely exceeded in a day in Smyrna.

Turkish cavalry arriving near the Konak. Their car had gotten caught in the crowd of Turkish celebrants, and when they finally broke free, they encountered four Turkish soldiers with rifles raised to execute a bare-chested man in the street. Their driver hit the accelerator to save the man, but the car stalled, and they were immediately besieged by people climbing onto the car. They had managed to move ahead slowly in the car, and in the commotion, the man to be executed slipped away. The medical team had then gone on to the Greek hospital, which they rejected as their base because the swift evacuation of the wounded Greek soldiers had left the facility a mess. At the Armenian hospital, Turkish officers, who were moving patients out to make room for Turkish soldiers, sent them away. They had ended up at a small Dutch hospital near the YWCA and begun treating refugees for gunshot and stab wounds.

On this night, Sunday, when it was her turn to make the rounds of the YWCA building and the grounds, Miss Evon walked among the women and children in the courtyard and then went to the roof of the building for a view of the grounds. She looked out over the city, which was dark except for a few small lights that seemed to move stealthily through the streets. They were handheld lanterns. Occasionally two or three lights came together and stopped, and then there was a sound of smashing doors and human screams and shots. Then, after the shots, she saw the lights go from window to window, up through the house, and she heard other women shrieking and children screaming and more shots. The killing was enacted in silhouette as a gruesome show of sound and shadow behind lantern-lighted curtains. When the screaming stopped in one house, Miss Evon saw the lantern lights move to the next house and then again heard the crashing of the door, the shrieking. At the same time, hundreds of dogs were barking and yelping throughout the city, adding to the ghoulish scene. "When no one could see me," she later wrote, "sometimes I clenched my hands over my ears and stood there hanging on to self-control. I said to myself, isn't there enough decency in all humanity, is it possible that the decency of the world isn't strong enough to keep such things from being done on this earth in this century?"

Back at the theater, where Knauss was posted for the night, the refugees were huddled with their carts, donkeys, and bundles. They seemed to him pitiable "small heaps" hardly stirring except to occasionally ask the guard for some water. Nonetheless, Knauss directed the sailors to prepare a metal screen that could be pulled down over the theater's front doors in the event that refugees were overcome by their anxiety and attempted to rush the theater. At 2 A.M., he was glad he had taken the precaution. Several Turkish soldiers on horseback rode into the crowd and grabbed a man from the group—his name must have appeared on a list of traitors. They wanted specifically him. The American sailors barely had time to drop the screen as the crowd attempted to force its way into the theater to escape the Turkish soldiers.

Merrill, who had tagged along on the security loop to the American institutions, displayed a different response to the fear of the refugees. "No one could imagine without seeing them 'under fire,'" he wrote in his diary, "what a chicken-liver lot these 'Christian minorities' are."

CHAPTER 14

Garabed Hatcherian

y Saturday, September 9, the city's Armenian neighborhood was in high excitement about the approaching Turkish army. Many of those who could not afford to leave Smyrna were choosing instead to leave the Armenian district and move closer to the Quay with friends or family outside of the neighborhood—at least until the storm passed. If there was going to be trouble, the Armenians—everyone in Smyrna for that matter—knew the Armenian neighborhood would bear the worst of it. Better not to be there; many locked their doors and left.

Dr. Hatcherian decided it would be prudent for him and his family also to leave the district, at least temporarily. One of his patients was a woman whose family lived in a big house on the Quay. She was pregnant, and Dr. Hatcherian had been engaged to deliver the baby. He asked her if, in lieu of a fee, he and his family could stay in a room in their house for a while. It would assure his availability for the birth of her child and provide him a measure of relief from worry. She happily assented.

The doctor returned to his home and retrieved his family. He put on a Turkish fez and pinned his Ottoman military decorations to his chest. He thought they would offer him protection. Then, he, Elisa, and the five children and Araksi, their maid, walked to the house on the Quay, where they spent the night.

The next day, Sunday, September 10, Dr. Hatcherian was consumed with worry about his house and family's possessions in it. (This was the day after the arrival of the first contingent of Turkish troops into the city.) He decided to check on things. He left the Quay house with Araksi and two companions with property in the neighborhood. Once again, Dr. Hatcherian pinned his Ottoman military medals on his shirt as protection against harassment by Turkish soldiers. As he, Araksi, and his companions approached the Armenian district, they found the streets deserted except for Turkish soldiers milling about. The two companions decided the trip was too dangerous and turned back.

Dr. Hatcherian and Araksi continued toward his house, which was on the far side of the neighborhood, nearly a mile from the Quay. As they walked, he was twice stopped by Turkish soldiers who were lost and asked him for directions to the Turkish barracks. He pointed the way to them and continued toward his house. He saw that many houses on his street had been broken into, with windows and doors smashed, and some places along the street were splattered with dried blood, but his home, to his great relief, was not damaged, except that the lock on the front door had been forced, making it impossible for him to use his key. He pulled on the knob and rattled the door but couldn't get inside. He told Araksi to stand by the house as he checked nearby houses of friends. He knocked on the door of the house of his neighbor, Levon Arakelian, and got no answer. He checked other houses and found them broken into and rummaged. He walked around the corner and out of sight of Araksi. His diary records what he saw:

> First I see the house of the Balikjians, where the doors are broken and the furniture is a jumbled mess in the courtyard. The doors of the houses on the Grand Boulevard have been broken one by one and there are traces of blood all over. The stores, too, have been broken into and looted. I see Turkish soldiers ransacking houses. I hear gunshots coming from the Diocese area. . . . The local Turks and the soldiers who pass by take me for a Turk, judging by my appearance. But it is not wise to stay here any longer.

He went back to get Araksi. He tried the door of his house again without success. There were more soldiers in the street. He kept his composure—giving no sign of his inner turmoil. On the return, he and Araksi walked by the YWCA and saw the American guards out front.

He returned to the Quay and reported to the others what he had seen. Upstairs, where his family was staying, he tried to calm his wife, and occasionally he walked out to the balcony, where he saw Turkish soldiers marching groups of refugee men toward the military barracks beyond the Konak. In the days that followed, Dr. Hatcherian learned that Christian men were being rounded up and taken to the prison at the barracks—Armenian men were being singled out, he was told, because they were resisting the Turks.

CHAPTER 15

Noureddin Pasha

The city's new military commander, Noureddin Pasha, had a reputation even among the Turkish military for brutal methods.

Forty-nine years old and a veteran at suppressing indigenous revolts against the Ottoman state in Macedonia and Yemen before World War I, Noureddin too had been groomed by German military advisers hired by the Sultan Abdul Hamid II to modernize and train the Ottoman army. Like Mustapha Kemal, he had played his part in a British humiliation during World War I—the British defeat at Kut Al Amara.

In November 1914, soon after the war had begun, Britain had landed a force at the head of the Persian Gulf to protect its oil supplies in Mesopotamia. The landing was successful, and the force moved to Basra, which it soon occupied, giving the British control over the region's oil fields. The British troops were then ordered—more to demonstrate prestige to Muslim inhabitants of the British Empire than for military necessity— to march farther north and take Baghdad. On the way, following the Tigris River, the British came under attack by Ottoman troops led by Noureddin. The battle was inconclusive, and both sides retired after five days of fighting, but the British, under General Charles Townshend, began a retreat toward the city of Kut Al Amara, twenty-five miles south of Baghdad. Noureddin, seeing an opportunity, pursued the British and trapped them at Kut, where they were unable to escape or be resupplied despite several attempts to break the siege. Three months later, suffering from disease and diminishing food, the British surrendered—13,100 men were taken prisoner. They were marched through the desert to Aleppo. More than half of the British troops died in captivity, and the cruel conditions led British officers including T. E. Lawrence to try to gain release of the soldiers with a payment of two million pounds. The Ottomans rejected the offer. The British eventually reorganized their forces in southern Iraq and took Baghdad in March 1917, by which time British forces under General Edmund Allenby were moving north from Egypt through Palestine to Aleppo, forcing an Ottoman surrender.

After the Ottoman collapse and defeat of the Central Powers, the Ottoman government in Constantinople named Noureddin military governor of the Smyrna district, but the British successfully demanded his removal. Noureddin then left the Ottoman army and passed over to the nationalist camp and was appointed to lead the nationalist Central Army in the Black Sea region. In 1921, he put down a Kurdish revolt against the nationalists with such fury and cruelty that the Nationalist Congress in Ankara, no hotbed of sympathy toward minorities, sought to put him on trial.

Throughout the period of his command, tens of thousands of Ottoman-Greek subjects were slaughtered and deported along the Black Sea coast.

Noureddin had kept his command of the Central Army only through the intervention of Mustapha Kemal. And while Noureddin's ego and ambition posed a threat to Kemal's leadership during the war with the Greeks, Kemal had retained Noureddin because of his savagery in battle. He had proved his worth in the drive from Kocatepe to Smyrna, commanding the First Army.

One of his first orders of business in Smyrna was to settle a score with the city's Greek Metropolitan Chrysostomos, a religious and civic leader among the Ottoman Greeks but also a Hellenic nationalist who mixed Greek territorial ambitions with his spiritual duties. He was the bishop who had led the Greek troops on their landing in 1919. The fifty-five-year-old religious leader was no stranger to conflict—he had been removed by the Ottoman authorities as the city's bishop in 1914 and was only reinstated with the Greek occupation, and even then Governor Stergiades had chastised him for his incessant nationalism. During a church service, Stergiades had risen from his seat and forced the bishop to stop a sermon that was blatantly political. A British naval officer described him: "The Metropolitan, short, thick-set, with gnarled face, looking like a hard-headed business man who had arrived at prosperity only after a hard struggle, and having attained the top of the tree, was determined that those under him should have a taste of the hardships he had once endured."

Chrysostomos and Noureddin were old antagonists: the bishop had successfully pressed the British for Noureddin's removal in March 1919 ahead of the Greek landing, and Noureddin had not forgotten.

Late in the afternoon on Sunday, September 10, a French patrol called on Chrysostomos to offer him sanctuary at the French consulate. Chrysostomos declined, saying he wanted to remain with his flock, and as the French force was leaving the Greek church, a carriage with Turkish soldiers arrived and ordered him to climb in. He was told Noureddin wanted to see him, and he was taken to the general's office at the Konak. In their meeting, Noureddin reminded the bishop of an argument that had occurred between them in 1919 when Noureddin was the military governor. "On the last occasion that I had the pleasure of seeing you," Noureddin said, "you were good enough to say that I ought be shot. I have sent for you, Lordship, to tell you that you are going to be hanged."

Guards took Chrysostomos into the street where about fifteen hundred excited Turkish residents had gathered. Noureddin came to the balcony overlooking the street and, realizing that an alternative to hanging Chrysostomos had presented itself, said to the crowd that he was giving the bishop to them to do as they pleased. "If he has done good to you, do good to him. If he has done harm to you, do harm to him." The mob dragged Chrysostomos by his beard to a nearby barbershop, where they wrapped him in a barber's apron and beat and stabbed him. His eyes were gouged out and nose and ears cut off. The French patrol watched the scene, the men furious at what was happening but under orders not to intervene. Eventually, a bystander shot the bishop to end his misery.

ON MONDAY, SEPTEMBER 11, Captain Hepburn sent Lieutenant Merrill to arrange a meeting with Noureddin.

While waiting to be called in, Merrill was "cooling his heels" in the office of Noureddin's aide, Brigadier General Hassam Pasha, who, like Noureddin, projected the image of a German officer: he spoke fluent German, made a crisp and stern military presence, and delivered his orders and remarks to subordinates with a Teutonic finality. Merrill, in typical form, chatted him up in French and asked him about care of the refugees. The Turkish general said feeding his troops came first, then he led Merrill to a window where they watched Turkish guards lead six thousand Greek soldiers past the government building, forcing them to shout "Long live Kemal" as they passed by. After an hour or so, Noureddin saw Merrill and assented to a meeting with Hepburn. The time was set for 3 P.M.

Hepburn arrived on time with his delegation but was forced to wait an hour before entering Noureddin's office. In his white uniform and white shoes, Hepburn encountered the khaki-clad rugged and bearded man. He looked at Hepburn through small dark eyes, round and nicked like the bottoms of expended rifle casings. His ears were turned slightly forward at their tops. Noureddin was forty-nine years old, seven years older than Hepburn. He wore a stiff tunic, still dusty from the field, and a Sam Browne belt that girdled his waist and crossed his right shoulder.

Hepburn planned to introduce the relief committee and explain its goals, but his real intent was to gain insight into the general's attitude toward the refugees and Americans in the city. The captain introduced Barnes, Davis, Jaquith, and Dr. Post, who served again as the interpreter. The conversation would be in Turkish. Hepburn congratulated Noureddin on his military success and explained the work of the committee, which he said had been organized by Admiral Bristol in Constantinople and operated under his auspices. The American navy's mission, he said, was the ordinary one of looking after American lives and property. Based on the guidance he had gotten from Bristol, Hepburn told Noureddin that he hoped the refugees would soon be able to return to their homes in the interior. Noureddin interrupted. No, he said, the refugees could not return to their homes. The devastation by the Greek army made that impossible. The refugees would be killed if they went back, Noureddin said. "Bring ships and take them out of the country," Noureddin added. "It is the only solution."

The response caught Hepburn by surprise. Once again, the script failed to follow what Bristol had laid out for him. (Jennings and the relief committee, of course, had already reached that conclusion based on the momentum toward a general massacre.)

Forced to improvise, Hepburn continued to engage the general and made the point that a removal of hundreds of thousands of people would take time, and that in the meantime food and medical care must be made available. This required bringing the refugees into safe areas, under the protection of Turkish guards; in addition, the relief workers would need a Turkish liaison officer with whom they could coordinate the compli-cated work. Hepburn handed him a note listing refugee collection points suggested by the relief committee. These included the warehouse at the Point, the football stadium, and the barracks at Balchova. It made no mention of Jennings's string of safe houses, which Hepburn appears not yet to have noticed. Noureddin said he didn't have time to read it and the details should be taken up with his commandant but there would be no liaison officer assigned to the relief committee. Dr. Post was translating Noureddin's words for Hepburn, and soon the general and Dr. Post en-gaged in a rapid back-and-forth that sounded hostile to Hepburn, who sat and listened in exasperation, guessing at what was passing between them in Turkish. He was reluctant to interrupt more than occasionally for fear of showing discord within his delegation. In one of the pauses, Post told Hepburn that Noureddin was going over an incident from last year that Noureddin said had proved missionaries in Marsovan had supported an Ottoman-Greek rebellion against the Turks.

The Marsovan incident was well known in the missionary commu-nity and had turned into a serious point of conflict between the Ameri-can Board of Commissioners for Foreign Missions and Admiral Bristol. Marsovan, a town in the Black Sea region, was home to Anatolia College, a missionary school, as well as a big missionary hospital and orphanage. During the First World War, thousands of Armenians had been deported from the city, and the Turks had demanded that the college's president,

Dr. George White, a Congregationalist minister, turn over Armenian faculty and students. White refused, and the Turks threatened to execute the American missionary staff. White relented, and the Armenians were taken away; the men were executed and the women deported. The school was closed. After the war, White had returned and reopened the school. In 1921, nationalist authorities who controlled the territory around Marsovan suspected the school was sheltering Greek students who were plotting against Turkey. They raided the school and discovered documents and letters that they said proved that the students—and by extension the school—were involved in subversive activities. Among the evidence were a map labeling the area "Pontus," a Greek word that had been applied to the region for two thousand years, student essays about Pontic autonomy, and a letter written by White, in which he expressed his hope to convert Turks to Christianity. Three teachers, an alumnus, and two students—all Ottoman ethnic Greeks—were arrested and executed. The executions spread, and soon five hundred more ethnic Greeks were put to death. The school was closed again. Dr. White protested the actions to Bristol, who, in his diary, suggested the problem was with the school for allowing a student "debating" society.

As Hepburn listened in bafflement to the back-and-forth between Noureddin and Dr. Post, Noureddin had specifically referred to Dr. White's letter about Muslim conversion. Noureddin, his temper rising, told Post that he had the letter that proved missionary collusion with Greek subversives. (It was a detail that stuck with Merrill. A letter of that sort would be valuable to Bristol in his campaign to discredit the missionaries.) Noureddin asked Dr. Post if the Americans had brought priests—"the Americans are always bringing priests." (Post was both conversing rapidly with Noureddin and giving Hepburn snatches of the translated conversation.) Post would later say that Noureddin had told him, "You have a saying in your country, 'America for the Americans.' We say 'Turkey for the Turks.' You have another saying, 'The good Indian is a dead Indian.' Well, we believe that the good Armenian is a dead Armenian."

Hepburn was getting a good insight into Noureddin's antipathies, but he did not get an answer to his specific question about Noureddin's disposition toward the refugees: Would they be protected until their evacuation was arranged?

He tried again, being less oblique. The refugees, he told Noureddin, had flocked to American institutions but it was not the American intent to protect them; the intent was to remove them to a place where they would be safe. He put the question again to Noureddin, and this time the general shot back that he resented the question: "Of course they will be protected." At that moment, the sound of cheers from the street entered the room through an open window, and Noureddin walked to the balcony overlooking the square, the one from which he had spoken to the crowd about Chrysostomos. He gestured to the Americans to watch with him as Turkish soldiers passed by. "Look at them," he said with pride. "They have come five hundred kilometers in twelve days. Praise Allah."

Noureddin concluded the meeting by giving Hepburn a copy of a proclamation he had just prepared. It ordered civilians to turn in their guns, prohibited looting, and declared that anyone who harbored a Greek soldier or "functionary" would be executed. The proclamation was posted throughout the city the next day.

BACK AT THE CONSULATE, Hepburn found the relief committee further discouraged. The looting and shooting remained flagrant, and it was obvious by now that the Turkish command had no intention of stopping it. The Americans—principally Davis and Jaquith—feared that the disorder was sliding toward a slaughter of all Christians in the city. The refugees were packing into any building that put them out of sight of the Turkish army and roaming civilian bands with clubs and guns. They were hiding even in mausoleums and in stone-covered graves. (One survivor would remember the smell of the ptomaine gases coming up from a putrefying corpse in the tomb where they stayed for two days.) Jennings's safe houses were overflowing. So far, Turkish soldiers had left the safe houses untouched.

But the Turkish soldiers had begun pulling the refugees out of their hiding places, including churches, and marched the Greeks and Armenian men they collected out of the city to face firing squads or behead-

ings. As for the women, "Armenian women were to be seen in groups
being guided towards the Turkish quarters," according to a British account. "What became of them? At the last day it shall be known." Near
the Anglican church at the Point, Rev. Charles Dobson reported that he
saw two hundred Christians kneeling and sitting on the road guarded by
Turkish soldiers: "I afterwards learned from an absolutely unimpeachable
source that these men were subsequently butchered. The method of killing, my informant told me, was by steel to avoid rifle fire."

At the American Girls' School, Knauss arrived to find that a band of
Turkish soldiers was attempting to break down an inner door. They had
gotten past the outer door by claiming they wanted to deliver a Greek
priest to the school. When the door finally gave way, American sailors
met them inside with lowered rifles. They backed out. Knauss also received a report from one of the sailors who witnessed a rape outside the
school: "The Turks had taken a girl of fifteen from her father and mother
into an alley. Her shrieks were plainly heard, then the Turks returned and
one of them wiped a bloody knife on the mother's forearm then led them
down the street."

Cabling Bristol, Hepburn reported that he could "not understand attitude (of) military authorities who could suppress disorder in two hours
if so determined." Davis was more direct. Explaining Noureddin's decision to expel Christians from Turkey, he messaged his headquarters and
Bristol, "Believe this is final decision (of) Nationalist Government as
solution to race problem."

The relief committee pressed Hepburn for evacuation of the most vulnerable Americans, the naturalized citizens and women and children—
but Hepburn demurred. Horton had even suggested an interim plan
worked up by him and Lamb at the British consulate—refugees would
be moved to an old Ottoman fort just south of the city and housed and
fed there until an evacuation from the country could be arranged.

Hepburn had two concerns that blocked his growing inclination to
act. First, an American evacuation would be badly received by the Turkish authorities as a demonstration of a lack of American confidence in
their good intentions, and consequently, Bristol would likely be opposed
to it. Bristol had made a point of warning Hepburn in their talk before

his departure that Hepburn should be careful not to jeopardize the property and businesses of Americans in the city by antagonizing the Turks. Hepburn had another equally worrisome consideration as a military commander: the Turks might object to an evacuation of ethnic Greeks and Armenians who were naturalized Americans on the grounds that they had cooperated with the Greek administration and were therefore traitors, for which the penalty was death. In such case, Hepburn would be faced with a standoff. It would be impossible for him to hand over American citizens, even naturalized ones. (He and Merrill made the distinction between "natural born" and naturalized American citizens, treating the second group as less entitled to American protection.) American prestige—not to mention the American public—would not allow it. Hepburn desperately wanted to avoid a confrontation that would require military force, and he knew Bristol surely would disapprove if one were to arise.

The captain grew increasingly uneasy in his predicament. He was caught between the alarm expressed by the Americans with long experience in the city, toward whom he was being increasingly drawn, and the views of his superior officer in Constantinople, with whom he was unable to communicate. His own judgment was in flux. He still had not sent his assessment of the relief supplies that were required in the city. The relief committee by now was unanimous in its view of evacuation, and Horton and others with the longest service in the country worsened Hepburn's dilemma by pointing out to him that an evacuation would take time to accomplish, and if Hepburn asked for permission, negotiations would ensue and probably last at least a week. In the end, permission would likely be granted but on a person-by-person basis with a demand for names and papers—it would not be a general release for all persons. This would inevitably result in an impasse that would require either American force or capitulation.

Hepburn listened closely to the relief committee's reasoning and then in his head ran through the arguments for and against evacuation. He decided that for now he had the stated, if not actual, cooperation of the Turkish authorities, and lacking an "emergency" involving Americans, he would maintain the current situation: no evacuation. If an emergency arose, and he still thought it was unlikely, he would act to remove the naturalized Americans to American ships in the harbor. He gave no consideration to the evacuation of the city's Ottoman Christian residents or refugees.

MEANWHILE THE RELIEF WORK continued. The bakeries remained closed, food that had been brought on the *Lawrence* was running low, and the Turks had shut the water supply.

Nurse Evon had found her own way to deal with the lack of food. Each morning, she went to the YMCA, gathered a group of Armenian men, and led them through the Armenian Quarter to look through the rifled shops and homes for food that had been left behind. The American flag was her only protection, though she was easily recognized wherever she went by her big black-rimmed hat. The men collected sacks of beans, flour, and canned milk. Turkish civilians abused the men as they followed the American nurse, but they refrained from attacking them. After gathering the food, she led them to the YWCA, where they visited their wives and daughters, delivered the food, then returned them to YMCA. "They were, I think," Miss Evon wrote, "the only living Armenians on the streets from Saturday to Wednesday, and the only Greek men I saw were gangs of prisoners, bound together, being driven through Turkish crowds that cursed and struck them."

Misses Evon and Corning and Dr. Post also continued to move each day between the YWCA and the Dutch hospital in a car that had been supplied to them by the relief committee. Miss Evon walked ahead of the car with a cane, pushing discarded goods out of the way with a stick, and when she encountered a body, she and Post would carry it to the side of the street.

Jaquith cabled Near East Relief headquarters that no food was reaching the city and that seven hundred thousand people faced possible starvation: "Many deaths attributable starvation/typhus out broken and local hospitals overflowing/Appalling need doctors nurses medicines foodstuff/Deplorable conditions worsened by wailing pleading women babies be safeguarded."

Then there came an odd and ambiguous warning. The Turkish command told Lamb that the foreign nationals in the city would be safe until the twelfth, Tuesday. After the twelfth, there were no guarantees. By making a submerged threat, the Turks had given him a deadline to remove British nationals. What, Lamb wondered, would happen on the thirteenth?

MONDAY, SEPTEMBER 11, had been a long and trying day for Captain Hepburn, but it held one more surprise.

Throughout the previous week, George Horton had grown exasperated with the way the reporters in Smyrna had been reporting events to the outside world. They were reporting for both American and British papers. Generally, they conveyed a sense that the city had been swiftly and competently occupied by the Turkish army, and an expected massacre of Christians had not occurred. Violence was scattered and light, they reported, and mostly due to hooliganism. Typical of the reports was this from John Clayton: "The apprehension of fear-ridden Smyrna has turned to amazement. After forty-eight hours of the Turkish occupation the population has begun to realize there are not going to be any massacres. Apart from a few looters, who have been shot by the patrols, and a few snipers (who) executed Armenians, Greeks and Turks amongst the victims as a result of private feuds, there have been few killings." After several days in the city, Ward Price, a correspondent for the *London Daily Mail*, filed a story that said, "There are rumors of considerable slaughter of Armenians, but, though there has certainly been some occasional killing and looting, inquiries made lead one to believe that the total has been much exaggerated by the panicky population of Smyrna."

Horton saw the situation as a Bristol-inspired whitewash. The Smyrna consul general claimed to have heard one of the American reporters say of a story describing the true conditions: "I can not send this stuff, it will queer me at Constantinople." Surely, a story about Jennings's effort to save Christian women who had been raped by Turkish soldiers was a legitimate story for the reporters to send back to the United States. When Sweeny had shown up and begun agitating for access to the backcountry to report on Greek atrocities, Horton again saw the hand of Bristol. The old man fumed. In a report to the State Department, Horton later wrote, "Early in the development of this gigantic horror, I heard several of these correspondents say they must hurry away to Constantinople as it was necessary for them to get back into the interior of Asia Minor through that city in order to write up the Greek atrocities. It struck me as curious that men, in the presence of one of the greatest and most spectacular dramas in history, should think it their duty to hurry away in order to write something which would offset it."

Horton saw an opportunity to change the press narrative on Monday. During the day, he had learned from a source at the British consulate that the British were likely to declare war on the nationalists. Horton went to Constantine Brown at the home where he and the other reporters and Merrill were staying (down the Quay from Jennings) and passed the information along to the reporter, adding that the British would cite the need to protect the Christian population as the cause of the war. Horton may have put his own spin on the tip, reasoning that the Christian element in the story would have forced the reporters to acknowledge the killings in Smyrna. Rather than the Turkish atrocities in Smyrna, it was far more likely that British consideration of hostilities was tied to the incursion of the nationalist army into neutral territory at Chanak, threatening the straits. In Brown's upstairs bedroom, Horton encouraged him to not downplay the Turkish cruelty. Brown listened to Horton without making a commitment. He understood the conditions under which Bristol had allowed him to travel to Smyrna, and he had no intention of writing the story Horton was insisting on. Brown revealed the conversation to Merrill when Merrill returned to the house from the late-night rounds with Knauss. Brown knew that Merrill was Bristol's man in Smyrna. He also understood the bigger game, and the outing of Horton as a tipster surely would put Brown in Bristol's good graces.

Merrill saw immediately that Horton was surreptitiously undermining Bristol, and despite the late hour, 10:30 P.M., he went to Hepburn aboard the *Litchfield* and reported Horton's leak to the press. The breach between Horton and Bristol was now out in the open. Rather than attempting to report this information in code via radio telegraph, which was a chancy matter at best, Hepburn decided it was important enough to dispatch Merrill back to Constantinople. He told him to be ready to leave on the *Lawrence* in the morning.

Hepburn was angry with Horton, but now he had a bigger worry, worsening his dilemma: a declaration of war by the British might result in Turkish closure of the port, and that meant American citizens would not be able to leave, nor would the valuable cargo of tobacco that had just been loaded onto an American cargo ship, the SS *Hog Island*.

THE NEXT DAY. TUESDAY. September 12, Hepburn went ashore and saw that violence against the refugees was worsening. His officers reported it from their rounds, and he personally saw the bodies of three refugees, only recently killed, at the Basmahane station.

Nearby, about eight thousand refugees had taken shelter in the gated grounds of St. Stephanos, the Armenian cathedral. Turkish soldiers had tossed grenades into the churchyard, killing and wounding several people. The Turks wanted the gate opened and the people to come out. The Armenian bishop refused both demands. There was a standoff until a Catholic priest arrived with an Italian officer and Italian troops, and they took the women and children from the church to the Quay, where they dispersed into the mass of people. The men were arrested and the soldiers led them away.

At midmorning, Hepburn and Vice Consul Barnes called on General Kiazim Pasha, the city's military governor, to select areas in which to concentrate refugees for protection and feeding. The meeting was interrupted by a Turkish officer who informed the general of a serious incident at International College, which, astonishingly, Hepburn was unaware of. His ignorance of the event suggests he was isolated from the worst of what was happening in the city—and not communicating well with his officers.

On the previous day, a member of the school's staff had seen Turkish soldiers looting the college's settlement home, a kind of Christian community center, and he awakened college president Alexander Mac-Lachlan from his afternoon nap to report it. MacLachlan decided to investigate and told Crocker, the senior American guard at the college, that he was going to drive to the house, about a quarter mile outside the school's grounds. Chief Crocker tried without success to persuade Mac-Lachlan against it. MacLachlan prided himself on his good relations with the Turks. During World War I, MacLachlan, a British subject, had chosen to remain at the college, technically as a prisoner of war. The war had raged in the Near East—at Gallipoli, in Syria, Palestine, and Mesopotamia, and even along Anatolia's Aegean coast, including occasional aerial bombing and naval strikes at the old Turkish fortress overlooking Smyrna harbor—but MacLachlan had sought to keep the school open as a redoubt of civility and good relations with the Turks. When the Ottoman army had turned the campus into a prison camp for British soldiers captured in the Mesopotamia campaign, MacLach-lan, who spoke Turkish as well as Greek and Armenian, received Turk-ish military officers in his home for afternoon tea and cultivated their friendship and goodwill.

Stubborn and unwilling to heed the advice of Crocker about the dan-ger of confronting the looters, MacLachlan was determined to chase the unruly soldiers from the school's property. Crocker decided to go with him and brought several sailors along in case help was needed. They stopped their car about one hundred yards from the settlement house, and MacLachlan and Crocker approached it as the sailors, arrayed in a line and armed with a machine gun, stayed near the car. At the settle-ment house, MacLachlan shouted in Turkish, "What are you doing here? This is an American house, American property!"

Six Turkish soldiers came out of the house with their guns pointed at MacLachlan. One of them whistled, and another six soldiers ap-peared from another house that was being looted. The second group of soldiers took a position between MacLachlan and Crocker and the sailors. The American sailors were about to fire when Crocker, realizing that his men were outnumbered and likely to lose in a firefight, threw his pistol to the ground.

"Don't fire," he shouted to his men. "Retire!"

The sailors backed away, and after covering about thirty yards, Crocker shouted to them again, "Run." They did, with the Turks firing at them, and reached the college unharmed. The action left MacLachlan and Crocker alone with the Turks but within sight of the college. (An American sailor in the college's clock tower was watching all this.) One of the Turks went up to MacLachlan and demanded his watch, then his wallet and coat. Two other soldiers beat MacLachlan with the butts of their guns, and he fell to the ground, temporarily losing consciousness. He got back up and one of the Turkish soldiers told him to start running. MacLachlan stood in place, taking the beatings, fearful that the order to run would provide the soldiers with an excuse to shoot him. Speaking Turkish, MacLachlan explained that he was trying to protect American property. Some of the soldiers listened, but others were goading him with their rifle barrels to run. The first soldier demanded his shoes. At this moment, a Turkish boy from the school appeared and appealed to the soldiers to stop the beating, explaining that MacLachlan was his teacher. He had no effect on the soldiers and ran off to find help.

The soldiers asked MacLachlan what was in the car, and he said nothing, but they found a stick inside and beat him with it. They took the wedding ring from his finger. Crocker was getting the same treatment, beatings with gun butts and the stick, and the soldiers forced both men to strip and stand naked. The beatings continued. The boy who had run off had found a Turkish cavalry officer nearby, and when the officer appeared, he asked MacLachlan who he was, and what was going on. MacLachlan explained he was the president of the nearby college, and the officer dispersed the soldiers. Both men were injured, MacLachlan seriously, but Crocker was able to help the president back to the campus.

It was a humiliating incident—and a serious sign that order was breaking down even further and that the situation was dangerous not just for naturalized Americans. Even American sailors might be attacked. It seems inexplicable that Captain Hepburn would not have been informed of the incident immediately, but Hepburn's own report says he learned of it a day afterward at the meeting with the Turkish military governor. (Rhodes was the officer detailed to making the rounds of guarded American properties and keeping Hepburn informed.)

Even for the cautious Hepburn, it was clear that the city was approaching a crisis. There were other troubling signs: Noureddin had issued another proclamation, which, by requiring passports and Turkish permission, made it difficult to remove refugees and naturalized Americans; none of the Turkish guards that had been promised for the refugee encampments were provided; and news of the beatings and killings of Europeans and their servants in Boudjah and Bournabat was finally reaching him.

Knauss also brought him reports of worsening violence. "On my round at 5 A.M., I found looting in full progress throughout the Armenian quarter with desultory firing everywhere and many new dead in streets especially about the Collegiate Institute (Girls' College)." In the afternoon, he spotted Turkish soldiers on rooftops in the Armenian Quarter sniping at refugees inside the Girls' School. He went aboard the *Lawrence* to report it to Hepburn, who was meeting with a Turkish officer. The Turkish officer gave Knauss a note to take to the city's district police commander, who, the officer said, would intervene to stop the sniping. Knauss departed with Jaquith, who spoke Turkish, and after a runaround at the police station, a Turkish army officer said he would go with them to the school to investigate. At the school, the offficer gathered some nearby Turkish soldiers from the street and told Knauss he wanted to enter the school to investigate. Concerned about the Turk's intentions, Knauss stalled and told one of his sailors guarding the school to hide the refugees inside the building.

"I could see that he (Turkish officer) desired to enter the building and kept him on the stairs until I felt all refugees would be out of sight and when he remarked that it was cooler within than without we entered and while there 1050 refugees in the building not a head was in sight." Knauss introduced the officer to his men, said he would feed the Turkish soldiers a meal, and quickly escorted him out. The Turkish officer said he would post guards at the school to prevent the sniping, and Knauss returned to the Quay.

On his way back, Knauss saw a French officer and two French sailors backed against the wall by Turkish soldier, and the French officer was talking furiously to save their lives. Knauss slowed down, and a Turkish soldier in front of the car pointed his gun at him. Knauss pressed the accelerator and the soldier jumped out of the way. Knauss pulled out his revolver but was able to get away while the Turk was still off balance and unable to shoot. Later in the day, the Turks held a parade on the Quay to celebrate their victory, and Americans along the parade route were forced to remove their hats as it passed by. To make matters worse, small unexplained fires were breaking out in the Armenian Quarter, where the stench of rotting bodies had become overwhelming.

"On Tuesday, a visit to the Armenian quarters was, literally, like entering a 'city of the dead,'" wrote a British officer. He went on:

In the first Armenian street were one or two dead bodies, but turning into the main street the whole place was strewn with them. It was impossible to proceed without going over them. A cart outside a house was being filled with loot from one of the top-floor windows. A Turk held up a flaming-red woman's petticoat, grinned, and threw it to his companion below.

The shutters of some of the houses, that had been pushed to, were opened. The same story everywhere. Families of six and seven dead in a room; the women had suffered; and the place had been looted. Not a sign of life anywhere, except the Turks taking away what they could find. And the smell of putrefying bodies was terrible.

George Horton reported that nine cartloads of bodies were removed from the Konak and three cartloads near the Aydin Railroad station.

"In the early hours of the twelfth," wrote Knauss, "squads of Turkish soldiers were sent out to collect the dead bodies exposed to view in the streets, and by ten o'clock no bodies were to be seen on the more important streets of the Armenian quarter. However, at three o'clock in the afternoon, fifty bodies were seen on one street in this quarter by an American."

The frustration and alarm among the relief committee was growing more intense, the pressure on Hepburn to act more severe. Charles Davis sounded the alarm in a cable to the Red Cross: "Only way to picture this refugee situation imagine refugees some single, families, groups few to five thousand hidden in institutions or huddled here, there moving panic stricken when irregulars begin shooting them."

Hepburn was getting smiles and pleasant receptions from the Turkish command even as the Christian refugees were being terrorized and shot, and he came to see that the Turks were working him. Late Tuesday night, Hepburn talked the situation over with the relief committee's leaders, who strongly favored immediate evacuation. Jaquith pledged Near East Relief money to charter a merchant ship if it was necessary to remove the naturalized Americans. Hepburn, keeping his own counsel as they spoke, made up his mind to evacuate the vulnerable Americans, and he decided too that George Horton would be among those he would send away. He said nothing to the relief committee; he would make his decision known in the morning.

PART
TWO

CHAPTER 16

Fire Breaks Out

I n summer, a north wind blows in a ceaseless rhythm over the eastern
Mediterranean, gusting to a gale in the afternoon but nearly always slow-
ing to a whisper in the evening. Stirred in the vast spaces of the faraway
Russian steppe, the wind—the Meltemi, as it is known—sweeps down the
Balkan peninsula, ruffles the blue surface of the Aegean, and bends the
wild grasses of the Anatolian littoral into undulating waves of green and
brown. As timeless as the ancient landscape it scours, the wind once filled
the sails of Greeks on their way to Troy and Persians on their way to Athens.

In the first weeks of September 1922, the north wind brought a small
measure of relief to the hundreds of thousands of people crammed into
the hot and fetid streets of Smyrna.

On Wednesday morning, September 13, something strange happened.
The north wind died, and almost immediately a new and unfamiliar wind
lifted out of the south. The shift was at first imperceptible. For a brief moment, the air in the city's streets was motionless. Curtains that had been
lofting in open windows went slack and the trembling leaves of the hillside
olive trees went still, but soon the south wind—"Samyeli," in Turkish, the
Damascus wind—was gusting with force, bringing with it the heat of the
desert. The city already was hot, but the new wind was hotter. It was a
strange wind for Smyrna in summertime, and it came as an alarming portent. A few men lost their hats. People felt something unfamiliar without

knowing what the unfamiliar thing was that played at the edges of their senses. The surface of the harbor turned to white chop, the flags of the Allied warships in the harbor snapped to the north, and donkeys and horses standing among the crowds in the hot morning sun lifted their heads and flexed dry nostrils to sniff the danger in it. The danger was fire.

Hepburn came ashore early, on this, his fifth day in Smyrna, went to the American Theater, and met with officers who had made the morning's rounds of the guarded checkpoints. They told him they had seen less looting and fewer corpses, but, in Hepburn's judgment, the change had come because nearly all the shops and homes already had been cleaned out and residents killed or driven off. He motored through the city to have a look. He traveled along the Quay, then into the Greek and Armenian Quarters. Smashed-up furniture and broken doors and windows filled the streets; the arms and legs of corpses were bent and turned in lifeless and unnatural gestures on the pavement. It was a scene to make a man sick, and the captain could no longer avoid concluding the obvious. The Turkish command had encouraged the sacking of the city. He made a note for his diary: "Few patrols were in evidence, and these paid no attention to the wandering chetahs and rowdies that were obvious looters and probable murderers."

Hepburn seems not to have traveled north on the Quay, toward the Point and Jennings's safe houses. It was an area untouched by looting, and there so far had been little violence on the upper area of the Quay in sight of the foreign consulates. Hepburn turned onto Galazio Street and arrived at the American consulate at 8:30 A.M. He found George Horton meeting with British consul Harry Lamb. The two had been close colleagues, brought closer by recent events, and they would continue their friendly relations after both had departed Smyrna. Horton momentarily excused himself from the conversation with Lamb and told Hepburn privately that he now had confirmation that Britain was about to go to war with the nationalists.*

---

* In his London trial testimony, Lamb said Britain had not decided on war, but Horton's account is consistent with naval activity and other reports. It seems the truth was somewhere in between: the British anticipated war but had not settled on it.

As Hepburn absorbed the important news, Horton explained to him that the British action would require closure of the British consulate, and Lamb was requesting that Horton handle British interests in the city as he had done during the early years of World War I. He felt it was his duty as a State Department employee to inform Washington of the request. Once again, Hepburn and Horton found themselves in conflict. Hepburn objected to the British request on principle, but he also told Horton (falsely) that he should decline the British request because the American consulate too could be closed at any moment. Hepburn, in fact, had received no instructions about closure of the consulate, nor had he previously considered it. There was no reason to expect the Turks to demand it.

The situation now was tightening around Hepburn. The prospect of war between Britain and the nationalists—along with the accumulation of Turkish provocations and other indications he was receiving that morning—confirmed for Hepburn that an evacuation was the prudent decision. He was persuaded that he needed to bring it off this day, or very soon. Without having resolved Lamb's request, Hepburn ordered Horton to prepare for departure from Smyrna by packing his personal possessions for transport to a destroyer. Hence forward, as he had been doing for the last several days in his meetings with Turkish authorities, Hepburn would work with the young vice consul, Barnes, the barely experienced twenty-five-year-old Grinnell College graduate from Minnesota. The request took Horton by surprise, and he replied that he was reluctant to exit Smyrna if it would leave the impression he was abandoning his post. Hepburn, soft-pedaling his reasons, told Horton it was his duty as consul general to ensure the safe landing of Americans in Athens. Hepburn said he would personally explain the necessity of Horton's departure to the State Department. Horton had no choice but to assent. No mention was made of Hepburn's anger over Horton's leak to the press.

Hepburn initiated the practical details of an evacuation. He gave orders for the *Simpson* to move from the Standard Oil dock to the Quay, and for both the *Simpson* and *Litchfield* to prepare to lower their whaleboats at his command, perhaps later in the afternoon. Then, with Vice Consul Barnes, he called on the city's latest vali, Abdul Halik Bey, with two requests, the first a mere formality—permission to keep the American consulate in Smyrna open on an informal basis until the United States could establish diplomatic relations with the nationalists; and (more urgently) permission to evacuate Americans, which both he and the vali knew included naturalized Americans who formerly had been Ottoman subjects. Hepburn tried to finesse the issue by pointing out that the naturalized Americans were in the same condition as the refugees in the streets, and he had already had been told by Noureddin that all refugees should go. To demonstrate good faith, he also said that he had waited until the Turkish command had established civil order in the city before deciding to evacuate Americans so as not to provoke fear among other foreign nationals. He wanted to leave the vali with the favorable impression that the United States had concluded civil order had indeed been established. The vali said he would consult with Ankara.

Just as Hepburn returned to the theater to check on evacuation preparations, one of his officers came back back from Paradise and reported that, en route, he had seen fires burning in houses in the city's Armenian neighborhood. He'd seen no effort by the fire department or the Turkish army to extinguish them. The freely burning buildings posed a danger to the rest of the city, the officer said, noting that a hot south wind was blowing, and it was bound to push a fire in the direction of the main part of the city. The houses in the backstreets were mostly of one or two stories, with frail walls of thin, sun-dried bricks, sustained with wooden posts and beams, which easily caught fire. A second officer then appeared and reported that fires had been set near the American Girls' School. He said he thought the fires had been set to smoke out the refugees who had taken shelter in the school. By the time Hepburn received these two reports, at about noon, the fires had grown sufficiently large for smoke to blanket the back section of the city near Basmahane station.

In the meantime, French admiral Henri Dumesnil had summoned Charles Davis aboard his flagship to discuss the refugees. Davis found it a gruesome ride through the harbor. The shootings may have diminished, but the number of victims floating in the harbor was appalling, and the launch that carried him to the French vessel had to steer around them. "The whole harbor was strewn with the most ghastly looking corpses floating out to sea," a crewmember of the *Iron Duke* wrote to his parents on the thirteenth. Hepburn's reluctance to coordinate with the Allies required Davis to serve as a go-between. The Italian admiral Guglielmo Pepe was present at the meeting and said the Italians were guarding seven buildings with six thousand refugees and sanitation was very bad. Dumesnil reported two thousand refugees were sheltered in the Catholic cathedral, also with intolerable sanitation. Neither the French nor the Italians had formed a relief committee; they were concerned solely with their own nationals and protégés. As Davis talked with the French and Italian admirals, two columns of smoke rose from the back of the city, from the area near Basmahane, where the officers had reported the fires to Hepburn. When Davis returned to the consulate, Hepburn informed him that he had made the decision to evacuate Americans and ordered him to stay at the consulate. Davis would remain there until the very last minute.

Clayton of the *Chicago Tribune*, meanwhile, had scored a scoop: an interview with Mustapha Kemal. He immediately sent his story via a merchant ship departing for Alexandria, Egypt, where it could then be relayed by telegraph to his editors. "You can say order has been completely restored from today," Kemal told Clayton. "We do not wish any acts of revenge. We are not here to regulate past accounts. For us past acts are finished."

JENNINGS HAD SPENT THE NIGHT in Paradise with his family and returned to the city on the train in the morning. He got off at a stop before the Aydin station, and as he walked toward the YMCA office through the Armenian Quarter he encountered an armed Turkish mob moving up the street. The poorest and roughest elements of the Turkish population, from the edges of the city, and even from outside the city, were roaming the Greek and Armenian Quarters in search of loot and victims. Jennings took an American flag from his pocket and pinned it to his jacket, hoping it would offer some protection. As the mob passed him, he was absorbed into it and it carried him along like a cork in a stream. He made his way out, flattened himself against a wall, and escaped without harm. At that hour, the fires were still small and widely dispersed, and the fire department was making a modest effort to extinguish them. Soon, however, more had been lit, and they had spread along several blocks. Jennings by then had limped his way back to the YMCA building, which the sailors continued to guard.

By early afternoon, the city generally was becoming aware of the fires. The smoke was visible, and the acrid smell and the fine dust from the tchatma—the local building material, a mix of plaster and wood—filled the air.

People ascended to high places where they could get a look—Colonel Reginald Maxwell of the Royal Marines looked from the roof of the Oriental Carpet Company on the Quay; George Helzel, the Czech manager of the Hotel Splendid, watched from the hotel's roof, also on the Quay but several blocks north; Dimitrios Marghetti took his view from atop a carpet factory in the Mortakia neighborhood, in the industrial north end; Haralambos Spanoudakis, an accountant for the Aydin Railroad, looked from his second-floor office near the Point; Rene Guichet, a French engineer for the Casaba Railroad, watched in the north center of the city from the roof of the French hospital where his wife was a patient; Lieutenant Heaton Lumley of the Royal Marines gazed from a warehouse, nearer the Quay, which was being used as a semaphore station next to the British consulate. Each observer had a different line of view, but it was clear to all of them that the fires were spreading, and Smyrna was in danger.

By midafternoon, the smaller fires had joined together—fires spreading through adjacent houses, crawling over the cotton fabric commonly stretched between roofs and over narrow lanes to provide shade, then jumping streets and lighting still other houses—to create three distinct bigger fires. They were distributed in a quarter-mile arc across the outer boundary of the Armenian neighborhood.

Under the force of the south wind—shifting sometimes slightly east or west—the bigger fires, after sweeping through the Armenian district, would soon merge and roar as a single mass of flame into the southeastern flank of the Greek Quarter, begin to consume the European district, and press along a broad front toward the Quay.

By late afternoon, the crowds along the Quay grew denser and more chaotic as Italian, French, and British nationals assembled for loading on naval launches. The French and Italian efforts were poorly planned and confused. Guards from the two countries were having difficulty moving their nationals through the crowds, which were packed along the waterfront and made even more alarmed by the sudden decision of the French and Italians to evacuate. These were the two nations that had been counseling calm and the good intentions of the Turkish authorities. The refugees wanted desperately to be taken aboard the ships, asking for mercy and claiming false French and Italian national connections, but they were denied passage and pushed back.

The British showed better preparation, and their officers had even rehearsed a smaller evacuation earlier in the week. Turkish soldiers mustered British nationals in batches at the British consulate, and marched them down Galazio Street past the American consulate to the Quay and then along the waterfront to the Passport Office. The Turks checked their identification a second time before allowing them to embark on the British ships.

For the present, Hepburn decided against bringing American boats to the Quay. He was waiting for permission from the vali and for the other navies to clear some of the Quayside congestion.

THE SPEED OF THE FIRE forced Hepburn to pick up the pace of the American evacuation. Jennings and Lawrence had driven out to Paradise at noon and spread word that all American women and children should be ready by 3 P.M. to travel to the city so sailors could take them aboard a destroyer. Hepburn had decided only Americans would be evacuated, not servants or staff at the school, and only hand baggage could be brought along.

Many of the families at Paradise counted housekeepers and cooks as members of their families—these were often long and close relationships— and they protested against having to leave them behind, fearing for their safety. Knauss had arrived at Paradise to supervise the transportation of the Americans into the city, and the American women pleaded with him to bring along their household staffs. Knauss weakened. He said he could not give permission to the non-Americans to join the evacuation, but he would not object if the American women happened to bring them along without asking his consent. (This loosening of his orders would infuriate Hepburn.) The American women ended up bringing their servants, members of the servants' families, and Greeks and Armenians attached to the college. There were about 125 Americans, and they brought along at least 60 others.

Jennings drove his family back to the city in the Chevrolet, which he had draped for protection with the American flag. He steered around refugee corpses in the road and refused to stop when a group of Turkish irregulars—bandits, really—stepped in front of the car. He swerved to avoid them and continued toward Caravan Bridge and then the movie theater. The route took him past the fire, and near the Quay, the car had to pass slowly among the crowds. He dropped off Amy and the children and returned to Paradise for others. The sailor driving the car with the Jacob family and their servants told his passengers to look at the car's floor or close their eyes to avoid seeing the bodies, some of which had been stripped naked. The sailor swerved sharply several times to avoid bodies, but occasionally the passengers felt a bump when the tires rolled over one. The stench of decomposing bodies was sickening.

The Paradise Americans (and their entourage of servants, friends, and families of friends and younger students from the college) waited nervously inside the theater for Hepburn to decide when they should depart for the whaleboats that would carry them to the ship. After Jennings, Jacob, and Kingsley Birge (a teacher at the college) had finished ferrying the people from Paradise, they stayed at the theater to reassure their families and help with the evacuation. Jennings, who had been moving between his safe houses, Paradise, and the YMCA, then decided to make one quick check of the YMCA before his family departed. He hurried back to his office there. The fire had not yet reached the building, but he found an Armenian employee inside, frightened and unsure how to save himself. He was reluctant to leave the building. He appealed to Jennings for help, and Jennings decided to take him to the theater with the others that were being evacuated. Together, they made their way through the crowds to the theater. Jennings told the guard at the theater door that the young Armenian was a servant he had employed in Paradise, and the guard allowed him to join the people being evacuated. "As long as I live I shall never forget the gratitude, almost devotion, that lit up his face," Jennings later remembered.

The American sailors sorted the people into groups of ten, which were the limit for each whaleboat, and each group was set apart and assigned to a boat.

By midafternoon, Hepburn had directed the *Litchfield* to tie up, stern-to, at the Quay. Its anchor, at the bow, was dropped, and the stern was swung around so that it was only thirty yards off the seawall. The ship was made fast to the Quay with two lines as big around as a man's arm, both tied with knots that could be slipped in a hurry. The *Simpson* was brought to within fifty yards of the seawall and anchored, and it swung naturally with its bow pointing south, into the wind. The plan was to bring the Americans to the *Simpson*. He planned to have two motor sailers (each destroyer was equipped with one) tow the whaleboats, two at a time, from the Quay to the *Simpson*. Given the numbers of people the Paradise families had brought along, Hepburn, who thought he was evacuating 125 Americans, estimated it was going to take maybe nine trips to get all the people, Americans and non-Americans, aboard the destroyer. He was not pleased, and he demanded an explanation from Knauss for his failure to follow his order to bring back only Americans. Knauss said the Paradise Americans must have misunderstood his directions, and some of the Americans, seeing that Knauss's concession to them had landed him in trouble, told Hepburn that Knauss had conveyed an Americans-only order but they had chosen to violate it. Anna Birge had brought along four boys who were students at International College and when challenged about them said they were her sons. There was nothing Hepburn could do at this point. The fire was approaching, and the Americans were sup-

porting Knauss, and everyone was already in the theater. He agreed to
load them all.*

Both ships were in position by 4 P.M.

THE SITUATION AT THE AMERICAN Girls' School had grown even more
desperate. The building, which wrapped around a gated courtyard, was
in the neighborhood where most of the looting and killing had taken
place. The school had twelve American sailors as guards and was directly across the street from the Basmahane station, though its front
door opened onto a side street, Tchinarli Street. The teachers had witnessed shootings and stabbings since Saturday when the Turkish cavalry
had first arrived, and the streets outside the buildings had become impassable, piled high with rummaged goods, broken carts, and bodies.

Minnie Mills was the school's director. She had deep experience
in Turkey. Born in Magnolia, Iowa, and a graduate of Olivet College, a
small religious school in Michigan, she had been a missionary teacher in
Smyrna since 1897—this was her twenty-fifth year since arriving at the
Girls' School. She was fifty years old.

That morning, she had seen Turkish soldiers break into nearby homes,
light fires, and spread them with petroleum they poured from tins. The
fires flared under the accelerant and drew close to the school, but Miss
Mills had decided to remain with the students and her colleague Annie
Gordon, a fifty-five-year-old missionary teacher from Canada.

On that Wednesday, the two missionary teachers had responsibility
for the school's students and staff as well as twelve hundred refugees,
mostly from the neighborhood, who had taken refuge in the gated courtyard. Some were also inside the school. Miss Mills had given them sanctuary when they began arriving the day of the Turkish cavalry's entrance
into the city. The people were all women and children. (Hepburn had
ordered the men removed earlier in the week.) The school's staff had

---

* Mrs. Birge's boys placed a plaque at her church in Bristol, Connecticut, upon her
  death in 1925. It reads, "Placed here by her boys, to whom she was a protector and
  friend in the hour of peril. . . ." Haroutoun Casaprian, one of the boys, graduated
  from the University of Virginia Law School in 1928.

counted eight new babies among the refugees—one woman had given birth while at the school—and several women were expected to deliver on this day. Many of the refugees were camped in the courtyard; the locked iron gate separated them from the soldiers in the street. The school had been feeding them as best it could with soup and bread. Turkish soldiers had tried several times to enter the courtyard but were frustrated by the gate and the American sailors.

At about 3 P.M., Dana Getchell arrived at the school. Getchell, as a member of the relief committee, had been moving between the American consulate, the Armenian orphanage, and the Girls' School. He arrived as the fire was moving along Tchinarli Street toward the school, and new fires were breaking out in nearby streets. He saw the city's fire department attempting to put out some but without success. Getchell and some of the sailors brought water buckets and wet carpets to the roof, hoping they could prevent blowing sparks from setting the building on fire, but a Turkish soldier on the street pointed his rifle at them and ordered them to desist. When the building next door was set afire by a group of Turkish irregulars, Getchell decided his effort was futile and the situation too dangerous to carry on. He descended to the courtyard below and told the refugees that he and the teachers would stay with them awhile longer, but there was nothing more that the school could do for them. The Americans would soon have to abandon the building. For the refugees, this meant either staying inside the courtyard as the building caught fire—or attempting to leave and enter the streets, where they were likely to be killed by the soldiers.

At about 4 P.M., navy ensign Thomas A. Gaylord (a red-haired recent Annapolis graduate from Pittsfield, Massachusetts) and four additional sailors arrived to evacuate the teachers. The navy men told Miss Mills that they had come to take only Americans, but she refused to depart without the school's children, principally Greek and Armenian. Ensign Gaylord told her she would come along on her own or a sailor would carry her back, but in any event, he said, she would be evacuated. These were his orders. Miss Mills was determined to stay with the children. The standoff continued and the fire touched the building. Miss Mills planted herself; she wasn't moving without the children. Gaylord had four of the sailors carry Miss Mills to the truck they had parked outside the door and promised her that he would leave a contingent of sailors to lead the children and school staff to the Quay. The truck with Miss Mills and other teachers departed.

The remaining seven sailors, including Petty Officer J. W. Webster of Omaha, brought the children and staff together and led them out the door. "When we left," Webster wrote in a letter to his sister, "we could hardly get out of the door, and some of the Turks fired into the crowd and killed a few people."

The group started toward Rue Rechidieh, the main avenue leading through the Armenian Quarter toward the Quay, but the fire stopped them. They turned back toward the school to find a different route, and as they passed the school the sailors saw that the Turkish soldiers had begun shooting the refugees in the courtyard. The group followed Tchinarli Street in the opposite direction for a short distance, then turned left toward the Quay, wending its way through the cross-hatched neighborhoods without any clear sense of where it was. The streets, which sometimes jogged right or left, were not arranged in neat squares or rectangles: they crossed each other at acute angles as well as right angles, and sometimes the streets dead-ended at masonry walls.

At about the same time, Dr. Post and nurses Agnes Evon and Sara Corning decided they had to leave the Dutch hospital, where they had been treating refugees, to retrieve children at an American-assisted Armenian orphanage, near the Girls' School. They walked about a half mile in the direction of the fire to reach it. Coming through the smoke and litter of the streets, they arrived at the orphanage to find the children—one hundred and fifty little girls in black-and-white aprons—waiting quietly under the protection of Jean Christie, director of the Smyrna YWCA, and Bertha Morley, a teacher at the Girls' School, who, in the mayhem, had taken responsibility for the children. The orphanage also had a courtyard, and hundreds of refugees had gathered there, behind its gate.

Miss Christie, born into a missionary family in Turkey, was a Wellesley College graduate and thirty-nine years old. Miss Morley, from Oberlin, another school with a reputation for turning out missionary teachers, was five years older. Preparing to depart, Miss Morley and Miss Christie lined up the orphan girls two by two to form a column to march to the Quay. Miss Christie and Miss Morley were at the front. Sara Corning took position in the middle, and Agnes Evon and Dr. Post at the rear. Miss Morley carried an American flag on a pole. Because it was officially an Armenian and not an American institution, the orphanage had no American guard.

The women and children stepped from the school's door into the street. At this point, they became visible to refugees in the courtyard, and it was obvious to the people that the orphanage was evacuating the children. Turkish soldiers were standing outside the courtyard gates, and soon the fire would force the refugees into the street. Knowing their probable fates, the refugees came crashing out of the courtyard to join the evacuation party and overwhelmed the column of girls. About one hundred of the orphan girls had passed into the street by the time of the rush, and in the chaos, many of the children were pushed aside, some trampled underfoot. The women and Dr. Post tried to separate the refugees from the children, and Turkish soldiers joined the fray. One of soldiers was about to drive his bayonet into a male refugee when Miss Corning struck him in the face with a fat Bible she was carrying. He went down in a heap.

The women pushed through the crowd and rounded up the girls, who had remained quiet through the ordeal, reassembling the column of black-and-white aprons. Then, the children followed Miss Morley with her flag, as the women led the orphans through the burning streets toward the Quay. The group found its way to the YWCA, which lay in the direction of the consulate and the Quay. Another young American missionary teacher, Myrtle Nolan, was there preparing to evacuate the women and children with the help of American sailors who had been placed there as guards. Miss Morley had planned to stay at the YWCA, but as the fire approached, she departed and took the children, on her own, toward the Quay. Some would be lost along the way.

The medical team went back to the Dutch hospital, which was about four blocks from the YWCA, and found that many of the patients had been removed. Others were too badly injured or sick to be moved, and the Greek medical staff said they would stay with them. The hospital was made of stone and occupied the inside of a courtyard, which offered protection from the fire. Dr. Post directed Agnes Evon and Sara Corning to return to the American consulate with the sailors; he said he would go to the YMCA.

It was close to 6:30 P.M. by then, and the southeastern part of the city and much of Smyrna's midsection were engulfed in flames.

ALL THROUGH THE AFTERNOON, the fire had forced people from homes, churches, and schools, all the places they had been hiding. They filled the streets, moving toward the Quay and away from the burgeoning mass of the fire. From above, they must have seemed like animals trying to outrun a rapidly moving forest fire. It was becoming clear to all Christians in the city—residents and refugees, Greeks and Armenians—that the Allies and Americans had no intention of evacuating or even protecting them. They were being left behind with the fire, the Turkish army, and the lower class of Turkish residents that had turned into a mob.

At 5 P.M., the American sailors at the American Theater carried the evacuees' luggage to the whaleboats and ferried it to the *Simpson*. Then at about 6:30 P.M., Hepburn prepared to give the order to begin moving people. The transfer needed to happen quickly. The sailors moved the assembled groups into the theater's lobby, and then, with a double line of sailors forming a passageway, the whaleboats were made ready at the seawall. Hepburn gave the order, and when a sailor at the seawall saw that the whaleboats were in position, he signaled the sailors in the theater to send the people to the street. The evacuation began. The Americans moved through the line of sailors and to the whaleboats ten at a time. The refugees pushed and pulled and attempted to pry themselves between the sailors; women shrieked and begged to be taken along. The sailors were sickened at the duty, and they were forced to beat them back.

Among the last to pass through the line of sailors was Asa Jennings, his wife, Amy, and their three children. Jennings was near total exhaustion. He had not slept in two days and barely had taken anything to eat. He took Amy and the children to the lip of the Quay, passed them to the waiting sailors, and said good-bye. He had decided to stay in Smyrna to maintain the safe houses. He stepped back from the Quay's edge and watched his wife, who had suffered an emotional breakdown in the chaos, ride through the harbor's chop with the other Americans toward the destroyer. From the deck of the ship, Amy saw Asa melt into the crowd of refugees on the Quay. It would be nearly a year before she would see him again.

Some time after 7 P.M., the theater was empty of Americans.

Hepburn now wanted to get his sailors aboard the ships. He sent Roger Griswold to retrieve the guards that remained at the bakeries and then to the consulate to help load files for transport to the ship. Davis and the consulate staff, including Horton, were still at the consulate. Hepburn wanted them to depart as well. It was time for everyone to leave. There were still sailors guarding the Standard Oil property and International College but since they were safe from the fire, Hepburn decided not to recall them. They would remain at their posts for the night. (He had left guards at International College because some of the American families had decided to remain.) He sent other sailors to move several of the relief committee's cars to an area near the Konak, which appeared to be outside of the fire zone. Eventually, the fire would be over, and he wanted to preserve the vehicles for his and the relief committee's use. At a minimum, he would need the cars to retrieve the Standard Oil and International College guards.

Next, Hepburn had sailors clear a small section of the Quay, just astern of the *Litchfield*, as a collecting place for the Americans who had not yet come in from the Girls' School and the YWCA. It was after 7 P.M. and they had not yet arrived.

THE SITUATION IN WHICH HEPBURN found himself was chaotic. It was impossible for him to know precisely what was happening around him, except as he could see it. He was not communicating with the Allied navies or the Turkish authorities, and his men had ceased making their rounds of inspection. The fire made movement through the city impossible. The heat, the flames, the smoke, the cacophony and panic of refugees— all of it conspired to create an atmosphere of confusion. A kind of fog of war prevailed. The captain was sensible only to the world that contained the theater, a small section of the Quay, and the destroyers.

It would later be established that Turks, both soldiers and civilians, had begun starting fires late Tuesday night and very early Wednesday morning. A lookout at the city's fire station (a few blocks east of the American consulate) had spotted the first fire at 1 A.M. in a house on Rue Rechidieh, the thoroughfare through the Armenian district (and quite probably the route Hepburn and others traveled when they drove out to Paradise). Ten minutes later, another fire was reported nearby, next to the Basmahane station, in a house next to the Armenian Club. At 1.45 A.M., another had sprung up in the same general area at Rue Suyane, in a tight grid of small streets southwest of Basmahane station. As the fire brigade extinguished the Rue Suyane fire, they spotted smoke nearby at yet another fire. And so it went through the early hours of the morning—the fire brigade would douse one fire only to have others set behind them. There were at least five fires by sunrise.

The fire that had threatened (and ultimately consumed) the American Girls' School was reported at 11 A.M.—at about the time that Hepburn's officer was returning from Paradise. It was one of the fires that would not be extinguished and would spread toward the main part of the city. (Hepburn's officer was correct in his prediction about the danger posed by the south wind.) The fire brigade responded to the numerous early-morning blazes, each involving one, two, or three houses, and hooked its fire hoses to hydrants that drew water from a storage tank above the city. Around noon, the fire brigade was forced back to the central station because of faulty equipment—their hoses had sprung leaks. The brigade was sent back with new hoses to meet the spreading fires but forced to withdraw again as the blaze threatened to surround them. By late afternoon, the fire was past fighting in the Armenian Quarter.

THE FACTS ABOUT THE FIRE were established at a London trial in 1924 in which the American Tobacco Co. had sought to collect on its losses from the Guardian Assurance Co. The trial lasted fourteen days, and forty-two witnesses were called to testify under oath, and many more people, including George Horton, were deposed. Lawyers cross-examined nearly all the witnesses; the judge also put additional questions to them.

Everyone with knowledge of the fires concurred that they had begun in the Armenian Quarter. Firemen said they had seen Turkish soldiers and civilians lighting fires with kerosene-soaked rags and furniture cushions. One said that Turkish soldiers had forced Armenian families to remain in their homes as they caught fire, burning them alive. The court stenographer summarized one fireman's testimony this way: "Witness went on to describe he found dead bodies in all the houses he entered in the district and spoke to having seen in a cupboard the mutilated body of a woman. He also saw [the] body of a woman hanging from a lemon tree."

The lawyer for the insurance company called as a witness an Armenian woman, Arouskiak Sislian, who was in Smyrna to visit her parents. She was a nurse, and her parents lived around the corner from the Basmahane station. The insurance company sought to establish that Smyrna had been beset by civil disorder, which exempted it from liability. This excerpt describes her experience in the days and hours leading up to the evacuation of the Girls' School, which was only three blocks away.

> Mr. A. T. Miller [Defense Counsel]: Do you remember the
> Saturday on which the Turkish troops came into Smyrna?
> A: Yes.
> Q: On the Sunday did you see any serious incidents?
> A: Yes.
> Q: Will [you] just tell us about them?
> A: They were stopping people and taking everything that they
> had upon them as regards valuables. In Bouchon Street [four
> blocks from the Girls' School and about eight blocks from Dr.
> Hatcherian's home] two men caught hold of either a Greek or
> Armenian; they killed him and took everything he had on his
> body.
> Q: How did they kill this man?
> A: Two men caught hold of this man, whoever he was, a Christian; 6 shots were fired at him. I heard the sound of 6 shots
> having been fired.

Q: What was the next thing that you saw at this time?

A: After that, in front of our house they caught hold of another man and took everything off him, and after a long discussion between them, they killed the man; they knifed him.

Q: Did you see any other incident of that kind on that day?

A: At the corner of Tchukour Street and Fethie Street [in the same general district at Bouchon Street], they caught hold of another man and they sabred him in about five or six different places, and killed him as well.

A: What was the night like between the Sunday and the Monday; that is to say, the Sunday night?

A: We were very frightened, and kept on praying the whole night.

Q: Could you hear noises outside?

A: Yes, rifle fire—gunfire.

Q: I am sorry to have to bring your mind back to the incident of the next day, the Monday, but will you please tell us what took place on that day, because it is important that we should know it from you. On the morning of that day, were you still at home?

A: Yes.

Q: Did you see any Turks?

A: Yes.

Q: What were they doing?

A: They opened 3 houses.

Q: Were these people soldiers or civilians?

A: They were mostly soldiers but there were civilians as well.

Q: How did they break into your house?

A: They tried many times to get into our house, but we had a big strong iron door. They began to knock at the door with big stones.

Q: Yes?

A: They put bits of iron under the door and pried the door open, and when I got down, the door had just fallen inwards.

Q: Did many Turks come into the house?

A: As I turned my face toward the door I saw at least 100 to 150 people coming into the house.

Q: What did they do?

A: Some of them got into the rooms, and they opened cupboards and tried to do different kinds of things to all of us.

Q: Did they take you anywhere?

A: Two soldiers said that I was to point out the men, and tell them where the men were.

Q: Did you take them round the house?

A: Yes. They thought there was somebody up on the terrace, so they took me up to the terrace.

Q: Was there anybody there?

A: Behind the door there was a lawyer, Dikran by name.

Q: Did the soldiers find him?

A: Yes.

Q: What did they do?

A: As soon as they found him, one of them smacked my face.

Q: Did they do anything to him?

A: He (the Turk) had a big knife in his hand and with one slash he cut his head off, the head falling to one side and the body to the other.

Q: Did you see anything happen to your sister?

A: Yes. I saw three soldiers. They raped her.

Q: Did your sister recover from that treatment. .

A: No, she went to Athens and died.

Q: Did anything of the same sort happen you?

A: Yes.

Q: Were you in great trouble also about one of your daughters?

A: A 3 year old girl, one of the civilians got hold of her and was taking her towards the water-closet; I shouted out with all my strength, "If God sees this he will not allow it."

Q: Was this girl saved?

A: On that a man came in from the outside with a rifle in his hand.

Q: What sort of man?

A: Rather a well-dressed man; he appeared to be a superior officer, or a superior person.

Q: A Turk?

A: Yes, a Turk.

Q: What did he do?

A: He said, "Are you not ashamed of yourselves, you have done quite enough to the bigger people, what do you want with a small child," and he gave the little girl to me.

Q: How did you get out?

A: I took my daughter on my back, and a small one, a sister, and two soldiers took us to another house.

Q: What was that house?

A: On Tchukour Street; they killed my father, he was lying in front of the door, I said, "My father," and they would not let me go near him.

Q: In front of the door to your house?

A: Yes, the street door.

Q: Did you see his body?

A: Yes, I said, "My father," and they would not let me go there.

Q: Then the soldiers took you to another house, as you have told us?

A: Yes.

Q: Were there many of you in the house?

A: My sister, my two children, my mother, and myself.

Q: What was going on outside?

A: Looting and stealing.

Q: Did you remain there during the night?

A: Yes.

Q: Did you see any incident in the streets?

A: A big (burning) pillow or cushion was thrown into the balcony of a house we were standing in. I caught hold of the cushion or pillow and threw it out.

Q: Did you remain in the house?

A: No; after I threw the pillow out I heard people saying, "The house is occupied," and I got afraid and went to the house opposite.

A: Could you tell us who threw the pillows?

A: They were Turkish young men, young Turks.

Q: Were they civilians or soldiers?

A: They were civilians, and they said in Turkish, "There are some Christians here."

Q: Then you told us you went to another house?

A: Yes.

Q: Did you remain in this new refuge of yours?

A: No. We saw the fire was getting closer so we were obliged to leave.

Q: Did you see any incident?

A: We saw two Turkish civilians with a pail and a long piece of stick which was passed through the loop of the pail. Another man got hold of a pillow or cushion and dipped it in the pail, set fire to it, and threw it into the house next to the school through the window.

Q: Did you succeed in getting down to the Quay?

A: Yes.

Q: Where did you take refuge?

A: At the Point.

AS IT HAPPENED, the sailors (including Petty Officer Webster) who were leading the group that had left the American Girls' School had gotten lost on the way to the Quay.

With the fire raging and dense smoke making it difficult to see more than a few feet in front of them, they had pushed on toward the Quay as best they could determine its direction. The setting sun was a bright red ball behind the smoke, and it showed the way westward toward the waterfront. The fire often blocked their way, and they encountered crowds of people who were also trying to find their way to the waterfront, and the crowds pushed them off their intended course. It was like being caught in the middle of cattle drive except instead of dust and dirt there were smoke and cinders.

As they moved along, Turkish irregulars shot at them, and they took cover behind walls or inside buildings. The American sailors returned the shots. The sailors picked up children who fell and carried them. One sailor carried six children through a burning section of the street. It was difficult to keep the group together in the chaos and smoke, but the teachers continually pulled the children who had become separated back into the line—or the semblance of a line. From time to time, to their horror, they lost children along the way. The group had to keep moving—it was impossible to stop for more than a few moments and search for them. And there was yet another macabre element to the chaos: the fire was dislodging innumerable squeaking rats from the buildings, and they had formed into packs and were moving away from the heat and toward the waterfront.

"We were about a mile from the docks," Webster wrote, "and none of the sailors knew the way, and people that did were so scared they couldn't talk. When we went out, we had to go through streets that were on fire and some of the front of the buildings had fallen into the streets. We had all the people in back and every little bit we had to stop and fire over the heads of the crowd to keep them from running over us. It took me about an hour to get to the docks, as I got lost from the rest of the crowd. There were a couple of hundred people following me."

The group needed to move west toward the Quay, but the fire kept pushing them north until they reached Galazio Street, which ran east to west, from the waterfront to the back of the city. They turned left on to Galazio, passed the British consulate and the American consulate, where they were spotted by Charles Davis, who hailed them, and then to the Quay. The sailors led them toward the theater and spotted the staging area that had been cleared astern of the *Litchfield*. Meanwhile, Petty Officer Webster finally reached the waterfront. "I could hardly get to the headquarters building (movie theater), as the people were packed on the docks like sardines in a can. We began picking out girls that had been at the school and sent them to the *Litchfield*."[*]

The staff and some of the children from the YWCA also had arrived and gathered there, and the number at the staging place including the children from the Girls' School was about two hundred. Hepburn was still mindful that he had decided—and had communicated to the Turk-

---

[*] There are at least four first-person accounts of the evacuation of the Girls' School, the YWCA, and the orphanage. They vary slightly in their details but agree on key elements.

ish authorities—that he would only embark Americans. Now he was faced with two hundred Greek and Armenian children and the presence of four very determined missionary teachers. He was confronted again with a decision that brought him in conflict with his orders. "It was necessary on the score of humanity," he later wrote, to remove the children. In his report, he felt the need to justify the decision. He ordered the *Litchfield*'s motor sailer to take the teachers and children to an American merchant vessel, the SS *Winona*, which had arrived two days earlier for a cargo of tobacco and figs.

In the meantime, members of the relief committee, without authority, were ferrying refugees from the Quay to the *Winona* as well. Miraculously, among those who were taken to the *Winona* were Arouskiak Sislian, the Armenian nurse, and her children, sister, and mother.

Still missing, however, were Horton and his wife, Catherine.

AS THE SUN DROPPED below the horizon, the white banks of smoke over the city turned purple. It was an odd bit of beauty—a lilac sky over a burning city—that would be remembered by many who were there.

The scene at the Quay was frantic. People were throwing themselves in the water. Where it was shallow enough, in just a few places, they stood in water up to their shoulders away from the heat, but in most places along the seawall the water was deep, and it was either swim or drown. Some tried to swim to the navy ships. Others deliberately threw themselves into the water to drown. Turkish soldiers on the Quay were terrorizing the refugees by whetting their bayonets on the pavement, working the bolts of their rifles, and drawing their hands across their necks. An officer on a British ship made a note in his diary, "The sea front is a seething mass of wretched people of all ages begging to be taken off."

By 7:30 P.M., the fire was more than a mile long, and spreading rapidly, a single mass of smoke and flames.

Consul Horton was still missing. Hepburn assumed he was supervising the loading of his substantial collection of books, carpets, and antiquities, but he actually had departed the consulate at the last minute to save an elderly Greek physician, who, he had been told, was hiding with his family in a Smyrna factory. The old doctor was among the prominent Greeks in the city the Turkish soldiers had been searching for, and Horton knew him well. His name was Dr. Ippokratis Argyropoulos, a Vienna-trained physician, veteran of the Greek army, and president of the Smyrna Greek Club. It was an ill-advised mission at best; it put Horton in danger and complicated the evacuation. Horton clearly had lost his bearings. He no longer was acting simply as the American consul general. It was a grand final gesture of paternalism toward the Greeks that Horton could not resist. He hurried to the factory, where he found Dr. Argyropoulos, his family, and several Turkish soldiers. Horton demanded the doctor's release, and the soldiers, confronted by the American consul, waving his cane, allowed the doctor's family to carry him out on a litter. They took him to the Quay, where he died. Horton made his way back to the consulate. He was lucky to return alive.

While waiting for Horton, Hepburn had decided to get one last look at the fire from the top of the Gary Tobacco Co. warehouse near the consulate. The fire had not yet reached the building, and he had a little time to have a look. From the roof, he saw three distinct lanes of fire— two had originated in the Armenian district and a third, to his left, in the Armenian district but very close to the Greek Quarter. The fires in the Armenian district originated near the Basmahane station and the Girls' School. He estimated that the fire, by now a single trident moving on three fronts, would reach the American Theater in about two hours and the American consulate sooner.

Hepburn returned to the street, where the crowds where growing even larger. People were streaming from additional back-section districts as they caught fire. "The tens of thousands of terrified people," Hepburn wrote in a navy report, "moved between the Custom House and the Point, and still people continued to pour to the waterfront and soon it was one solid and congested mass of humanity and luggage." Hepburn hurried on foot back to the consulate to check on Horton and the guards, who had not yet returned. He found Barnes, Griswold, Davis, and the sailors pulling documents from the consulate's files and packing them in boxes. It was now about 9 P.M. Dr. Post and Agnes Evon and Sara Corning arrived from the

Dutch hospital, which had caught fire. Finally, Horton appeared back at the consulate. His wife, Catherine, was upstairs in their apartment.

Hepburn gave him ten minutes—no more—to get in the truck, and then he returned to the staging area on the Quay, where he waited for them. Horton grabbed a few additional items, including twelve ancient Lydian coins that had been entrusted to him by American archaeologists and the copy of *Leaves of Grass* inscribed to him by Walt Whitman. He was leaving behind an entire library, and he had trouble pulling himself away. Finally, he, Catherine, his stenographer, an Armenian girl, and his clerk, a Greek—and Horton's Gordon setter, Tye—went to the waiting truck, and they made their way slowly through the crowds toward the Quay. The fire was now only blocks away. Horton's stenographer had put her hand on a wall in the consulate before leaving and found it too hot to touch. Davis left at about the same time with navy guards, and as he departed he saw Turkish soldiers pouring a liquid into the street. Davis dabbed his finger in the liquid and examined it, confirming it was gasoline.

With all the Americans, including Horton, accounted for and in the whaleboats or aboard the destroyer, Hepburn also left the Quay to board the *Litchfield*. He ordered the ship's stern lines slipped from the Quay's bollards, and the *Litchfield*'s hull, catching the south wind, immediately swung around to anchor and lay about 250 yards off the seawall. The evacuation was complete. Only one American civilian remained ashore in the city—Jennings.

The *Simpson* was already under way and steaming out of the harbor toward Piraeus. The Paradise families and their entourage of servants, children, and college employees and the reporters were on the afterdeck watching the city burn.

" . . . as we headed for the harbor entrance one could hear the shrieks of women and report of rifles," Knauss noted in the ship's diary. "The flames and glow of the burning city were plainly visible for over fifty miles."

In Athens, Clayton filed a story with a Smyrna dateline reporting the fire. "The loss of life it is impossible to compute," he wrote. "The streets are littered with dead. Thus, despite Kemal Pasha's assurances, Turkey has regulated past accounts."

CHAPTER 17

"All Boats Over"

With the wind still blowing out of the south, sometimes shifting to the southeast, the *Litchfield* tugged at its anchor chain with its bow pointing south, and it quartered slightly away from the Quay, so that its port side afforded an uninterrupted panorama of the burning city. The sailors and officers gathered at the rail.

The fire by now raged along nearly two miles of waterfront, and in some places it was nearly a mile deep. It had moved diagonally across the city in a mass of explosions and reached the Rue Parallele just behind the Quay. It gained ferocity with each passing hour, and by the time the American evacuation was complete, the flames were shooting hundreds of feet into the air, and the explosions launched fiery towers of glowing red cinders followed by oily clots and columns of black and gray smoke. The smell was nauseating; the sound of crashing buildings and bursting stores of ammunition was deafening. Even aboard ships far out in the harbor, the pneumatic pulses of exploding kerosene drums thumped in the chest and ears of the sailors.

Hepburn stood on the wood-plank deck of the *Litchfield* and felt the heat on his face and arms and brushed away the cinders and ash carried by the wind. Ships a quarter mile out in the harbor had to remove flammables, including canvas awnings, from their decks, lift anchors, and retreat to avoid the blast of heat and fall of ash. The screams of the people followed them.

Backlit by the crimson light of the giant fire, the refugees appeared to Hepburn as a single swaying swarm—a dark snake a mile long filling the narrow space between the line of waterfront buildings and the seawall. Mixed among the people were animals, carts, and crates. Some of the people, crazed with fear, refused to let go of their parcels even though they had burst into flame. Hepburn and his officers and men had been too busy evacuating Americans to appreciate the full scale of the disaster until the ship had been repositioned away from the Quay. Now they stood at the rail and watched in awe. In his report, Hepburn noted the tremendous noise of the fire—explosions and rifle fire—but there was one auditory detail more than any other that stayed with him: "High above all other sounds was the continuous wail of terror from the multitude."

In places, the people were so tightly packed that those who were crushed to death or asphyxiated by the crowd did not fall to the pavement. The people closest to the seawall kneeled and lifted their arms, begging to be rescued by the warships. Their screams and moans merged into a mournful drone that reached the destoyers, the rails of which were lined with sailors appalled and sickened by the sight. Some hundreds of the refugees threw themselves off the seawall, standing up to their chests in the shallow places, the women's skirts blooming around them in the black water as they held their children aloft. Many drowned. Turkish soldiers shot others as they swam toward the ships.

The Turkish cavalry moved among them, sometimes individually or in small groups, stealing rings and watches and snatching young women. Herded together by mounted soldiers, some of the refugees seemed to have lost the capacity for panic. Their exhaustion was complete. Mothers made their blankets wet in the seawater and put them over their children and awaited their own deaths. Some women went into childbirth. It was impossible to calculate the number of people on the Quay—three hundred thousand, four hundred thousand, a half million.

Hepburn could not understand why the refugees did not leave the Quay by moving left or right, either toward the Standard Oil tanks or the

Turkish military barracks, both of which were outside of the fire zone. He guessed they were paralyzed with fear. What he didn't know was that Turkish soldiers were positioned at the two exit points to keep the people on the Quay. The soldiers were armed with machine guns, rifles, and bayonets. On the north end, in the direction of the oil docks, the soldiers were only a few hundred yards from Jennings's house at No. 490. Deeper in the city, in the back sections, in places not yet reached by the fire, some groups of refugees had attempted to leave by finding the road east to Bournabat, the so-called Daragatch Road, but they had been driven back by soldiers who put their rifles and bayonets forward in the fashion of troops breaking up a labor strike.

"I sat up all last night watching the whole city of Smyrna burning fiercely," Arthur Duckworth, a radioman aboard the *Iron Duke*, wrote to his parents. "No one could go to bed. The wind caught the flames and huge houses were burnt in five minutes to ashes and dust. Loud explosions and crashes from falling roofs continuously. Above all the steady screams and yells of thousands of terror stricken people."

The American men (besides Jennings) who had decided to continue the relief work were aboard the *Litchfield*. The American reporters had departed on the *Simpson*; none were present to see the conflagration. On board the *Litchfield* were Davis, Prentiss, Jaquith, Lawrence, and Barnes. Standing with Hepburn and the crew, they watched the city burn.

Then, at about, 10 P.M. the horror intensified. Davis saw Turkish soldiers pouring pails of kerosene on the side streets that led down to the Quay, just north of the Hotel Splendid. The kerosene flowed down the slope of the streets to the places were the refugees were packed together, bringing with it dancing blue flames. He saw another group of Turkish soldiers throwing accelerant onto the barges where many hundreds of refugees had been living for days.

Davis was also convinced that Turkish soldiers had formed cordons at either end of the Quay to prevent the refugees from exiting the narrow zone ahead of the fire. (His hunch was correct—Turkish officers would later corroborate it at the London trial.)

The prospect of the people being set afire was too much for Davis. He asked Hepburn for his permission to use the *Litchfield*'s motor sailer to tow the empty barges in the harbor to the Quay so that the people could climb aboard and get towed away from the fire. He proposed doing it himself with Prentiss. Hepburn judged the ploy too dangerous—the *Litchfield*'s motor sailer lacked the power to pull a barge, and any approach to the Quay by a whaleboat would invite a mass of people to try to board it, which would end with its being capsized. He told Davis he could not take the risk.

Davis persisted. If the *Litchfield*'s motor sailer was incapable of the task, what about asking the British or French to use theirs? Their battleships were equipped with heavier boats. Hepburn realized that it was a reasonable suggestion, at least technically. But he was stuck: Bristol had specifically told him there were to be no joint operations with the Allied navies, and he had received nothing from the admiral since his arrival that freed him of his original orders. An officer in Hepburn's position did not have to guess at the consequences of defying Bristol even indirectly. It would be a career-ending move even in these circumstances.

Hepburn only had to consider the case of Commander Victor Stuart Houston to know the price an officer under Bristol's command would pay for showing sympathy to the Greeks. Stuart had been commander of the destroyer USS *Brooks* a year earlier when it was in the Black Sea port of Samsun. Greeks living along the Black Sea coast were being deported and killed by the thousands, during the Noureddin military command, and missionary and press reports of the brutality had reached Constantinople and the wider world. In July 1921, Houston and another officer on a second U.S. destroyer at Samsun were made aware of a planned deportation order of fifteen thousand Greek women and children from Samsun, a certain death sentence. Realizing that thousands of lives hung in the balance, Houston steamed back to Constantinople determined to deliver the news to Bristol, who, he hoped, would send a message of protest to the nationalists in Ankara. Bristol refused to see him. Bristol's chief of staff said the admiral was too busy. Days later, Houston was at dinner in a Constantinople restaurant with a group that included the Greek Orthodox patriarch, the writer John Dos Passos, and others, and he described the pending deportations in Samsun. Understanding the seriousness of the deportation order, the Greek patriarch left for the embassy and appealed to Bristol to try to stop it. Bristol was furious at Houston for having revealed the information to the Greek cleric, insisting that it was a violation of his order to remain neutral in the war between Greece and the nationalists. He attached a letter to Houston's fitness report that criticized his lack of discretion and his failure to follow orders. Bristol ultimately did send a letter of protest to the nationalists; under the circumstances, he had no choice. But the letter in Houston's file ended any chance of Houston's promotion to captain. Nonetheless, Houston filed a response to Bristol's letter, defending his action in the name of humanity. Houston ultimately was relieved of his command, and he retired from the navy four years later at the age of forty-eight.

In contrast, Hepburn had no intention of destroying his career to take a chance on saving refugees. He nursed ambitions of rising even further in the navy; and if he were to choose to retire, he had only to wait four more years to qualify for retirement at three-quarters pay, at which time he and his wife, Louisa, could return to their town house in Washington and enjoy their lives. He was taking no risks.

After putting the rescue request to Hepburn, Davis stood before him on the *Litchfield*'s deck and awaited an answer. Again, Hepburn struggled with his conscience. He was there to protect American lives and property and gather information. Those were his orders: protection and surveillance. From the time he had arrived, he had been presented with circumstances that had seemed to him to be slowly slipping toward disaster—and it was clear that Bristol's orders were fully insufficient to the situation Hepburn was now confronted with. Already, he had put Greeks and Armenians aboard the *Simpson* and *Winona*. Davis's request was a bigger proposition—a combined American-Allied rescue effort in defiance of the Turkish authorities. It was a step too far, and he would not do it. But he saw a way out: alluding to his situation as "delicate," he asked Davis to approach Admiral Dumesnil on an "unofficial" basis to explain the inadequacy of the *Litchfield*'s boats and ask the French admiral to undertake the rescue operation with the bigger French boats. Hepburn's plan may not have had the virtue of candor, but the gambit would take full advantage of what Hepburn knew to be Davis's rapport with the French admiral. It was not, strictly speaking, a violation of Bristol's order—it was an adroit way around it. Davis immediately agreed, and Hepburn provided the motor sailer to take him to the French ship.

While Hepburn waited for Davis to return with the French response, a message came from the captain of the *Winona*—the refugees he had aboard needed emergency medical care. Miss Evon and Miss Corning were aboard the *Litchfield*. Hepburn sent them to the *Winona*, which was anchored farther out in the harbor. The nurses found that many of the two hundred people who had been brought on board had bayonet and bullet wounds. The two women had only rudimentary first aid kits, and the problems of sterilization and bandaging were severe. Making matters worse, the *Winona*'s captain was in a foul mood, cursing the loss of cargo space and the delay caused by the refugees. The *Winona* had come to Smyrna to load tobacco and figs, and he wanted to know who was going to pay for the ship's losses. Agnes Evon told him the Near East Relief would pay passage for the refugees.

At about 11:30 P.M., while Davis was on his errand, the wind shifted strongly out of the east, and like the breath from a bellows it pushed the fire more rapidly toward the waterfront. The baggage that the refugees had deposited along the Quay's edge caught fire, creating hundreds of bonfires in a long line along the Quay. The people now had to contend with the fires breaking out among them. "The spectacle was magnificently terrible," a British seaman wrote in a letter home. "The stench of human flesh burning was appalling." With the smoke blowing almost directly into the harbor, the waning moon, now only a half disk in the southern sky, came in and out of eclipse.

The only reporter left in the city was Ward Price of the *London Daily Mail*, aboard a British ship. "What I see as I stand on the deck of the *Iron Duke*," Price wrote, "is an unbroken wall of fire, two miles long, in which twenty distinct volcanoes of raging flames are throwing up jagged, writhing tongues to a height of a hundred feet. Against this curtain of fire, which blocks out the sky, are silhouetted the towers of the Greek churches, the domes of the mosques, and the flat square roofs of the houses. All Smyrna's warehouses, business buildings, and European residences, with others behind them, burned like furious torches."

Another British observer, a twenty-nine-year-old seaman aboard the

Maine, the hospital ship, described an even more horrible sight: refugees hanging in the water from the piers along the Quay and "Turkish soldiers coming along and deliberately severing the victims' arms resulting in hundreds of bodies falling to their death in the sea."

Within the hour, Davis was back on the *Litchfield* and reported that Dumesnil was still ashore, directing the French evacuation, which like the Italian effort was a mess. After talking with Hepburn, Davis got back into the launch and went to the *Iron Duke* to appeal to Admiral de Brock. Again, Hepburn distanced himself from the request and remained on board the *Litchfield.* His principal worry was the safety of his guards at the Standard Oil pier and at Paradise. It was now past midnight, and he had been out of communication with them for about twelve hours. At 1:30 A.M., the fire breached the line of buildings along the waterfront just south of the American Theater near a second smaller movie theater, the Cine Pathé. It burst into a ball of flame and sent the fire moving north along the Quay. It reached the American Theater, and the sailors aboard the *Litchfield* who had been inside it only hours earlier watched the flames wrap around the theater's marquee. Referring to the final dance scene in the film *El Dorado,* the sign advertised, LE DANSE DU MORTE, THE DANCE OF DEATH.

About this time, Davis boarded the *Iron Duke,* a dreadnought battleship that was twice as long and wide as the *Litchfield.* At roughly twenty times the tonnage of the *Litchfield,* it carried a crew and officer corps of a thousand men. A serious floating edifice wrapped in twelve inches of armor, the battleship's very presence was intimidating. It bristled with ten 13.5-inch guns in five turrets, and a secondary battery (for close engagement) of twelve 6-inch guns. It also carried antiaircraft guns and four torpedo tubes.

Davis asked to speak with de Brock. He was told that the admiral was sleeping but that he would be awakened. De Brock was not only the senior British naval officer at Smyrna—he was commander of the entire British Mediterranean Fleet, the biggest force in the British navy. A veteran of North Sea engagements during World War I, including the Battle of Jutland, where he had served as chief of staff to the fleet commander, de Brock had movie-star good looks: He stood tall and straight and had a strong jaw, square face, thick dark hair. He had been a brilliant student and remained a voracious reader, fitting out a room on the ship as his private library. But he was not without his critics—most especially his chief of staff Captain Barry Domvile, who considered him moody, difficult, and mercurial. Davis went below and put his proposition to de Brock. As Davis and de Brock talked, they made their way to the ship's deck from where they could see the fire, and Davis told de Brock that Turks had blocked the exits from the Quay with machine guns and that they were pouring kerosene into the streets.

Davis put the rescue request to de Brock—could he employ his motor sailers to bring the barges around to the Quay?

Like Hepburn, de Brock was in a tight spot—though a much more dangerous one. De Brock's problem was that Britain might soon be at war with the Turkish nationalists. Only the day before, Mustapha Kemal had insulted Lamb when Lamb had called on him to protest the destruction of British property. After making Lamb wait to see him, Kemal had insinuated Britain and the nationalists were at war. The slight had been telegraphed to the Foreign Office, and de Brock had sent Domvile to Kemal that morning with a stiff note asking him to confirm or deny whether a state of war existed between Britain and the nationalists. In a note delivered to the *Iron Duke* only seven hours earlier, Kemal had retreated, saying it had been a misunderstanding. Nonetheless, circumstances pointed toward imminent hostilities between Britain and the nationalists. De Brock had been in regular cable communication with London about war preparations. The British cabinet had decided that British troops should be moved to Gallipoli to hold the peninsula if the Turks attempted to take it. (French troops were already garrisoned there, but the British had plenty of reason to wonder if the French would fight the nationalists, with whom they had developed warm relations.) The cabinet had decided that the nationalists should not be allowed to cross the Dardanelles, even if it required sinking their transports. "The maintenance of the deep water separating Asia and Europe was a cardinal British interest," London told de Brock, "and any attempt of the Kemalists to occupy the Gallipoli Peninsula should be resisted by force." To add urgency, de Brock had just received a radio report from the battleship

Ajax, positioned in the Dardanelles, that Turkish cavalry and two divisions of infantry were approaching Chanak. The British were preparing to engage them. With all this on his mind, the admiral was not inclined to risk a rescue operation. It was not in his nature—nor was it a wise military decision. A rescue attempt would create an extended moment of British naval vulnerability. He declined Davis's request.

Domvile was present and listened to the American, whom he had met earlier in the day aboard the *Iron Duke* and didn't especially like. He considered him slovenly and fat, and he was irritated that the ever-earnest Davis had mooched his pipe tobacco at their earlier meeting. But Domvile was aware of the suffering on the Quay and he knew de Brock to take a painfully long time to make decisions though he would admit that those decisions usually turned out to be correct. Domvile also knew de Brock was a worrier, obsessed with the second-guessing of his superiors. Picking up where Davis had left off, Domvile made a passionate appeal to de Brock to save lives. The elder officer listened, and as he was listening, another officer came to him and declared, "My God, Admiral, they are throwing kerosene over the women and children. We have got to send in the boats." As it happened, the officers and crew of the *Iron Duke* had been looking to shore through binoculars as Davis, Domvile, and de Brock were discussing the situation and witnessed the splashing of an accelerant on the Quay.

De Brock was moved and assented to a rescue, but he judged that even the *Iron Duke*'s motor sailers were inadequate to the task of moving the barges. He would try to bring boats directly to the seawall. It would be impossible to evacuate all the people on the Quay—Brock knew this, of course—but he and his officers and men would attempt to bring off as many as they could. At 2:40 A.M., he gave the order: "All boats over." It was immediately transmitted to the other British ships in the harbor, and then spread to the crews by the blasts of the bosun's whistles.

In minutes, British boats—a few with motor power, most with oarsmen—were in the harbor moving toward the Quay. It hadn't taken long to launch the boats—nearly all the British sailors had been out of their hammocks and on deck watching the fire. The commanding officers of the British ships also boarded the boats and joined the rescue.

Captain Thesiger, the officer who had halted the column of Turkish cavalry on its entrance to Smyrna and commanded the battleship HMS *King George* V, was among those in a picket boat sent to the Quay. At the same time, Domvile went ashore with forty British marines and a crew of stretcher bearers to evacuate a British maternity hospital between the Point and the Aydin Railroad station that had been missed earlier in the day.

Watching from the *Litchfield*, Hepburn admitted that the alacrity with which the British boats were launched and the vigor displayed by the oarsmen made a "stirring spectacle." The British sailors had their hearts in it—as undoubtedly the American sailors would have if they had been allowed to participate. Within minutes of Davis's return to the *Litchfield*, the first British whaleboats and power launches reached the Quay. The warships aimed their searchlights on the Quay to help with the work, though the fire provided plenty of light.

The British boats were met by frantic men and women, and the rush made the loading dangerous. The boats tried different techniques and found that the best approach was to put armed men ashore to separate out a single boatload of people at a time; then a boat would come to the seawall and board the refugees who had been separated. Each boat was loaded to its full capacity and sent off. Sometimes the refugees on the Quay could not stand the disappointment of being left behind and jumped into the water and attempted to hold to the sides of the boats. Fearing that the boats might capsize, the sailors had to beat their hands loose from the gunwales.

Lieutenant Commander C. H. Drage of the HMS *Cardiff*, a battle cruiser, approached the Quay in a whaleboat when a cutter (a larger power boat) came alongside and made first contact with the seawall. The men in the boat jumped to the Quay but were swept back by a wave of terrified people who ended up in the boat on top of the sailors. Drage, twenty-five years old, brought his bow to the seawall and put ashore a sailor, who continued to hold the boat's painter—the short rope attached to its bow. A woman took the painter from him, and she and others jumped in the boat. The sailor was left onshore as the boat pulled away. (The woman had also taken his pistol.) He was picked up by another boat.

As Drage and his men took their first load of refugees to a Swedish merchant ship anchored in the harbor, they met a motor sailer from the *King George* circling a capsized caique, searching for survivors. Drage and his men joined the search, and Drage spotted a woman in the water. Her throat had been slashed, though apparently not enough to kill her. She had drowned. A baby was bobbing next to her just below the surface. He pulled it from the water by one leg and shook and slapped it. "Look out, sir," said one of the oarsmen. "That baby's alive. It's crying." He took it aboard the *Cardiff,* where the men cared for it, and eventually it was deposited, on a subsequent sea cruise, at a Russian monastery.

On yet more trips to gather more refugees, Drage went ashore with his men and a few stretchers at the hottest part of the Quay, where there were few or no refugees, reducing the likelihood of people jumping into the boat. He found them "stupid with fear." He and the men held the stretchers between them, cutting off the ten or so people that they could safely load and pushed them along the Quay until they reached the boat, giving them one final push over the seawall and into the boat.

The British boats took the refugees to all ships in the harbor that would take them—merchant ships, British warships, the British hospital ship, the *Litchfield.* In the early hours of the morning, British whale-boats, motor launches, and a picket boat crisscrossed the harbor. (The picket boat, a substantial steam-powered vessel, had been lowered from the *Iron Duke.*) In many cases, the motor launches towed a line of British pulling boats.

Once the refugees realized the warships would take them aboard, they didn't wait for the boats to pick them up—they used every means possible to get out to them, overloading small fishing boats or lying on floating wood and paddling with their hands. Refugees swam to the *Litchfield* and begged to be brought aboard. The crew dropped lines, and they were hauled up. One American sailor went over the side of the ship with a rope and hung in the water to help refugees climb to a metal ladder that had been lowered but did not quite reach the waterline. Drage and his crew brought a load of refugees to the *Litchfield* that included an old woman who could not walk. She had been carried on her sister's back to the Quay. With difficulty, the men carried her up the metal ladder.

At the same time, the French and Italians were continuing their ill-planned evacuation, and the motor sailers from their ships were also pulling whaleboats to and from the Quay with their nationals and protégés. Near the Point, not far from Jennings's house at No. 490, where Turkish soldiers were posted, British sailors saw soldiers pouring more kerosene on the pavement. Shots were fired, and a British officer was wounded in the leg.

"One of the saddest cases I met," a British sailor remembered, "was that of a little girl of nine who was with her father, mother and baby in arms were making their way to the (British) boats when their parents were shot dead. This little girl picked the baby up off the ground and dashing through the flames reached the boat. She was attended for burned legs." A British officer described an "Awful scene with hysterical women as they crept up the ladder to the quarter deck, embracing every sailor and officer they could see, kissing the deck, etc. Water was provided for all. Some women wouldn't let anyone near them and moaned and yelled in terror that we were Turks."

Before daybreak, about twenty thousand refugees had been taken off in the British effort, and the *Iron Duke* had departed for Chanak to face the mounting crisis with the nationalists. HMS *Cardiff* and HMS *Serapis*, a destroyer, remained at Smyrna to assist in further evacuation of refugees.

Hepburn had limited the American participation to clearing the propeller of one of the British launches (debris and corpses were a problem) and serving coffee to British sailors who had worked themselves to exhaustion. The refugees aboard the *Litchfield* were fed, but Hepburn—still conflicted—faced the question of whether he should return them to shore after the fire had died down.

At about 4 A.M., the captain called together Davis, Jaquith, Barnes, and the others to discuss options. The relief workers strongly opposed returning the refugees to the Quay. Hepburn decided he would put the refugees on board the USS *Edsall* when it arrived and send them to Salonika with enough flour to last several days. (The *Edsall* had been dispatched from Constantinople with more relief supplies for Smyrna.) Hepburn knew he was taking a fateful step by transporting Ottoman subjects. He had already composed his defense: under the extreme circumstances, it was a necessary act of humanity. (That had also been Commander Houston's justification.) As Hepburn met with the relief committee, the *Edsall* was steaming through the Dardanelles at an "economical speed," as ordered by Bristol, with four hundred bags of Near East Relief flour and eight thousand loaves of bread—a fraction of what would be needed. It expected to arrive in Smyrna at 8 A.M. Merrill and four men from Standard Oil were aboard. Hepburn radioed the *Edsall*'s commander, Lieutenant Commander Halsey Powell, with a message directing him to steam more rapidly—he wanted the ship in the harbor by first light.

On its way to Smyrna, the *Edsall* passed several Greek steamers ferrying refugees across the Sea of Marmara, and as it reached the Dardanelles, the crimson glow of Smyrna appeared in the night sky. The smoke from the giant fire, carried on the south wind, soon reached Constantinople, and the Smyrna catastrophe would be revealed there as an acrid smell in the back of the nose.

CHAPTER 18

Morning After

The sun rose Thursday morning, September 14, on a city that was still burning and a harbor whose surface was pocked with the bobbing bodies of refugees. A British ship spotted the body of a Greek soldier who had been nailed to a wood door, in the manner of a crucifixion, and set adrift. A burlap bag containing the form of a standing body unsettled the crew of another British ship when it became fixed against the ship's hull. Some of the sailors added weight to sink the bag and remove the gruesome sight.

The fire had turned the line of waterfront buildings along the middle section of the Quay into a charred carcass, and the flames now were chewing their way north and south of the American Theater, though they remained at least a quarter mile from Jennings's first safe house. New fires were being lit, and areas that had seemed spent roared back into flames.

It was not to be a one-day fire. It was a natural thing for the people to hope that the inferno would have exhausted itself in the fury of the previous night, and that somehow the fire would fit itself into the comprehensible unit of a single day and night—one turn of a wheel of suffering, beginning and ending with the rising sun. But the morning of Thursday, September 14, did not dawn on a blaze that had gone out. The fire would last another two days, and after new fires were started this day, the fury of the fire on Thursday night would surpass the previous night.

The only solace for the refugees was that they had gained new places to hide from the flames. In distressed and fatigued packs, they moved down rubble-strewn streets to burned-out areas, where they sought safety in the interstices of collapsed buildings. Not all of them left the Quay. From the ships, sailors watched women who walked up and down the promenade, laughing; one was fully naked, holding her child. They had gone mad, broken by the night of fear and panic.

The British rescue effort of the previous night started up again in the morning, fitfully, and on a more modest scale now that the refugees could get out of the way of the fire. Until midmorning, the British boats continued to take refugees to merchant ships. British sailors, in their white pith helmets, hauled them up ladders; sometimes the refugees were naked, and the sailors placed them half dead on the decks of the vessels. Some refugees attempted to gain the ships on their own. A woman and her young son approached the merchant ship SS *Sardegna* in a small boat and begged to be brought aboard. With the ship full, the captain refused. Exhausted, she threw herself into the water to drown. The crew fished her out and brought her and her young son aboard.

AGNES EVON, DEFYING ORDERS and feuding with the *Winona*'s captain over his unwillingness to take more refugees aboard, went ashore in the early morning and found more than fifty orphan girls in their black-and-white blouses and aprons who had been lost on the previous day's march from the orphanage. They were huddled on the southern end of the Quay with Miss Morley. As it happened, Miss Morley had arrived at the Quay the previous night without knowing the evacuation plan; she intended to spend the night with the children on the waterfront. Vice Consul Park also was apparently confused by the evacuation planning, and seeing her on the Quay with the children, told her to bring them to the Passport Pier, where they would be put aboard boats and taken to the *Winona*. Miss Morley had fought her way toward the pier, unsuccessfully, losing children along the way. The crowd made it impossible for her to reach the pier. So she turned back in the direction of the consulate, where she saw the space cleared by Hepburn for late arrivals, and she was taken aboard the *Litchfield* but without many of the children, who had become lost in the chaos. "Those in the crowd I could find were taken," she later wrote, "but I could not see many." In the morning, she had gone ashore, weaving through the mass of people rounding up the children she had lost, and now she had them gathered by the pier.

Hepburn sent navy boats to the seawall to fetch her and the children, but the wind had come up, and waves in the harbor made the job difficult. The boats rose and fell and slapped against the seawall, making the footing dangerous and everyone wet. Nonetheless, the sailors, working carefully, loaded them all one by one and took them to the *Winona*.

By now, Hepburn had acknowledged, at least to himself, that Bristol's orders were obsolete. The situation that had unfolded before him overnight mocked those orders. Either through naïveté or the admiral's unwillingness to acknowledge the consequences of a nationalist occupation of Smyrna, the orders had proven to be destructive—to human life as well as American property. The Standard Oil docks had been spared, but tens of millions of dollars of American property had gone up in flames.

The enormity of the relief operation that would be required was apparent to Hepburn. So was the need to evacuate the entire Christian population of Smyrna—in fact of all Asia Minor. It was an extraordinary thing to contemplate, removing an entire population, but an unavoidable conclusion for an officer who considered himself a realist. If these people remained, they would die of starvation or disease or be killed by the hostile population around them. An undertaking of such magnitude was far beyond the capacity of the relief committee—maybe even of a single foreign government. Even after a decade of slaughter, there were more than a million Christians remaining in Anatolia.

"It appeared to me now," Hepburn later wrote, "that the fire had entirely changed the aspect of the matter." The only feasible path forward was cooperation between the Allies and the United States. Still, Hepburn was reluctant to act on his own. In the morning, he sent Charles Davis to the other senior naval officers aboard the Allied ships to convey his view that an international effort was needed and they should meet for a conference to discuss the proposition. Always proceeding with caution, Hepburn would later note in his report, "My instructions forbade any joint action with foreign naval forces, but I felt sure that they did not contemplate inaction in the face of a purely humanitarian emergency almost without parallel in history and which, in my opinion, could be met in no other way."

The USS *Lawrence*, returning from Constantinople, steamed into the harbor at 10 A.M. It had passed Greek merchant ships moving toward the Turkish coast of the Sea of Marmara to pick up the tens of thousands of refugees who were stranded there. Hepburn directed the *Lawrence* to the anchorage by the Standard Oil pier, where it was able to report to him that all was well with the navy sailors who had spent the night guarding the facility. He was relieved at the news.

At noon, Davis returned from his meeting with the Allied admirals with disappointing news: they had declined a joint conference for now and suggested instead that each of the officers forcefully present the case for a coordinated relief effort to his respective government and wait for directions before initiating a relief plan. The Allied admirals had also concluded that it would be necessary, before proceeding, to obtain assurances from the Turks that a relief effort would be allowed and relief workers and sailors from the three nations would be given unmolested access to the city and the refugees.

The relief committee members who had spent the night aboard the *Litchfield* returned to shore. Jennings, who had remained on the Quay looking after the women and children in his safe houses, was exhausted and tormented by his pain and fevers, but he was safe. The fire had not traveled as far north as No. 490. The medical supplies that had arrived on the *Lawrence* would be put to good use there. Jennings was more or less operating these homes on his own. He was a member of the relief committee, but his work, as the days wore on, grew more detached from the work of the committee. He was feeding the women and children in his shelter bread and water, and access to the food would have come through the committee, which was the principal contact with the navy, but Jennings had assumed management of the safe houses on his own. The gap between Jennings and Jacob, the boss who didn't want him from the start, seems never to have closed. Jacob remained a leader of the relief committee, but he seems to have had little contact with Jennings in the days leading up to the fire and immediately afterward. In a detailed memo that he later sent to YMCA headquarters describing events in Smyrna, he never mentioned Jennings's safe houses or his walking circuits of the city to find and rescue women and children. Jennings appears to have made the best of Jacob's indifference. "We gathered in here [the house at 490] also many children left alone without protection on the streets as the result of the death of their parents, many of whom were massacred in the presence of their children," he later wrote. "It became evident that one house could not hold all who expected our protection so we also assumed the supervision of several other houses along the Quay . . ." In all this, Jennings had the help of a prominent Greek resident of Smyrna, a lawyer, who joined him at the safe houses after Jennings had rescued him following the Turkish entry into the city. The lawyer took control of one of the safe houses and served as a translator for Jennings. (Few of the people in his houses spoke English.)

Davis and Jaquith made arrangements to feed the refugees, but they intended to set up feeding stations only on the Quay. The roaming bands of irregular soldiers and rough civilians made it too dangerous to venture away from the sight of the ships and into the smoldering ruins, even though that's where many of the people had drifted in search of safety. The committee had flour but insufficient bread—the supply had been exhausted.

Fear of the Turkish soldiers had not subsided, and some refugees sought to hide in wrecked buildings or the basements of homes that had burned. Those who had family or village connections had tried to stay together, and the Americans searched along the Quay for those who had been under their protection before the fire. Incredibly, the Paterson warehouse on the Quay, which the committee had used to store flour and other items, had not been destroyed, and Hepburn placed guards at its entrance to protect its contents.

The situation was more than discouraging. It was a monumental calamity without any semblance of an adequate response—or even the plan for an eventual response or a path toward a plan. Jaquith told Hepburn that the Near East Relief would pay the costs of evacuating Greeks and Armenians who had been associated with the American charitable organizations in the city. The problem was finding ships to charter. The job was given to Vice Consul Barnes, who would be singularly unsuccessful. He seems not to have sent any messages to Bristol requesting transports.* The captain of the *Winona* agreed to take more refugees on board, but he demanded a letter from Hepburn justifying his deviation from orders. He also wanted to be paid. Hepburn provided the letter, and children who had an American connection, through the school or the orphanage, were taken to the *Winona*. The Turks did not interfere. The *Winona* departed at 4:30 P.M. with two thousand refugees aboard.

Jaquith radioed a message to the Near East Relief office in New York: "The survivors perhaps 250,000 must be removed. Turkish officials forbid repatriation. Fifty thousand should be removed immediately." He said he needed at least a million dollars for relief and repatriation. "Bring all possible pressure," he advised his New York colleagues, who had repeatedly demonstrated an ability to raise large sums of money from the sympathetic American public. The condition and treatment of the refugees appalled Irving Thomas, the managing director of Standard Oil in the Near East now back in the city, and he cabled the Laura Spellman Rockefeller Foundation for financial assistance. His anger over the Turkish actions at Smyrna would open a split between him and his close friend Bristol. Charles Davis, for his part, pressed the American Red Cross for additional help—beyond the $50,000 that Bristol had sought.

It seemed impossible that the situation could worsen, but the relief committee brought Hepburn the message that the murderous attitude among the Turkish soldiers and civilians had grown even more ugly. "The impression they had," Hepburn wrote, "was that every able-bodied Armenian man was being hunted down and killed with even twelve-year-old Turkish boys joining in the killing with clubs." It was not hard for him to believe: aboard the *Litchfield* Hepburn himself had watched

---

* The State Department subsequently investigated charges that Barnes had shown a callous attitude toward the refugees, an assertion repeated by American sailors interviewed by Marjorie Housepian in her book *Smyrna 1922: The Destruction of a City*.

through binoculars as a man was searched and beaten by Turkish soldiers on the Quay, then bound with rope and thrown into the harbor and shot. Walking on the Quay with a private personal guard, Barnes saw groups of Turkish civilians circulating among the refugees in search of Armenian men. They found one and clubbed him to death. "The proceeding was brutal beyond belief," Barnes reported. "We were within ten feet of the assailants when the last blow was struck and I do not believe there was a bone unbroken in the body when it was dropped to the edge of the Quay and kicked into the sea." Unsettled by what he had seen, Barnes decided to return to the *Litchfield* and saw three Armenians shot on the way back.

Merrill also went ashore—to get a closer look at the burned city and retrieve from the Washburn house, his former lodgings, Washburn's Victrola and two bird dogs (puppies) that Washburn had given him. The intelligence officer maintained his inexplicable disdainful attitude toward the refugees and their plight. In his report to Bristol, Merrill scoffed at estimates that put the death toll from the fire at more than a thousand and officially dismissed as a false rumor the report that Turkish cordons had blocked the Quay's exits on the first night of the fire. But he was clear on the fire's source. He cabled Bristol, "Am convinced the Turks burned Smyrna except Turkish section conforming with definite plan to solve Christian Minority problem by forcing Allies to evacuate Christian Minorities."

By midafternoon Thursday, the fire had consumed the Hotel Splendid and reached the southern end of the Quay and the Oriental Carpet Co., the British onshore headquarters. British sailors were sent to the roof to try to save the five-story building, which was at the head of a half-mile stretch of carpet warehouses. Despite the British efforts, it caught fire later in the day when the wind lifted. Soon the entire carpet-warehouse district was ablaze, burning, as a British officer put it, a million pounds' worth of carpets "with a fierceness unbelievable." The warehouses were "one roaring seething mass of writhing flames rising to an enormous height," and the smoke and smell of burning wool enveloped the city.

At about 9 P.M., Barnes and Jacob, on the stern of the *Litchfield*, watched a man light fires around the big storage building on the Passport

Pier. Turkish soldiers were stationed around it and did not interfere with the arsonist. After several attempts, the building caught fire and an enormous blaze broke out. The building, which had been a holding place for Armenian men, was packed with barrels of kerosene and ammunition. A witness said the series of resulting explosions created waves of oily flames four times as high as the building. "The explosion must have been repeated fifteen times, of which the first seven or eight went straight up through the building and yet left the walls standing. The eighth or ninth explosion took the centre of the building clean away, and only the end walls afterward remained standing."

Yet fires were not the worst of it. Captain Hepburn and the relief volunteers noted what seemed to be a thinning of the refugees' numbers. He sent a message to Bristol about the ominous development—previously feared and still not fully confirmed. "Number of refugees in sight much less than yesterday. Believe being herded into interior and all such definitely beyond hope relief or evacuation. Within week under present conditions relief workers generally agree there will be no relief problem."

Had deportations begun? It was a terrible echo of the past.

CHAPTER 19

Garabed Hatcherian

D r. Hatcherian had awoken on the morning of Wednesday, September 13, in a good mood. He decided again to check on his house—it was always on his mind. He walked through the Greek Quarter and asked an old Greek man if he had any news of the Armenian district. The man said that some sections of it had been ransacked; other sections not. He advised Dr. Hatcherian against going there. He went anyway, and on reaching the neighborhood he saw that it was under siege. He continued far enough to see the balcony and door of his home, which appeared closed. The house seemed untouched, but the neighborhood far too dangerous to enter. He returned to the house on the Quay.

Then, in the afternoon, he saw smoke billowing over the Armenian district, and he and his family watched from a window in the attic. He wondered if the fire had come near his home—he seemed not able to put his home out of his mind. He decided again to check on it, and again he put on his Ottoman medals. Dr. Hatcherian walked toward the house and found people were pouring out of the Armenian neighborhood. It was as if he was walking into the current of a swift river. He was running into and around people who were intent on one thing: moving away from the fire. He fought his way upstream. Women were fleeing with infants in their arms, pulling young children along; men followed with bags and bundles of household goods. As he got closer, he saw two fires, one spreading on either side of St. Stephanos, the Armenian cathedral. He was still at least ten blocks from his house. A Turk who took him for a compatriot said to him, "We did what was due. You turn back." Not wanting to create suspicion about his identity, Dr. Hatcherian answered, "Very well." He waited for the Turk to move twenty or so steps away, then followed him step for step out of the neighborhood, keeping the same distance between them. At the Greek hospital, the Turk went right, Dr. Hatcherian left. He took a deep breath.

Back at the Quay house, he watched the course of the fire from the upper floors into the night. "Gradually," he wrote, "the flames approach our house. The crackle of burning materials and the transformation of explosives into flaming clouds produces an infernal sight the likes of which I have never seen before. In Istanbul and other cities, I have seen huge fires. During the battles in the Dardanelles and in Romania, I have witnessed the burning of so many cities and villages, but none of those fires has made such a strong impression on me. This fire in Smyrna is indescribable and unimaginable."

The blaze reached the Quay, but not the house in which the Hatcherians were staying. It was unclear whether the fire would take the house or not. It seemed a dangerous proposition to leave the house and join the masses of people moving back and forth on the Quay. He and his family stayed in their upstairs room. In the morning, fearing the fire, the owners of the house said they were departing, and Dr. Hatcherian felt obliged to leave with them. He carried his chest of medical instruments, his wife held their infant daughter, and each of the older children carried a sack; they walked along the waterfront among the frightened people, terror-stricken themselves but without any place to go. They moved toward the Point but heard gunfire and turned back. (He passed Jennings's safe house at No. 490. It was full.) The children began to cry, and his wife lamented his decision to keep them in Smyrna. The children joined in blaming him. "Alas, I have nothing to answer. I join their lamentation and confess that I am the only one to be blamed and, with tearful eyes, I ask for forgiveness."

Dr. Hatcherian saw the foreign navies loading people into boats along the Quay and begged for his family to be taken aboard, but his requests were repeatedly denied. Only people with foreign passports were taken. He was still carrying his doctor's chest, and the weight of it strained his arms. His wife suggested that he throw it into the harbor, but he insisted on keeping it, seeing it as their only hope for a future. Tired, hungry, and without hope, the family walked back and forth along the Quay under the hot sun, jostling among the people and looking for some escape. They found none—they were among tens of thousands of others doing the same thing. People were wailing, pushing, and jumping into the sea, attempting to swim out to the big ships in the harbor.

In the afternoon, the wind shifted and came off the sea, pushing the fire back from waterfront toward the inner sections of the city. Somehow, Dr. Hatcherian found the owners of the Quay house and together they returned to it. From the balcony, Dr. Hatcherian saw a group of American sailors leading a group of Armenian children toward the Passport Pier, and he decided to try to join them. (These would have been the orphans who were brought aboard the *Winona*.) He summoned his family and grabbed his box of instruments and ran to the pier, but the American sailors refused to take them. The whaleboats were full, and even some of the orphans had to be left behind.

"On the open sea, we see an American transport ship and look for a way to get on board a boat to get to the ship; it turns out to be impossible. The waves are high and we are wet again up to our knees. On the Quay, along with household items, one can see valuable objects and human corpses strewn everywhere and we walk through them almost stepping on them."

Unable to get to the *Winona*, the Hatcherians returned to the Quay house and found that the owners had admitted more people, and now there were many people inside the mansion. Everyone waited and carefully marked the progress and direction of the fire, which skirted perilously close to the big house, but somehow, miraculously had not yet touched it.

The next day, Friday, September 15, one of the people in the house on the Quay where Dr. Hatcherian and his family had taken shelter told him that he had heard that not all the Armenian neighborhood had burned—some houses were still standing. Tortured with indecision and perpetually desperate to determine if his family's home and possession remained, Dr. Hatcherian foolishly went back to check on it a third time. He again put on a Turkish fez and pinned his Ottoman medals to his chest; he was joined by his friend Aram Arakelian, an Armenian who had obtained false papers identifying him as a Turk with a different name. Aram also had a home in the Armenian section.

The two set off to check on their properties, and as they entered the Armenian neighborhood a Turkish soldier called out to them to turn back, then, suspicious of them, summoned the two to come to him. The soldier asked their identities to which Aram said, "Thank God we are Muslims." Suspicious, the soldier turned to a group of Turkish boys standing nearby amid the rubble and asked if they knew the two. The boys identified Dr. Hatcherian as an Armenian. Not sure who to believe, the boys or the men, the soldier took Dr. Hatcherian and Aram to the Basmahane station, which had been turned into a military quarters. Dr. Hatcherian showed his Ottoman military papers and service medal, and Aram took out the fake papers that identified him as a Muslim. Aram's papers created more suspicion, and a soldier ordered the two men arrested.

CHAPTER 20

Oil, War, and the Protection of Minorities

The destruction of Smyrna has several backstories. Oil is among the most important. It was the pursuit of oil that led to the decisions that led to Smyrna.

The serious pursuit of oil in the Near East had begun twenty years earlier in a remote region of sand and cream-colored rock in southwestern Persia (now Iran) about 350 miles north of the apex of the Persian Gulf. In the late nineteenth century, European geologists explored the region, and one Frenchman in particular, Jacques de Morgan, published papers and maps that extolled its oil potential. Until the turn of the century, there had been no serious attempts at oil drilling in the Persian Gulf, but the history of the Near Eastern oil industry soon would begin with the encounter of two remarkable characters.

In 1900, a British socialite was introduced through an intermediary to the shah of Persia. The socialite was leading an extravagant life that was drawing down his considerable wealth. The Persian shah was a dandy who had a taste for luxury. The socialite was William Knox D'Arcy, and he was seeking an investment that would float the life that he and his second wife, an actress, were leading in London and at their two country estates. One of those estates was near D'Arcy's favorite haunt, the Epsom racetrack. The Persian shah was seeking an investor who could turn what he suspected was his country's reservoirs of oil into a steady stream of royal expenditure. The shah especially liked to travel to Paris, where he enjoyed the movies. D'Arcy and the shah were oddly compatible in their need to find money to support their lavish tastes. One wanted to make an investment; one had an investment to offer. Out of that compatibility, the Near Eastern oil industry came to be born. The two never met in person—their communication was through the shah's Armenian business agent—but they soon would strike a deal and ultimately trigger a rush for Near Eastern oil.

D'Arcy sent a team to investigate oil prospects in Persia, and when it reported back favorably, D'Arcy and the shah, Muzaffar al-Din Shah Qajar, signed a deal. For twenty thousand pounds cash, another twenty thousand pounds in company stock, and the promise of 16 percent of the profits, D'Arcy got a concession to all the oil in Persia, except for a few northern provinces near the Russian border. It wasn't exactly the purchase of Manhattan for trinkets, but the comparison is irresistible. Following the sale, the shah immediately went on a Paris vacation and caught the latest movies.

After financing the costs of two wells over the next two years, which produced no oil, D'Arcy grew discouraged. He decided in 1904 to unload his concession. A bettor by nature, he decided he had put his money on the wrong horse. But a coincidental meeting with British Admiral John Fisher, a second sea lord and a forceful advocate of new naval methods and technologies, proved to be the encouragement that D'Arcy needed to continue drilling. With Britain considering conversion of its naval fleet to oil, Lord Fisher (and many others in British naval circles) did not want D'Arcy's Persian oil concession to slip out of British control. Britain needed a reliable source of oil since it had none of its own. Fisher would help D'Arcy hold on to his concession, which ultimately would prove extremely, fabulously, and unbelievably profitable. Its success would ignite an oil fever at the very time Europe was organizing itself for a very big war.

THERE WAS THE UNEASY FEELING among many in Britain that war with Germany was inevitable, and there was very little time left to prepare for it. Lord Fisher was one of those who saw the conflict ahead. The help he gave D'Arcy came in the form of a well-financed syndicate with D'Arcy as a director, but no longer the controlling interest. The syndicate, with capital provided by the Burmah Oil Co., chose to drill farther south, and closer to the Persian Gulf, and after two more dry wells, it too lost hope. An order was mailed to end the work, but D'Arcy's stubborn geologist, convinced that there was oil below the sand, drilled a third well, at Masjid Sulaiman. Fortunately, the mail arrived late.

At 4 A.M. on May 26, 1908, the drill struck oil, and it gushed fifty feet over the rig. A young British lieutenant who was present, along with twenty riflemen to protect the operation against bandits, sent the news back to the British government in code: See Psalm 104 Verse 15 Third Sentence. The passage read: "And wine that maketh glad the heart of man, and oil to make his face shine . . ."

Gusher followed gusher, and the Near Eastern oil industry was born. In 1909, the British syndicate was reformulated as the Anglo-Persian Oil Co., later to be named BP, British Petroleum.

ALL THIS, BY WAY OF A WINDING ROAD, led to World War I, the breakup of the Ottoman Empire, Smyrna, and Bristol's inexcusable response to a humanitarian disaster.

D'Arcy was not the only person who had sniffed oil. In 1908, a retired American admiral, Chester Colby, had gone to Constantinople to negotiate an oil and railroad concession on behalf of a New Jersey corporation. He was granted preliminary approval, but the concession was never ratified by the Ottoman Parliament and withered, though it would revive and die again over the next fifteen years.

In 1909, at about the same time that the Anglo-Persian Oil Co. had been formed, a group of well-placed British bankers established the Turkish National Bank in Constantinople. The bank was a front for an initiative to gain an oil concession in Mesopotamia, the place now called Iraq, to the west of D'Arcy's concession. The British bankers worked through a mysterious and brilliant young Armenian business-man named Calouste Gulbenkian. There were no Turks involved in the Turkish National Bank—just the British and Gulbenkian, an Otto-man subject but not a Turk.

Gulbenkian, with good contacts in the Ottoman government, was adept in the negotiating skills of the Near Eastern carpet trade and he understood the oil business. Mesopotamia had drawn the British, Germans, and Americans, and they had each negotiated competing claims to oil rights and concessions from the Ottoman government. It was a tangle that needed a patient deal maker. Astonishingly, after long negotiations, Gulbenkian was able to bring together his British business partners, assigning their interest to the Anglo-Persian Oil Co., with representatives of Deutsche Bank and the powerful Royal Dutch Shell Co. into a single entity. It was called the Turkish Petroleum Co. (again, no Turks involved). On June 28, 1914, the Ottoman government granted the hugely valuable Mesopotamia concession to the Turkish Petroleum Co. The Anglo-Persian Co. got 50 percent; Deutsche Bank, 22.5 percent; Royal Dutch Shell, 22.5 percent; Gulbenkian, 5 percent. His personal piece of the deal would make Gulbenkian the richest man in the world.

On the day the concession was granted, the Austrian-Hungarian arch-duke was assassinated in Sarajevo. The big forces of colonial, military, and industrial competition that had been building for decades among the powers of Europe, and especially between Britain and Germany, were about to burst. Suddenly all bets were off on oil in the Near East.

ON THAT DAY of the assassination, June 28, 1914, Captain Mark Bristol was in Washington as head of the new Office of Naval Aeronautics; George Horton was in Smyrna as consul general, documenting the ter-ror campaign against Ottoman Greeks in western Anatolia; Dr. Garabed Hatcherian was in Bardizag, his Armenian hometown on the Sea of Marmara, practicing medicine as a private physician and teaching hy-giene in the local Armenian school; Theodora was four years old and living with her family in Gritzalia; the Reverend Asa Jennings, recently recovered from his illness, was preaching at the Richfield Springs Methodist Church.

BY THE FALL OF 1918, sixteen million people were dead as a consequence of the war, and the continent of Europe was a shambles. World War I lasted four years and two months and ended in a series of rolling armistices toward the end of 1918: the Bulgarians first, on September 29; the Ottomans next on October 30; then, Austria-Hungary on November 4; finally, Imperial Germany on November 11. "The Allies had floated to victory," Lord Curzon said after the war, "on a sea of oil." He might have added, "American oil." The war had made it clear that Britain needed its own source of petroleum if it wanted to remain a world power.

Oil had twice the thermal content of coal, and an oil-powered battleship required one-third the engine weight and one-fourth the fuel weight of a coal-powered battleship to achieve the same horsepower. Its range was four times farther. Speed was essential to winning naval battles, and oil gave a battleship an extra four knots—decisive when big ships with big guns slugged it out at sea. There were other advantages—it took five hundred men five days to fuel a coal-powered battleship while just twelve men in twelve hours could refuel an oil-fired battleship.

So obvious was the military advantage to a nation with ready access to oil that the United States, beginning in 1910, established oil reserves for its navy, places of naturally abundant supply in the American West that could be tapped in times of war. One of these was at Teapot Dome in Wyoming, a rock formation that soon would become synonymous with graft in the Harding administration. The secretary of the interior took a bribe to let the Sinclair Oil Co. pump oil from the reserve. The first dirty money passed hands in November 1921.

When Britain had met with its allies at Sevres to divvy up the Ottoman Empire in 1920, its eyes were on Iraq—the oil prize of the war. The Sevres Treaty assigned the Iraq mandate to Britain—with 25 percent of Iraq's oil production pledged to France. American oil companies immediately objected. The loudest objection came from Walter Teagle, president of the Standard Oil Co. of New Jersey, the biggest single piece of John D. Rockefeller's old empire, which the Supreme Court had broken up in 1911. (It was later named Exxon.) Teagle—all three hundred determined pounds of him—charged that the British were monopolizing oil in the Near East. The State Department also conveyed its objection to Britain and held fast to the American policy of an "Open Door" on all commerce, including oil exploration.

Britain claimed the mandate did not lock up Iraq's oil for Britain alone and pointed out that Britain accounted for only 4.5 percent of the world's oil production while the United States accounted for 80 percent. The American opposition to the Iraq mandate was so noisy that Britain produced a densely reported and reasoned document, "Memorandum on the Petroleum Situation," that dissected and disputed the American concerns of a British monopoly. Mark Bristol had a copy of it on his desk. He considered it British bunk, and it only further inflamed his antagonism toward Britain—and, by some extension of geopolitical overthink, the Greeks, whom Bristol considered a British client. Secretary Hughes suggested that the seven big American oil companies form a consortium to negotiate their piece of the Iraq oil reserves—and the State Department would back it up with tough-minded diplomacy. (Hughes was no apologist for the oil companies: he had voted to break up Standard Oil as a member of the Supreme Court back in 1911. But he knew America needed oil.) Hughes was true to his word. America would remain engaged, through diplomacy and hard bargaining, on the issue of oil, and eventually a compromise would be found in which the American oil companies and the British divided Iraqi oil.

AS FOR THE NON-OIL ELEMENTS of the Sevres Treaty, including the provisions intended to protect the Christian minorities, the European allies had lost interest, and Americans were staying out of the matter entirely. Harding stood firm on the issue of American military engagement in Turkey. There wouldn't be any. Harding was no enemy of the Ottoman Greeks or Armenians; on the contrary, it was in his nature to sympathize with people. But he had not the slightest inclination to protect them from

Turkish cruelty—either as a moral imperative or as an obligation under a treaty to which the United States was not a signatory.

It was in this political atmosphere of business first, international humanitarian ideals last, that Bristol operated in his own inimitable way as high commissioner. The admiral flattered himself with the notion that he was influencing American oil policy. He was not; others at a higher level managed that important matter for the nation. As for American-Turkish relations, they would travel on a track laid down by forces of political economy and geopolitics far more profound than the admiral's personal conception of a "square deal" and his preference for Turks over Greeks. In all likelihood, Washington saw Bristol as running an expensive but useful taxi service for oil and tobacco executives in the Near East.

But Bristol was not without influence, and the Smyrna catastrophe offered him his one opportunity for a genuine legacy. He could have responded with speed and compassion; he might even have saved the city with mediation. But Bristol was no Henry Morgenthau; of course, there was no room in the Harding administration for a Morgenthau.

Idealism was out; the missionary impulse and rural Protestantism was fading. Consumerism, oil, and public relations were in. Power was shifting. The America that was emerging in 1922 was not the America of 1914.

CHAPTER 21

Bristol's Resistance

After World War I, the navy had sent Mark Bristol to Belgium to help watch over German naval disarmament. He was then sent to Turkey with the title of Senior Naval Officer in Turkish Waters, a modest assignment given the small contingent of American vessels assigned to the region.

As a naval officer, Bristol understood that America's sea power required oil, and he was an advocate of America's oil companies in the Near East from the moment he had arrived in Constantinople on January 28, 1919. He was also an advocate of America's mining companies, tractor and locomotive companies, sewing machine companies, banking companies, car companies, alcohol companies, and tobacco companies. He was for American companies, pure and simple, but oil was his priority.

Bristol's ties to business were a point of pride with him, and he eagerly enumerated them in listing his achievements to his navy superiors. When he was denied a promotion in June 1920 that would have made him a permanent rear admiral, he wrote to his superiors with characteristic confidence, "With my complete file before the board I can not believe it possible that my brother officers of that board could have passed me over unless there was some information attached to my record that is not known by me." (There was nothing hidden in his file.) He had followed up with a five-page single-spaced memo detailing his accomplishments and citing numerous letters of praise from oil executives and especially Standard Oil of New York, where his close friend and confidant Lucien Irving Thomas was a director.

In his advocacy of American commerce, Bristol was no different from legions of others in military and government service. The point that separated Bristol from others was the nasty edge he brought to his advocacy. He wasn't just for America; he was against its competitors, notably and almost singularly, Britain. Earlier American representatives to Turkey, including Morgenthau, had championed American business, but they had done so without Bristol's acidic touch. He nurtured a distrust of the British and a disdain for the local commercial "races" of Greeks, Armenians, and Jews. Bristol believed Britain wanted to lock the United States out of Near Eastern commerce and oil exploration. Like many of Bristol's assertions, there was a grain of truth in his indictment of the British, but he carried it too far, and with Bristol everything ultimately became personal.

All this mattered for one important reason: Bristol was the American decision maker in Constantinople, and it was Bristol who would make the early decisions about how to respond to the Smyrna crisis when it began. He was not going to damage the good relationship he had built with the future rulers of Turkey (and the owners of its oil) to conduct a humanitarian mission on behalf of Greek and Armenian refugees.

IN THE FIRST HALF of September, in the days leading up to the fire at Smyrna, Bristol had carried on his routines at the embassy and Therapia. He had his usual rounds of meetings with American businessmen and minor American officials passing through Constantinople. American businessmen wanted assurances about the safety of their property in Smyrna, and he gave it to them.

He told the agent of the Gary Tobacco Co. not to worry and reassured the manager of MacAndrews & Forbes when they called on him at the embassy. As usual, he didn't miss an opportunity to expound his views, and he continued to take his lunch at the Pera Palace Hotel, a few steps from the embassy.

The hotel was a masterpiece of belle epoche design and a favorite among passengers arriving from Vienna on the *Orient Express*, sometimes carried to its door on the Rue Grand de Pera in a sedan chair. The hotel's ceiling domes were made of turquoise-flecked glass that admitted shafts of colored sunlight into the grand hall, and its restaurant offered an Ottoman-French menu—Tournedos Rossini, Poulet Mascotte, Asperges See Mousseline, Souffle Rothchilde. Bristol had lunch at the hotel on September 8, 1922, with Lord Beaverbrook, owner of the *London Daily Express*. He had traveled to Turkey on a secret mission to make contact with the nationalists on behalf of the British government. Over the meal, Bristol got in a dig at Rumbold but he had to endure Beaverbrook's support of the Greeks. "They had been supported by us and we had left them to be wiped out by the Turks," Beaverbrook told Bristol, whose dark eyes were sizing up the publisher across the table. "Short man with a rather large head compared to the rest of his body," Bristol noted with condescension.

In the afternoon, Bristol rode in his admiral's barge back to the *Scorpion* and in the evening attended a dinner party at the home of a prominent Turk and his princess wife, a granddaughter of the sultan. As usual, the Bristols carried on a busy social life. His war diary often noted the social events of the week: September 6: "In the evening Mrs. Bristol and I dined with Prince and Princess Serge Gagarine in the gardens of the Russian Embassy." September 9: "After dinner we attended the regular dance at the Yacht Club at Prinkipo."

THROUGHOUT THE FIRST TWO WEEKS of September, Bristol rationed his cables back to the State Department, and each was reassuring in its own way. He drummed at three points: the Turkish occupation of Smyrna was orderly and Turkish authorities were acting responsibly; the Greek army had committed atrocities in its retreat toward the sea and Greek soldiers had threatened to burn Smyrna; the Greeks and Allied powers, most especially Britain, were refusing to accept their responsibility for solving the refugee problem created by the Greek defeat.

These assertions were not altogether untrue, but they came with a good deal of spin, exaggeration, and even misinformation laced in. Bristol simply was in no hurry to help Britain, Greece, or the refugees. One of the noncommissioned officers at Smyrna remarked that he thought he had been sent there to protect the American tobacco company warehouses—an attitude that reflected Bristol's actual point of view.

Bristol was deliberately slow to dispatch ships, and the aid he had sent aboard those ships was insufficient. The *Litchfield*, then the *Simpson* and *Lawrence*, had been dispatched to Smyrna primarily to gather information and protect American property. It was not until later that they began to carry significant amounts of food aid to the city, and at no point does the record show any attempt by Bristol to requisition American shipping to deliver supplies or ferry refugees to safety. Bristol had become aware of the Turkish offensive days after it had commenced on August 26. George Horton's urgent cable asking for assistance had come on September 2, the same day Harry Lamb had cabled Admiral de Brock, who had decided to immediately make a run for Smyrna. Bristol had not shown any inclination to send a ship until September 5, by which time he had been directed to send a destroyer by the Navy Department. That first ship, the *Litchfield*, didn't arrive until September 6.

Bristol's go-slow and do-little attitude soon would become a headache for the State Department, and for Acting Secretary Phillips in particular. Faced with a stubborn admiral, Phillips's stiff Boston exterior of courtesy already was showing some cracks.

Bristol was also finding reasons not to work with Britain, France, and Italy on what was clearly a crisis that Britain, France, Italy, and the United States had helped to create. In his cabled repetitions to Washington about Britain's responsibility, Bristol conveniently forgot his country's role—Wilson early on had accepted the division of the Ottoman Empire, approved the Greek occupation of Smyrna, and failed to engage the problems of the postwar Ottoman Empire. Even Harding, as a candidate for president, had thrown his support behind Greece's aspirations. "You may be assured that to do my just part to further the righteous cause of the Greek Nation and of the splendid element of citizenship it has contributed to our country," candidate Harding had locuted, "I will continue to help in every possible way."

Bristol seems to have believed that his personal influence with the Turkish nationalists was strong enough to prevent a massacre at Smyrna. The memorandum he had handed to Hamid Bey when the two had met in his office on September 7 appealed to the nationalists on the basis of his personal friendship. His belief that he could steer nationalist policy seemed boundless. "I am convinced," his memorandum to Hamid Bey said, "that this is the greatest opportunity that Turkey has had to show the world that a new regime has been established and is successfully maintaining the highest principles of civilization and humanity."

Bristol waited three days to send his first cable to Washington following the arrival of the *Litchfield* at Smyrna on September 6. It focused on the problems presented by the Greek army—not on the refugee problem: "Smyrna situation most alarming. Greek troops in panic and pouring into city. Population fears violence between time Greek troops ordered to evacuate and temporary arrangements of Turks. Repeated threats by Greek officers to burn town." Nothing about refugee hunger or homelessness or the prospect of trouble for the Christians in Smyrna at the hands of the Turkish army appeared in the cable. The next day, September 10, Bristol sent another cable reporting Turkish forces had occupied Smyrna and Turkish celebrations had erupted in Constantinople.

ON THE FOLLOWING DAY, September 11, Dr. William Peet, the missionary administrator in Constantinople, was back in Bristol's office at the embassy with Jeannie Jillson, a fifty-three-year-old missionary teacher from Boston who operated a Mission Board school in Broussa, a city in the Marmora region southwest of Constantinople.

Broussa had a lineage reaching back to ancient Greece and Bithynia, the kingdom of a warlike tribe that had crossed the Sea of Marmara from Thrace in the sixth century BC and held the region until about the first century, when it had become a Roman province. Broussa, or "Bursa" in Turkish, had powerful historical resonance for the Turks. It was an early capital of the Ottoman Empire, and many of the early sultans were interred there. In 1922, it was a city of eighty thousand people and the center of Turkey's silk trade. The fertile plain that stretched from the Sea of Marmara to the snow-capped mountain Asian Olympus, on whose slopes Broussa was partially built, was densely cultivated with mulberry trees, which fed the all-important silkworms. Broussa was principally a Muslim city, but Greeks and Armenians who had survived the deportations of the previous ten years remained a presence, and it had long been an important missionary station.

Miss Jillson wanted permission from Bristol to travel to Broussa to check on the mission school and Christian refugees who (it was being reported) had gathered at Mudania, the city's port. Bristol approved her travel aboard a navy sub chaser, a vessel smaller than a destroyer, which was leaving that day. It was a short trip by boat from Constantinople.

On approaching Mudania, the captain of the sub chaser, Lieutenant Andrew H. Addoms, noted that three destroyers, one British and two French, were lying off the harbor and flying battle flags. He went up alongside the British ship, and the captain told him that Turkish artillery had fired on him. The British destroyer had taken aboard a hundred Greek soldiers who had swum out to the ship. They were standing on deck naked, and fifty more were in the water attempting to reach the ship. Lieutenant Addoms retreated offshore with the sub chaser and sought permission to land, which was given. Addoms was thirty years old and from Kansas City, where his father had been in the cattle business. He had thick dark hair and eyebrows and a cleft chin, and he was powerfully built. At the Naval Academy, where he had been a gymnast, he had impressed his classmates with one-arm chin-ups. Ashore, Addoms and Miss Jillson found the situation at Mudania similar to that at Smyrna. Forty thousand refugees had fled to the waterfront hoping for evacuation or protection. They were without food; sanitary conditions were bad.

Miss Jillson and Addoms were discovering what others soon would learn: Smyrna's suffering was not an exception; it was the rule. Along the Sea of Marmara and down the west coast of Anatolia, Greeks and Armenians by the hundreds of thousands had fled, and were continuing to flee, toward the coast, where they met rough treatment—or worse—from Turkish civilians and the nationalist army.

Two hundred French troops were ashore in Mudania, protecting a French railroad terminal at the port. The refugees had crowded close to the soldiers for protection. "The Turkish soldiers have told them," Addoms reported, "that they are all going to be massacred and that everything is going to be stolen from them. The result of this is that all of the refugees are now in a terror stricken state, so that it seems that something must be done at once if they are to be saved."

Miss Jillson and Lieutenant Addoms managed to hitch a ride on a truck driven by a French soldier. They made slow progress on the fifteen-mile road from Mudania to Broussa. It was littered with the bodies of naked Greeks, and from time to time they encountered columns of Greek prisoners, stripped to their underwear, being marched down the muddy road. In Broussa, they found the streets empty except that Turkish women had come out of their homes to watch the passage of Greek prisoners of war. The Armenian Quarter had been ransacked but it was not burned. They went to Miss Jillson's school, saw that it was undamaged, and returned to Mudania, where they found some of her students among the refugees at the harbor. After much searching, she and Addoms located a boat that she could charter, and they arranged through a Turkish official for the refugees from her school to depart for Constantinople. The next day, Addoms received orders to return to Constantinople. Miss Jillson wanted to remain at Mudania, so he put her aboard the French destroyer until she and the refugees could leave on the chartered boat.

BACK AT THE EMBASSY, Bristol, on September 12, was berating a correspondent for the *Christian Science Monitor* for its coverage of the Greek-Turkish war. The reporter, Chrys Danos, a Greek woman based in Athens and graduate of America's Constantinople Women's College, had told Bristol she wanted him to give her the facts about the current situation in the country; he replied he was glad to hear that because the *Monitor*'s coverage so far had been inaccurate and slanted. The *Monitor* had written extensively on the situation in Turkey and singled out Bristol for criticism, accusing him of covering up Turkish abuses against Christians: "He thinks that in that way there can be obtained concessions and other business advantages." The *Monitor* had been especially forthright in its coverage of the deportations of Greeks along the Black Sea.

Bristol suggested the newspaper was in league with the Greek government, and he wanted to know why the *Monitor* had not published the findings of his report on the Greek landing at Smyrna. Mrs. Danos had no answer. (As a correspondent, she was not in a position to know. Those decisions were made by her editors.) Annoyed with her, Bristol handed her off to an assistant and noted in his diary, "Mrs. Danos was typical of the races in this part of the country. She is obsequious and cringing and says she wants the truth but she probably couldn't write the truth if she knew it."

Afterward, Bristol had lunch at the Constantinople Club with Irving Thomas, who asked Bristol for a ride to Smyrna to check on Standard Oil's property. A ride on a destroyer was a courtesy Bristol was happy to provide, and he suggested to Thomas that he go on the *Edsall*, which was leaving that afternoon. But when Bristol learned by radio later in the afternoon that the *Lawrence*, unexpectedly, was on its way back to Constantinople, bringing Merrill and his report on Horton's leak to the press, Bristol delayed the *Edsall's* departure. This information would have to come first. He and Thomas went down to Therapia at day's end, had a big dinner, and waited up late for Merrill. The *Lawrence* arrived after midnight, and Merrill made the trip to Therapia by navy launch. Aboard the *Scorpion*, Merrill described the situation in Smyrna as stable and related the story of Horton's attempt to focus press attention on Turkish cruelty by leaking information to Brown, the Chicago reporter. The three of them talked into the early hours of the morning. It now became imperative that Bristol not only maintain control of the narrative of Smyrna as the result of Greek and British fecklessness; he needed to do something about Horton, who obviously was intent on undermining him.

Merrill and Thomas were up early in the morning, September 13, and met the *Edsall*, which departed at 7 A.M. for Smyrna with Merrill, Thomas, three other Standard Oil managers, and flour and bread. But first, they would steam north to Salonika, where Standard Oil had a facility. There was no hurry.

Back at work that morning, Bristol took the occasion of another British request for the Americans to help the refugees, this time from a British army commander, to send another cable to Washington thrumming his favorite theme. Bristol wrote: "Allies and Greeks seemingly shirking all responsibility and assuming we will handle entire situation." Bristol knew this was not entirely accurate: Three days earlier, a cable from the Greek patriarch in Constantinople to Jaquith in Smyrna passed through Bristol's hands. It reported that the Greek patriarch was asking Near East Relief to help pay for coal to send the steamship *New York* to rescue refugees at Smyrna. Bristol described Rumbold's request for American aid for the refugees and the more recent British request. "I informed him (the British officer) very frankly that I considered it [the] duty of Allies and Greeks to undertake this work, and when he stated no British organization existed for this purpose I told him it was time one was formed and that a short time ago we had not any either."

This of course was not true—private American relief agencies had been providing relief for years. Bristol also reported to Washington, "Generally speaking conduct of Turkish troops of occupation extraordinarily good, discipline perfect . . ."

Bristol ended September 13, the day of the fire, with some pleasant exercise at Therapia: "In the late afternoon I took part in a Tennis Tournament at the French Embassy. I played a match which was very amusing. Madame Arlotta, wife of the Italian Counsellor of the High Commission, and myself played against General Pelle and his wife. They won the match and it required three sets to determine it."

PART THREE

PART
THREE

CHAPTER 22

Halsey Powell

I n 1904, when he graduated from the Naval Academy, Halsey Powell had made a reputation among his fellow midshipmen as "a fine soldierly lad of real old blue-grass stock." Slightly built with freckles and alert brown eyes under gracefully arched, even feminine, eyebrows, Powell was descended from Kentucky pioneers. One of his forebears had entered the Kentucky territory before Daniel Boone. The men in his family had fought in the Indian wars, the American Revolution, the War of 1812, and the Civil War. John West Powell, his father, a Union army officer and slave owner, was a doctor-turned-planter with 550 acres of sweet Kentucky farmland in McAfee, thirty miles southwest of Lexington. The senior Powell married twice; his second wife was Halsey's mother, Margaret Halsey Powell. She too was Kentucky pioneer stock.

McAfee was a place of gently rolling farms that naturally grew the smooth meadow grass whose flower pods turned blue in late summer. As a boy, Halsey would have stepped out the door of the family's white-frame farmhouse and seen "bluegrass" pastures enclosed by rough plank fences and fields of tobacco and corn. The nearest neighbors, a half mile away, were the Dunns, the family of his father's first wife, in their Greek Revival plantation house, Lone Pine. Halsey lived in the woods and fields of Mercer County—hunting fox or raccoon and fishing in the nearby Salt River. Young Halsey grew up as the son of a prosperous and aristocratic family in a place where racial lines were strictly observed but where river trade with northern and southern states had created an atmosphere that was neither Democratic Deep South nor Republican North. Mercer County had its racial haters, but it also had men and women of broader views, and it had come through the Reconstruction period following the Civil War without the hard-edged resistance to slavery's abolition shown by its Confederate neighbors. Halsey's father possessed a reputation as intellectual and courteous. He was a gentleman in a place that reared gentlemen. Halsey's older sister went to Vassar College. The uncannily prophetic letter his mother's uncle sent her upon Halsey's birth shows the sort of family that Halsey came from: "This my hope and prayer that your son may be worthy of both his parents; that he may be heir to the best qualities of the best of the Halseys and Powells combined; that he may be healthy, strong, good, brave and generous; that he may be a lover of truth, a friend to the unfortunate, a defender of the oppressed, and a strong friend of his country in war and peace . . . and that he may leave a good record of himself as citizen, a patriot and a Christian."

And so he was stamped as a young man. He emerged from his boyhood at Dunlora, as the family plantation was called, with a strong sense of duty and an impulse toward helping others—and ultimately a choice of career that would provide him opportunities for both.

From the beginning, Halsey was bright and independent. At seventeen, he went off to Centre College, a Presbyterian school in nearby Danville, where he won the entrance prize for the highest score on the admission tests in English, Latin, Greek, and mathematics. The next year, he entered the Naval Academy, where he was successful in his course work and sports and well liked by his fellow cadets. (One of them was his cousin, through his mother, William "Bull" Halsey, who would go on to command the Third Fleet in World War II.) Halsey was comfortable with himself, and this made others comfortable with the athletic young Kentuckian whom friends called "Tuck."

In his first fifteen years of naval service, Powell logged only eleven months of shore duty. As an ensign in 1908, he joined the USS *Yankton* and the around-the-world cruise of America's Great White Fleet, dispatched by President Theodore Roosevelt to demonstrate America's new sea power. (The *Yankton* was a converted double-masted steam yacht that had once belonged to the French actress Sarah Bernhardt.) In December 1908, a giant earthquake struck Sicily, killing 125,000 people. The fleet was in Egypt, and the *Yankton* steamed to Italy, where Powell got his first taste of rescue work, digging survivors from the rubble. In 1914, the navy assigned him to command the destroyer USS *Reid*, an event brought about by the American occupation of Vera Cruz during the Mexican revolution—an act of gunboat diplomacy, which had been triggered by threats to an American oil-drilling district around Tampico, Mexico, and further escalated by worries about a German arms shipment to Mexico's dictator, Victoriano Huerta. Before the incident was over, seventy American warships were in Mexican waters. (Many of the officers at Smyrna had served there, including Bristol. It was a formative experience for a generation of naval officers.) Mexican oil had become crucial to the American economy—drilled in Tampico, refined in Texas, and consumed by factories in the Northeast. President Wilson had taken no chances on an interruption of its flow. Halsey Powell was thirty-one when America put marines ashore at Vera Cruz and he got a close look at the navy's role in protecting American commercial interests in a foreign country—not the last time in his career.

Several commands followed the *Reid*, and in 1916, Powell was assigned to command the USS *Jouett*, another destroyer, which was at the Naval Shipyard in Norfolk, Virginia. By then, Norfolk was already a navy town, though the giant naval station at Sewall's Point had yet to be built. For naval officers stationed in Norfolk, there was a lively social life ashore of dances and parties at country clubs and the homes of its leading residents. Halsey met Virginia Perkins, the daughter of a prominent Norfolk doctor, and they were married in June 1916 in her father's home on York Street, a gracious but eccentric wood-frame home with a turret. Virginia's family was present for the simple ceremony. Halsey was granted twenty-five days' leave, and he and Ginger, as he called his bride, traveled to Hot Springs, Virginia, for a honeymoon, then to McAfee, where Halsey showed her Dunlora, and she met his family.

When they returned to Norfolk, Halsey resumed his command of the *Jouett*, and they lived in the big house on York Street. The following June, three months after the United States had declared war on Germany, Lieutenant Commander Halsey Powell was sent to Europe as commander of the USS *Parker*, another destroyer. Ginger remained at Norfolk. The *Parker* was assigned to protect troop convoys against German submarines. On August 3, Powell's thirty-fourth birthday, the *Parker* engaged and damaged a German submarine, an action that won him the navy's Distinguished Service Medal. A year later, he and the crew of the *Parker* staged a hazardous rescue of survivors of a British hospital ship, HMHS *Glencart Castle*, that had been sunk by a German sub. The rescue was a display of seamanship and courage in rough seas and gale-force winds that brought Powell praise in the British Parliament and a letter of commendation from the assistant secretary of the navy, Franklin D. Roosevelt. (Many years later as the nation's president, Roosevelt would remember the bold young officer with an important and much bigger reward—a promotion to rear admiral.)

After the war, Powell returned to the United States, and he and Ginger visited his parents again in McAfee—he would be drawn back to the Kentucky countryside throughout his life. Then, with new orders, the Powells traveled to Newport, Rhode Island, and the Naval War College, where Halsey became an instructor, mostly marking up the correspondence course exams of officers who were far from Newport. The Powells rented a small wood-shingled cottage in nearby Jamestown, a pleasant small town amid old New England farms with a view of Newport and upper Narragansett Bay. Halsey planted a garden and commuted on a ferry to the War College across the bay. At Jamestown, trouble entered the couple's happy life with the slow deterioration of Ginger's health. She had an undiagnosed wasting disease and lost a dangerous amount of weight. In April, Halsey sent a note to his mother that Ginger was down to one hundred and six pounds. In September 1920, she grew more desperately ill and slipped into a coma. She died in Rhode Island on September 22, 1920. She was twenty-eight years old; they had been married only four years. Halsey traveled with her body back to Norfolk, where she was buried. His sister Mary joined him there, at the house on York Street, caring for him during his grief.

Powell soon left Newport and returned to sea, and in June 1922 he took command of the USS *Edsall*, which was assigned to steam to Constantinople. He was thirty-nine years old. The *Edsall* was identical to the other "flushdeckers" in the Turkish detachment—the *Litchfield*, *Simpson*, *Lawrence*, and *MacLeish*. Like the other destroyer commanders working under Admiral Bristol, Powell patrolled the waters of the eastern Mediterranean and Black Sea, ferried oil and tobacco executives around the Near East, and supported the American famine-relief effort in southern Russia.

But unlike others, Powell was a genuine war hero—a boast not even Bristol could make. In looking back for an explanation of his future conduct at Smyrna, the status that his war record had conferred on him might offer a clue. Maybe it gave Powell the confidence to operate from a sense of right and wrong without the blurring considerations of rank or career. The scant record that he has left—crisply written naval reports and detailed ship's diaries that show not the slightest turn of self-aggrandizement—suggests a man who was supremely capable on the bridge of a ship or in its engine room. He took his own counsel. Surely that had been the case, during World War I, when he had picked up the distress signal from the *Glencart Castle* and steamed to its last-known position and circled the survivors clinging to debris in high seas and a February gale, always moving his ship to avoid German submarines, while he sent five of his crew overboard to make the rescue. His report back to the navy was brief and without adornment or drama. It said, essentially, the *Parker* answered a distress call and rescued eight men from the sea. Nonetheless, so daring had the operation been that members of Parliament had sought an adequate way to acknowledge the American commander and his crew. He received Britain's Distinguished Service Order cross.

IN AUGUST 1922, Powell took the *Edsall* to several ports on the Black Sea. He called on Varna, Bulgaria, where Standard Oil had a terminal and American tobacco agents bought tobacco leaf, and Novorossisk, Russia, another Standard Oil depot, where he picked up Miller Joblin of the

Standard Oil Co. And then the ship made a clockwise cruise of the Black Sea, stopping at Batoum, the port from which Russian oil from Baku was shipped, then to Trebizond, on the north coast of Turkey, where an American destroyer was often positioned to watch the port, important to American tobacco companies. In that last week of August, it became clear to Powell that something big was afoot inside Turkey. He was denied permission to land at Trebizond. The *Edsall* then moved west to Samsun, another Turkish Black Sea port.

He would soon learn that the nationalist army, opening its offensive against the Greeks at Afyon Karahisar, had closed the country's northern frontier, including Trebizond and Samsun. From the *Edsall*'s deck at Samsun, Powell, with his officers and crew, watched the city celebrate the nationalist advance with fireworks, a parade, and machine gun and artillery fire, some that came too close to the *Edsall* for Powell's comfort. He demanded the shellfire near his ship immediately cease. The Turkish battery complied.

After three days of waiting, the Turkish military governor allowed Powell to come ashore, and he learned that the nationalist army had advanced as far as Ushak. A Turkish officer showed him nationalist communiqués that alleged Greek army atrocities in the line of its retreat. Powell made an inspection of the city, toured the Near East Relief orphanage and hospital, met the Turkish governor, and went pheasant hunting with two Americans in the city. During the day afield, Powell upheld Kentucky's reputation for producing marksmen: the day's bag was twelve birds. Powell had a navy commendation for small-arms proficiency. (McAfee, Kentucky, is only a short ride from Pall Mall, Tennessee, home to Sergeant Alvin York, the most famous marksman of World War I.)

The *Edsall* departed Samsun on September 7 (a day after the *Litchfield*, the first of the American destroyers, had arrived in Smyrna) and, delayed by a broken steering cable, arrived in Constantinople late the next day at the Standard Oil docks, where it took on 104,000 gallons of bunker oil. On September 9, the *Edsall* moved to the buoy opposite Dolma Bahtche palace, and on September 10 it steamed fifty-five minutes to Prinkipo Island, one of Bristol's favorite destinations for recreation. The ship loitered at Prinkipo on Sunday, September 10 (the day Kemal entered Smyrna), as Bristol and a party of eighteen, walking and riding on mules, went on a picnic and climbed to the picturesque St. George Byzantine-Greek Monastery. By his own account, Bristol enjoyed the day, though he was disgusted with a Greek priest who had related the legend of an ancient priest who had been directed in a dream to discover a lost icon on the island. Bristol bristled at anything Greek: "It makes you rather angry," he noted in his diary, "to have these Greek priests tell you such stories with a straight face and think you are fool enough to believe it."

The next morning, the *Edsall* ferried Bristol and his group on the short trip back to Constantinople, took aboard flour and stores from the Near East Relief pier, then, early on September 13, headed to Smyrna, by way of Salonika, with Merrill and the Standard Oil men aboard.

After getting Hepburn's urgent radio message early in the morning of September 14, as the fire raged at Smyrna, Powell increased the *Edsall*'s engine speed and arrived in the city at 6 A.M. By then, Hepburn had already made his decision to send the refugees he had on board the *Litchfield* to Salonika. The *Edsall* came alongside, unloaded flour and bread, and took aboard the *Litchfield*'s 671 refugees as well as Mark Prentiss, the publicist from New York, Dr. Post, and nurse Sara Corning. They departed for Salonika at 8 A.M. A careful record keeper, Powell noted the ethnicity of his bedraggled passengers: 500 Greeks, 170 Armenians, and one Jew. The refugees were crammed on the narrow deck of the ship. Powell had his men string lines fore and aft along the ship's rails and stationed sailors at the lines to make sure none of the children went overboard. "During the trip," he noted in the ship's diary, "the refugees were easily handled, obedient to instructions and caution about keeping back from the rail, and about keeping their children off the forecastle." He gave them two meals at sea—the first food many of them had eaten in days.

On the way to Salonika, the *Edsall* radioed Bristol with a message from Prentiss, the first transmission in what would eventually form a controversial record of the Smyrna fire and its aftermath. It began, "Prentiss requests following telegram be sent N.Y. Times corrected as you deem best." The substance of the cable was a proposal to write a story about the burning of Smyrna. Bristol approved the message and had it relayed from the radio room of the American embassy in Constantinople to New York, and the *Times* agreed to take an article written by Prentiss.

Prentiss's first story appeared on the front page of America's most important newspaper two days later: EYEWITNESS STORY OF SMYRNA'S HORROR. In it, he described the city's suffering during the fire, but he played down the brutality leading up to it. "I personally saw Turkish officers escorting a wounded old lady to a hospital. I saw Turkish soldiers giving food and water to dying Armenians and Greeks. I saw officials arrest junior officers for brutality to prisoners." Throughout the *Times* story, Prentiss stands at the center of the action as a principal character in the relief effort. There was no mention of Jennings, his shelter, or the women brutalized by Turkish soldiers. Over the following months, Prentiss would make himself into the hero at Smyrna. Once again, he was inventing a résumé.

The *Edsall* reached Salonika at 11 P.M.

Powell put the refugees ashore. The Greek civil officials and military officers at the port warmly received him, and he responded with his own hospitality, inviting them and the U.S. consul at Salonika, Leland B. Morris, aboard the ship. Morris was a thirty-six-year-old Foreign Service officer from Texas.* Powell, Morris, and the Greek officials descended to the *Edsall's* tight wardroom, under the forward deck, and a Greek officer in halting English rose from his seat to thank America for its kindness in helping his stricken countrymen. The Greek officer, in his heavily accented English, said he was not surprised that America had come to the aid of Greeks since America was a friend of Greece—perhaps now America was its only friend. His words brought similar speeches of gratitude around the table from the officer of the port and the Greek naval officers. Powell was moved by the display of appreciation.

The two hours he had spent alongside the *Litchfield* on Smyrna's

---

* Morris would become American's first ambassador to Iran and the American chargé d'affaires in Berlin when Hitler declared war on the United States. Ribbentrop delivered the war note to Morris.

waterfront earlier in the day had been enough to convince Powell of the urgency of an evacuation. As the *Glencart Castle* episode had demonstrated, he had an instinct for rescue. In the *Edsall's* wardroom, he raised the question of how to organize an evacuation of Smyrna's refugees. There was a lot of talk among the men, and the outline of a plan began to emerge. Powell suggested using Greek merchant ships. One of the Greek officers said the Greek military would make Greek merchant ships available at Chios but the Turks would not allow the ships into Smyrna's harbor. Powell considered the man's comments and responded in his soft Kentucky drawl that he thought it would be impractical for the Greeks to bring in their own ships. He suggested an alternative—to have the American chargé d'affaires in Athens request Turkish permission for the Americans to take over Greek merchant ships and conduct the evacuation. Someone at the table suggested that Bristol might be able to work it out; everyone knew Bristol had good relations with the Turks.

On its face, the idea was far-fetched. It would require American intervention, and the U.S. government had been disinclined to get involved, even as an interlocutor between the Greeks and Turks for the handover of the city to prevent its destruction. Authorizing American naval officers to take indirect command of Greek shipping and work between the Turks and Greeks to direct a large-scale evacuation seemed even less likely. Besides, Bristol was downright opposed to an American-led evacuation. He was hewing to his line of neutrality and the sole mission of protecting Americans and American property. As the conversation continued around the table in the cramped quarters, lit by an electric light powered by the ship's generator, Powell offered an alternative to relying on Bristol. Why not have the senior Allied and American naval officers in Smyrna work out an agreement with Mustapha Kemal directly? It eliminated layers of decision making and potential opposition. The obstacle to this approach was that it violated Bristol's order against working in concert with the Allies. Still, it seemed to Powell as workable if handled in the right way. The men talked past midnight.

At 1:30 A.M., Powell broke up the gathering. The *Edsall's* boilers were fired for the ship's return to Smyrna, but a gasket in a steam pipe blew out, and the ship was forced to remain at the pier until morning. The engine crew made temporary repairs, and the *Edsall* departed Salonika at 9:30 A.M. firing a single boiler, which meant the trip to Smyrna would take nearly twenty-four hours. It arrived the next day, early Saturday, September 16.

As the ship came to the Quay, the fire in the city was still burning, though not with the intensity of the first three nights. On the previous two days, it had spread north and south along the waterfront, leaving wreckage from the mansions at the southern end of Bella Vista all the way to the Custom House Pier—well over a mile and a half of jagged black walls, smoldering piles of masonry and wood, and barely discernible streets. Refugees remained on the Quay, sitting on the remains of their bundles, many partially burned. Turkish soldiers on horseback patrolled up and down the waterfront, and refugees attempting to swim the ships were shot. Jennings's safe house at 490 flew an American flag, and children continued to occupy the space outside the front door, but there was no American guard posted there.

HEPBURN HAD BEEN BUSY in Smyrna on Thursday and Friday, September 14 and 15, while Powell had made his way to Salonika and back.

The day before Powell's return, on Friday, September 15, Hepburn had joined a meeting aboard the *Galileo*, the flagship of Italian admiral Pepe. British admiral Reginald Tyrwhitt, Harry Lamb, the French and Italian consuls, and Dumesnil's chief of staff were present. The group agreed that a meeting with Kemal was needed to get answers about the Turkish attitude toward the relief and evacuation of the refugees. Pepe suggested that the consuls call on Kemal, but Lamb favored the naval officers as emissaries, and Lamb's view appeared to prevail when the French officer who had been silent through the meeting finally spoke up. He surprised everyone with the news that French admiral Dumesnil was at that moment meeting Kemal. Clearly the French were working their own channels and agenda, and the group realized there was nothing to do but await the outcome of the conversation between Kemal and Dumesnil. The shipboard meeting broke up, and as Hepburn departed, Admiral Pepe said to him, "There shall be no refugees problem to worry about by the time we get through conferring."

Over the previous several days, a storm of diplomacy had been blowing among the Allied governments in London, Paris, and Rome. None of it was a secret to the men aboard the ship except possibly Hepburn—the U.S. State Department itself was staying abreast of the shifting Allied positions through leaks in the embassies at London and Rome. The French had announced that they supported the firm British position that a nationalist incursion into the neutral Dardanelles Strait would trigger war, but the French commitment to force was thin. It would soon disappear, and French foreign minister Raymond Poincaré would fly into a rage at his British counterpart Lord Curzon over an ultimatum to the Turks issued by Lloyd George and Winston Churchill. Even more conniving, Italy openly opposed the British position and had proposed a conference between Turkey and the Allies. The Italians had been trying to broker a Greek-Turkish armistice for a month and had sent a series of questions to the nationalists including one marked confidential: "What oil concessions would Italy get in Turkey in a peace settlement?" The French were slipping toward the Italian position. It was the same old story: the Allies could not agree among themselves on how to deal with Turkey.

Having heard nothing about Kemal's response, the next morning, Saturday, September 16, Captain Hepburn decided to call directly on Dumesnil. Hepburn wanted to return to Constantinople to consult with Bristol and he needed to know Kemal's position on the fate of the refugees. On board the *Jean Bart*, Dumesnil had no answers for Hepburn—either he had not asked Kemal, Kemal had not answered, or Dumesnil was not saying, choosing to withhold his response. The refugee situation was now less serious, the French admiral said, though on what basis he made the judgment was not clear. Nonetheless, in response to Hepburn's suggestion, Dumesnil said a meeting between Kemal and the naval officers would be useful, but Dumesnil could not attend because he was returning to Constantinople to consult with his government. Dumesnil warned Hepburn against making demands of the Turkish supreme commander. There should be no ultimatums, he insisted. Dumesnil was making clear his deference to Kemal. Hepburn left the French ship frustrated.

Then later in the day, a proclamation went up around the city, in Turkish, that settled Hepburn's question. It announced that all Christians must be evacuated by October 1—two weeks away—or they would be deported to the interior. Women, children, and old men could leave, but all Greek and Armenian men between the ages of eighteen and forty-five would be held as prisoners of war. The Turkish authorities also declared that the names of refugees who wanted to depart must be furnished in advance. Given that at least 250,000 refugees were in the city, the overwhelming number without documents, the requirement was a logistical impossibility. The Turks seemed to be setting up a situation that had no logical outcome except the erasure of the refugees through death or deportation.

To Hepburn, the situation was moving backward toward some sort ultimate catastrophe.

Hepburn decided to call on Kiazim Pasha, the city's military governor, to work out a compromise to the demand for refugee lists and documents. By now, Powell was back in Smyrna, and Hepburn brought him along, but the Turkish governor was absent. Hepburn returned to the *Litchfield*, and Powell, who was ashore in Smyrna for the first time, went to have a look at the refugee concentration sites. The largest group was at the Greek cemetery at the north end of the city, where about twelve thousand people milled about, sat on their blankets, and huddled with their children. As Powell walked among the crowd, the refugee men, mostly elderly with thick broad mustaches and dressed in farm clothes, removed their hats as Powell passed by, stood at attention, and gave him military salutes, offering to escort him through the makeshift camp. "There is no doubt that they knew and appreciated what our visit was for," he wrote in his ship's diary. The suffering and the obvious appeal for help touched and made an impression on him.

THE BURNED CITY THROUGH which Powell walked was a ghastly scene—a vast plain of rubble and destruction, leveled almost entirely by the fire except for the shafts of naked chimneys, brick arches where once there had been grand entrances, and blasted churches without roofs. The twisted metal and cinder-filled streets were discernible only by the broken lines of standing walls of masonry, the remnants of capacious buildings. The blackened warehouses and hotels that still stood at the perimeter of the fire zone showed floorless vacant interiors—the rectangles that once were tall upper windows afforded a view to more ruins beyond, or the sky. The scene resembled those places in France that had been devastated by artillery fire in the Great War, except this was worse because it was not a Picardy village or a town that been shattered by exploding shells but an entire city that had been broken, burned, and flattened. Jagged and partially standing walls resembled headstones. The spread of it was appalling—nearly a mile deep and more than a mile wide. The blasted cityscape smoldered still, smoke rising from the piles of mortar and stone at various places, and it gave off the smell of wet ashes, tobacco, and death. The corpses of the people who had been trapped by the inferno or shot in its aftermath lay in distorted positions, blackened, on the pavement. Dogs roamed, pulling at the putrid flesh. It was surely a piece of hell reconstructed on earth. Here and there, Turks picked through the ruins for unburnt booty, or a pod of refugees took shelter in the shade under an overhang of scorched masonry. Occasionally, under the wind, in a pile of rubble or a tumbled building, flames would flare back up. The only part of the city undamaged was the Turkish section at the base of Mount Pagus, the small adjoining Jewish section, and the terminus of the Point. Turkish residents had taken to fishing along the Quay with hooks and strands of salvaged telegraph wire for submerged bodies from which they could remove valuables: rings, coins, or gold teeth. The water was remarkably clear, and the corpses could be seen waving like seaweed below the surface. For years afterward, a big fish would be caught and opened and a bag of jewels would come out of the stomach.

Throughout the day, Merrill had been busy, pursuing his own agenda for Bristol. Bringing along Brown from the *Chicago Daily News*, Merrill also had called on Kiazim Pasha, who told him the police had arrested twenty-two Armenians for starting the fire. He said they had confessed and belonged to an organization of six hundred Armenians that had plotted the city's destruction. Merrill asked to interview the fire starters. Ki-azim agreed but was unable to produce them. Merrill continued to press for them, but they were never produced. He also visited Noureddin at the Konak, seeking a copy of the letter written by Dr. White that proved American missionaries had conspired with ethnic Greeks in Marsovan against the Turkish government. This was the letter that Noureddin had described in the conversation five days earlier in the meeting with Hep-burn and Dr. Post. Merrill told Noureddin he wanted to take it to Admiral Bristol. (It would make an excellent talking point for the admiral in his press campaign against the missionaries.) Noureddin said he didn't have the letter in Smyrna but he would send for it and have it delivered to one of the destroyers for transmission to Bristol. (If the letter was ever delivered, it appears not to have made its way into Navy or State Department archives, and even if it had been, it hardly could justify the killing that took place in Marsovan.)

Hepburn finally had concluded he had the information he needed and decided to return to Constantinople on the *Litchfield* early that night to report back to Bristol. As he prepared to leave, Jaquith and Davis came to him with a request to evacuate Armenian orphans who had been left behind by the *Winona*. The children had spent three nights on the Quay. (They were not among those under Jennings's care.) Turkish soldiers, Jaquith said, had already taken some of the orphan girls from the group. It was imperative, he argued, that the children be evacuated to save their lives.

Hepburn did not want to evacuate anyone without Turkish permission—in fact, he was reluctant to evacuate anyone under any circumstances. He had made exceptions on the night of the fire and the morning afterward, but he was not inclined to make yet another. Bristol was adamantly opposed to bringing orphans to Constantinople. Jaquith and Davis assured Hepburn that they had secured Turkish permission (with bribes), and Jaquith said the Near East Relief would pay for their support. Hepburn played the issue back and forth. The dreadful events of the previous week had softened his attitude, and, while it would be impossible to keep the news of it from Bristol, he agreed reluctantly to take them along.

At about 5 P.M., just before Hepburn's departure, the *Simpson*, with Knauss in command, returned from Athens, where it had delivered the American evacuees, including Consul Horton. It anchored near the north end of the Quay, almost opposite Jennings's safe house at 490, where it could keep watch over a new and temporary consulate in a mansion that had been the home of an Armenian family before their departure. Powell brought the *Edsall* in front of the new consulate as well. No doubt the presence of the two warships in front of the string of safe houses gave Jennings some comfort. The *Lawrence* was anchored in front of the Standard Oil pier, where ten sailors remained ashore as guards. At 6 P.M., Jaquith arrived, at the place where the *Litchfield*'s whaleboats had tied up at the Quay, with the orphan children—nearly five hundred of them, more than twice as many as he had asked Hepburn's permission to bring along. Nonetheless, they were all put on board the *Litchfield*, and Hepburn departed. Also on board were Aaron Merrill; Irving Thomas and Miller Joblin of Standard Oil; Yantis, the tobacco agent; Harold Jaquith; Myrtle Nolan of the YWCA; and Mark Prentiss, the publicist.

On the way back, Prentiss wrote another story for the *New York Times*, which he cabled to New York from Constantinople. He blamed the violence in Smyrna on Greek snipers, who "exasperated the Turks beyond their officers' control," and the role he ascribed to himself in the relief effort outshone any of the other Americans, including Jennings, who did not get a mention in the story. Prentiss's reports continued to play down Turkish actions. "I made a personal investigation," he wrote in the *Times* story, "and could find nothing resembling an organized massacre by the troops on the Quay."

AS HEPBURN AND THE LITCHFIELD passed Pelican Point on the way back to Constantinople, Halsey Powell became the senior American officer in Smyrna.

His first act was to answer an invitation to go aboard the French vessel *Jean Bart* for another meeting of the discordant admirals: Pepe of Italy; Levasseur of France (representing Dumesnil, who had departed); and Tyrwhitt of Britain. Each of the officers had been ashore, and each had witnessed the suffering. The French still had five thousand proté-gés gathered around French-owned buildings at Cordelio who awaited French help in departing. The Italians continued to have problems gathering and removing their nationals and affiliates.

Powell was not caught in the crosscurrents of competing national interests, as were the Allied officers, all of whom outranked him, and he cultivated a working relationship with all of them. He was the trim, practical, and straight-talking Yank. The British in particular took a liking to him. The officers decided among themselves that the only acceptable path forward was evacuation of the refugees and that Admiral Pepe should approach Kemal with a request to allow Greek ships into the harbor to remove the people. It was a bold plan—simple and straightforward: bring in Greek ships, and take away refugees. It was the idea that Powell had raised in the *Edsall*'s wardroom back in Salonika. At the meeting on the French ship, the officers decided to inform their home governments of their decision rather than to seek their permission. Of course, no arrangements had been made to obtain Greek ships. The naval officers would cross that difficult bridge when they got to it.

Powell included the French summary of the meeting in his naval diary. It read, in part:

An intervention must be done if we want to save some refugees. Mustapha Kemal Pasha's intention is to send them in the country's interior. . . . Admiral Pepe is willing to secretly ask the Excellency Mustapha Kemal Pacha if he would consent. . . . Admiral Pepe is willing to ask also, at the meeting with S.E. Moustapha Kemal Pasha, if the occasion occurs, what are his thoughts about the removal of the bodies in town.

The Italian admiral had been the obvious choice among the officers to approach Kemal. Italy's policy was the most favorable toward the nationalists. (In a few days, the *Times* of London would report that Russian agents were in Italy purchasing arms for the nationalists and had placed an order with Fiat for armored cars, trucks, automobiles, and machine guns. In other words, the Italians were helping the Turks prepare for what soon might be war with the British.) No timetable was set for the meeting with Kemal. It would be up to the Italian admiral to work it out. There was yet more waiting.

That night, some of the fires flared up again, but for the most part the city appeared burned out.

OVER THE NEXT SEVERAL DAYS, Powell attempted to assess American property losses and intercede with the Turkish military on behalf of the relief committee. The losses were big. The fire mocked Bristol's reassurances about the safety of American property. Horton's proposal for American mediation to ensure an orderly occupation was beginning to seem prescient.

The fire had destroyed or damaged millions of dollars of inventory and buildings owned by the big American tobacco companies. All the big tobacco companies bought tobacco in Smyrna: the American Tobacco Co., Liggett & Myers, and R. J. Reynolds. Most American cigarettes were made with a blend of Turkish tobacco. It was crucial to the American tobacco industry.

In 1900, before the widespread introduction of Turkish tobacco, Americans consumed two and a half million cigarettes each year. In 1920, when nearly 85 percent of American cigarettes were blended with Turkish tobacco, the consumption grew to more than fifty billion cigarettes per year. The luxury brand was American Tobacco Co.'s Pall Mall—made from 100 percent Turkish tobacco.

The American companies had their own buyers in the city; they also purchased tobacco through agents such Alston Tobacco Co. or Standard Commercial Trading Co., which was owned by Ery Kehaya, an Ottoman Greek born in Turkey who had lived an astonishing life. As a young man trained for the priesthood, Kehaya made his way to America, where he had become a citizen and a waiter at a Greek restaurant in New York. One day some of his customers, who happened to be in the tobacco business, learned that Kehaya had been born near Samsun, one of Turkey's rich tobacco-growing areas, and soon one of those customers asked him to help sell a load of tobacco. Kehaya made the sale and used the commission to go into business for himself. That was in 1912. Ten years later, he was one of the largest tobacco dealers in the world, and R. J. Reynolds was a principal customer. Young Kehaya built a fortune and an international company, married the daughter of a prominent North Carolina cigarette manufacturer, listed his company on the New York Stock Exchange, and sent his son to the St. Paul's School and Yale.* Such was the money to be made in tobacco.

Standard Commercial had lost two of its five warehouses and about $900,000 worth of tobacco in the fire. (A million pounds of leaf were in the two warehouses, and Smyrna tobacco was selling for about 90 cents a pound.) The local American manager for Standard American, William P. Dortch, had quit after the fire and refused to leave the *Edsall*. A Standard Commercial manager, E. P. Rogers of Richmond, Virginia, who had been on his way to Macedonia, diverted to Smyrna, hired an armed Turkish guard, and went to inspect the warehouses. He found Turkish bandits sifting through the ruins for loot. Gary Tobacco, which had twenty-seven warehouses in the city and supplied Liggett & Myers, the makers of L&M and Chesterfield cigarettes, lost about $1,000,000 worth of leaf. The American Tobacco Co., manufacturer of Lucky Strike, lost about $500,000 in stock, but its agent had wisely advised the company to buy insurance coverage that protected it against losses due to war or civil insurrection. Also hard hit was MacAndrews & Forbes, whose stock, warehouse, and offices were destroyed.

Some of the big warehouses were on the unburned edge of the fire line, near the northerly industrial section of the city, and Roger Griswold and Jehu Archbell, both members of the relief committee who were living at the American consulate, quickly formed a shipping agency, hired workers, and began soliciting ships to carry away undamaged tobacco. It was a chance for them to make some money. By September 17, they already had six million pounds of undamaged tobacco ready for shipment. American Tobacco sent away 1,400,000 pounds on

---

* In 2005, Standard Commercial merged with another tobacco company to form Alliance One. EK's grandson is chairman of the board of directors.

a French steamer; Standard Commercial sent away 900,000 pounds.

But not all tobacco dealers were so lucky. Several days after the fire, Turkish authorities showed up at Socrates Onassis's home in Karatash and arrested him as an enemy of Turkey. He was taken to the prison in the Turkish Quarter to await trial. Aristotle, his son, had been present when his father was arrested but the Turkish authorities had left him behind, possibly because of his youthful appearance. His small stature and smooth face made him seem younger than his age of eighteen. By this time, one of the uncles and his favorite, Alexander, who had been in the countryside on business, had been hanged, and two others had been arrested and were being held in deportation camps. The Turkish officer who had arrested Socrates took the Onassis villa as his residence, and Socrates managed to persuade the man that he needed Aristotle to maintain the big house. Aristotle cadged whiskey from around town and took it to the general along with good tobacco, making himself indispensable. Soon, Aristotle had a Turkish pass to move freely through the city, including to the jail. The father told him where he had hidden a substantial amount of money, and Aristotle retrieved it. Next, he needed to find a way to gain his father's release through bribes to the right people. It was a tricky affair that could end with both their deaths.

ON THE MORNING OF SUNDAY, September 17, Powell came ashore at a landing place that he had established on the north end of the Quay, near Jennings's safe houses, and, as he did each day, he walked the length of the Quay to the Konak, where he called on Turkish military and civilian governors. On this morning, he found that there was yet another military governor at the Konak, Nadja Bey, and Powell noticed that he was meeting with a man who wore a French officer's kepi, the raised cap with a short visor. It was General Maurice Pelle, the French high commissioner from Constantinople. His appearance was a significant diplomatic contact. General Pelle, former commander of the French army, was in the city to negotiate the removal of the Allied ships from Smyrna. It was obvious that the French were working at cross-purposes with the British.

Powell transacted his business with the governor's assistant and departed.

On the Quay, Powell passed refugees sitting among their belongings, saw shootings, and heard gunfire in the streets behind the broken and burned walls of the Quayside buildings. Turkish soldiers patrolled the Quay and shook down refugees who appeared to them to still have valuables. He also saw refugees being marched in work battalions into the city's ruins. "Bodies can be seen daily floating around the harbor," he wrote in his ship's diary after one of the walks. "The smell of burning flesh is at all times noticeable." On the block behind the new consulate, corpses had been stacked for transportation by the work crews to graves and pyres.

It was during his walk on Sunday that Powell encountered Jennings for the first time. Until then, Powell had been dealing with the leaders of the relief committee—Davis, Jaquith, Jacob, and Griswold, who was particularly adept at getting results through bribes to the Turkish officials. Powell had met with these men at the American consulate relocated since the fire—now in a Quayside mansion that was owned by the Spartali family, wealthy Armenians who had departed the city. By September 17, Jennings had filled the several vacant mansions along the north end of the Quay with women and children and in some cases their fathers or brothers who had managed to escape Turkish capture. Jennings's first house at 490 was two blocks north of the relocated American consulate; another one of his houses was next door to the consulate. Powell saw the refugees packed tightly around the entrances to the safe houses, and he noticed also that Jennings had become a favorite of the American sailors and junior officers who had come ashore as guards. He joshed with them, and they lent him a hand when he asked for their help. Powell had probably seen him earlier but had not stopped to take notice.

Walking up and down the waterfront, the little man with the hunched back, peculiar gait, and straw boater on his large head had become a fixture on the Quay, tending to injured refugees and greeting the young sailors with a smile and a hello. "I must say the Navy crowd was exceedingly kind in every way," Jennings later wrote. "In my attempt to save people from drowning and many other of my activities, my friends of the Navy simply let me go. I was not even restricted in giving orders." In one instance, he directed a sailor to save a drowning refugee. The sailors had orders not to engage in rescues, but Jennings insisted on it and the sailor complied. But most of Jennings's orders were more in the nature of getting the young American swabbies to help him bring injured women he found on the streets to his shelters. It was work they were happy to do.

There was something both reassuring and endearing about the little man with the hunched back. Maybe part of his appeal *was* the hunched back—which suggested a kind of magical figure to the poor Greek women, who were overwhelmingly agricultural peasants. A favorite character in Greek folklore had been a likable little hunchback—Karagiozis (Kar-a-gee-O-zees). A poor man of the people who survived on his wits during the Ottoman rule of Greece, Karagiozis had imparted wisdom and laughter—usually without realizing it—to audiences throughout Greece and Asia Minor, including Smyrna. Represented in shadow-puppet theaters with a long right arm and raggedy clothes, he was a beloved figure who had given the Greeks a way to laugh at themselves—and their Islamic masters. A rich Turkish pasha was a regular character in the corpus of Karagiozis stories, known to the refugees by heart.

Jennings was no fool nor was he barefoot, black eyed, and big nosed, as was Karagiozis, but he would become beloved. Powell was among those who saw the good work he was doing—sheltering people who had been frightened beyond endurance and gently treating their wounds and sicknesses and saying his prayers among them.

On this Sunday-morning walk of the Quay, Powell saw that an American flag was hung on the house at No. 490, and he decided it had to come down. It was likely to attract Turkish attention and provoke trouble. Powell asked Jennings to have someone haul it down, and he went inside for an inspection. The house was full on all its floors; people were spread everywhere, and many of the women were pregnant or holding newborn babies. It smelled of sick and unwashed people. They were dirty and frightened, but they were safe—or safer than on the street. The mansions along the Quay were the products of great wealth—their entrances typically opened onto a large foyer and grand staircase, the ceilings were high, the rooms capacious, the floors made of marble tiles or polished wood. There were four big rooms on a floor, and there would be two main floors, top and bottom, with a tighter floor squeezed between the first and second floors for servants and household chores. The mansions were filled with red Ushak carpets, tall mirrors, bronze statuary, high beds, and mahogany wardrobes the size of arks. Each had a big balcony protruding from the third floor that overlooked the harbor. Powell walked through Jennings's small hospital, though the scarcity of medical supplies hardly justified the name, and checked the other safe houses, and he saw the same scenes spread among the luxury of former residents—women who had been raped and stabbed, others who appeared emaciated and were speechless—but he also saw that there were men present, some of them sick and wounded, others healthy relatives of the women who were being sheltered. Powell did not know what the Turkish attitude toward these safe house was—so far there had been no trouble—but he wanted to see them continue operating until he could arrange an evacuation, and he worried that the presence of the men would bring down a Turkish order to empty them. He directed Jennings to remove the men. Powell also learned from Jennings that he had been sleeping in the safe houses since the night of the fire. Powell's orders were to protect Americans—he ordered Jennings to sleep aboard the *Edsall* or in the American consulate (the Spartali mansion) at night for his own safety.

In the ship's diary that night, Powell recorded the names of the American Relief Committee members as they had been given to him, and it showed that the committee continued to assign Jennings little importance, listing him as an assistant after young Robert Trueblood, a recent graduate of Whittier College who had only just arrived in Smyrna to teach at International College.

Director and Acting Chairman: C. C. Davis
1st Assistant Director: H. C. Jaquith
2nd Assistant Director and permanent chairman—Prof. Lawrence
Director of General Relief—Mr. Jacob
Assistants—Mr. Trueblood, Mr. Jennings
Director of Supply and Transportation—Mr. Griswold
Assistant—Mr. Archibell [*sic*]

Director of Department of Health—Dr. Post.
Assistant Director—Dr. Magulis [*sic*]
Director of Evacuations—Mr. Parks

THE RELIEF EFFORT WAS SPUTTERING. The fire had destroyed nearly all the bakeries, and there was no gas or water service to the few that remained on the city's outer edges. The fire had melted the underground pipes that brought water through the city. The committee was producing only eight hundred loaves a day. The only vehicles were those few that Hepburn had saved on the night of the fire, and the relief workers couldn't travel safely on foot without guards to protect them—the risk of being robbed or shot by Turkish soldiers was too high. Some of the soldiers had come from deep inside Anatolia, and they had no idea who or what an American was and why they should care. Jennings was now staying close to his houses and not wandering the city.

Feeding was restricted to stations along the waterfront. People thronged the volunteers when they arrived with food, rushing the feeding stations like pigeons to a crust thrown on the street. Refugees were given flour with which they tried to make their own bread by finding water and improvising ways of cooking it. Some made flour patties and placed them on the blades of shovels, which they held over hot spots in the ruins to make something that resembled bread. The American destroyers had brought Near East Relief foodstuffs from Constantinople, and the relief committee was distributing them, but it was having difficulty because the refugees were scattered not just on the Quay, but throughout the burned city, on the roads out of they city, and in the nearby suburbs. The refugees had taken to wandering like frightened animals in search of food and shelter. Many families would walk miles in one direction, only to turn around and walk miles in another—the wandering might turn up some food or a way to escape. The continuous movement seemed instinctual.

John Clayton, back in the city, filed a story on Sunday, the seventeenth: "The horrors of plague have been added to the terrors of Smyrna. The disease broke out yesterday, and, owing to the impossibility of taking sanitary precautions among the thousands of refugees, scores of victims are being added to the toll of starvation and massacres. . . . The city is almost entirely without food today, practically the only visible supply being a little formerly in possession of the various relief organizations but now being held for the Turkish population."

The only efficient way to get what little food there was to the refugees was to concentrate them at several locations that could be reached by a vehicle, but the relief committee and Powell found the Turkish officials were unwilling to follow through on promises of establishing concentration points. The Turkish army either allowed bandits to roam through refugee camps or dispersed the refugees without notice to the committee. Powell made several attempts to intervene, and while he did not meet overt opposition, his efforts went nowhere—he was either told that the decision he sought must be made at a higher level or he was given a promise of assistance that never materialized. He could not get past the smiles, insincere promises, and delays. Often, the people in charge changed, requiring a new set of negotiations and explanations.

The Turkish authorities made two points clear to Powell: the Turkish army would be fed first from available supplies, and the Turkish military was determined that all Christian men of military age would be arrested. Powell could see that the Christian men were being hunted down. Nadja Bey, the military governor, made his own trip to the biggest refugee camp, outside the city at Balchova,* to determine whether any men of military age were present. He walked among the refugees carefully checking men and boys, examining their faces and pulling them out of the crowd if they were even close to the dangerous age bracket. They were arrested and taken away by soldiers.

Powell also visited the Balchova camp and found the conditions appalling: no water for most of the people and hardly any food. Ernest Jacob came along with him. "The worst sight I have seen thus far are the 8,250 old men, women and children in the military barracks at Baldjoba," wrote

---

* Ironical, perhaps: Balchova was the location of Agamemnon's Baths, the place in legend to which the Greeks who fought at Troy were led by an oracle to heal their wounds.

Jacob. "There is almost no water, and they had no food for five days. We gave them over thirty sacks of flour, promised bread for tomorrow, and arranged to repair the pumps."

To make matters worse, the nights were turning cold, and the rains would soon begin. The refugees huddled and slept on the ground at the city's football field and the big Greek cemetery, both near the Point, or anywhere else where they could find safety, either by blending into a large group or hiding amid the ruins. Frightened and defenseless, they responded like vulnerable animals on an African plain, seeking safety from predators in sheer numbers. "On account of the continued moving of the refugees," Powell observed, "it is difficult to keep track of them and relieve them. Only one camp has been permanent for three days, that at Belchova, where the conditions are very bad." Powell did find the committee's American businessmen skilled at bribing Turkish officials; they provided helpful to him as he tried to get answers and the authorities' cooperation.

Powell was also aware of friction inside the relief committee and the general unhappiness (including his own) with one member in particular, who, as he put it in his ship's diary, was seeking the limelight. No doubt it was Prentiss, who had returned to Smyrna after filing his second story to New York. His articles ignored the work of others, and he continued to magnify his role and cast himself as an expert and the leader of the relief effort. He also had the annoying habit of blowing a whistle in the concentration areas to bring the refugees to order or get their attention—this, while wearing a helmet, making himself look ridiculous as well. He also arranged to have his photo taken as he threw bread to the scrambling refugees, and another committee member reported that Prentiss had come into a large amount of unexplained cash while in the city.

Powell had other worries. It had become dangerous for Americans to wander from the Quay, out of the sight of the ships. Jacob and Trueblood had been roughed up and robbed at gunpoint near the remains of the YMCA building just three blocks back from the Quay. They complained to a Turkish officer, who took what money the first bandits did not. Powell also had received the report of the murder of a Greek American in his home in a farming village south of Smyrna near Aydin. Powell intended to take every incident seriously—it was essential for the maintenance of American prestige and the protection of American lives. He let nothing slide. He ordered Vice Consul Barnes to write an official letter protesting mistreatment of Greek and Armenian naturalized Americans. Powell said he wanted the Turks to investigate each incident and provide him a report of the details, including the statements of witnesses.

For the Greek American killed near Aydin, he also wanted the city's military governor to provide a caisson for the return of the man's body and a Turkish officer as an escort to ensure its safe return. Both were supplied. Powell also sought the release of a naturalized Greek American, fifty-three-year-old George Carathina, who he knew to have been arrested and shuffled among the city's jails until his whereabouts were unknown. Mr. Carathina had returned to Turkey from California, where he had immigrated, to retrieve his family in Smyrna. Powell was not making distinctions as Hepburn had between native-born Americans and naturalized Americans. Americans were Americans, and he was there to protect them all. Powell's inquiries into Carathina's whereabouts were met with the predictable reassurances and—the same lack of results. Carathina, by now, Powell concluded, was probably being marched into the interior.

In line with the decision to protect all Americans, Powell decided to reverse Captain Hepburn's decision to allow Americans, if they chose to accept the risk, to remain at International College in Paradise, which no longer had American guards. It was an untenable situation in his view, since he could not stand by if they were molested. Cass Reed, a professor at the college, was among those who had remained. Powell ordered them into the city and aboard the destroyers, where he housed and fed them. He also set his mind to evacuating the orphans and American missionary director of the orphanage in Boudjah that was sheltering four hundred children under the auspices of the relief committee. He intended to put them on the *Simpson* when it returned from Constantinople and send them to Salonika. A young American missionary, Raymond Moreman, a graduate of Pomona College and teacher at International College, was supervising the orphanage. Moreman had hoisted an American flag over the orphanage and told the Turkish soldiers, "I shall die with them if they are killed."

Powell preferred to avoid the young American's martyrdom. The *Simpson* had just returned to Smyrna, but Bristol almost immediately ordered it back to Constantinople, scuttling Powell's plan to remove the orphans. Powell was unwilling to give up on the orphans' evacuation, though, and let Bristol know, via the ship's telegraph, that he was seeking to position one of his ships so that it could watch over the consulate and the Standard Oil docks at the same time, freeing a second ship to remove the children. Either his message was not received, or Bristol elected to not respond.

On Sunday, September 17, Powell also got word back from Admiral Pepe through a subordinate officer that Kemal was unwilling to allow evacuation of the refugees on Greek ships. It was obvious that Kemal had the authority to do as he pleased in Smyrna—he was the uncontested leader of both the army and the nationalist government—but he chose to tell the Italian admiral that the decision must be evaluated by a committee and submitted for consideration in Ankara. Admiral Tyrwhitt got the same news and sent it back to London. Lord Curzon immediately cabled British ambassador Auckland Geddes in Washington. Kemal's decision, the cable said, was "tantamount to condemnation of quarter of million people to death by starvation." The note directed Geddes to ask the United States to join Britain in issuing a protest and pressing again for permission to evacuate the refugees. The State Department did not respond.

Theodora[*]

Theodora opened the door of the rooftop locker where she had been huddled with her little sisters. They had been in the locker, a small storage room, for days, hiding from the soldiers who had killed their parents, brothers, and aunt and uncle in the rooms of the house below. The bodies were still there, bloated and the flesh putrefying.

The man who had brought Theodora and her family to the house from the church had left with his family the morning after their arrival. He had given the Gravos family no warning of his departure. They had waked to find themselves alone in the house. The Turkish soldiers had come soon afterward.

It was hard for Theodora to remember how many days had passed since the soldiers had come banging on the door of the house, and her parents, frightened, had sent her and the other two youngest children up the steep stairs to the roof. She knew only that she was very hungry and thirsty. She had not eaten in days, and the only water she had drunk had come from the leaky faucet of a dirty sink in the locker. Staying silent, she had wet the hem of her dress in the puddled water in the sink and brought it to her lips. Each time she drank it she had felt that she would

---

[*] The substance of this narrative comes from an interview with Theodora Kontou in the collection of the Asia Minor Research Center in Athens.

vomit. In the days that the children had hidden in the locker, people had come into the house to take away its contents. Theodora had heard the voices of Turkish women, and the clatter of them taking pots from the kitchen and chickens from the back of the house. Always, Theodora and her sisters had remained silent in the locker. The baby sister had a bullet wound to one of her feet—it was unclear how this had happened. Had a bullet from one of the Turkish rifles passed through the ceiling of the house? The wound was festering, and it too had a terrible smell but the child remained silent as the house was ransacked.

Theodora heard no sounds on the rooftop and she sensed that there was no immediate danger outside the locker so she stepped out and looked around, down to the street and among the tightly packed homes and shops of Smyrna's Greek Quarter, near Daragatch. She crossed herself in the manner of an Orthodox Christian: she instinctively put her thumb and first two fingers together and her other two fingers flat on her palm and then she touched her forehead and her stomach, making the tall line of the cross, then she touched her right shoulder and left. The cross was now placed upon her. In church, she often crossed herself—it was what a person did in church.

In peace let us pray to the Lord. Kyrie Eleison, Kyrie Eleison. For the peace of God and the salvation of our souls, let us pray to the Lord. Kyrie Eleison, Kyrie Eleison.

Theodora's mother had often crossed herself in church and at home. So Theodora did what her mother had done: she placed the cross upon her body for protection. It was what she and her mother did in church.

Theodora looked down from the roof. It made her a little dizzy. The street was empty. This seemed strange to her, though she could not say why for sure. It would have been unusual to see empty streets in Gritzalia—people would be moving about, going to the fields, or returning from the church—and Smyrna was a much bigger village than Gritzalia. It had bigger churches. Maybe it had bigger fields. Smyrna was such a big and strange place to her, and so full of danger. It was not at all like her village, where her family had surrounded her, and she knew the small houses and the people who lived in them and even the animals, the goats and the sheep and the little donkeys.

From her perch on the roof, she could see the sea sparkling in the sunshine, and she heard the rumble of people and ships in the distance. She was terrified that a soldier would appear. She waited silently, watching, and as alert as a mouse before it dashes across an open floor. Satisfied that the house was empty, and feeling the pain in her stomach, she decided to take her sisters down the stairs and into the house. They all needed food. She put the younger child on her back and held the hand of the older one. She hurried down the stairs, passed the bodies of her family, and emerged into the light of the street, and when she got there, she saw a group of people—they were speaking Greek—passing hurriedly by. She ran after them.

At the corner, she saw a girl who was sitting upright on a pile of rocks. Theodora wanted to have a friend now. She felt alone. Maybe this girl would be her friend and she could tell her what had happened to her and her family. She approached her and asked how she could find a place to get food. She wanted to talk to someone—and now she had found this girl, but the girl didn't answer her questions. Theodora walked closer and saw that there was a piece of wood that had been shoved into her body from behind and had reached inside her mouth. It was what had kept her in the sitting position. Theodora could not move when she saw the piece of wood. It was a horrible thing to die this way, and now to see it, this piece of wood that went from her behind to her mouth. Theodora's mind was telling her to run, but her legs were not listening. They were stone. Then she found that she was running and she came to a church. It was a Greek church. She went inside, but it was full—completely packed with no room inside—and she and her sisters who smelled so badly were pushed out.

Theodora had two possessions, both given to her by her mother—her mother's purse and a photograph of mother. She looked at them and held them tight, remembering the words of her mother in the house of her father's friend: "When you see things are getting really bad, throw yourself into the sea." Theodora didn't want to throw herself into the sea, and she had her two sisters to care for. They curled like puppies outside the church and slept like puppies on the street.

Theodora awoke for who knows what reason—she had been sleep-

ing in the daylight—and she moved with a crowd of people toward the
Quay. She had one child on her back, and she carried the other in her
arms. Eventually, they reached the great mass of people, and she sat
down among the throng at the waterfront. She saw Turkish soldiers on
the Quay and ships in the harbor. Later, a truck came through and bread
was distributed to the crowd. She was able to get a piece, and she shared
it with the children.

It was several days later that she heard the people around talking
about a fire. It was coming toward them, they said, and they might have
to jump into the sea. Theodora smelled the fire before she could see it.
In time it reached them and she saw the giant flames. She ran with the
others up and down the Quay to escape the heat. She had been sure
many times that they would die, but somehow God had delivered them.

Always, she held the children's hands tightly; always she prayed; and
always she remembered her mother. She made the sign of the cross.

Kyrie Eleison, Kryie Eleison.

The days of the fire passed in confusion, and somehow Theodora and
her little sisters had survived and they were back on the Quay, and they
found a place where they would be given bread to eat and water to drink
by people who did not speak Greek, nor any language that she could
understand.

CHAPTER 24

Days of Despair

And so it went on September 17, 18, and 19—days of utter helplessness and hopelessness.

As the suffering worsened, Powell and his officers began to have trouble making sure the American sailors remained neutral and did not interfere with the Turkish soldiers. The sailors wanted to do something for the refugees.

A sailor posted as a sentry at the American consulate allowed two Greek priests being chased by mounted Turkish soldiers to duck into the consulate building for protection—this was strictly against orders. The priests were Ottoman subjects. Powell put more officers ashore to watch the sailors, but controlling the officers became a problem too. Lieutenant Commander Knauss had helped the two Greek priests who had escaped into the consulate by offering them clothes (in place of their long black gowns and toadstool hats) and a chance to slip out a back door. The sailors also had begun taking Greek and Armenian girls from the Turkish soldiers and escorting them to Jennings. *She's my girl,* they told the soldiers, and the soldiers surrendered them. Powell did not object—the Turkish soldiers did not put up much trouble in surrendering the girls to the sailors, maybe because there were plenty of others, easily plucked from the crowds. Jennings took them all and found space in his houses. Some of the sailors lingered with Jennings to provide a uniformed American presence to dissuade the Turks from retrieving the women.

Unfortunately, not all the women were rescued: "From the military bakeries," Ernest Jacob recounted, "comes direct and detailed testimony of what has been reported from many another place. . . . The Turkish guards took five girls from among the refugees, stripped them, made them dance, violated and then killed them."

The relief committee continued to distribute food delivered by the destroyers and to provide emergency medical care where it could. The city's hospitals had been destroyed, and Jennings's houses were the only sheltered locations for medical care. Refugees suffered from burns, gunshot and bayonet wounds, and rape, and typhus had broken out in the city. The fleas on rats carry the bacterium that causes typhus, and the fire had dispersed the city's rat population. Cholera, the consequence of the lack of toilets in the city, had also broken out. Weak from hunger, thirst, and fatigue, refugees—especially the oldest and youngest—readily succumbed to the diseases. Rape had left women not only mentally traumatized; they suffered severe physical injures—tearing of tissue, bleeding, and contusions. Some committed suicide. Dr. Post (who had returned from Salonika) cared for pregnant women throughout the city and went out to the refugees on a barge and a derelict schooner anchored in the harbor. He delivered a baby on the barge. A local doctor, Dr. Margoulis, a Jewish resident of Smyrna, assisted him in his medical work. The committee found it difficult to keep track of the locations of the refugees as the Turkish command chased them from place to place, or the refugees moved en masse without notice, driven by terror.

Passenger ships that had regularly called on Smyrna mostly avoided the city now because of the fear of disease, but a trickle of refugees was able to leave by buying passage on the few steamers that had called on the city or on merchant ships chartered by the British, French, and Italians to remove their nationals and protégés. By demanding passports and visas, documents that were next to impossible for refugees to produce, the Turkish army had essentially closed off the possibility of refugees surreptitiously departing on the vessels intended to take away European nationals. In some cases, the French and Italians supplied documents to refugees who had found a way to make a personal or compelling appeal based on the ability to speak French or Italian. For the overwhelming mass of people there was no escape.

NIGHTS ON THE QUAY invited terror. Emboldened by the darkness, Turkish soldiers came onto the Quay, looted refugee possessions, and took away girls. There were many more refugees than soldiers, and while the refugees carried only a few household items with them, it was enough to lure soldiers back night after night.

Some of the Allied ships swept the searchlights on their decks over the Quay to disperse the soldiers. Oddly, it worked. The Turkish soldiers seemed not to want to be seen by the Allied and American navies as they preyed on the people. There is probably no better description of the nights on the Quay than the one offered by Ernest Hemingway, through the voice of a British officer, in his short story "On the Quai at Smyrna."

> The strange thing was, he said, how they screamed every night at midnight. I do not know why they screamed at that time. We were in the harbor and they were all on the pier and at midnight they started screaming. We used to turn the searchlight on them to quiet them. That always did the trick. We'd run the searchlight up and down over them two or three times and they stopped it.

Hemingway actually never got to Smyrna; he had heard the details from a recently returned British officer, most likely at the bar of the Pera Palace Hotel.

While he was in Turkey and Greece Hemingway produced twenty-six chiseled pieces for the *Toronto Star* related to the Greek-Turkish War. The genius of the young novelist rings in each of them. The opening passage of his Smyrna short story matches other first-person Smyrna accounts, though Hemingway's version distills the suffering into timeless language. If the voice of modern American literature—detached, ironic, cynical, piercing—can be traced to Hemingway, then it is no exaggeration to say that Hemingway found the expression of that voice, or at least the perfection of that expression, in the suffering at Smyrna.

> The worst, he said, were the women with dead babies. You couldn't get the women to give up their dead babies. They'd have babies dead for six days. Wouldn't give them up. Nothing you could do about it. Had to take them away finally.

And so it was: in the daytime, the women grasped their dead children; in the night, the warships in the harbor ran their lights over the crowds to dissuade Turks from the worst of their brutality. The refugees understood this, and when the lights passed over them, they felt a little safer. Their screaming ceased.

ON SEPTEMBER 19, a dirty and ill-kept tramp steamer, the SS *Treaty of Versailles*, came into Smyrna harbor and dropped its anchor. The Orthodox patriarch in Constantinople, with help from Near East Relief, had chartered the vessel to carry away refugees. It had a British registry, and the senior British naval officer in Smyrna negotiated the ground rules for bringing it to the railroad pier to load refugees. The British officer asked Powell for the assistance of his crew, which Powell eagerly provided, and the ship was loaded with people from the Quay, departing on September 20 for the island of Lesbos. A second British-flagged merchant vessel, the SS *Worsley Hall*, equally foul from carrying cargoes of coal, arrived, and it too was loaded with refugees. The vessels removed forty-eight hundred people to Lesbos, but the departures seemed to make very little difference in the numbers of people on the Quay. The Near East Relief also had arranged for a Russian freighter to steam to Smyrna to carry away refugees, though it would take several days for it to arrive. In addition, Bristol sent a message to Powell that said the SS *Manhattan Island*, an American freighter in Constantinople, would make the trip to Smyrna if an American agent in the city could guarantee a cargo of tobacco. There might also be room for refugees, he said, but the tobacco came first.

Powell estimated that about twenty-five thousand people had been evacuated in the days since the outbreak of the fire—three thousand by the American ships (the *Litchfield* and the *Winona* on the first night and following day of the fire), six thousand by the French, six thousand by the Italians, and fourteen thousand by the British on British merchant ships carrying away British nationals, as well as the refugees on the SS *Versailles* and *Worsley Hall*. Hundreds of thousands remained. In fact, more people had come into the city than had been removed.

There was next to no food, water supplies were damaged, disease had broken out, but it was the lack of sea transport that proved most troublesome to the relief committee. Evacuation had emerged as the only way to save lives, and the American Relief Committee was the only group trying to get ships. No international effort had been launched, and Bristol was not making an effort in Constantinople. The absence of ships seemed to seal the fate of the people. Jennings continued to minister to the refugees in his houses, but he, like the other relief volunteers, understood that their efforts were not the answer—they were simply buying a little more time until starvation and disease prevailed. "We therefore became more and more anxious and determined for boats," Jennings explained in a letter afterward. Jennings directed his daily prayers to finding ships.

THEN CAME THE CHILLING EVIDENCE that the Turks had indeed decided to dispose of the refugees by marching them out of the city. Several days earlier, Jennings, on a trip back to Paradise, had seen Turkish soldiers marching hundreds of refugees eastward, toward the interior. Captain Hepburn had taken note of Jennings's report, and worried about it, but he had held open the possibility the Turks were marching refugees that Jennings had seen back to their homes.

But additional sightings by American officers made it clear that by September 17, forced deportations had begun. American patrols saw refugees being herded in large groups out of town and eastward toward the mountains and desolate tablelands of the Anatolian interior. Other witnesses confirmed the deportations, and soon the Turks made no secret of it. A feeling of horror descended on the Americans. Dr. Post was among those who had witnessed the Armenian death marches of 1915

and 1916. While running the American hospital in Konya in the fall of
1915, Dr. Post had been one of the missionaries who had alerted Ambassador Morgenthau to the scope of the forced marches with descriptive
letters documenting the death and suffering.

The Young Turk government had employed the forced marches to
kill hundreds of thousands of Armenian women and children. The killing had begun with Turkey's entrance into World War I, but the organized top-down orders for the systematic removal of Armenians came
in April 1915. The typical method was for soldiers or police to round
up Armenians in the cities, towns, and villages where they lived. The
roundup then proceeded to the killing—males were killed outside of the
settlement by sword or bullet, and women and children were led on long
marches to wastelands to the south, deserts in Iraq or Syria. Most died of
starvation, thirst, exhaustion, and outright slaughter along the way.

At Trebizond, on the Black Sea, the Italian consulate remembered
the scene:

> The passing of gangs of Armenian exiles beneath the windows and
> before the door of the Consulate . . . the lamentations, tears, the aban-
> donments, the imprecations, the many suicides, the instantaneous
> deaths from sheer terror, the sudden unhinging of men's reason,
> the conflagrations, the shooting of victims in the city, the ruthless
> searches through the houses and in the countryside; the hundreds
> of corpses found every day along the exile road; the young women
> converted by force to Islam or exiled like the rest; the children torn
> [a]way from their families or from Christian schools, and handed over
> by force to Muslim families, or else packed by hundreds on board
> ship in nothing but their shirts, and then capsized and drowned in
> the Black Sea and River Deyirmen Dere—they are my last ineffable
> memories of Trebizond, memories which still, at a month's distance,
> torment my soul and almost drive me frantic.

Of the fourteen thousand Armenians who had lived in Trebizond,
fewer than one hundred had survived at the time of the Italian consul's
departure.

The nationalists had used similar methods to dispose of Greek and Armenian women and children from towns and cities along the Black Sea and central Anatolia. In May of 1922, Dr. F. D. Yowell, director of the Near East Relief unit at Harpoot, a city in central Anatolia, reported, "Conditions of Greek minorities are even worse than those of the Armenians. Sufferings of the Greeks deported from districts behind the battlefront are terrible and still continue. These deportees began to reach Harpoot before my arrival last October. Of thirty thousand Greek refugees who left Sivas, five thousand died on the way before reaching Harpoot. One American relief worker saw and counted fifteen hundred bodies on the road east of Harpoot."*

In Smyrna, the relief committee saw the nightmare of deportations being repeated. The refugees—women, children, and old men in some groups, men of military age in others—were rounded up, formed roughly into lines, and marched out of the city, herded along by the Turkish cavalry.

Traveling through the city and estimating the numbers of people in the key concentration areas, Jacob was unable to account for large numbers of people. "It seems almost impossible to estimate how many refugees there are," he wrote. After the fire, there had been hundreds of thousands on the Quay—and still more in the unburned back sections of the city. He estimated that from 40,000 to 125,000 men had already been deported to the interior. "But," he asked, "where are the rest?" The answer was that the women and children—as well as the men—were being removed and taken into the backcountry for execution.

The American officers saw the Turkish soldiers collecting and moving the refugees in large groups. There were five roads out of Smyrna, one north, two east, one south, and one along the coast toward Chesme. Relief workers and sailors observed refugees on the roads going east and south—towad Magnesia, Nif, and Paradise. Each day, the numbers of people on the Quay and in the concentration areas fell. Soon, Powell witnessed it himself. "About a thousand refugees were seen being marched

---

* Bristol had tried unsuccessfully to suppress the report, which had been delivered to the consul general in Aleppo.

along the waterfront to the southward under a small guard," Powell recorded in his ship's diary. "Deportations are continuing and are acknowledged by the Turks."

Most were driven toward Magnesia and beyond. Many were killed at a deep canyon along the Magnesia Road called Buyuk Dere.

News of the deportations spread through the exhausted hordes of people and created a new panic. Tens of thousands gathered around the American consulate and Jennings's safe houses, trying to get as close to them as possible. Even if they could not get inside, they hoped that simply being near an American institution would protect them. The consulate and safe houses, combined with the destroyers anchored close to the Quay, created a strong American presence near the tip of the Point. America had a reputation for justice among all the peoples of Asia Minor—Greeks, Turks, Armenians, Jews, and Arabs—and the refugees, who knew their tormentors, felt that the very presence of Americans would be an obstacle to Turkish cruelty. They were mostly correct—an incident was less likely to occur in the presence of an American.

But out of the sight of the Americans, the deportations continued—and none of the Turkish authorities offered information about the ultimate fate of the people who were being removed. "Turks were proceeding with evacuation of refugees in wholesale manner," Knauss noted in his diary. "At the cemetery and football field the refugees had been evacuated and the road to Dadagatch [actually, "Daragatch," north and east of Smyrna to Bournabat—Author] was filled with women and children being driven towards the interior." Knauss saw that the Turks were gathering refugees at the Quay and in the small and unburned northern sections and moving them toward the back of the city and then toward the Daragatch road "in order to escape notice from the Quay." The lieutenant commander, who had been moved by the refugee suffering from the beginning, added, "Some very pitiful sights were noted. It is said that the Turks keep them on the go until they drop."

Jacob also witnessed the roundups. "The seizing of all men of military age, and on both sides of the age line," he wrote, "is being energetically pushed. The process complete in a given camp, the women and children are thrust into the streets, the prey of both soldiers and civilian Turkish rabble." Even Lieutenant Merrill, who had been indifferent to the suffering, took note: "The Turks never miss an opportunity to frighten the Armenians and Greeks. In passing through crowd of refugees they will invariably feel their bayonet points, whet their sabers or work the bolts of their guns."

Powell was doing his best, with the scant capacity he had to work with, to remove at least the orphan children who were collected in several places around the city under the protection of the relief committee, including at an unburned brewery. He sent another message to Bristol on September 19, this time via a British vessel, HMS *Serapis*, explaining that he was trying to get by with one destroyer so he could evacuate the orphans. Powell's note did not seek permission; it declared his intention to remove the children. He would eventually get it done, though it would take a few more days to work it out. He couldn't get the children off his mind.

CHAPTER 25

"We Are Celebrating Smyrna"

Mustapha Kemal fell in love soon after he entered Smyrna.

He had established his residence at a grand seaside home in Cordelio in one of two houses that had been selected as his headquarters, and, ironically, the same house that King Constantine had used when he had come to Smyrna in 1921. It was there that two elderly Turkish women cared for Kemal, preparing and serving his meals, laying out his clothes, emptying his overflowing ashtrays, and attending to his comfort. He smoked three packs of cigarettes and consumed fifteen cups of strong Turkish coffee each day. He did most of his work at Cordelio in the days soon after his arrival, concentrating on Chanak and talks with the Allied powers.

On September 11 or 12, a young woman who lived nearby—the daughter of Smyrna's richest Turkish resident, Muammer Bey—called on him. She was dressed modestly in European clothes but wore a black scarf over her head, the minimum of what was expected of a Muslim woman. She was petite, though not fragile; her hair was black and cut short into a style that was close to a bob, though not so daring. She had dark eyes, under dark eyebrows, that turned down slightly at their outer edges, which gave her a sleepy look, and a soft round face and high prominent brow. She was twenty-three years old and not particularly attractive except in a sensitive and intelligent way that invited a longer look. There was something oddly beguiling about her appearance.

Her name was Latife. Her family, with the exception of her father's mother, was living in exile, having departed soon after the Greek landing, and they were staying at their home in Paris. (They had another at Biarritz.) Latife had returned to Smyrna four months earlier on a steamer, by way of Marseille and Constantinople. She was living in the family's Cordelio house with her grandmother and their servants. She had returned from France with a single objective—to meet Kemal, whose successes she had followed in the newspapers. She was smitten before she met him.

Her call on Kemal at his headquarters in Cordelio was ostensibly to offer him the use of her family's second house in Smyrna. The aide told her that Kemal was too busy to see her, but she insisted on seeing him. It was clear to the aide that she was an upper-class woman, and being unable to persuade to her leave, he went to Kemal and reported that there was a woman in the anteroom who was asking to see him. Kemal declined to see her, but she walked into his office. She introduced herself and showed him a locket that she wore around her neck that contained a newspaper photograph of him.

"Do you mind?" she said.

"Why should I mind?" he answered.

He smiled and rose from his chair.

She said she had come to offer him the use of her family home in Göztepe, a district of summer villas just south of the city. She explained that her family was in France and the home was empty and available for his use. It was in a peaceful location; the air was known to be fresh. He would find, she said, that there were additional houses on the property that could be used by his staff. They talked some more, and Kemal was struck by her confident bearing and her direct eye contact. It was immediately clear to him that she was well educated. She had, in fact, studied law at the Sorbonne and attended a British boarding school. She had a quick mind and a pleasant voice. Her talk was clever and informed. Kemal was intrigued. He thanked her for the offer of her home and said he would consider it. Later in the day, he told Halide

Edib, who was among his staff at headquarters, that he had met a most unusual woman. He was in a very good mood.* Latife, for her part, later described the meeting in a letter to her uncle: "I met a pair of beautiful blue eyes."

Latife's family, known by the name Ushakizade, was commercial royalty in Smyrna. Her great-grandfather, Haci Ali Bey, had come to Smyrna from Ushak, where he had begun a carpet manufacturing business. One of his company's carpets had won the gold medal at the 1869 Paris Exhibition, and Emperor Napoleon III had given it as a gift to his wife. Ali Bey brought the business to Smyrna, where he lived as a cultivated businessman, and his book-filled home was an Ottoman salon. His son (Latife's grandfather), Sadik Bey, extended the family's holdings into transport between Aydin and Smyrna. He was said to own a camel train that reached nearly the entire seventy miles between the two cities. Sadik Bey held a seat on the New York Cotton Exchange. On a trip to Constantinople, Sadik fell in love with a Circassian concubine and married her. (Concubinage—slavery for sex with both women and boys—remained legal in the nineteenth century in Turkey; Circassian women, from the Caucasus, were considered the most desirable due to their light skin and perfect proportions.) Like his father, Sadik Bey also was a cultivated businessman, an aesthete. The house was full of books, music, and tutors. Sadik Bey's son and Latife's father, Muammer, further built the family's wealth and took a leading position in the city. He had been Smyrna's mayor and for a time was chairman of the district's Young Turks organization. He was a member of the Sporting Club and an avid bridge player, an obsession he shared with his close friend, the French consul general, with whom he often played in the garden of the house at Göztepe. The family lived in splendor—their home in Cordelio was decorated as an English manor house. They traveled to Europe for vacations.

Muammer spent lavishly on his children's educations. Latife had an

---

* An alternate description of their meeting is offered in a Turkish biography of Latife. In that account, she sent Kemal a note offering the house. This account is taken from Lord Kinross's magisterial biography, *Attatürk*. It conforms with the account of Halide Edib, who was with Kemal at the time.

English governess and tutors in German, English, Latin, French, and Arabic. The family had Greek servants, and when Latife came of age, her father hired a Greek girl to be her companion. At fourteen, Latife traveled to Constantinople and lived with her uncle, a chamberlain of Sultan Abdul Hamid, while she attended the American College for Girls. From there, she went to a British boarding school. Latife had taken a strong interest in all things German—language, music, and culture—and could recite long passages from Faust. She was tutored by the niece of the German poet Rilke, who said "she was the most talented of all my students" and looked like a "Murillo Madonna."

In addition to being an indulgent father, Muammer—a big man, bald but suavely handsome—had a reputation as a ladies' man and was connected, at least in Smyrna gossip, to a Greek cabaret dancer who performed in the decidedly downscale Quarantine district of the waterfront, where sailors sought amusement. The dancer's name was Despina, and Muammer fell hard for her. He carried on an affair with her but she ultimately threw him off for a handsome young Greek officer. Muammer was heartbroken, and the story made the rounds of Smyrna society, high and low, and found its way into song and a poem by one of Turkey's most famous poets, Atilla Ilhan. It suggests the exotic potion that was Smyrna, simultaneously mixing and separating its people against a sensual backdrop of entertainment and pleasure.

> With a rose in her hair every night
> You would feel an earthquake when the brunette canto girl
>   started.
> Goblets would tremble; glasses would break from the applause
> —Muammer Bey's favorite, Despina of Karantina.
>
> With a coquettish smile, she'd take a swift carriage from
>   Cordelio.
> How different she was of all women in every way,
> She would lull Muammer Bey with endless happiness
> distilled from her many affairs.

Invasion confused everything in Izmir.
But Despina learned to draw upon this nefarious night
To make love to Colonel Zafiru at the Splendid
Before the Greek battleships in the gulf.

Reflection of ship lights on gardens,
Milky Way's mode, song by the pool,
As his solitude brews, Muammer Bey realizes
It is not possible for one human to understand another.

KEMAL DID NOT IMMEDIATELY ACCEPT Latife's offer of the house.

On September 12, he moved his headquarters to the Quay and occupied the home of an Armenian who had left city. He was at work there
when the fire broke out, and he stayed as the flames approached the
Quay. Then when the home caught fire, at about the time Charles Davis
left the *Litchfield* to seek Allied help in rescuing refugees, Kemal and his
staff abandoned the Quay headquarters, Kemal and a few others in the
big Mercedes and others in a truck. They returned to the first headquarters, at Cordelio.

Kemal remained there for several days until the smell of the corpses
and dead animals decomposing in the harbor forced his departure. The
south wind brought the putrid odor into the big windows of the Cordelio
house. He and his staff moved to Latife's Göztepe home on September
17—the day Powell walked the Quay to the Konak and met Jennings. It
was also the day General Pelle was in Smyrna, suggesting that Kemal
likely stopped at the Konak to talk with Pelle—or brought him to Göztepe for talks about the Allied naval presence in the harbor.

The house that Latife had offered Kemal was a four-story white mansion set on a steep hill back from the harbor and among tall trees. It had
two curving sets of front steps that led around and over a first-floor arched
doorway to a second-story veranda and the home's main entrance. The
veranda was hung with jasmine, roses, ivy, and wisteria, and there were
flower gardens spread among the grounds. Kemal took it as his home

and headquarters. His office was in a big room at the front left of the second floor, and his bedroom was directly above the office. At first, Latife remained with her grandmother in Cordelio, but soon the two moved with their servants to the white mansion. She looked after Kemal and ensured his comfort, making sure his favorite foods were served, fresh flowers were in the vase on the table next to his bed, and his photos from the newspapers were prominently displayed in his office. Soon she was serving as his secretary—translating documents, writing letters, and offering ideas. Right about this time, Kemal—whose health from military life, hard drinking, and chain smoking was precarious—suffered some sort of cardiac spasm, and Muammer's doctor was called. He proscribed tobacco and alcohol, and Latife tried to limit Kemal's indulgence. She placed only two cigarettes next to his bed at night.

It was clear to the people around Kemal that he was infatuated with Latife. He talked of her continually to Halide Edib, extolling her good manners, education, and ideas. Kemal was impressed too by her patriotism—she dismissed her father's losses in the fire as less important than the nationalist victory.

But the situation for Kemal was complicated. Most of his experience with women had been as a soldier, and he had a reputation for a voracious sexual appetite, which he satisfied casually, often with prostitutes. He possessed, as a confidant said, an instinct for the harem. Latife, as an upper-class Muslim woman, guarded her modesty.

Since boyhood Kemal had displayed an uneasy relationship with women, especially with his mother, against whose religion and control he had rebelled as a boy but to whom he had shown unfailing Muslim respect and deference as an adult. There was one sexual relationship that had figured importantly in life. It was with a woman who was a cousin through marriage. Her name was Fikriye. Slim and attractive with dark eyes and a long face, she was sixteen years younger than Kemal. His mother had taken in the girl, who was essentially an orphan, when they had lived in Salonika. Mother and adopted daughter moved to Constantinople after Salonika had passed to Greece. Kemal and Fikriye were lovers in Constantinople soon after the end of World War I. Kemal was thirty-six; she was twenty. She worshipped him. During the

Greek-Turkish War, she had followed him to Ankara and lived with him as a companion. Kemal was affectionate to her, though he continued his loose life in Ankara. He enjoyed the comfortable home life she had made for them, but standing between Kemal and Fikriye was Kemal's mother, who did not approve of her as a match. Fikriye was educated, played the piano, and was an expert rider, but Kemal's mother wanted a woman of higher social standing for her son, and the son was mindful of his mother's opposition.

On September 19, Latife put together a party for Kemal at the white mansion and invited his closest commanders and the Turkish journalists who had arrived from Constantinople. Kemal and the guests drove to the mansion from the city in the early evening. They came up the curved steps and were greeted on the veranda by Latife. Among them were Halide Edib and Ismet and Falih Refki. (None of the accounts place Noureddin at the party, suggesting that Kemal had relied on his military prowess but felt no affection for him.) Latife, dressed in black, met them at the veranda and offered each a greeting of peace, "As-salamu, alaykum." Kemal disappeared briefly to his room upstairs and returned to the main sitting room on the second floor wearing a white Caucasus Mountain tunic with a belt, his hair brushed back, eyes gleaming. "She was dazzled by him and he was frankly in love," wrote Halide Edib. "So the strong current of human attraction between the two enlivened the evening."

At one point, Kemal, who was standing next to a table of drinks, said to Halide, "We are celebrating Smyrna—you must drink with us." Halide refused his raki, but accepted a glass of champagne. She raised her glass and wished the two of them happiness. Latife also refused Kemal's raki, which upset him—a minor moment of unpleasantness that would suggest much trouble ahead between the two strong personalities.

But it was a night of celebration, and Kemal's spirits soared. He reminisced about his life in Salonika and told stories of the many battlefronts he had experienced. In the night's conversation, Kemal had dismissed the fire that had burned Smyrna as the cost of war. He showed no particular concern for the refugees. (Latife would later quote him as having said, "Let it burn. Let it crash down.") The Victrola was wound, music was played, and Kemal sang Roumeli folks songs—the peasant songs of Macedonia and the southern Balkans. As he commanded the table with his stories and songs, Halide Edib was thinking of Fikriye, and of the pain she would experience on learning of Latife's entrance into Kemal's life. (In a few months, Fikriye would put a pistol to her head and commit suicide.) Kemal carried on at the table, laughing, talking, and singing. He dominated the room. Halide was beginning to find the night tiresome.

Kemal continued to drink raki and talk expansively, and, finally, overcome by his feelings—in the traditional manner of the rough men of the Anatolian hills and Aegean Islands—he got up to dance the zeybeck, in which a lone dancer wanders the floor with his arms spread until he feels the nine-beat rhythm of the music and the inner force of his wild soul and begins to dance—making himself into an eagle, proud and fierce, the predator that drops out of the sky.

CHAPTER 26

Jennings and the Hand of God

I t is difficult to know precisely what happened to Asa Jennings on the morning of September 20.

It was a Wednesday, his birthday, and he was turning forty-five years old, though the day would pass uncelebrated. It was one more hopeless and breathless day in a long string of hot, hopeless, and breathless days on the Smyrna waterfront. The sun came up behind the city and baked the red roofs and gray cobbles of the street. Hollow-eyed women and skinny children crouched where they could find shade—in the lee of a standing shattered wall or under a blanket hung between two upright sticks. Dogs limped through the rubble, heads down, and tongues out, jackal-like. Occasionally, a breeze worried the surface of the harbor.

Jennings stood in front of his safe house at No. 490 and looked down the length of the Quay. He saw refugees, mostly motionless except to pick lice off their children. There were mounted Turkish soldiers whose horses occasionally shook their heads against the flies. Lieutenant Commander Powell and a few American sailors were outside the nearby consulate, and the *Edsall* was anchored in its usual place, just off the Quay. The British ships *Curacoa* and *Serapis* and several merchant vessels also were in the harbor, all at anchor. The atmosphere was static, desultory, tired, and hot, and whatever movement occurred seemed to be formed without intent or consequence.

The deeper motivation behind the action Jennings was about to take, setting far-reaching events in motion, had been present throughout his life, but Jennings himself did not seem to know its immediate cause. Maybe it was the consequence of his powerful empathy encountering unimaginable despair. Possibly the fever that he lived with every day had spiked in the hot morning sun and caused some dislocation of his thinking and, as a result, loosened his normal restraint. Did he have a vision of his imagined Jerusalem, the place as well as the meaning of it? Maybe he'd had a moment of clarity brought on by his awareness of advancing age and declining health. Time was running out on his chance to achieve the importance he told Amy he had wanted his life to embrace. Asa had been inclined toward a religious life since boyhood, and his deep faith coupled with a strong sense of personal duty. Maybe this was the moment for which he had been allowed to live twenty years earlier when the abscess had broken in the Adirondack cabin. He stood alone on the Quay, but he felt (he would later say) God's hand placed on his shoulder.

He described the sensation that surged through him as an "uncontrollable desire" to save the lives of the people who had come under his protection. There were about two thousand of them now, women and children, spread among a number of safe houses at the north end of the Quay. In the two weeks since the relief committee had relegated him to messenger-boy status, Jennings had pulled women from the streets where some had begun to give birth and others from the water where they had tried to drown themselves. He watched refugees being beaten and shot and carried off to be raped.

Jennings had been fully occupied with the care of the people in "his houses," as he called them, not getting much sleep and suffering with his own broken body. Lack of sleep can also be a powerful drug, so it might be said that on Wednesday morning, September 20, 1922, Jennings was drugged into action.

He was nothing if not respectful of authority and he had accepted the directions he had been given—and not given. The relief committee had assigned someone else to find ships to remove the refugees to a safer place. So, being a man who understood obedience, he had left that job to another, though every day he had prayed privately for ships.

As he scanned the harbor, Jennings saw a passenger ship that had arrived the previous day. It flew the French flag from its stern, and it was taking on passengers. Jennings was unaware of it, but the ship had been a Russian navy vessel until it was sold to a French steamship company for passenger service in the Levant. It was named *Pierre Loti* after the French naval officer of the same name, a passionate Orientalist and novelist.

Jennings went to Powell, pointed to the ship, and said he would like a sailor to take him out to it. He wanted to see if he could get the ship to take away some of the people in his care. There were other ships in the harbor, but Jennings had fastened his attention on the *Pierre Loti*, and he asked Powell for a launch and a sailor to ferry him to it. Powell gave him a long look, then consented and sent him off in a motor sailer. Powell and Jennings were friends by now, and Powell had come around to helping Jennings in his mission by assigning sailors to bring women to his shelter.

Do your darnedest, Powell said to Jennings as Jennings limped to the seawall.

Jennings got into the launch with the sailor and motored toward the *Pierre Loti*. He went on board and met the captain, who told him that the vessel was full. The captain would not—could not—take more passengers. Unable to shake the "uncontrollable urge" that had seized him on the Quay, Jennings again surveyed the harbor. He saw a second steamer, the *Constantinopoli*, which was flying the red, white, and green flag of Italy. A tramp steamer, it was a twenty-four-year-old 330-foot-long single-screw vessel with a long fantail that hung over an exposed rudder. It had a cabin amidships, one stack, and two masts, one fore and aft. It looked like a cross between a Chinese junk, a city bus, and a scrap yard. It was primarily a cargo ship, but it held a few well-appointed cabins for passengers. In its first life, as the *Citta Di Torino*, it had carried thousands of poor Italian immigrants to New York and Buenos Aires from Genoa, Palermo, and Naples, but since America had tightened its immigration laws, *Citta Di Torino* had made a new life, principally as a cargo ship, plying the Levant. Today, it was scheduled to sail from Smyrna to the city for which it was named.

Jennings directed the sailor to take him to the *Constantinopoli*. He went aboard, and the Italian captain told him the ship was scheduled to sail in a few hours and without refugees. It was carrying cargo and a few paying passengers. Jennings put his request to the captain: Would he accept two thousand refugees for passage to Lesbos, which was on the way to Constantinople? No, the captain said, it was impossible; there were too many obstacles to taking aboard refugees. His orders would have to be changed by his employer, the steamship company Servizi Marittimi. It was impossible to reach them from Smyrna. Anyway, even if the company allowed him to take the refugees aboard, what assurance did he have that the harbormaster at Mytilene, the port at Lesbos, would permit them to be unloaded? And what about the Turkish authorities? the Italian captain wanted to know. Would they countenance the transfer of two thousand people from the Quay to his ship? And, even if these obstacles could be surmounted, who would pay for their passage? Jennings had to know that his ship was not a philanthropic organization.

The captain's last question suggested that he was keeping an open mind—based possibly on the quiet exchange of some cash. What would Jennings be willing to pay him if the obstacles could be overcome? Jennings understood that he was being felt out on a bribe—*baksheesh*, the universal language of the Levant. Let me work on this, Jennings told him. If things could be worked out, the captain said, the refugees would need to be on board for a 10 A.M. departure the next morning. The deadline was firm; he would delay only one day.

Elated, Jennings went ashore and told Powell and Davis of his meeting with the Italian captain. Davis approved the expenditure. The captain wanted $5,000. Money for the passage would be collected from the refugees who had it, and the rest (including the bribe) would come from Near East Relief. As it turned out, many of the refugees had sewn money into their clothes or had been able to hide it from the bandits and soldiers on the street, and most ended up paying their own passage. Davis gave Jennings papers that identified him as a member of the American Relief Committee at Smyrna and told him to determine whether additional refugees could be landed at Mytilene, whether there would be housing for them, and what supplies would be needed if others were sent. Overnight, Jennings, Davis, and Powell prepared the refugees for departure. The Turkish authorities had granted permission for the evacuation, but only women, children, and old men would be allowed to depart. The women pleaded for their husbands and brothers to no avail. In the morning, Thursday, September 21, Turkish soldiers appeared at the house at 490 and formed a row from the front door to the Quay to be sure no men joined the evacuees. "It was heartbreaking to see the grief," Jennings later recalled.

Powell provided the whaleboats to ferry the refugees to the ship. It was a lot of people. Hepburn had transported about two hundred on the first night of the fire, but Powell needed to move two thousand with fewer boats and men. To make matters worse, a wind had come up—the "donkey wind," which often came up in the afternoons when the heat of the land pulled in air from the cooler sea and created an updraft. The harbor had turned rough and sloppy. Powell put his men to work in the whaleboats and motor cruiser moving back and forth between the safe houses on the Quay and the *Constantinopoli*. The job was not complete until the late afternoon, well beyond the Italian captain's announced sailing time of the day before at 10 A.M., but with the money in hand, the captain held the ship.

Powell told Jennings he would have the *Litchfield* pick him up at Mytilene, the main port at Lesbos, the next day. Powell had finally been able to send the *Litchfield* to Salonika, earlier that morning, with the orphans he had wanted so much to evacuate; it was returning to Smyrna the following day. Like Davis, Powell instructed Jennings to investigate the feasibility of Mytilene as a trans-shipping station for refugees.

Jennings and the *Constantinopoli* departed Smyrna at 5 P.M., September 21.

THE CONSTANTINOPOLI WAS PACKED with women, children, and old men— from stem to stern, above and below deck. No space was left unoccupied, and Jennings had been barely able to pass from the gangway to his cabin. "I could scarcely get through the mass of people that crowded around me," he later said. "They fell at my feet in gratitude. They kissed me. Old men got on their knees kissing my hands and feet, tears streaming down their faces. They did everything they could to show their thanks."

As the people mobbed him, they wept for family members left behind and begged Jennings to find a way to bring them away too. Jennings was overcome with emotion and embarrassment and disappeared
into his cabin. "When I finally reached the cabin assigned to me," he
recalled later, "I dropped on the berth and burst out crying." He said his
prayers and thanked God for the ship. "There in that cabin," he told a
reporter a year later, "I thanked Him for His guidance, and asked Him
to continue it." After he collected himself, Jennings left his cabin and by
happenstance met a passenger who had booked one of the cabins for the
trip to Constantinople. He was Ernesto Aliotti, a twenty-five-year-old Italian Smyrniot with fine features and dark hair parted at the middle. The
Aliottis were among Smyrna's most successful families and had piled up
a fortune from, among other things, carpets. Ernesto's grandfather had
been a founder of the Oriental Carpet Co. It was a fortuitous meeting.
Aliotti spoke English, and he and Jennings talked as the ship steamed
and rolled ever so slowly toward Mytilene.

The trip from Smyrna to Mytilene was only about one hundred
miles. Lesbos, a big island shaped like a triangle with rounded edges, had
been an Ottoman possession until ten years earlier, when it had passed to
Greece after the First Balkan War. Mytilene, a small but prosperous city
of twenty-five thousand people, was its principal harbor, on the southeast
point of the blunt triangle. In the daylight, Turkey was visible from the
port city as a line of low brown hills only six miles distant. Now, at night
from the deck of the *Constantinopoli*, the Turkish headland was dark
except for the flicker of a few lights at Aivali. No moon was visible in the
sky; it had waned since the first week of the month, and on this night it
finally disappeared. The night was black.

On the trip, Jennings described to Aliotti his mission to deliver the
refugees and determine whether others could be brought from Smyrna.
Aliotti was helpful, and it didn't take much effort to persuade him to join
Jennings. Aliotti spoke Greek as well as English and Italian, so his presence would make Jennings's task much easier. He was also a man of important reputation and wide acquaintance; he had contacts on the island
who could assist a relief committee. His name assured instant credibility.
The *Constantinopoli* arrived at Mytilene at midnight, Thursday, Septem-

ber 21. Jennings and Aliotti continued to formulate a plan of tasks and committees, which would be made up of the people on Allioti's list. At 5 A.M. the two men went ashore. It was still dark.

A rock breakwater with a narrow entrance that admitted only smaller vessels protected Mytilene's harbor. The *Constantinopoli* was too big and its draft too deep to tie up at the inner harbor's dock so it waited at anchor offshore. Soon, the sun was rising over the Turkish headlands and threw its bright rays on the white façades of Mytilene's harborfront and the dome of St. Therapon Cathedral. It was a picturesque port, gathered in a curve around the small harbor, with many pink and white villas among palm trees along the shorefront, but the pretty picture on that morning contained thousands of refugees and soldiers who had been evacuated from Smyrna and other Aegean ports in the days before the Turkish capture of Smyrna. Mytilene and Chios had been the two main holding areas as the army awaited its return to Greece. The streets, churchyards, and empty lots of the city were full of refugees, and soldiers camped in the open areas at the edge of the port.

Jennings and Aliotti went first to the harbormaster and woke him. He gave them the names of the people to whom they needed to talk to get permission to disembark refugees—the island's governor, the city's mayor, and General Athanasios Frangos, the commander of the First Infantry Division who had attempted to pull together the shattered forces at Dumlupinar for evacuation at the coast. In addition, Jennings and Aliotti found others who could help, including Percival Hodgkinson, a retired British intelligence officer and septalingual Smyrna businessman who had been vacationing at Mytilene, and Panos Argyopoulos, a Greek naval officer who had been cashiered by the Royalist government in 1920. They turned wherever they could for assistance. By 7 A.M. Friday, Jennings and Aliotti had arranged for a doctor to board the ship to inspect the refugees for disease, and soon thereafter, tugs were provided to take the people ashore to join the crowds who were already there.

Jennings, with Aliotti's help, spent the day meeting and making arrangements. The island's authorities welcomed them and reported that a Home Defense Committee already had been formed to assist refugees, but it had exhausted its funds. The authorities deferred to Jennings and his new now-forming committee, and they were willing to accept more refugees on the island if food could be provided to feed them. Jennings learned there were already about 75,000 refugees in the city, and 35,000 soldiers. The supply of flour was expected to last only three more days. Jennings made an executive decision—he promised deliveries of Near East Relief flour to the island. The governor said he would open the city's hospital to refugees and provide warehouse space for supplies, and the mayor said he would ask the island's residents to open their homes to the refugees; it was acknowledged by all that most refugees would sleep in the open, but as Jennings noted, "Any place would be better than on the Quay at Smyrna."

These meetings occurred near the city's harborfront and within view of the Greek merchant ships that had evacuated the Greek troops. They lay at anchor offshore in the same vicinity as the *Constantinopoli*. Their presence raised the obvious question of their use to evacuate more refugees from Smyrna. The refugees he had just landed were the first to make a plea to Jennings to put them to use. He counted ten empty ships quietly at anchor in the offshore haze. He took the proposition to Frangos, who declined it, saying he feared their seizure by the Turks. Jennings asked him if he would release the ships if the American navy guaranteed them protection, a proposal Jennings had no authority to offer, nor had he discussed it with Powell.

Under those circumstances, American protection and a guarantee of safety, Frangos said, he could release six of the smaller vessels, which had a capacity of about six hundred persons each. (Frangos, it would be learned later, had only nominal control over the troops on the island. A revolution was brewing in both the officer corps and the ranks.)

At about 6 P.M., Rhodes and the *Litchfield*, back from Salonika, arrived at Mytilene to pick up Jennings, as Powell had arranged the previous day. Rhodes went ashore to find him. He brought with him Cass Reed, the International College professor who had accompanied the college staff and orphans to Salonika. The two men had no idea where Jennings was, so they walked to the Grand Bretagne Hotel, a waterfront landmark with an impressive neoclassical façade and steeply sloped tile roof. It was a meeting place of the city's prosperous business class. There,

Rhodes and Cass Reed met several people Reed knew from Smyrna—Griswold's partner in the fig business and some of the Whittals and Patersons, two wealthy Levantine families. Paterson owned the warehouse that the Smyrna Committee had drawn upon to feed refugees. Paterson had been on his yacht *Cleo* when the troubles had broken out. Rhodes also met an American Tobacco Co. agent, but he didn't find Jennings.

Rhodes and Reed waited in the hotel about an hour, then began walking back to the ship when they spotted Jennings in his straw boater and loose jacket near the harborfront. Jennings said he wanted to stay longer at Mytilene—he had set up a final meeting before his departure. Rhodes told him the *Litchfield* was leaving and he needed to be aboard.

On the way back to Smyrna, sometime after 6:30 P.M., Friday, September 22, Jennings prepared a summary of his visit for Powell, reporting that four to six ships were available to transport refugees if they were assured protection and if flour was sent along with the refugees. The *Litchfield*'s telegraph operator tapped it out to the *Edsall*.

WHILE JENNINGS HAD BEEN AWAY, Powell had continued to meet with the Allied naval officers, though no progress was being made toward an evacuation plan, mostly because of stalling by the French admiral. Powell, Admiral Pepe, and Admiral Tyrwhitt had met again with Admiral Dumesnil, whose obfuscations left the three baffled; the Frenchman was making no sense.

Powell continued to put requests to the Turkish authorities on behalf of the relief committee but with even less success than before. The Turks had begun to insist that the refugees present visas even to buy bread, which Turkish residents were peddling. Most of the concentration camps had been closed, which created another frustrating dispersal of the people, and conditions at the Balchova camp remained bad. He met with Nadja Bey, the military governor, to arrange the concentration of refugees at the city's football field and Greek cemetery, but he said he had to check with the civilian governor before agreeing to Powell's proposal. And so it went, nodding heads, promises, and more delays. In the meantime, the wind had shifted back to the north and picked up speed, restarting the fires, and

threatened the Paterson warehouse, the committee's larder, but they soon
died down again and the warehouse remained unburned.

On the same day, September 22, Powell, Davis, and the teacher J.
Kingsley Birge drove to Bournabat late in the afternoon, the soft time
of day when the plain and hillside behind Smyrna took on its red glow.
They wanted to meet with Halide Edib, the nationalist propagandist who
had traveled with the army to Smyrna, to enlist her help with gaining
the cooperation of the Turkish command. They met a petite woman,
thirty-six years old, with thick brown hair, whom Kemal had promoted
to the rank of sergeant in the army. She met them cordially, and in the
conversation that followed, blamed Greeks and Armenians for the fire
and described the Greek army's devastation of towns and villages in the
interior. Davis responded with an offer to send food aid to the devastated
districts and asked permission to visit them. She was noncommittal about
his access but sent her "very kindest" regards to Admiral and Mrs. Bristol. She hoped to join them soon, she said. The Americans returned to
Smyrna without having made any progress toward Turkish cooperation.

In a cable, either late on September 22 or early September 23, by
which time Jennings had returned from Mytilene, Powell informed Bristol of the evacuation of two thousand refugees on the *Constantinopoli*,
but he left out Jennings's name and adroitly backed into the sequence of
events:

> *Litchfield sailed Salonika 8 a.m. with 400. Will return via*
> *Mytilene and investigate necessity and possibility of relief work,*
> *and possibility of evacuating refugees there to be repatriated*
> *by Greece. Will make recommendation. Evacuated 2000 in SS*
> *Constantinopoli to Mytilene. Relief paid passage.*

It would be almost a week before Bristol was fully informed about
how Powell and Jennings were negotiating with the Greeks to bring off
the evacuation for far more refugees.

In Jennings's absence, Powell also had been trying hard to get a reliable answer on whether the Turks would allow Greek ships to evacuate
refugees. As early as Wednesday, September 20, Powell had gotten infor-

mal information through a Turkish liaison officer that Greek merchant ships would be allowed into the harbor if they did not fly the Greek flag. It was a breakthrough, if it was true, and Powell was cheered by the news, but he wanted confirmation. Too many promises had been made and never kept for him to trust the liaison officer's information. Late on the same day, under State Department pressure, Bristol had given Powell the okay, if he had Turkish permission, to use destroyers to embark refugees to vessels chartered by Near East Relief or the Greek Patriarch. The next day, Thursday, September 21, the day Jennings had departed for Mytilene, Powell, with Davis, had called on the military governor to get confirmation of the permission and ask for an extension of the evacuation deadline. Powell got the usual answer: the governor said he would take up the questions with his superiors. So he had been right to be cautious: nothing had been settled.

The next afternoon, September 22, Captain Hepburn arrived back in Smyrna on another destroyer, the USS *MacLeish*, the fifth to call on the city. He was focused on making arrangements for the SS *Manhattan Island* to pick up American tobacco whose shipment had been arranged by Archbell and Griswold and to take away refugees if it had room. Hepburn met with Powell and Barnes over dinner aboard the *MacLeish*, and they made a plan to have the *Manhattan Island* come first to Smyrna, pick up the tobacco and refugees, and then sail to Kavala, a city in northern Greece, where it would deliver the refugees and pick up more tobacco, before returning to the United States. Tobacco was the priority, and refugees would be taken aboard only if the cost of carrying them was guaranteed by someone in a position to pay, most likely Near East Relief.

Soon after dinner, Hepburn received a telegraph calling him back to Constantinople. Bristol wanted him to return with two destroyers. He departed at 9:30 P.M. on the *MacLeish*. Charles Davis joined him for the return. Hepburn told Powell to send the *Litchfield* back to Constantinople when it returned from Mytilene later that night.

At some point on September 22, probably very late, Powell got the message he had been waiting for. It came as a memorandum signed by Noureddin: "Your commission is informed that Greek steamers can come to Smyrna, but not under their own flag, and provided they do not tie up to the Quay or piers. The embarkation of the refugees is to be under the control and protection of the government of Great National Assembly."

It's not clear from the record whether he received the message before or after Hepburn departed for Constantinople, but it seems likely that it came afterward since Powell doesn't mention it as a topic he discussed with Hepburn while he was in the city, which they most certainly would have done. In any event, this was what Powell wanted—written confirmation from the Turkish command granting permission to Greek ships to enter the harbor. It was the real breakthrough, not flimsy hope of a breakthrough. Events were unfolding out of sequence: Jennings had managed to get the promise of ships before Powell had gotten permission to bring them in, but now Powell had both permission and ships, and the way was cleared for an evacuation. This is what mattered, and it was an even simpler version of what he had envisioned at Salonika when he had discussed possible evacuation scenarios with the Greek officers. It was beginning to look like a single U.S. naval officer and a Methodist minister who had felt the hand of God on his shoulder were pulling off the entire operation.

The *Litchfield* arrived back in Smyrna with Jennings at 10:30 P.M. Powell directed Lieutenant Rhodes to bring the ship alongside the *Edsall*. He did not want it to drop its anchor; he wanted a quick conference with Rhodes and Jennings so he could slingshot them back to Mytilene. He heard them out—Jennings confirmed the availability of ships, Rhodes described the conditions on the island—and ordered Rhodes to return with Jennings, then proceed to Constantinople as ordered by Bristol. Powell told Jennings to bring the six Greek ships to Smyrna as fast as he could. The commander wanted to lose no time in pressing the evacuation.

The *Litchfield* departed, and Powell waited for Jennings to radio him when he got to Mytilene. It had been a good day—except for one thing. The day, September 22, was the second anniversary of Ginger's death.

CHAPTER 27

Garabed Hatcherian

At the police station in the Turkish Quarter, Dr. Hatcherian and Aram were being held as prisoners of war.

A policeman led them upstairs to a small dark and airless room. There were about eighty Greek and Armenian prisoners in it—there was not room for another person. The men were squeezed inside, all standing, with no room to sit. So Dr. Hatcherian and Aram were placed on a bench in a hallway, and a policeman stood guard over them and the men in the dark room. In time, more men were brought upstairs, and soon about forty men were standing in the hallway. Soldiers beat the new men who were brought into the hallway and searched their clothes for valuables. Other soldiers came up the stairs with loot and traded among themselves. Now and again, Dr. Hatcherian or Aram was asked his nationality, and each time Aram answered, "Thank God we are Muslims." Late at night, the station became quiet except for the shuffling of the men's feet and their coughing. Aram put his head back against the wall and fell asleep sitting on the bench. Dr. Hatcherian was wakeful—listening, watching, and reproaching himself for the stupidity of returning to his house. He later recorded in his diary:

> After midnight, when I am lost in my thoughts, my attention is
> drawn to the begging voice of a woman, coming from the floor

below. Her voice is mixed with the threatening voice of a Turkish
soldier and the plaintive screaming of a three to four year old child.
The woman, whose voice sounds young, implores the soldier to
spare her honor; but the soldier orders her threatingly to submit
without a word. The child screams and the woman begs, but the
Turk is merciless. One can also hear the voice of an older woman
who appeals to the compassion of the soldier, saying "Honor be-
longs to Padishah." The Turk orders the old woman to shut up
unless she wants to become a corpse at once. The old woman stops
but the child continues to cry.

After a period of silence, Dr. Hatcherian heard the voice of a second
Turk, and again pleadings from the woman. She was raped again, and
the child was still crying. There was a third soldier, then another, and the
rapes continued until sunrise.

The next day, soldiers brought more men to the hallway where Dr.
Hatcherian and Aram sat, but they removed other men. A policeman
came upstairs and checked the documents of Dr. Hatcherian and Aram
and wrote down their names and ages. Unfortunately, Dr. Hatcherian's
military document listed him as forty-four years old, not his actual age
of forty-six. After waiting several hours, they were summoned to speak
with the police chief on the floor below. Dr. Hatcherian did not hide
his Armenian name, and they pleaded their cases. Dr. Hatcherian's
military papers showed that he had served with honor as a physician in
the Ottoman Army. He asked to be released, saying he had done nothing wrong, but the police chief said it was impossible. He told them
that his duty was to turn them over to the army, which would make the
decision.

They went back upstairs and waited, and while they were waiting
soldiers brought an Armenian man in a brimmed railroad cap upstairs
and forced him to undress. The soldiers beat him with the butts of their
guns. Writhing on the floor, the man tried to explain that the cap was
for the railroad, and he was not a revolutionary. When the soldiers were
done with the man, he crawled to a corner of the hallway. Later, more
Armenians in railroad clothing were brought upstairs, and the soldiers

began a rant against the prisoners, mocking the Armenians and telling them they were finished. Eventually, they departed and the hallways became silent again.

The next day, Dr. Hatcherian's third as a prisoner, a soldier called out the names of all the men under forty-five, and Dr. Hatcherian's name was among them. They were taken outside, formed into a column, and marched through the Turkish Quarter, taunted along the way by Turkish residents, and taken to the Turkish military barracks at the southern end of the Quay beyond the Konak. The soldiers placed the men in the barracks courtyard. The officer at the barracks acknowledged Dr. Hatcherian's status as a physician, calling him "effendi," a respected person, and apologized that he did not have a place suitable for him. The officer sent him to stand against a wall where there seemed to be people of higher status—a priest, another doctor, others. The barracks smelled of human filth—there were no toilets. Dr. Hatcherian looked around and recognized other Armenians from the city.

The courtyard contained about five hundred people. Soon, they were all marched out, leaving just the people against the wall, including Dr. Hatcherian. He wrote:

> I survey the ones who are left behind in the barracks and see friends and acquaintances; there is Armenang Magarian from Bardizag, Stepan Kevorkian, Aram of Ödemish (from the Elmassian Street), Gh. Gharzarian's aged father-in-law Assadour and others. On one side of the barracks, there is a group of women, among whom I see Mrs. Köleyan and her daughter, Arshalouys, and I talk to them.

In the afternoon, a soldier took the men to a wall with a hole that opened on to the harbor, and they were told to go out to the beach and take care of their needs. Toward evening, Dr. Hatcherian went out but quickly returned—the beach was covered with filth, and corpses floated in the water. As Dr. Hatcherian came back through the hole, a soldier demanded that they trade shoes. Dr. Hatcherian refused, saying the man's shoes would not fit him, and he showed the soldier his military papers with his rank of captain. Dr. Hatcherian summoned the courage to tell the soldier he wanted to see his captain to settle the matter, and the soldier, confused about what to do, let him go.

Before sunset, another soldier, a man with a whip, ordered all men over forty-five into another line, and Dr. Hatcherian moved to the older group. The man with the whip checked some of the men's papers in the line but passed by Dr. Hatcherian, satisfied that he looked to be over forty-five. The men were left to wait until dark, and then they were sent back to their places. Dr. Hatcherian sat with a group of Armenians that he knew, and they made a pact to protect each other. They hid the money they had among then under stones. Soon soldiers reentered the courtyard and began searching prisoners for money and valuables.

In the night, the raping of the women began again.

Not far from us, women and girls are lodged who are visited by the soldiers. Holding electric torches, they approach the women and rape the most attractive ones publicly, next to their mothers and sisters. The loud screaming of the females cannot help the victims break free from the clutches of the bestial soldiers. I think of Arshalouys Koleyan, who had told me that day that she had been untouched so far. The plunder and rape continues until midnight. From the first day of the arrest until today, I have not slept for one minute. Unable to withstand the long sleeplessness and the suffering any longer, my head gets heavy, my body weakens, I crouch in a corner on the bench and forget myself. I go to sleep.

Another day and night passed. More men were brought in, some were badly beaten and half dressed; others, between the ages of eighteen and forty-five, were marched out. Dr. Hatcherian continued to pass for over forty-five. His documents were not checked.

The next day about two thousand more people were brought into the barracks, bringing the total in the courtyard to about ten thousand. The stench from the filth was so strong that Dr. Hatcherian vomited and grew dizzy, leaning against a wall not to collapse. Periodically, soldiers passed through and searched the men for valuables and kicked them in the legs, demanding money.

Toward evening, after several repetitions of the beatings, some of the men in the barracks began to raise their voices. The protest brought a Turkish officer into the courtyard and he asked the prisoners what they wanted. There was no answer. Then, in an angry voice, the officer said to the prisoners, "You have burned down Muslim cities and villages, you have plundered and massacred the people, you have spared neither children nor elders, you have tarnished Islamic honor and you have raped our virgins. Now that you are sitting quietly in the barracks, enjoying every kind of protection, instead of being pleased with your situation and instead of moving our compassion, you are staging rebellious demonstrations. You deserve all of you to be crushed and to be burned."

Then, soldiers pulled about fifty men from the courtyard, to what fate Dr. Hatcherian did not know. The pillaging began again.

During this night, I have spent the most dreadful hours of my imprisonment and perhaps my entire life. It is impossible to describe the horrors and the emotional chills we felt each time we saw a soldier approaching us. Not even for a minute did we close our eyes, and the hours felt like months.

The next morning, September 21, the men over forty-five were called to line up, and a Turkish officer walked up and down the line and examined them, pulling out any man he considered under forty-five based on his appearance. After he was done, younger soldiers were permitted to go up and down the line doing the same, but also questioning the men as to whether they had ever done harm to a Muslim. Once this was complete, the men were left to stand in the sun for several hours, before finally being brought into the street. They were then marched toward the remains of the Passport Pier on the Quay.

We walk very fast to avoid stampede. The ones who fall behind are whipped. We traverse the government square and arrive at the Quay. The shore is crowded with Turkish idlers from the bloodiest and lowest class, Kurdish porters in bestial appearance, the bottom of the barrel. They mock us, grinning from between their fangs, saying, "Congratulations! You are going to Agia Sophia. Your wishes and dream have come true. Good-bye, etc." We arrive at the scene of the fire. The imposing building of Oriental Carpets and all the once-magnificent buildings in the same row lie flattened in ruins. The caravan proceeds and arrives at the dock of the Cordelio Steamship Lines. At that point, the soldiers order us to shout, "Long live Mustafa Kemal Pasha, long live."

Soon Dr. Hatcherian and the shouting men noticed that the guards who had brought them to the pier were gone. He hurried up the Quay, toward the house where had left his family six days earlier, hoping they were still there.

CHAPTER 28

Washington Feels the Pressure

On Friday, September 15, two days after the fire had broken out, and as it was still burning, Acting Secretary of State Phillips cabled Admiral Bristol and directed him in no uncertain terms to work with Britain, France, and Italy to develop a joint plan to aid the refugees at Smyrna. It was an order, not a request. He sent a copy of his directions simultaneously to the British, French, and Italian governments.

Immediately upon receiving the message, Bristol's tone turned agreeable and conciliatory. "I concur absolutely with the Department's opinion that situation clearly beyond the scope of any private charity." His tone changed, but his actions remained the same. He would continue to find reasons not to cooperate with the Allies.

In Washington, the pressure was building on President Harding for intervention in Turkey to save the Christian population. Bristol was managing the American reporters in Turkey, but shocking reports of the suffering at Smyrna still found their ways into American newspapers. Day after day, Smyrna was the lead story in the *New York Times*: SMYRNA BURNING, SMYRNA IN RUINS, SMYRNA WIPED OUT, KILLINGS CONTINUE. Prentiss's reports of Turkish moderation were overwhelmed by reports of cruelty. The *Times* carried a French observer's account of the torture and killings of Armenians. "How long will Christian America stand by?" a New Haven minister thundered in the newspaper.

It was not just the coverage in the *New York Times* that captured the nation's horror. In towns and small cities across the country, Smyrna was big news: in the *Bismarck Tribune*, TURK ARMY MASSACRES 2,000; in the *Tulsa Daily World*, TURKS BEGIN MASSACRE IN GREEK CITY. The press was responding to the reservoir of American sympathy for the Christians in Turkey, and especially for the Armenians.

Protestant clerics reacted to the press reports with resolutions and telegrams to President Harding. The presiding bishop of the Episcopal Church read a letter to Episcopal bishops gathered for a convention in Portland, Oregon, that described the fate of a half-million "breadless and roofless Christians" who were "exposed to unheard of torments." The bishops passed a resolution calling for ministers and Sunday schools to make time for presentations on the suffering at Smyrna. The presiding bishop said the church supported the president in any effort he would make in response to the suffering, "diplomatic, naval or military." Many churchmen were ready to go war with the Turks to protect the Christian minorities.

Henry Morgenthau and Oscar Strauss, Jewish Americans with reputations as human rights advocates and former U.S. ambassadors to Turkey, added their voices to the calls for action. So did James Barton, head of the Foreign Missions Board and one of the founders of Near East Relief. In a telegram to Harding, he wrote: "Turkey has entered Smyrna and is conducting the affairs of that city true to form."

The American Federation of Churches of Christ sent a petition signed by twenty of its leading members to the State Department. Allen Dulles passed it along to Phillips with a note that said he was working on a reply, adding, "At the same time, we have received a mass of telegrams from all over the country from various kinds of and conditions of people requesting various types of action, involving war, intervention and general protest. These telegrams are being answered as rapidly as possibly [*sic*] by the form letters which you have seen."

The conflict between religious leaders and the administration grew more intense when James Cannon Jr., bishop of the Southern Methodist Church, stepped forward with powerful public criticism of Harding's policy. Cannon at the time was a big figure in American politics. H. L.

Mencken, from his perch at the *Baltimore Sun*, would call him "the chief figure in American public life today." Cannon was the leader of the Anti-Saloon League and the embodiment of the nation's conservative and rural Protestant values.

Cannon represented the old order with a forceful, reasoned, and articulate presence. He was also an internationalist in the Wilson mold. He had been traveling through the Near East in the summer of 1922 and had included Admiral Bristol in the list of people he had interviewed about the status of the Christian minorities. (Bristol seemed not to know who he was in their meeting, asking him to explain his background and credentials. The two sharply disagreed on America's Near East policy in their meeting.) Cannon was appalled by the conditions of refugees he had witnessed in Constantinople and moved by the sickly Armenian orphans he saw laid out in the city's bleak warehouses. He directed his anger against Islam itself and inveighed against the "Terrible Turk."

As Smyrna spiraled toward intensifying violence, Cannon, in Britain as he made his way home to America, wrote a heated letter to the London *Times*. He called for American military force to protect Christian lives in Turkey. "The blood of millions of Armenian and Syrian Christians cries to heaven," he wrote, "and any massacres that have been perpetrated in the last few months by the Greeks in retaliation for Turkish massacres is as dust in the balances compared with the practically continuous massacre of Christians by the Turks." The administration was forced to respond, and Secretary of State Hughes eventually detailed the administration's efforts on behalf of the Christians in Asia Minor but defended Harding's unwillingness to send the American military. Cannon—speaking for millions of churchgoers, especially in the South—had put the issue at the steps of the White House.

By the middle of September, the rail and coal strikes were coming to an end, easing pressure on Harding. On September 15, the first poststrike deliveries of anthracite coal, the principal fuel for heat in those years, were made in New York. At the White House, Mrs. Harding was recovering from her illness. President Harding was sympathetic to calls for helping refugees, but he firmly resisted demands for American intervention in Turkey. He was sure that the public's support for the Christian minorities did not extend to sending troops to Asia Minor to protect them. "Frankly," he had written to Hughes earlier in the year, "it is difficult for me to be patient with our good friends of the Church who are properly and earnestly zealous in promoting peace until it comes to making warfare on someone of a contending religion. It is, of course, unthinkable to send an armed force to Asia Minor. We would have open rebellion in this country if we attempted it."

Harding was not against providing relief—he showed far more willingness than Bristol—but on the question of steering events through military force or ultimatums, Harding was opposed. The president, in fact, had worked to reduce America's military expenditures and had called history's first disarmament conference in 1921. It slowed battleship construction by the world's leading powers. He was a noninterventionist from head to toe.

With Secretary Hughes still away, Phillips continued to handle matters with a cool hand. Bristol was not his sole source of information about Smyrna. The State Department had received intelligence from its officers in other capitals, who had their own information networks and perspectives. The cables from well-regarded Jefferson Caffrey, the chargé d'affaires in Athens, painted a picture different from Bristol's. Greece, he said, was in no position to finance the relief effort: it was broke and had food stores that would last less than a week. Caffrey also reported that he had received reports of the Greek army burning crops and villages in its retreat, but other reliable reports were skeptical of the widespread civilian atrocities by Greek troops, which were reported as a fact by Bristol. Reports from London described the Turkish occupation in cruelest terms. In London, the U.S. ambassador to Britain, George Harvey, cabled the State Department: "Foreign office states that is no longer possible to doubt there has been a deliberate and wholesale massacre of the Armenian quarter."

On September 15, Phillips sent Hughes (still traveling) a memorandum that said Britain and the Allies were close to war with the nationalist Turks and that such a war was likely to bring in Bulgaria, Serbia, Yugoslavia, Italy, and Russia. Troop movements already had begun in the Balkans. Once again, southeastern Europe seemed to be the tinderbox that would burst into a major European war. The British had concentrated their Atlantic and Mediterranean fleets for the defense of the Dardanelles and called up troops from its Dominions. Phillips wrote to Hughes,

> Department action has been limited to protection of American lives and property and facilitating relief work of private organizations, the Red Cross and the Near East Relief. I have also instructed Bristol to consult with Allied colleagues and submit a comprehensive plan for meeting the appalling situation among thousands of refugees whose evacuation from Asia Minor will probably be necessary. . . . Confidential reports received from many officials at Smyrna and British Foreign Office indicate that Turks burned the city in conformity of definite plan to solve the Christian minority problem by forcing the evacuation of the minorities.

As the week passed, and Bristol plied back and forth between the *Scorpion* and the embassy, he seemed oddly detached from Washington's demands and actual events in Smyrna. He was hewing to his own plan, which was to let the Greeks flounder and events to unfold in favor of the nationalist Turks. "I have received," Bristol cabled the State Department, "no reports up to the present time of atrocities committed by Turkish forces, and all are agreed that the Turkish occupation of Smyrna—even during the first few days when that city was practically in a panic and when disorders of all kinds were to be feared—was carried out in a most orderly and peaceful manner."

The State Department's attitude toward Bristol during the previous two or three years had been tolerance of an ornery old salt who was something of a character, but one who was also a fierce proponent of American interests. He was a son of a bitch, but he was their son of a bitch. Now its patience grew short, and Phillips's tolerance for Bristol's inaction had worn thin.

Bristol was viscerally opposed to working with the Allies, and his reports back to the State Department distorted the directions he had given his commanders. He left the false impression that he had ordered an evacuation of refugees by U.S. destroyers. The only refugees removed by American warships were those that had been brought to the *Lawrence* on the first night of the fire by the British and the orphans taken away on the *Litchfield* through Jaquith's insistence, and others through Powell's unstinting efforts to juggle ships. Most astonishingly, as the days progressed into the third week of the month, Bristol would appear uninformed about details of the plan Powell and Jennings were formulating to evacuate the refugees through the use of Greek merchant ships. Keeping his plans hazy to Bristol may have been Powell's intention.

Bristol's first thought on receiving Phillips's cable directing him to work with the Allies was to seize the initiative and call a meeting of the Allies at the American embassy. But he decided against it and mulled his next move for the next several days. His mind was a hive of bees. He fussed about who should make the first move—he or the Allies. Bristol was taking a position not articulated in Washington. Before he joined a mutual effort, he wanted the Allies to declare their willingness to evacuate refugees (something they already were engaged in to a limited extent) and identify the place to which they intended to evacuate them. The latter point seemed intended to squeeze Britain and Greece on the fate of the Greek province of Thrace, a place to which some refugees from Asia Minor already had fled and that the nationalists wanted to take back for Turkey.

Bristol's sympathies resided with the Turkish claims to eastern Thrace, and he was essentially suggesting that the Allies decide on the national boundaries of a new Turkey before a rescue could begin, an impossibility. It was a point that could only be settled through extensive negotiations among all the parties at a peace conference. He also wanted Britain and Greece to take primary responsibility for the expense of a relief effort. His position ignored the economic position of Greece, and to a large extent, that of Britain.

Bristol insisted the Greeks could afford a relief effort if it demobilized its army, notwithstanding the fact that the Turks were now threatening to cross the Dardanelles to seize some of its territory. If war broke out in the Balkans, the center of it would be Greece's easternmost province. Yet Bristol wanted Greece to disband its army.

The admiral carried these ideas around as he traveled back and forth between the *Scorpion* and the embassy and as he moved about the crowded streets of Constantinople in the Cadillac that bore the license plate of the U.S. Navy on its front grille.

Constantinople at the moment was a mix of Allied tension and Turkish hopefulness. The narrow streets, filled with the usual assortment of street vendors and hamals carrying huge loads on their backs, were hung with bright red Turkish flags displaying the star and crescent. The British had moved nearly all of their troops out of the city to Chanak, where the clash with the Turks was likely to occur. Left to patrol the city were a company of the Irish Guards and about eight hundred infantry of the Royal East Kent Regiment, the Fifth Battalion of which had fought at Kut in 1917. The city's Greek population was glum and keeping a low profile; many were departing.

The Turkish population, well armed with guns smuggled into the city from the Asiatic shore, was intent on driving out the city's Christians. Turkish nationalist officers slipped into the city in civilian clothes, preparing for what might be a battle for Constantinople. Bolsheviks from Russia were active in the Stamboul section to stir an uprising. Bristol was getting queries from Americans asking if they should evacuate. When the sultan's mounted guard clambered through the streets with Turkish banners on September 15, frightened Greeks and Armenians thought they were the vanguard of Kemal's army and went into hiding. Soon, they began leaving the city in large numbers. For the first time since the Turks had captured Constantinople from the Byzantine Empire in 1453, the sultan paid a visit to the tomb of Mohammed II the Conqueror. Turks waving flags lined the streets, and Turkish flags hung from minarets, including the spires at St. Sophia Mosque. Turkish nationalism had merged with Islam, creating a belligerence that frightened the city's Christians.

On the fifteenth, the same day he had gotten Phillips's cable telling him to get moving on a rescue plan, Bristol declined an offer of assistance from A. C. Ringland, director of the Constantinople office of the American Relief Administration. On September 16, he stiff-armed a request by two YMCA officers in Constantinople to transport more staff to help at Smyrna despite the pressing need in the city.

By September 17, Sunday, Hepburn and Merrill were back in Constantinople and they briefed the admiral. After meeting with them, he
wrote, "It appeared to come clear to me that the burning of the city was
an accident so far as the large area and great loss of property was concerned. . . ." The roughing up and robbery experienced by Jacob and
Trueblood, which Powell had protested to the military governor, struck
Bristol as funny. He considered the briefing from his chief of staff with
equanimity. "The actual destruction of life will not prove to be great,"
Bristol wrote, "and later when one's emotions are calmed will be considered on par with many happenings that have taken place in Ireland
within the past two years. [In 1922, Ireland was engaged in a civil war
over establishment of the British-backed Irish Free State.] There is no
need to have any surprise over what the Turks did. In fact, I am only
surprised when these different races out here do something to commend
than when [they] do something that one condemns."

He was back to his bedrock view—none of these people were worth
a damn, but there was a hierarchy of worthlessness and the Greeks were
the worst of the worst.

As Phillips in Washington waited for a response from Bristol, the *New
York Times* ran a story with the headline: WASHINGTON PREPARES BUT HAS
RECEIVED NO REPLY FROM BRISTOL ON PLAN FOR INTERNATIONAL ACTION.
The story said, "The State Department is tonight without a reply from
Constantinople to the American proposal that this government cooper-
ate with the Allies for the relief of refugees in Smyrna and other points
in Asia Minor. No dispatches of any character had been received from
Admiral Bristol, American High Commissioner, up to a late hour this
evening."

Bristol's relaxed attitude contrasted sharply with the emergency along
the coast of Asia Minor. The Allied consuls in Smyrna cabled their high
commissioners in Constantinople on the eighteenth, "About two hundred thousands totally destitute Christians still lying on seashore Smyrna
awaiting help to leave. . . . Unless pressure or drastic measures be immediately taken no one will survive."

Bristol finally responded to Phillips on September 18. In his cable, he
reported Hepburn's conference with the Allied naval officers in Smyrna

on the fifteenth in which they had decided to have the Italian admiral seek Kemal's permission to allow Greek ships to carry away the refugees. He told Phillips that he planned to wait for an answer—yet another delay: "I am awaiting result of this conference before taking further steps to consult with Allied colleagues." It was on the eighteenth that Kemal declined to admit the Greek merchant ships.

Phillips responded to Bristol the next day, September 19, with frustration. He wanted to know what relief stores were available and whether any provision could be made for the refugees on the Aegean islands. He asked for an immediate response, and with the American church organizations turning up the heat, he added this: "Advise Department frankly and fully of facilities which you need in order that this Government may dispatch its full part and more if necessary in helping to meet tragic situation at Smyrna as described by press reports received yesterday and today."

Then Phillips sent Bristol another cable, asking for a response to the State Department's order of September 15 to cooperate with the Allies on a plan. "If your answer is delayed by inability of Allies to agree with you on a general program of relief, submit your own views immediately as to plan of action to meet refugees problem."

In the middle of this strained back-and-forth, Bristol presented the State Department with another headache. He had sent one of Constantine Brown's news stories to the State Department in the navy's secret code, asking the department to pass it along to the editors at the *Chicago Daily News*. The dispatch presented two problems: a comparison of the coded message with the text of the story could disclose the navy's cipher; it was also a breach of State Department protocol. The State Department was not a messenger service for newspaper reporters—even reporters who were serving Bristol's interests. Bristol's request bounced around the State Department for several days and finally it was sent by Edward Bell, the department's chief press officer, to Bristol's friend Dulles with a note that Bristol's request could embarrass the government: "I think it would be as well if you drafted this telegram as you know the admiral and how best to approach him." Bell was more than a little sensitive to the matter of codes since he had been the American diplomat in London in 1917 to whom the British had delivered the notorious Zimmermann Telegram—the telegram in which Germany had offered Mexico territories in Texas, Arizona, and New Mexico if it entered World War I on the side of the Central Powers.

Finally on the nineteenth, Bristol, with his mind settled on how to proceed, called on two of the Allied high commissioners. He went first in his barge to the Italian high commissioner's palatial summer residence at Therapia. Commissioner Marquis Eugenio Camillo Garroni, a seventy-year-old and sleepy-eyed veteran for whom Bristol had little respect, greeted him with high courtesy. "Garroni is always cordial, in fact very cordial," Bristol wrote in his diary, "but like most old diplomats does not know much about what is going [on] in his mission." Interestingly, British Admiral De Robeck, former British high commissioner, had a different view: "Leisurely, courteous, experienced in Turkish affairs . . . but withal a cunning old fox, who feigns a certain torpor, but is really wide awake."

Bristol went through his oft-repeated points: the British and the Greeks had created the refugee problem, the Greek army had been guilty of civilian outrages, which prevented return of the Christian refugees to their homes and farms, and the Americans had already spent too much money in the region on refugee relief. The monologue seemed even too much for the Italian embassy's translator, who, without prompting from Garroni, interrupted and asked Bristol what he suggested should be done. Astonishingly, given Phillips's requests, Bristol responded that he did not think it was proper for him to make suggestions. He asked what the Italians thought should be done. "We would look to America to come forward in her usual bountiful way and take care of the refugees," Garroni told him. Bristol responded that Americans "were tired of putting their hands in their pockets" and that they "would like to see something done to stop this manufacture of refugees in the Near East." The old and crafty Italian blinked sleepily and smiled. There was some small talk and Bristol departed.

Bristol then traveled to Yenikuey, down the Bosporus on the way back to Constantinople, where he met with his nemesis Rumbold, at the summer residence of the British embassy. Rumbold's polished manners seemed to annoy Bristol more than usual. Bristol set the tenor of the meeting by telling Rumbold that since it was close to lunchtime and he had a long trip back to the American embassy, he would get right to the point. He described the cabled directions he had received from Washington and repeated his discourse on Greek guilt as he had delivered it to Garroni. Rumbold listened and replied that London had not passed the American message about joint action along to him. Neither man chose to pursue the matter further, and Bristol departed. The next day, Bristol cabled Washington about his two meetings: "I met with no encouragement for drawing up a joint plan for Smyrna emergency."

The volley of cables between Washington and Constantinople continued.

On September 21, Phillips informed Bristol that Harding had requested $200,000 from Congress to help naturalized Americans displaced by the war in Turkey. Phillips said also that the American Red Cross, Near East Relief, and the YMCA would double the amount. "Success of Department's efforts will depend largely upon full information from you. . . . Department is still hopeful that you will succeed in drawing up with Allies a general plan for relief but in absence of such a plan you will submit as specific information as is possible as to what you need to cope with the situation." (This was never done.)

In the morning of the next day, Bristol fired back with some testiness of his own. "Department is being promptly, fully and frankly advised as it is possible under the present ever rapidly changing conditions. I sympathize with Department's anxiety for news and desire that our Government take its part to relieve this tragic situation. The situation changes so rapidly and completely from day to day that it is practically impossible to give any comprehensive plan for relief. Thus we have attempted to meet the situations as they have arisen and have done so with much success."

This of course was nonsense: the "situation" had been on a steady trajectory toward disaster for weeks, and resources at Smyrna fell far short of the need. At the moment Bristol was sending these messages to Washington, Jennings was struggling without adequate medical supplies to treat the wounded women and children in his safe houses, and the relief committee lacked sufficient food to feed the refugees.

As this diplomatic cat-and-mouse game continued, Bristol met with

Hamid Bey, the nationalist representative in Constantinople, flattering him and appealing to the honor of Turkish troops not to harass refugees in Smyrna. Hamid Bey, according to Bristol, said the "Turks were always brought up with the ideas of the French revolution before them and with the fundamental idea of that revolution, namely that each man had a right to live, and he only wished that the Christian minorities were given a little of the same instruction." Bristol noted in his diary, "I agreed with him entirely as to the latter point." Bristol renewed his request for newspaper correspondents to travel to the interior of the country to tell the story of the Greek atrocities.

The next day, September 22, was a busy day for Bristol—and the day when events began to seriously run ahead of him. He had a number of visitors at the embassy, and he called on the French high commissioner Pelle, who was back from Smyrna and his meeting with Mustapha Kemal, the previous night—the meeting that Powell had accidentally happened onto. Pelle invited Bristol to a conference of the Allied high commissioners to discuss a refugee relief plan but, unbelievably, Bristol declined. Despite Washington's prodding, he was sticking to his decision to let the Allies first develop a plan of their own, then he would decide on his response.

In the meantime, Bristol had some advice for Washington—a little PR was in order. Bristol cabled Phillips and suggested that the State Department issue a press release assuring the American public that the reports they were reading in American newspapers and hearing from the pulpits of their churches were exaggerations.

I suggest Department issue a statement to the press along the following lines, "American officers who have been eye witnesses of all events occurring Smyrna from time of the occupation that city by Nationalists up to the present report killings which occurred were one for the most part by individual or small bands of local rowdies or soldiers and that nothing in the nature of a massacre has occurred. During the fire some people were drowned by attempting to swim to vessels in the harbor or falling off the Quay wall but the number was small. When mass of people was gathered on the Quay to escape fire they were guarded by Turkish troops but were at no time prevented by such troops from leaving the Quay if they so desired. Impossible to estimate number of deaths due to killing, fire and executions but total probably does not exceed two thousand."

So there the relief and evacuation effort remained, stalled, at least among the high commissioners in Constantinople, with Bristol applying the brakes whenever possible. Meanwhile, as Bristol's proposed press release moved on the wires back to Washington, Jennings was boarding the *Litchfield* at Mytilene with news that Greek ships were available for transporting the refugees, and Powell was eagerly awaiting his return.

On September 23, the State Department cabled Bristol that it wanted someone else to take charge of the relief effort for refugees who were U.S. citizens, and it picked a person who could not have been more different from Bristol, Oscar S. Heizer. A consul in Constantinople, and as such Bristol's subordinate, Heizer had served in Trebizond on the Black Sea during the Armenian deportations in 1915 and had provided Morgenthau with some of the most detailed accounts of Turkish brutality, including the deliberate drowning of a boatload of Armenian orphan children. Phillips told Bristol that Heizer was to begin immediately and would handle the money appropriated by Congress for the relief and repatriation effort. Phillips added, "He should also telegraph fully his views and suggestions."

Phillips's patience with Bristol had run out.

CHAPTER 29

Jennings Negotiates
with a Prime Minister

Jennings had been as eager to return to Mytilene on Friday, September 22, as Powell was to send him back, but Jennings was worried about General Frangos's tepid commitment to provide ships for the evacuation. Jennings wanted something substantial he could carry back on his second trip to ensure that he would be taken seriously and get the ships. He asked Powell for a written order bearing the imprimatur of the United States Navy, which he could present to Frangos as a demonstration of his bona fides.

Powell agreed, and he directed Lieutenant Commander Rhodes to compose a letter for Jennings. The letter was written, though exactly when is unclear from the record. It probably was composed on the ship on the way to Mytilene, given Powell's push to get Jennings back to the island and the *Litchfield* back to Constantinople. Neither a record of the conversation between Powell and Rhodes aboard the *Litchfield* nor the order as Powell gave it to Rhodes appears to exist in the navy or State Department archives. Rhodes was not a diligent record keeper—he alone among the commanders at Smyrna did not keep a ship's diary. But the letter was written—dictated by Jennings and signed by Rhodes. It was a masterpiece of ambiguity and inference, conveying authority and implying more American protection than was actually present in the words.

> In accordance with orders received at Smyrna from Captain H. Powell, S.N.O., U.S. Navy (USS Edsall), the ships at Mytilene are ordered to proceed to Smyrna for the purpose of transporting refugees to Mytilene. Ships will not be molested in any way, providing they do not fly the Greek flag or tie up at the Quay or pier. If desirable, ships can be escorted in or out of the harbor. If possible send USS Edsall radio signal when ships leave Mytilene for Smyrna. Flour is on way to Mytilene from stores in Smyrna. USS Edsall call "NUPM." Signed J.B. Rhodes, Lieutenant-Commander, U.S. Navy, Commanding USS Litchfield.

It is difficult to comprehend how Rhodes could have signed the letter. Its text exceeded what Powell had agreed to in granting Jennings a letter stating his mission. Powell had no authority to order Greek ships anywhere, nor did he make any promises of safe transport connected to an American escort. He had no authority to assure it. Powell—and all his commanders—were still under strict orders by Bristol to make no displays of naval force. This "no-displays" policy was a directive that the president himself had approved during his exchanges with Acting Secretary Phillips in early September. There is no question that protection of Greek ships against Turkey, while Greece and Turkey were at war, would have been taken as a demonstration of American naval force.

To a person unfamiliar with the American position as articulated by the president, State Department, and U.S. Navy, the letter could easily be interpreted as a guarantee of American protection, especially in context of the proposition Jennings had put to Frangos less than twenty-four hours earlier. Jennings had asked Frangos if he would make Greek merchant ships available for the evacuation if American destroyers protected them. The suggestion of American protection was the factor that had moved Frangos to offer the six ships in the first place. Clearly, Jennings had intimated that he was returning to Smyrna to get the assurance Frangos wanted. Taken together—Jennings's proposition on his first trip to Mytilene and the response implied in Rhodes's letter—a reasonable person could conclude the American navy was declaring its willingness to protect Greek shipping during an evacuation.

Did Powell deliberately frame his directions to Rhodes in such a way as to go right up to the edge of Bristol's orders, communicating an assurance of American protection without actually breaching the admiral's orders? Or, did Rhodes, whose record as a navy officer had shown a certain degree of laxity and sometimes drunkenness, let the letter pass into Jennings's hands without a careful consideration of its contents? With the passage of time, it seems an impossible question to answer, though Powell would eventually supply some clues later in the week. In any event, the letter became a powerful lever for Jennings in dealing with Frangos and the Greek government.

The *Litchfield* arrived back at Mytilene just after midnight on September 23. Rhodes asked the Italian destroyer *Sulferino* to send a boat to pick up Jennings, and Jennings was quickly ferried into the port on an Italian motor launch. The *Litchfield* proceeded to Constantinople. Jennings was ashore by 1:30 A.M. He immediately roused his relief group— Ernesto Aliotti, Captains Argyropoulos and Hodgkinson, and Captain Cardos, the harbormaster—and together they called on the island's governor Bakas and General Frangos.

As Jennings had feared, Frangos now balked about his earlier offer to release the six smaller ships. His new position was that he had to consult with Athens, and he offered no timetable for getting permission. Jennings produced the letter and pressed him hard, as did the others, but Frangos held firm, and the meeting broke up.

Jennings's group decided to look for a way around Frangos's caution. Jennings was sure that the Greek government did not want to abandon the refugees, especially if there was a means of evacuation backed by the Americans. He decided he would try to get permission from Athens without the help of the general, which meant he needed another communications conduit to the highest level of the Greek government.

One of the ships anchored outside Mytilene harbor was the Greek battleship *Kilkis*, a heavily armored two-stack battleship. In its former life, it had been the USS *Mississippi*, built for the American navy in

1908 as a scaled-down and less expensive version of its *Connecticut*-class battleships. The navy was disappointed with it—it was a rough ride in high seas and difficult to stabilize for accurate gunnery. Battleship technology had been roaring ahead in the early years of the twentieth century, and the American navy abandoned the design and sold the *Mississippi* and its sister ship, the USS *Idaho*, to Greece in 1914, recovering most of its eight-million-dollar investment. The Greeks had wanted it as a counterweight to a Turkish naval buildup. Turkey and Germany had bitterly opposed the ship's sale, and the German ambassador to the Ottoman Empire had made a personal appeal to U.S. Ambassador Morgenthau to stop it. Nonetheless, the sale went ahead, and the *Mississippi* and the *Idaho* (renamed *Kilkis* and *Lemnos*) steamed from Newport News to Piraeus soon after the assassination of Archduke Ferdinand. The *Kilkis* had not seen action in the big war—the French had commandeered the Greek navy during Greece's neutral period prior to its entrance into World War I and removed the *Kilkis*'s gun blocks. After the war, the ship had patrolled the Greek coast, and it had been called upon to watch over the Greek landing at Smyrna. So, ironically, its two main employments had been to cover the landing of the Greek army in Asia Minor, then three years later to cover the army's exit from Asia Minor. In the week after the nationalist entrance into Smyrna, the *Kilkis* had laid down a barrage of artillery along the peninsula to Chesme to impede the Turkish cavalry as it pursued the retreating Greek army. After the Greek army's evacuation, the *Kilkis* had stayed for a few days at Chios, then moved to Mytilene. It had been the distant guns of the *Kilkis* that Captain Hepburn had heard on first entering Smyrna harbor.

Jennings had guessed correctly that, while General Frangos was the nominal military leader on Mytilene, whoever commanded a battleship with twelve-inch guns was not without rank and influence of his own. Jennings and his committee went out to the *Kilkis*, and Jennings introduced himself and the others to the ship's captain—a thin and severe figure with a receding hairline and dark mustache. He was dressed in his white Greek navy uniform with upright collar and brass buttons. His name was Ioannis Theophanides. He was forty-five years old and had served twenty-five years in the Greek navy, distinguishing himself as a tactician and gunnery expert against the Turkish navy in the First Balkan War. Born in Heraklion, Crete, Theophanides was a Royalist officer with a proud navy (and Greek) pedigree. Two of his ancestors had served as admirals in the Ottoman navy in the early nineteenth century, before Greece had won its independence, and he was married to the granddaughter of Theodoros Kolokotronis, the George Washington of the Greek War of Independence. Theophanides was both an electrical engineer and a classical pianist.

The Greek captain greeted Jennings and the committee warmly when they boarded the ship. It was still dark. Jennings produced the Rhodes letter and explained his mission. He asked Theophanides if he would make his radio telegraph available to send a message to Athens asking for use of the merchant ships at Mytilene to evacuate Smyrna's refugees. Immediately grasping the situation, Theophanides agreed to help—and he would have some suggestions of his own to help Jennings.

Theophanides was another stroke of good fortune for Jennings. He had found an officer who, like Powell, was independent minded, capable, and sympathetic to the refugees. It would be this unusual lineup of men—Powell at Smyrna, Theophanides at Mytilene, and Jennings moving between the two places—that would conjure one of the most unusual and dramatic naval evacuations in history.

Unknown to Jennings, but probably suspected by Theophanides, a Greek military coup was taking shape at that moment at Chios and Mytilene. Republican officers of the Greek army, humiliated by the Asia Minor defeat, were making arrangements to overthrow the Royalist government in Athens. Frangos, as a Royalist officer, was not part of the planning—in fact, he would soon be in jail with the island's governor.

The prime minister of Greece, Nikolaos Triantafyllakos, was serving on a temporary basis in Athens at King Constantine's request because of the resignation of the Royalist government following the Anatolian debacle. Triantafyllakos also held the position of minister of military affairs. So it was to him that the request for Greek merchant ships was sent. The prime minister and Theophanides, both Royalists and well placed in the small circle of Greek high society, most certainly would have known each other—another stroke of luck.

Jennings composed a message with Theophanides's help, and the captain directed his radio officer to send it in code to Athens. Marked "very urgent," it read:

> *Military governor of Mytilene Bakas and American President*
> *of Refugee Relief Near East report that 150,000 refugees are*
> *prisoners on the Smyrna Quay. Stop. Turkish terms for their*
> *departure are seven days from today. American destroyers*
> *according to the order of High Commissioner and Admiral Bristol*
> *will give protection to the Greek steamers without flag entering*
> *Smyrna taking refugees on board. Stop. American Committee*
> *will also care for shelter. Member of American Committee now on*
> *board ship and awaits answer. Stop.*

Jennings was taking serious liberties with Powell's orders and Rhodes's letter. He had even inserted Bristol's name—a flashing light to anyone with political savvy in Greece or Turkey.

The *Kilkis*'s radio operator received a quick response. He took it down on a sheet of paper and handed it to the captain. (It was a message that would make a non-Greek smile.) It said it was too early in the morning to conduct government business. Jennings and Theophanides were not amused. They responded with a demand for an immediate meeting of the Greek cabinet. If an answer were not forthcoming, the message would be repeated out of code. In other words, Jennings and Theophanides were threatening the government with embarrassment for failing to respond to an evacuation plan offered by the Americans. (Radio telegraph messages in those days could be intercepted by anyone with a receiver.)

Athens responded that it would call a cabinet meeting as soon as possible. Jennings and Theophanides responded by upping the ante. They wanted Greek merchant ships in Piraeus as well as in Mytilene for the evacuation. (This probably was a Theophanides touch, given his familiarity with the Greek merchant fleet, about which Jennings would have known little or nothing. Athens responded with a series of questions: Would the United States provide protection? Jennings attempted to finesse the answer to this question by referring to the language of the letter signed by Rhodes, but the Greek text received at Athens was more categorical: Yes, there would be protection. Would Americans board the evacuation ships? The response: "American President of Committee Mytilene will embark on first ship." This would be Jennings.

The messages continued to volley between the radio room of the *Kilkis* and Athens as the sun rose on the morning of September 23. Finally, Theophanides pressed Jennings to send an ultimatum: Acknowledge receipt of the demand and provide a favorable reply to the request for ships by 6 P.M. or the *Kilkis* would follow through on its threat to broadcast the American offer and the Greek rejection. Theophanides—aware of the discouragement of the army and possibly suspecting trouble in its ranks—may have been trying to hurry the negotiations. He soon would be in danger, and if the government in Athens was overthrown—or if he himself was removed from command as a consequence of the coup that was brewing—the opportunity to marshal the ships might be lost and so would the evacuation. He insisted on Jennings taking a hard line.

Jennings later wrote: "In this ultimatum, we showed them that the sympathy of the world would be with the Turks and no amount of explaining would ever justify the Greek government for not permitting the Americans to assist to evacuate their own nationals when the lives of thousands depended on the Greek government for furnishing the ships. . . . We assured them that if they would not give their ships, the American Relief Committee after using the few ships that had been chartered would wash their hands of the whole affair and put responsibility on the Greek nation and tell the reason to the world."

This was more of Jennings's creative bluster: he had no authority from the relief committee to threaten to withdraw its relief efforts in Smyrna. Jennings and Theophanides received a quick message that confirmed receipt of the ultimatum and promised an answer.

As they waited, Jennings sent a message to Powell in Smyrna: "12 ships and sufficient coal Mytilene with total carrying capacity of 18,000 persons each trip await favorable reply Athens to your generous offer before being released Stop Other ships also available Stop Expecting reply every moment Stop If favorable will send some of ships today and others tonight Stop Call me."

Powell confirmed receipt of the message.

Before the 6 P.M. deadline was reached, the *Kilkis*'s telegraph came alive. It clicked out an answer: the Greek government was ordering Frangos to turn over the ships at Mytilene to Jennings, and Greek ships from Piraeus were on their way, also to be placed under Jennings's command.

The bold gamble had worked. Incredibly, Jennings would soon find himself in command of a flotilla.

The *Kilkis* replied: "Mr. Jennings on behalf of American Relief Committee gratefully appreciates the Hellenic Government's prompt cooperation in connection with the transport of the Smyrna Refugees."*

Jennings then received a radio message from Frangos: "After communication with the General Staff I acknowledge you all the ships now in Piraeus harbor have been seized by the Government and have been ordered to Mytilene for the transport of the refugees from the Asia Minor coast. Stop. I acknowledge you also that the Commander of the Navy has ordered to be in communication with the American Admiral with reference regulation of the transportation.—Frangos, Brigadier General."

Since Bristol was unaware of what was happening and his name was being invoked as the enabler of the evacuation, there soon would be hell to pay.

Jennings then radioed Powell: "Capt Panos Argyropulos is hereby appointed to be in charge of transportation and direction of ships assigned to the American Relief Committee Mytilene during the emergency connected with the evacuation of Smyrna and elsewhere due to the advance of Kemal army." Argyropoulos was the cashiered Greek naval officer Jen-

---

* In later recounting the episode, Jennings wrote, "They insisted we guarantee their protection for their ships. We would not agree to go any further than the order and instructions we had received, but assured them that an American Destroyer would escort their ships into and out of the Smyrna harbor and that American officers and sailors would assist in loading the refugees." In any event, it seems clear that Bristol had no knowledge of the negotiations. He certainly would not have agreed to providing protection to the Greek merchant ships.

nings had met on coming ashore at Mytilene with Aliotti two days earlier and was among the group on the *Kilkis*. He and Theophanides were probably well acquainted with each other. Jennings needed Argyropoulos since Jennings barely new a ship's stem from its stern.

Theophanides immediately summoned the merchant captains at Mytilene to the *Kilkis*. He told them to be ready to depart at midnight for an evacuation of Smyrna. There was grumbling, and a number of the merchant captains explained why they could not join the evacuation flotilla, but Theophanides was firm. He threatened military action against uncooperative captains. Ten ships were made ready for the first trip to Smyrna. One of the merchant captains spoke a little English, so Jennings picked the captain's ship, *Ismini,* as the one on which he would travel. In the morning, it led the flotilla from Mytilene.

Powell soon received a radio message from Jennings, asking for an escort when the ships had entered the Gulf of Smyrna. Communication was roundabout: the *Edsall* radioed the *Kilkis*, which had already departed Mytilene or was about to depart, because of the rebellion, and the *Kilkis* in return relayed the messages to Jennings on the lead merchant ship.

Jennings to Powell: "15 ships are scheduled to arrive Pelican Spit 6:00 a.m. Stop. Meet with U.S. Destroyer. Stop. Confirm."

Powell designated the *Lawrence* as the escort, and the *Lawrence* radioed the *Kilkis*: "Reference your message to Edsall for Mr. Jennings. Am approaching Long Island (in Gulf of Smyrna)/have vessels ready to follow me/will escort them anchorage south and east of railway pier."

Powell, lacking barges to carry the refugees to the ships, had arranged (through Roger Griswold, expert at bribes) to bring the ships alongside the railroad pier. By early Sunday morning, thirty thousand refugees already had gathered outside its enclosure. The *Lawrence* met the Greek merchant ships with Jennings aboard the lead ship, the *Ismini,* at 2 P.M. Sunday, September 24. The ships proceeded in a line into the harbor. The *Lawrence* led the way, flying the American flag, and the Greek ships followed. "From quite a way out," Jennings later remembered, "I could see from my station on the bridge the smoking ruins of what had once been the business part of the town. It was the most desolate fearsome sight I ever saw. And at the water's edge stretching for miles, was what looked like a lifeless black border." As Jennings's ship drew closer, he saw that the black border was actually the crowd of black-clad women along the Quay, "suffering, waiting, hoping, praying as they had be[en] doing every moment for days—waiting, hoping praying for ships, ships, ships."

The ships moved closer. "As we approached, and the shore spread out before us, it seemed as if every face on that Quay was turned toward us, and every arm out-stretched to bring us in. I thought the whole shore was moving out to grasp us."

The refugees on the Quay, seeing the line of ships, knew immediately that help had arrived and that they might now survive. A great cheer went up from the crowd, and the many tens of thousands of people along the Quay reached toward the ships, tearful and exultant. Jennings would remember it as a cry of "transcendent joy." Among those watching were Theodora and her two sisters and the Hatcherian family. Their prayers had been answered.

The rescue was about to commence, but their suffering was not over.

CHAPTER 30

The Evacuation Begins

The Greek merchant ships tied up at the railroad pier four at a time. The seven that had arrived on the first trip were the *Ismini, Matheos, Atromitos, Thraki, Byzantion, Zakinthos,* and *Peneos.* The railroad pier was a big industrial space with cranes, train tracks, and storage sheds just past and around the bend of the Point at the very terminus of the harbor. In the morning, Turkish soldiers had herded 30,000 of the 250,000 refugees that still remained in the city toward the Point to board the ships. They filled the streets around the Point, to the north and south, and nearly all were women and children. They carried their sacks, straw baskets, carpets, blankets, and, sometimes, odd possessions—a wooden saddle, a piece of a loom, a roll of chicken wire. Many of the very young and very old were close to death. They had been without food for days.

The pier was made of rough wood planks and projected several hundred yards into the harbor, then broke at an angle to the right, forming a crooked digit that pointed toward the lower end of Cordelio. The ships docked at the crooked digit, two on either side. A seven-foot-tall iron-picket fence enclosed the rail yard behind the pier. There were three widely spaced gates in the iron fence, and refugees passed through each gate, inspected by Turkish soldiers. The three additional makeshift fences had been set up inside the main iron fence, and these interior fences channeled the refugees through the rail yard and toward the base of the pier, which led to the pier's crooked digit and the ships. The passages between the makeshift fences narrowed in some places with timbers to thin the line and allow closer inspection by the soldiers. All men of military age were pulled out of line, including foreign nationals without papers. The Turkish soldiers placed the men who were pulled out into wire pens on the pier, and when the pens were full, soldiers marched the men away. About 10 percent of the refugees were men of military age—husbands, brothers, and fathers of the women they were with.

A double line of Turkish soldiers loitered between the first and second gates, and from time to time some of them moved among the refugees, mostly to rob them of whatever money they had left or rummage their bundles for valuables. The third gate, distant from the two closer to the Point, admitted fewer refugees and was less well guarded.

Powell assigned sixty sailors to the rail yard and pier, twenty specifically to keep violence by the Turkish soldiers to a minimum. The sailors' only authority was their American uniforms and willingness to forcefully step between a soldier and his victim—they were not permitted to draw weapons for the protection of the refugees. The sailors were not shy about coming between a refugee and a soldier who was intent on extracting a last bit of punishment. Powell stood on the pier coordinating the flow of people, signaling to the Turkish soldiers to open and close the gates into the rail yard. He had to work fast. The Turkish deadline gave him only seven days from this morning to remove the refugees from the city. He wasn't entirely sure how many people were in the concentration camps and backstreets—there were likely tens of thousands more—but he operated on the assumption that those who failed to pass over the pier in the next seven days would be marched into the interior.

The loading was brutal and often chaotic. People were desperate not to be left behind, and they pushed and shoved one another and leaned into the fences and gates. Women were knocked down, children torn from their arms. Sometimes guards would hold back a woman to check her bundle but her family would be pushed through, causing her to be separated from her relatives. She would scream and attempt to push through a closed barrier as her family moved farther forward and disappeared into the tattered and dirty parade moving toward the ships, fully lost to her. The worst cases were when the women were separated from their children.

The Turks used leather straps, canes, rifle butts, and bayonets to control the crowd, and in a few cases Turkish guards shot male refugees who tried to force their way toward the ships or escape from the guards. "Robbing at the gates and in the yard was rather the rule than the exception," Powell noted in his diary. Posting sailors on the pier didn't stop the robberies—with scores of Turkish soldiers on and near the pier and thousands of refugees as targets, there simply were too many incidents for the sailors to intercede in all of them. Powell appealed to the Turkish officers to halt the brazen robberies by bringing their soldiers under control; and the request—officer to officer—slowed the worst of it for a short time near the ships, but the robberies continued among the long lines of people stretching into the streets and soon it was rampant again everywhere. Unable to get the officers present to act decisively to stop the thefts, he called on Noureddin and reported it to him. "It did not seem to interest him to any great degree," Powell wrote. Often guards at the gates demanded payment as a matter of course before letting people pass. If a refugee failed to produce money, the soldier sent her back to the street.

"Two sides of the Turk's nature," Powell wrote, "were evident every day of the evacuation: one in his treatment of refugees, both women and old men, was the robber and more or less of a brute, the other was a soldier doing his duty with a very humane side to him. I have seen them pick up a hat and an old man, or assist a cripple or elderly woman."

The first gate, closest to the Quay, was the main choke point. The crowd compressed as it squeezed through, leading to shoving, pushing, and pulling. There was the always-present fear of being left behind—of being the last person to reach a ship only to be told there would be no passage out. Women lost shoes, and their clothing was torn as they tried to get through. An old woman had become lost, and in her confusion she was unaware that she was naked from the waist down. She ran about calling for her family. Another woman was separated from her child when it was allowed to pass through the gate, but the gate was suddenly closed, preventing her entrance to the rail yard. She tried to force her way through and was beaten back by the soldiers. Wild, she climbed the picket fence, which was taller than a man. A soldier cornered her inside the fence and pinned her against the bars with the butt of his gun. She fought back, crazed to gain her child back, and broke away from the soldier, who ultimately let her run to it.

The Greek ships were built to carry cargo, not people, and the refugees were lowered into the deep vertical cargo holds with ropes, and when the holds were full, refugees were spread tightly on the decks, beginning at the aft end of the ship and working forward toward the bow for maximum stowage. Usually, the refugees' bundles were thrown into the hold first. At one point, a woman became hysterical when her bundle was taken from her and thrown into the depths of the ship. Sailors could not restrain her, and she jumped into the hold to retrieve it. Thirty feet down, she landed on other bundles, which cushioned her fall, and she unwrapped her bundle—it contained her child. The American sailors turned to the work with energy—cheerful even, in this unusual assignment—and carried bundles and rugs and stretchers to the ships. Some carried crippled refugees on their backs; others had a baby in each arm. Many of the bundles—big squares of cloth filled with household utensils and goods and tied at the corners—taxed the strength of the young sailors. The sailors marveled at the strength of some of the old kerchiefed and barefoot women who had carried these bundles for days over miles of rough roads and had kept possession of them through the fire.

The heat was punishing on the pier, with the temperature hovering near one hundred degrees Fahrenheit. There was no shade, and no water to share among the people. The stink was awful. There was a quarter-acre wedge of water between the pier and the Point in which an eddy caught and held the harbor's ghastly floatage—mostly garbage, sewage, and the carcasses of animals. The disgusting soup splashed against the stonework of the pier and released the smell of putrefying flesh. Occasionally a human body, swollen and naked, emerged among the dead animals and waterlogged garbage. From time to time, in the crush, a woman was pushed into the water, and she stood among the saturated carrion holding her child in the air until she could scramble to rejoin the crowd, the rags she wore absorbing the harbor's stench. The noise too was deafening: "The din was terrific," wrote an officer who was present, "winches rattling, women shrieking, children howling, shouted orders, and through all the steady undertone of shuffling feet and the murmur of a vast crowd."

THE RELIEF COMMITTEE had been relying on only two doctors—Dr. Post and Dr. Margoulis, the local Jewish doctor—throughout the postfire ordeal, but on the previous day, Saturday, a third doctor had arrived— Esther Pohl Lovejoy, an extraordinary woman who was the head of the American Women's Hospital Association. She had arrived on the SS *Dotch*, a broken-down tramp freighter that flew the flag of Imperial Russia, a defunct state. The Near East Relief had chartered the *Dotch* in Constantinople to deliver supplies and evacuate refugees. Packing a few cans of food and several Sterno burners, Dr. Lovejoy, then fifty-two years old, had jumped a ride on the freighter with another American, Ernest Shoedsack, an aspiring filmmaker who was in search of a big subject for a documentary. He was six feet, four inches tall, and Dr. Lovejoy called him "Shorty." "The trip to Smyrna was very distressing to Shorty," Dr. Lovejoy would later remember. "He was torn, as it were, between two massacres. The one which had already taken place at Smyrna, and the one which might take place at Constantinople."*

Dr. Lovejoy, born in a Pacific Northwest lumber camp, had grown up in Portland, becoming only the second woman to graduate from the University of Oregon Medical School. She practiced medicine in Alaska, during the Gold Rush of 1899, and Portland, where she became the city's health director. She had been a strong voice for women and children's health and an advocate of women's suffrage. She had turned Portland into a model of public health by writing its first milk- and food-handling ordinances, and she had kept bubonic plague, which was then appearing in West Coast cities, out of Portland by leading a crackdown on the city's rat

---

* Shoedsack was an innovative documentary filmmaker who also went on to direct *King Kong* and *Mighty Joe Young*.

population. Her first husband died in Alaska, her brother was murdered on the Dawson Trail, and her son had died at eight years old. A big-boned and beautiful woman, she had married a second time, but the marriage had ended in divorce. In 1917, she traveled to France to work with the American Medical Women's Association, which treated the war's civilian victims. She had stayed in Europe, helping to start the American Women's Hospital Association, which opened clinics in the Balkans, the Caucasus, and Turkey. Dr. Lovejoy had been in Paris, preparing to travel to Russia, when she had learned of the refugee crisis at Smyrna. She had immediately departed for Constantinople, where she had hopped on the *Dotch*.

On the railroad pier, she wore a long loose dress with sleeves to her elbows and a hat with full-circle brim against the sun. "In a city with so large a population," Dr. Lovejoy later wrote, "there were, of course, a great many expectant mothers, and these terrible experiences precipitated their labors in many instances. Children were born upon the Quay and upon the pier, and one woman, who had been in the crush at the first gate for hours, finally staggered through holding her just-born child in her hands."

Powell appreciated her presence and consulted with her about handling women who were in the worst conditions. Hysteria—uncontrollable screaming, wailing, and laughter caused by severe mental trauma—was a malady not uncommonly confronted on the pier.

THE HATCHERIANS WERE AMONG the tens of thousands of people on the railroad pier Sunday morning, September 24.

After he and the other older men had been released by the Turkish guards, Dr. Hatcherian had returned to the house on the Quay and discovered to his great relief that his family was still there, and while his wife appeared emaciated and his youngest child, Vartouhi, was suffering diarrhea from malnutrition, they were safe. The number of people in the house was now greater than before, and they had learned that Americans were transporting people out of the city and that tickets on the vessels were for sale at the American consulate. Mrs. Hatcherian, with another woman, bought tickets, ten liras each, and returned to the house.* Then, the Hatcherian family, with the tickets, went to another house, guarded by the Americans and next to the consulate, which served as a waiting place for departing refugees. (The house was one of Jennings's safe houses.)

On September 22, a launch had arrived at the Quay, opposite the house, and the Hatcherians and many others stood in line to board it to be carried to the freighter in the harbor. (It was either the *Versailles* or the *Worsley Hall*.) The smaller boat could take one hundred fifty people and it made several trips, filling the freighter. The Hatcherians were too far back in line to be taken aboard, and the ship departed without them. They returned to the Jennings house, where the Americans gave them bread and the children condensed milk.

The next day, September 23, the Hatcherians had arisen early and watched the horizon for another ship but none appeared. Dr. Hatcherian recorded in his diary:

> Outside the house where we are staying many thousands of miserable people are crowded together envying those of us living in the American building, but they, too, hope to benefit from the protection provided by the star-spangled banner. The whole day passes without change, and we realize that we will be obliged to be hosted for at least one more night.

On Sunday morning, September 24, the children were hungry but there was no food. So Hatcheres, Dr. Hatcherian's oldest son, had gone out to see if he could buy some. While he was gone, an American sailor announced that it was time for people to line up to go to the railroad pier to board the ships. Others prepared to leave, but the Hatcherians waited, worrying that they would miss the ship, but unwilling to leave without Hatcheres. After about an hour, Hatcheres returned—bloodied. He had ventured too far from the American building and Turkish soldiers had

---

* Near East Relief sought to defray its expenses by selling tickets, but refugees also were evacuated without them. There are indications that some of the ticket sales were an illicit and unauthorized attempt to extract money from the refugees.

stopped him, taken his money, and beaten him. With Hatcheres back among them, the family including Araksi, the housekeeper, joined the other refugees leaving the house for the walk to the railroad pier.

As they approached it, by the Aydin Railroad station, Turkish soldiers pulled Dr. Hatcherian and other men out of the crowd to clean the square. He complied but quietly sneaked away when the soldiers were not watching him and rejoined his family, and they moved with the mass of people toward the first gate. It was early afternoon, and the Hatcherians waited in the hot sun. At four o'clock, they saw the *Lawrence* coming into the harbor with Jennings's Greek freighters trailing behind. Dr. Hatcherian's heart pounded with joy—there were thousands of people waiting to depart but surely there would be room enough on those ships to take them all aboard. When the Turkish guard opened the gate, the crowd attempted to rush through, pushing and shoving, but the crowd was big and the opening narrow so the Hatcherians were unable to make their way inside.

> I have Vartouhi in my arms, my wife has my cane in one hand along with our only woolen blanket, and in the other hand, a bottle full of water. As for the maid and children, they each carry a bundle or bag. We, too, are mingled in the huge crowd, as we all attempt to reach the door of mercy. Many are forced to discard their bundles, bags and sacks over which me [sic] must climb in order to approach the door. It is impossible to change a step. I am squashed at my back and at my chest, and I fear that Vartouhi may choke. Some critical moments pass and I mobilize all of my physical strength to save my poor little girl from certain death. We are quite close to the door, but it is impossible to proceed over the goods scattered on the ground. I lose my balance and I fall down. Fear overcomes me that the crowd will stampede Vartouhi and me and we will be smothered. But I manage to get up making a superhuman effort. A few more steps and we reach the door, which we enter with great difficulty.

Inside the gate, Turkish guards stopped them and prepared to search them for valuables, but an American sailor interceded and they were able to continue moving in line. As they shuffled along toward the opening in a second makeshift fence, Dr. Hatcherian saw that some refugees were getting inside by scaling the fence. Incredibly, he decided to do the same, and with his wife's help he got over the top and she handed him the children. He was then faced with the problem of getting his wife over the top. He asked a Turkish guard on the other side if he would help his wife over the fence for money. The soldier agreed, got down so that Mrs. Hatcherian could step on his shoulders, and then the soldier stood up. Dr. Hatcherian reached for her at the top of the fence and helped her down. Now, the family was together inside the fence and they rejoined the line. As they moved toward the pier, another Turkish soldier asked him what he had given the other soldier, and Dr. Hatcherian said that he had rewarded him for some help and he offered the second guard money as well. The guard refused and put the point of his bayonet to Dr. Hatcherian's chest. He ordered him back out of the gate.

The children began to cry and Mrs. Hatcherian begged the soldier to allow her husband to remain with the family. Dr. Hatcherian appealed to an American sailor who stood nearby, but he responded that he could not intervene. The doctor was almost back out of the gate when the Turkish soldier decided to take the money Mrs. Hatcherian had offered him; he allowed Dr. Hatcherian to rejoin his family. Overcome by the tension, Dr. Hatcherian fainted. In a few moments, he regained consciousness and stood up. Then, from out of the crowd, a friend came to him and asked him to go outside the gate to attend to an old woman who had fallen in line and blacked out. It was an awful dilemma for Dr. Hatcherian— abandon his family or refuse to go to the woman's aid. He decided that he could do little or nothing for the woman without medicine and it was too dangerous to leave his family even for a few minutes. He told the friend that he could not go, and the Hatcherians moved closer to the ship. Now, they could see the people stepping onto the deck. Dr. Hatcherian felt again that he would lose consciousness. He rested, then began again with Vartouhi in his arms. He led his family toward the ship. There was one more Turkish guard to pass, and Dr. Hatcherian lowered his head and walked by him. There was always the chance he would be taken for being forty-five years old or less, arrested, and placed in one of the pens. The guard watched him closely. Dr. Hatcherian felt his gaze, but the soldier did not stop him.

> Without looking left or right and without disclosing the storm inside me, I quicken my pace and, finally, arrive in front of the ship. There I stop for an instant and check to see whether there is anyone missing. We are all here, eight people, including the maid. I breathe a sigh of relief. All that remains is to board the ship immediately. On the little bridge, a huge crowd is jammed. It will be very hard to pass through there. I climb the ship and manage to drag each of my family members up on the ship, one-by-one. We are all miraculously freed. After so much hardship and suffering, my being alive, is an absolute miracle.

The mad day wore on, and in four hours, Powell, his men, and the relief committee had managed to fill the six ships—sixteen thousand people. Dr. Hatcherian's family was among the last to be loaded.

Powell went aboard the *Ismini* to talk with Jennings, who had remained on the ship through the loading. The commander was handling the shoreside logistics; Jennings was controlling the ships in the harbor. Powell told him to unload the refugees at Mytilene as rapidly as possible and hurry back to Smyrna for another run. Time was short. Jennings departed with the ships, escorted out of the harbor by the *Lawrence*.

AMONG THE AMERICANS ON the pier was Mark Prentiss with his whistle and helmet. At the end of the day, he wrote another story for the *New York Times* and sent it via ship to Constantinople for transmission to New York. It was published later in the week. In the first paragraph of the story, he wrote that he was in charge of the ships moving between Smyrna and Mytilene. The story mentioned neither Jennings nor Powell. In describing the scene at the pier, he wrote, "I am certain no refugees were seriously hurt by the soldiers. . . ."

THE NEXT DAY, MONDAY, September 25, no ships arrived. The refugees scanned the harbor, waiting for a telltale line of smoke on the horizon or the glint of sun on a hull.

The problem was the turnaround time at Mytilene. It was taking longer than expected to unload the refugees—it had to be done with tugs, barges, and small boats. It soon became clear that a ship that left Smyrna with a load of refugees for Mytilene would not return to reload for at least thirty-six hours—this would be the cycle time, a day and a half, even though the round trip steaming time was four hours at most.

Jennings sent a message from Mytilene to Powell that the new arrivals had brought the number of refugees on the island to one hundred thousand, and the city was running out of food. He said he feared a riot if food did not arrive within twenty-four hours. This further complicated matters for Powell—he had flour at Smyrna, but the Turks would not allow it to leave the city. Food would have to be transported to the island from Constantinople, but there was the continuing problem of radio communication from Smyrna. Jennings also notified Powell that the *Kilkis* had set out to sea—though he did not know its location. Theophanides was gone from the city. The mysterious departure of the *Kilkis* was a quiet but ominous portent that Jennings did not yet understand.

Jennings also reported to Powell that there were refugees at other towns and cities along the coast—twenty thousand at Aivali just to the north of Smyrna and twenty-five thousand at Vourla, only a few miles to the south.* The Greek government had asked him, he told Powell, to attempt to evacuate them as well. They were close to starvation. This was another dilemma for Powell: it would be impossible for him to send a ship to either of those places—he needed his ships and men in Smyrna. His goal now remained the evacuation of Smyrna. "I gave Mr. Jennings orders to expedite in every way the arrival of the next Greek ships and to have them by 8 a.m. the next morning." (That deadline was not met because of the turnaround time.) Meanwhile, Powell observed, more refu-

---

* The Vourla refugees included the family of George Seferis, who later would win the Nobel Prize for his poetry, which drew on his nostalgia for Anatolia. Seferis was at school in Europe at the time of the evacuation.

gees were coming into Smyrna from the distant hills and villages. The crowds were again swelling along the waterfront.

At 11 A.M. Monday, while Jennings was unloading in Mytilene, Powell, taking along John Clayton and Vice Consul Barnes, called on Rauf Bey, the nationalist foreign minister, and together the group drove to Latife's home in Göztepe for a meeting with Mustapha Kemal. They climbed the same stairs that the guests had climbed the night of the party and entered Kemal's office. Powell was favorably struck with the Turkish leader: "He immediately impressed you as being a very strong man. . . . All of Mustapha Kemal's replies to questions were short and complete and answered entirely the question asked without evasion or without hesitation. . . . He informed us that the Nationalist army had already reached the straits and that his troops were now in Arenkiei [a town at Chanak on the Dardanelles Strait], and that, although rumored, there had been no contact with the British forces." Powell's interview with Kemal ranged broadly over Turkish nationalist intentions in the Dardanelles, the possibility of an exchange of populations between the Turks and Greeks, and the future of the Near Eastern oil fields. Powell specifically asked Kemal about exploitation of oil in Mesopotamia.

> **Powell:** Your excellency, those who have studied the oil question in its bearing on international politics, realize that Great Britain must have access to large petroleum deposits or cease to be a world power of the first importance. Therefore, to my mind the problem of the petroleum fields in Mesopotamia northeast of the Jebal Hamrin [a mountain range in northern Iraq] is certainly of greater importance than Constantinople, and possibly of as much importance as the Straits. Will you express the attitude of the Turkish Nationalist Government towards the British claims to the Mesopotamian oil?
>
> **Kemal:** All of the territories in question are in the Province of Mosul, which is part of the territory mentioned in the Nationalist pact [in other words, inside Turkey's borders—Author]. The great majority of the territory is Turkish. I don't think possession

of this territory is necessary for the exploitation of the oil fields in that region. For instance, there is nothing against American exploitation of oil fields in Turkey as America has no political ambitions in our country. If England would follow a similar attitude, it would be a most reasonable one.

The response was important enough for Powell to immediately dispatch the *Lawrence* back to Constantinople with a transcript. Oil had been Bristol's chief concern all along. It was precisely the answer that he would be pleased to hear.

On the same day, Powell received a note from Captain Hugh C. Buckle, commander of the British light cruiser HMS *Curacoa*, which remained in the harbor. The captain was concerned for the safety of the British manager of the Aydin Railroad, General de Candolla. (The general was the British secret agent whom Lieutenant Merrill had befriended a week earlier.) De Candolla had remained at the railroad office to avoid having the Turks seize the railroad by declaring it derelict. With war imminent, Buckle wanted the retired general and active secret agent to get himself aboard a British ship, but the captain was reluctant to send British marines ashore. Powell had one of his men deliver the message, and de Candolla returned to the *Curacoa*. Powell had been cultivating good relations with the British, and his rapport with the British officers would play an important part in the evacuation in subsequent days.

Five days earlier, when Powell had agreed to help Buckle load refugees aboard the *Versailles* and the *Worsley Hall*, Buckle had invited Powell and his officers to dinner aboard the *Curacoa*. The American officers had accepted the dinner invitation but said what they could really use was a drink. Of course, responded the British commander, and together the British and American officers had boarded a British launch and motored to the *Curacoa* for dinner and drinks in its wardroom, which was fitted out like a British men's club—leather armchairs, books, cupboard with trophies and awards, and a long green-cloth table over which hung a lamp with a yellow silk lampshade.

It had been a convivial evening. Powell was a good storyteller, and he had related his wartime experiences in the Queenstown flotilla during World War I with the British admiral Lewis Bailey, whom he admired greatly and called "Luigi" to the delight of the British officers present. It had helped the evening's good feelings that Powell had worn his Distinguished Service Order medal, a red and blue ribbon with a gilt-and-white-enamel cross. Another one of the *Edsall*'s officers entertained the British with his stories of odd characters, including a man who slept in his boots for obvious reasons, and there was a good deal of laughter among the men in the stateroom. "They (the Americans) went back to the ship," a British officer who was present later wrote, "leaving behind them the impression that if any trouble occurred, it would be pleasant to be in it with them. It was the beginning of a great friendship between the two ships."

THE NEXT MORNING, TUESDAY, September 26, Powell was up before 5 A.M. He had received word of the return of the Greek ships. This time, the *Edsall*, with Powell aboard, met them at the Pelican Spit buoy—nine had already arrived, and five more were approaching. Another trailed behind. Jennings had been able to increase the number of ships available for the evacuation—the flotilla was growing in size as the Piraeus ships joined the effort. About fifty ships were now involved—the fifteen now in Smyrna harbor, others at Mytilene, and still others on their way from Piraeus, including an ocean liner, the *Megali Hellas*, which had been making regular passenger runs to New York but was detailed to Smyrna.

The rising sun cast a burnished copper glow on the surface of the harbor as the *Edsall* steamed alongside the Greek ships at the buoy and led them toward the railroad pier. The air was still, the day already hot. From the *Edsall*'s bridge, Powell had a good view of the Quay from the rail yard on the far left to the Custom House Pier to the far right. The line of refugees all along the Quay was two miles long, and tens of thousands were already amassed at the rail yard gates.

Powell managed to tie up five ships at the pier by 8 A.M., working in the fifth ship at the tip of the pier's crooked digit, and the loading recommenced at 8:30. A small number of British and Italian merchant ships chartered by the American Relief Committee also came into the harbor to embark refugees, and the *Worsley Hall* departed for a second trip to Mytilene with its decks and holds packed with people. Then came another stroke of good luck—Admiral Nicholson, who was aboard the flagship *Curacoa* as commander of the Second Light Cruiser Squadron, sent a note to Powell asking if the British could lend a hand to the Americans in the loading of the Greek ships. Going ashore to help the Americans was a dicey matter for the British—two Turkish planes were buzzing Nicholson's ship, acting aggressively, and matters remained tense at Chanak. Powell happily accepted the request and got permission from the Turkish command to land British sailors on the condition they were unarmed and restricted to the pier. Admiral Nicholson sent all the men he could, about one hundred and thirty, retaining a small crew to man the cruiser's guns in case of trouble.

During the day, Powell broke free of the pier for a while to meet with the Allied officers aboard the French ship *Edgar Quintet* to discuss seeking an extension of the evacuation deadline—it was only five days off, and at least another 150,000 refugees remained. It was agreed to seek the extension. There was another matter Powell wanted discussed—the treatment of the men who were being removed from the pier. They were being routinely beaten and marched off without any explanation as to their fate, though most thought it was deportation (slow death) or execution (quick death). Powell wanted the naval officers to bring pressure on the Turks to stop the brutality. The subject was discussed, and Barnes, the young American consul who had replaced Horton, suddenly became an expert in international law and argued that it was an internal military matter and not a matter for the relief group or the foreign navies. Barnes, whom Bristol was supporting as the next consul in Smyrna, continued to show an inexplicable antipathy toward the refugees.

Powell was not persuaded by the young vice consul. "Knowing that the policy of the United States is at all times, and during the world war, while neutral, was to intercede for the sake of humanity where possible, and without overstepping the bounds of neutrality, I felt that no demands could be made but that Admiral Dumesnil when he went to Noureddin

Pasha could bring up the subject." Powell wanted Dumesnil to make it known to the Turkish command that the "neutrals" took an interest in the fate of the men. Maybe a show of concern would save some lives.

THE PHYSICAL AND MENTAL CONDITIONS of the refugees grew worse with each passing day. The sailors brought more refugees aboard on stretchers, and more were dying on the pier. The bodies were removed to the city for burial or burning. Many of the refugees appeared to Powell as if they would die en route to Mytilene. "One poor old thing sank exhausted on her bundle," wrote a British officer. "She was noticed by one of the seamen, who went up to her and put his hand on her shoulder to persuade her to lie down. She was already dead, and even in that short time the body was quite stiff."

The British sailors made a big difference—they were stationed closest to the ships, and they organized and packed the refugees onto the decks and in the holds so that more could be loaded. If the deadline of September 30 was to be met, Powell said, it would be because of the British help. "The fear and smell in that unwashed crowd were appalling," wrote a British officer. Captain Buckle of the *Curacoa* was on the pier every day with his men, and he and Powell got along well. "There was never a hitch or misunderstanding of any kind," Powell wrote in his report. The British captain deferred to Powell's directions on the pier, and Powell consulted with British Admiral Nicholson every day.

The refugees, even in their weakened state, remained difficult to handle. Panic from time to time would shudder through the mass like an electrical current. The robbery worsened. Rape had been a commonplace, and the women on the pier showed the trauma of it. A British officer who was present wrote, "The women were nearly all on the verge of hysterics. Those who were seen as passably young bore traces of the worst brutality; many were speechless, and those who could talk were unintelligible."

Some of the women, desperate to board the ships, were frightened of what awaited them even there. The same junior officer wrote:

It was quite obvious that the holds contained no further living perils; but the ladders were small and vertical, and to many of the poor crazed creatures it must have seemed that they were being forced down there so as to be deprived of all chance of escape from further outrage. I remember one girl well: a strong, buxom creature, her dusty face streaked with tears, fighting like a tiger cat against all the well-meant efforts to get her down the ladder. What she feared we never discovered, but her struggles held up all the work, and finally she was seized, pinioned, and lowered bodily on a rope, shrieking and struggling to the last.

In some cases, Dr. Lovejoy was called to help. Sometimes the refugees were beyond help. In one instance, a woman came on board carrying a baby in the fold of each arm. According to the British officer's account, she looked down at them lovingly and shooed the flies from their face as she sat crooning and swaying in the shade of the ship's bridge. The babies were strangely quiet and still. The officer touched the cheek of one, then the other. "In all the heat," he later remembered, "they were cold, icy cold. They had been dead for hours. But the mother hugged them to her breast and talked to them in baby talk."

For the British and American sailors, one of the most heartrending aspects of the evacuation was watching the separation of families—men from their wives, mothers, and children. Occasionally a man would dash from the crowd and past the barrier in an attempt to evade the guards—if he was able to get far enough past the barrier before being shot, the American sailors often made it difficult for the Turkish guards to pursue him. But these cases were the exception. Very few men escaped. Dr. Lovejoy observed:

As family after family passed those gates, the father perhaps of 42 years of age, carrying a sick child or other burden, or a young son or some-times both, father and son would be seized. This was the climax of the whole terrible experience for every family. In a frenzy of grief, the mother and children would cling to the father and son, weeping, begging and praying for mercy but there was no mercy. With the butts of their guns, the Turkish soldiers beat these men backwards into the prison groups and drove the women toward the ships, pushing them with their guns, striking them with straps or canes.

The Turkish soldiers sought men of military age, but they seized boys as young as sixteen and men as old as sixty. At the end of the day, the men (and boys) were marched into the city and put to work clearing debris and piling bodies into heaps and burning them. Later, they would be marched out of the city.

"They would be used as a labor corps in Smyrna for twenty-four hours," wrote a British officer from the *Curacoa*, "clearing up the filth and nameless things that still lay about and stank in the corners—relics of the fire and the massacre. Then they would be marched into the interior to a concentration camp. But none ever reached it." Describing "a convoy of these wretches starting off," the British officer reported, "they were surrounded by a troop of cavalry who, every now and again, broke into a sharp trot, belaboring the prisoners with carbines and swords to make them keep pace. The prisoners were kept without food and without water. When a man fell, he never got up again."

The same British officer offered a man in one of the pens a pack of cigarettes. According to his account, the man's response was, "'Tomorrow, sir'—a shrug of the shoulders, a little gesture of finality—'tomorrow, I die.'"

Through the chaos, heat, and shrieks, Dr. Lovejoy continued her work. She walked up and down the pier to watch for the sick, especially women in labor. A British naval surgeon had come ashore and performed emergency-trauma work at the end of the pier, and from time to time, Dr. Lovejoy presented him with the worst cases. The American sailors brought her the maternity cases. In one instance, a British sailor took her aboard a ship that was about to depart. They descended into the hold, packed with a mass of people humid with breath and stink. A woman was in labor. Dr. Lovejoy wrote:

With great difficulty we got her out and placed her on the deck behind a chicken coop. Her clothes were in rags, her hairpins gone and her long hair hanging loose. She had lost her shoes and her feet were bare and blistered. She was dirty like the rest of the refugees, but I noticed that her chemise was made of fine linen, hand embroidered. She spoke English, and when I asked her sister, who was with her, what they had to wrap the baby in, she opened a small bundle of baby clothes, which the young mother had clung to during the burning of Smyrna, and the subsequent two weeks on the Quay. Daintily made by hand, edged with fine lace and tied with ribbons, these little things aboard that refugee ship testified to a home life which seemed as remote and impossible as the Elysian age—the age of love, and innocence and joy.

ON TUESDAY, SEPTEMBER 26, Powell, counting down the hours to the deadline, refused to stop the loading even as it grew dark. The moon had returned to the sky as a thin crescent. Powell sent some ships away, brought others to the pier. He had the *Litchfield* shine its spotlights on the pier to allow the work to continue through the night. The *Curacoa* directed its beams on the pier too. Work that had been difficult in daylight proved almost impossible at night, even with the beams of the searchlights.

As Powell stood on the pier, one of the ship's lights revealed the forms of men swimming toward the warships. They had quietly slipped into the water and hoped to be taken aboard by the naval crews. Powell was standing with the Turkish captain of the port when the wakes of the swimmers became apparent, the disturbed water showing its phosphorescence. The Turkish police began firing at the swimmers, their bullets pocking the black water. The port officer asked Powell to pick the men up and return them to his soldiers. This surely meant execution. It seemed that one of the swimmers already had been struck by the firing. It was a tense moment. Powell was sympathetic to the men, but he also needed the cooperation—even permission—of the Turkish authorities to continue the evacuation. He had developed a good relationship with the port captain, in particular, and had found him helpful in the loading process. Powell did not want to endanger the partnership. It could bring the entire evacuation to a halt. He agreed to pick up the swimmers but said he would not hand them over to the soldiers. Instead, he told the port officer, he would return them to shore and the crowd. In deference to Powell, the Turkish officer consented.

At about the same time, some members of the relief committee attempted to sneak three refugee women and a man in a boat to the dark side of one of the Greek ships. The Turkish guards also saw this. Powell sent a boat around and brought the four back to shore and (like the swimmers) sent them back to the Quay. Powell assured the port captain it wouldn't happen again.

The loading ended that night at 9:30 P.M.—forty-three thousand had been sent away this day.

At night, the refugees who had not been loaded were pushed from the pier back to the streets. The American guards were withdrawn, with the exception of a few men who remained on the pier overnight. Despite the difficulty of moving the people back and forth each day through the gates, Powell judged it too dangerous for people to remain on the pier at night without a full complement of American guards.

The sounds of the night added their macabre touch. Some of the ships in the harbor were in the habit of playing music from their speakers, and the sounds of Caruso singing *Pagliacci* drifted over the still water. There was also the pitiful and mournful sound of refugees, praying, crying, and occasionally screaming. "A sudden wailing came down the wind like the shiver in the reeds when a gust strikes them," wrote a British officer who stood on deck one night. "It died away, then started again and became louder until it was like the sound of countless marsh-birds giving their lonely haunting cries."

The sad nighttime sound of the refugees remains one of the details most often found among the firsthand accounts of the evacuation. Dr. Lovejoy was one of those who had remembered it. She described it as she had heard from the balcony of the American house next to the consulate where she stood one night with an Armenian girl helping the relief committee: "There was a strange murmur of many voices rising and falling along the waterfront. The sound was mournful, like the moaning of the sea, increasing in volume as the darkness deepened. The language was unfamiliar, the tone minor and the effect weird and indescribably uncanny. 'What are they doing?' I asked this girl. 'Praying,' she answered simply. 'Praying for ships.'"

One morning, as the guards reassembled for the day's loading, the body of a Turkish soldier was found floating near the base of the pier. He was pulled out and recognized as one of the cruelest guards working the pier on the previous day. Apparently, one of the American sailors stationed on the pier overnight had quietly decided to end the soldier's career as a tormentor of refugees.

The American officers, struggling against their compassion, often had to keep the American sailors in line. The young men were responding as young men. In one instance, a husky young sailor had deposited a refugee girl in a niche of masonry in front of Jennings's house at No. 490 and brought her food each day from the ship. When he learned that his ship was departing, he asked that she be assured a place aboard a ship for evacuation. "She's my girl," he said. "I got her that place near the window with the blanket and the pillow. I've kept her there and brought her food for nearly two weeks, and I don't want no Turk to get her now. Give me God's truth, and promise me you'll watch her and get her aboard a ship."

EVEN AMID THE SUFFERING, there were lighter moments, and glimpses of irrepressible humanity flashed on the pier, ever so briefly.

While on the Quay, many of the old-men refugees had taken the precaution of putting on a fez, headgear typically associated with a Muslim. It offered no real protection, but to put it on was to grasp at a straw that might help in a dangerous moment. The old men wore the fez right up to their embarkation on the ships—and sometimes the British sailors on the pier, as a lark, took off their white pith helmets and put fezzes on too. But just as soon as the old men were aboard the ship and the ship let loose its lines, the men would snatch the fezzes off their heads, throw them on the deck, and stomp them. Sometimes, the British sailors joined in the fun. "It was always the crowning entertainment," a British officer recalled, "though what the Turks made of it we never knew."

CHAPTER 31

The Rhodes Letter Resurfaces

I t didn't take long for the ambiguity of Lieutenant Commander
Rhodes's letter to Jennings—and Jennings's overreach in his promise to the Greeks about American protection of its ships—to stir up
trouble for Powell.

A cable from the American minister in Athens alerted Bristol that
something was afoot. Bristol wanted an explanation, and responsibility
for the explanation landed squarely with Powell.

On September 24, the day following Jennings's negotiations with the
Greek government aboard the *Kilkis*, the Greek minister of foreign affairs
called on Jefferson Caffrey, the American chargé d'affaires in Athens.
The Greek minister wanted to confirm Jennings's promise of protection
of Greek ships. The request caught Caffrey by surprise. He was not aware
of any promise to protect Greek ships, nor was he aware of any plan to
evacuate the refugees with Greek ships. He immediately cabled Bristol.
Caffrey's message was sent at 3 P.M., September 24.

Caffrey did not receive a response from Bristol so he resent the mes-
sage of query the next day, September 25. It read, "September 25 11 p.m.
URGENT My 20 [20 is the cable number—Author] September 24 3 p.m.
Minister of Foreign Affairs called today to ask if American warships
would protect Greek vessels being sent to Smyrna to rescue refugees.
Please inform me of what action has been taken."

The late hour of telegraph transmission suggests that the Greek government was pressing Caffrey for an answer. Quite reasonably, after the unorthodox negotiations between the Greek prime minister and the *Kilkis*, the Greek government wanted to know if Greek ships could rely on U.S. protection.

Bristol finally responded to the first message late in the day, at 7 P.M.—a delay that is hard to explain but becomes understandable through subsequent developments; his cable also was sent before he received Caffrey's second cable, suggesting that he had received the first cable but was withholding a response. (Caffrey apparently didn't receive Bristol's response so he had sent his second query.) In any event, Bristol's answer to the Greek question of American protection of its ships was a firm no: "Action of American Naval Officers Smyrna confined purely to using good offices with Turkish authorities to obtain permission for Greek vessels to enter that port when not flying flag. We have not repeat not promised naval protection of any sort nor have [our] naval authorities given an assurances [*sic*] of assistance or care of refugees after evacuation."

Bristol's message to Caffrey in Athens makes it clear that Bristol was unaware of the full scope and detail of Jennings's mission as it was unfolding. Bristol's message to Caffrey makes no mention of the promise of a naval escort or Powell's attempt to send flour to Mytilene, which surely was an "assurance of assistance or care of refugees after evacuation." A cable Bristol had sent to Washington earlier on the same day was vague or silent on key points that Washington surely would have wanted to know about and Bristol would have felt compelled to mention had he know about them. His Washington cable makes no mention of escort nor does it explain that the Greek evacuation ships were obtained by a relief worker's negotiations with a foreign government.

No doubt, Bristol's response to Caffrey alarmed the Greek government. The Greeks thought they had a promise. Had they been duped by Jennings? The answer clearly was yes. Nonetheless, Athens continued to make Greek merchant ships available for the evacuation. Perhaps the success of the first refugee shuttle to Mytilene had reassured the Greek government that its ships were safe from seizure.

From Bristol's perspective, a promise by one of his officers to protect Greek ships would have been gross insubordination. He had not been consulted on the matter, and, in addition to his dislike of the Greeks, the promise had the potential of thrusting the United States between the warring Greeks and Turks. So what had happened?

Based on U.S. Navy and State Department records, Bristol's awareness of Jennings's mission seems to have unfolded this way:

1. On September 23, after dropping off Jennings at Mytilene, Rhodes arrived back in Constantinople at noon and remained there until 10 P.M. Then, he departed for Smyrna by way of Mytilene to pick up Jennings. In the ten hours Rhodes was in Constantinople, he most likely informed Captain Hepburn or Bristol that he had delivered Jennings to Mytilene. Rhodes may also have told Hepburn or Bristol that Jennings had gotten permission the previous day to bring six small Greek merchant ships to Smyrna to evacuate refugees. In addition, Rhodes may also have shown Hepburn or Bristol the letter he had given to Jennings.

   To Bristol, the offer of six Greek ships would have come as unexpected news, but it was not a problem since he had argued from the beginning that the Greeks should take responsibility for the refugees. Bristol also would have inferred from the six-ships development that Powell had managed to get official permission from the Turkish authorities for Greek ships to enter Smyrna harbor. Again, from Bristol's perspective, there was no problem.

   Undoubtedly, though, Bristol would have seen the loose language in Rhodes's letter as holding the potential for mischief by opening a path around his orders of strict neutrality. No doubt the artery in the strong-willed admiral's substantial neck was pounding in anger. Or so it would appear from subsequent events. His message to Powell of the 20th allowed Powell to load refugees onto Greek-chartered vessels but Bristol had not sanctioned escorts or protection of Greek shipping.

2. The next day, September 24, Caffrey in Athens sent his cable to Bristol conveying the Greek's government's request for confirmation of American protection. Caffrey received no response—either because it had been somehow delayed in reaching him or because Bristol was himself delaying until he could determine what was going on at Smyrna. No doubt Bristol would have connected the two troublesome dots: Rhodes's letter written for Jennings suggesting American protection and the Athens request for confirmation of the protection. If a promise had been made, Bristol would have wanted to put matters right before responding to Caffrey. Hence, a possible decision to delay a response. It surely was not Bristol's style to cable back, "I'm not sure. Let me find out what's going on."

3. On September 25, the *New York Times* carried a Reuters report from Athens that Bristol had offered to protect Greek shipping to evacuate refugees. The news story said the Greek government "has gratefully accepted the offer." The paper also carried a story reporting Washington's denial of a deal. Bristol, in his cable to Caffrey, also denied protection had been offered. But in Athens, Caffrey apparently did not receive the message, and he repeated his message to Bristol.

4. On September 26, Rhodes arrived back in Smyrna—and he had with him a formal memorandum, over his signature and dated September 26, indicating he had been directed to rescind any promise that may have been made to protect the Greeks' ships. It seems clear that the memorandum was prepared by Bristol once the artery in his neck had resumed its normal rhythm. Rhodes was not the sort to write memoranda—in fact, he had not been inclined to commit anything to writing since arriving at Smyrna. Nor was he the sort of person to communicate with his commanding officer (Powell) by handing him a memorandum with an official "cc" to the admiral.

The memorandum in full is worth including:

Navy 3713-22

File 169
JBR:WOG.

U.S.S. LITCHFIELD (#336),
Smyrna, Asia Minor,
26th September, 1922.

From: Commanding Officer.
To : Commanding Officer, (U.S.S. EDSALL).

SUBJECT: Naval Escort for Greek Ships.

    1.   A telegram to Stanav states that Greeks understand that U.S. Naval protection will be given to Greek Merchant vessels going to Smyrna for purpose of bringing out refugees.

    2.   I am directed to inform you that this is not correct and that any impression to that effect must be corrected. U.S. Destroyers may escort Greek merchant vessels assigned such duty. U.S. Authorities have obtained assurance from Turkish Officials that such ships will not be molested, but U.S. will make no Naval demonstration nor give any protection to these vessels. No responsibility for their safety can be assumed.

    3.   I am enclosing copy of letter given Mr. Jennings before he was landed at Mityleni.

J.B. RHODES.

COPY TO:
STANAV.

Courtesy of the Mark Bristol Papers at the Library of Congress

It was a heavy-handed rebuke of Powell, and it's impossible to know, from the official record, the nature of Powell's reaction to the memorandum. Did he become angry with Rhodes, express consternation with Jennings, or grow frustrated with Bristol? All would have been reasonable responses. For the previous ten days, Powell had been confronted with the near-impossible task of removing hundreds of thousands of starving women and children from a hostile city under an unreasonable deadline, and—having

found a way to do so—he had received a memorandum from a
subordinate officer (no doubt having been directed by his superior officer) ordering him to correct an error that had occurred on
his watch.

To his credit, Powell maintained his composure. He seems to
have taken the approach of "counting to ten" before responding
to Bristol.

5. The next day, September 27, Powell sent a cable to Bristol: "The
Greeks got the understanding that the U.S. Navy would protect
them from all molestation from their interpretation of the letter
written to Mr. Jennings by Commanding Officer of the Litchfield, or from Mr. Jennings' interpretation of paragraph 2 of that
letter." (Paragraph 2 said the U.S. Navy would provide escort.) In
his cable to Bristol, Powell said he had directed Jennings to correct the misunderstanding—though he did not say with whom
since a revolution was now under way—and he reported to Bristol
that he had sent a note to the governor at Mytilene clarifying the
U.S. Navy's role. By then, of course, the governor of Mytilene
was a prisoner of the revolution and Greek ships were running
regularly, under American escort, to the Smyrna railroad pier.

On the day Powell sent his note to Bristol, he had already evacuated
more than one hundred thousand people, and it was clear that his effort
was a huge success—at a time when Washington was clamoring for results. Nothing more was said by Bristol about the misunderstanding—at
least on the record. It would have been politically difficult for Bristol to
bring down the hammer on Powell as he had done with Houston in the
Samsun incident. The entire country was watching, and the navy was
emerging as the hero at Smyrna.

Later, much later, Bristol would extol Powell's action and efficiency.
In a letter to the secretary of the navy commending Powell on his work
at Smyrna, Bristol would excuse his delay in communicating the officer's
exceptional work because he had been occupied with other matters.

CHAPTER 32

Revolution

On his return to Mytilene on Tuesday, September 26, aboard the *Ismini*, Jennings found the island overcrowded, on the edge of starvation, and suffering outbreaks of typhus. As if that wasn't enough, he also learned that elements of the Greek army had launched a revolution against the military command, the government in Athens, and the king.

The revolt had begun on nearby Chios on September 23, during the very hours when Jennings and Captain Theophanides had been negotiating with the Greek cabinet. The leader of the revolt was Colonel Nikolaos Plastiras, commander of an elite Evzone unit, which was among the troops evacuated at Chesme about two weeks earlier. He was one of the few officers who had come out of the war with their honor intact—he had fought his way back and more or less held his unit together. (The Turks called him Black Pepper for his mustache and fighting spirit.) Through threats and appeals to their patriotism, he had rallied the army's officers and troops at Chios with the intention of overthrowing the government in Athens, deposing the king, and preventing Thrace from falling to the Turks. He and his followers recruited the Greek navy's junior officers at Chios into the revolt and arrested the navy's senior officers. The older men had continued to stand with the king and government, including the admiral of the fleet and the captain of the *Lemnos*, the *Kilkis*'s sister ship.

Only hours after Jennings and Theophanides had struck their deal with the Greek government for ships, the revolution had leaped from Chios to Mytilene under the direction of Colonel Stylianos Gonatas. The revolutionaries began rounding up Royalist officers including General Frangos and Governor Bakas. Theophanides, a staunch Royalist, put the *Kilkis* to sea and kept the battleship out of the possession of the revolutionary committee. All this had been happening as Jennings stood on the bridge of the *Ismini* on the way back to Smyrna with the first group of empty Greek merchant ships.

It was not until he returned to Mytilene late the same day, September 24, with the loaded ships that Jennings learned that his partner Theophanides was gone, and the revolt was under way. This of course presented him with the problem of working with two governments—the revolutionary government at Mytilene and the Royalist government still in place in Athens.

On landing at Mytilene, Jennings went to the revolutionary leaders and asked for their cooperation. It was immediately given, and he maintained command of his Greek merchant fleet. It was no doubt helpful that Captain Argyropoulos, whom he had designated to handle the merchant ships at Mytilene, was a former Republican naval officer.

As Jennings prepared to return to Smyrna, the revolution rolled forward around him. Three military transports carrying Greek soldiers put to sea and rendezvoused, off the island of Tinos, with the *Lemnos*, which was carrying the revolutionary officers from Chios. Together, the leaders of the revolt and the troops in the transport ships steamed toward Athens. Before they arrived, two planes from Chios dropped leaflets on Athens demanding the government's resignation and the king's abdication.

The troops landed the next day on the Greek mainland at Porto Rafti, Raphina, and Laurium—an easy march into the capital. Caffrey cabled Washington: "Troops have been landed this evening at a number of points near Athens. Government has not yet decided whether or not to oppose movement by force." Theophanides maintained his loyalty to the king and took the *Kilkis* to Phaleron, close to Piraeus, presumably to defend the government. With a civil war possible, the guns of the *Kilkis* would be important to the Royalist government.

Late on September 26, King Constantine abdicated, and Theophanides withdrew plans to resist. By then, Asia Minor refugees already were flowing into Athens. The city, packed with homeless people and humiliated by the catastrophe, sank into a sullen and angry mood that wanted retribution from the politicians and officers who had lost the war. It would come soon in front of a firing squad.

Meanwhile, Jennings continued to shuttle his flotilla back and forth between Smyrna and Mytilene. On the island, his right hand remained Captain Argyropoulos, and Jennings worked through his relief committee to care for the refugees. "The island is facing starvation within three days unless flour can be sent," he radioed to Powell. He reported that the city had put a hospital at his disposal as well as a warehouse for the storage of flour. Since the Turks were making it difficult to ship flour from Smyrna, Powell attempted to have it shipped from the Near East Relief supply in Constantinople.

CHAPTER 33

British Assistance

On Wednesday, September 27, a third group of Greek ships arrived at Smyrna, twelve of them, and the American and British officers and men loaded thirty-one thousand refugees onto the vessels at the railroad pier.

The loading began at 8:30 A.M. and ended at 7 P.M. Powell was also attempting to reconnoiter the situation up and down the coast near Smyrna based on reports he was receiving from Jennings that refugees needed evacuation from other towns and cities. Even though he did not have Turkish permission to enter other ports, Powell attempted to divert the *Litchfield* to Aivali on its return to Smyrna after delivering the Kemal-interview transcript to Bristol, but the ship failed to receive his radio message. He then tried to reach the *MacLeish*, which was on its way to Smyrna, behind the *Litchfield*. He had no success making contact with it either.

Powell hoped that he would be able to retain all four ships—*Lawrence*, *Litchfield*, *MacLeish*, and *Edsall*—for the evacuations at Smyrna and elsewhere. He wanted to keep the *Edsall* and *Lawrence* at Smyrna and send the *MacLeish* and *Litchfield* to Aivali, Vourla, and Chesme. Powell maintained his communication with Jennings at Mytilene via the *Edsall*'s radiotelegraph. Their plan was for Powell to telegraph Jennings if he was able to release a destroyer from Smyrna as an escort; then Jennings would dispatch the Greek freighter to the outlying coastal towns and cities for an escorted pickup of refugees.

On Wednesday, Powell learned that Kemal was preparing to leave the city with his cabinet for a conference at Ismid to negotiate an armistice and possibly to travel to Vienna to settle other big territorial questions now that the nationalists were in control of what remained of the Ottoman Empire. Final matters were congealing. The French minister, Henry Franklin Bouillon, was expected to arrive in Smyrna for talks with Kemal before his departure.

On Thursday, September 28, the situation on the pier took a belligerent turn. In the morning, the Turks were showing a nasty disposition. They began moving machine guns to the end of the pier. One possible explanation for the sudden Turkish aggression was the discovery of the body of the brutal Turkish guard that had been found floating in the water at the pier. The appearance of the guns alarmed the British, who had left their ships exposed to help load refugees. "Unarmed as we were, and with the ship denuded of men, we were helpless," wrote a British officer.

Powell responded forcefully to the provocation. He brought the *Edsall* broadside to the pier, uncovered the ship's deck guns, and put his men at their fighting stations. The Turkish guards were staring down the barrels of the *Edsall*'s four-inch guns, big enough around at the muzzle to take a man's fist. "To the eternal credit of the captain of the American destroyer," a British officer said, "he at once abandoned all thoughts of neutrality." The *Edsall*'s threat was a clear violation of Bristol's orders—no demonstrations of naval force—but it worked. The Turkish machine guns were removed, and the evacuation continued with the assistance of the British sailors and officers. (Not surprisingly, mention of the incident does not appear in the *Edsall*'s ship diary, nor did Powell communicate it to Bristol.)

On the same day, Powell got permission from Noureddin for American and Allied warships to enter Aivali and Vourla, but Noureddin denied permission for Greek merchant ships to enter those ports. Noureddin wanted Smyrna evacuated first and was withholding an answer on the request to extend the evacuation deadline past September 30. Powell sent the *MacLeish* to Aivali, and the British sent a ship to Chesme with a French escort. The commanding officer of the *MacLeish* went ashore at Aivali. The town seemed quiet, and the Turkish authorities, with a Greek priest present, assured the American officer that there were no people to evacuate. The authorities said the Greeks at Aivali wanted to stay. The *MacLeish* carried the news back to Powell, who later learned (through Jennings) that the Greeks had been fearful of requesting evacuation. There were thousands, kept out of sight, who wanted to leave.

By the end of the day, Powell had loaded thirteen ships with thirty-six thousand people. In an attempt to remove all the refugees before the deadline expired, only three days distant, he increased the number of ships being loaded at the same time by embarking refugees from the Quay with small boats from the Cordelio rather than waiting to tie up the ships at the pier. But the success of Powell's rapid loading of the ships had created a crisis at Mytilene, which was bursting with people. Mytilene was hardly much more than a town, and it now had 175,000 refugees—seven times its usual population. Jennings, in consultation with the new Greek government, was making arrangements for many of the refugees to be taken to other Greek islands and to the Greek mainland at Piraeus and Salonika.

The next day, Friday, September 29, eleven Greek ships came into Smyrna's harbor. The estimates of the numbers left to evacuate varied widely—at one point, Powell put the number as high as one hundred thousand. It was as if he was emptying a bathtub while the spigot remained open. People from the backcountry were still arriving, having traveled hundreds of miles, while many others came out of hiding. Then, rapidly, and oddly, Powell saw the size of the crowds on the Quay fall to an extent that could not be explained by the evacuation to the ships. (The bathtub drain had been unplugged.) A speeding up of deportations seemed the only explanation, and they were occurring despite the deadline still two days away.

By the end of the 29th, the number of refugees at the railroad pier dwindled dramatically. They came aboard two at a time, one at a time. Fortunately, the British sailors were not needed for loading the final ships.

The Turks had installed a field battery on a hill overlooking the harbor, forcing the *Curacoa* to shift its billet for safety. On this day, Prentiss and a young navy lieutenant were taken by Turkish escorts to the towns and villages along the line of the Greek army's retreat to gather evidence of Greek atrocities.

On the following day, September 30, the day of the deadline, nine Greek ships and an American shipping board freighter, the USS *Casey*, arrived, and the last six thousand refugees in the city were loaded. Meanwhile, the *Manhattan Island*, which had been chartered by Griswold and Archbell, waited at anchor with two hundred and fifty refugees because the Turkish authorities asserted that the tobacco on board belonged to a naturalized American who had been (and continued to be, in the eyes of the nationalists) an Ottoman subject. It might have been Ery Kehaya, the waiter turned millionaire.

On this last day allowed for evacuation, Powell received word from Admiral Dumesnil that Noureddin had extended the evacuation deadline one week. It was not needed—Powell and Jennings, the American officers and sailors, the relief committee and the British had done the impossible. They had evacuated about two hundred thousand people in seven days. Theodora and her two sisters were among them.

The gates to the railroad pier closed at 7 P.M., September 30. "Pieces of paper fluttered on the pier," wrote a British officer. "The flies rose in clouds; rags and a few forgotten bundles lay about; the cranes hung drunkenly over the side." The evacuation of Smyrna was over. The *Litchfield* departed with Dr. Lovejoy, Ernest Jacob, and John Clayton for Constantinople.

The next day, October 1, the *Manhattan Island* was released, and its refugees taken to Salonika. Powell called on the Turkish captain of the port in Smyrna to thank him for his cooperation. The port captain and Powell had often stood shoulder to shoulder on the pier during the evacuation, and the captain—not a member of the military—had kept his harbor police under control, refusing to permit robbery or harassment of the refugees. The two men had worked through several difficult incidents—including the matter of the swimmers who had been picked up by Powell's men—that could easily have led to a confrontation.

Powell drove around town and the outer areas looking for stray refugees. He wanted to leave no one behind. He had been told that some women and children were still hiding in half-standing incinerated houses and basements, refusing to come out. He searched among the ruins but was unable to find them. Fear kept them hidden. Eventually, they would come out, and he would put them on ships to take them away from Smyrna.

CHAPTER 34

After Smyrna

The evacuation of Smyrna was only the beginning of a more massive exodus that would ultimately involve more than a million people. In its scope and suffering, it stands as one of history's most remarkable forced migrations.

On that last day of September, when he had evacuated six thousand refugees, Powell had also dispatched the *MacLeish* with six Greek merchant ships to Chesme and Vourla. At Vourla, Turkish soldiers marched ten thousand refugees from the upper town to the pebbled beach below to be taken away. Mostly, they were old women and children. Their condition was so poor that about fifty died on the beach as they waited to be rowed to the Greek ships.

"The usual raping went on until finally one Turkish officer, a captain, stationed a strong guard about and stopped it," Commander H. E. Ellis of the *MacLeish* wrote. "One girl was taken aboard in a hazardous condition as a consequence and one woman died on the way out to the ships. She had been stabbed."

Up and down the Aegean coast, in the region from Aivali to Chesme, thousands of refugees waited to be rescued, and Powell continued to direct his destroyers to escort Greek merchant ships to places where people could be loaded. In some towns, there were no deepwater piers, and the American destroyers sent in their motor sailers and whaleboats to bring refugees aboard the merchant ships. It took hours to ferry them to the ships in some places; in others, it took days.

On October 2, the *MacLeish* escorted Greek merchant ships to Aivali, where ten thousand refugees waited. An officer and crew went ashore in a whaleboat flying the American flag. Turkish machine-gun fire snapped its flagstaff and dropped the flag in the water. The American officer landed the boat anyway. The Turkish gunners denied there were refugees in the town. The American officer insisted on seeing the senior Turkish officer, and eventually the American crew was allowed to embark the refugees who had gathered there, out of sight of the waterfront. The *MacLeish* then went on to Phocaea and Scala Nova (the port for old Ephesus), and the USS *Parrott*, sent from Constantinople, investigated towns opposite the island of Samos.

All along the coast, refugees continued to appear on the shoreline, awaiting the American warships that brought the Greek merchant vessels. Even at Smyrna, people from deep in the interior had continued to flow into the city. Some had been hiding in the hills, watching the evacuation from the nearby mountainsides and weighing the danger of making their presence known. "Thousands more had only just arrived from the hinterland villages traveling distances of several hundred miles," Harold Jaquith cabled Near East Relief headquarters.

At Smyrna, Powell remained in radiotelegraph contact with Jennings, who stationed himself at Mytilene. As Powell received reports of additional refugees from his destroyers and the British, he telegraphed Jennings, who dispatched Greek merchant ships, which were met by American escorts. Powell continued to work with Admiral Nicholson, who provided British escorts and sometimes British-chartered freighters. The *MacLeish*, *Lawrence*, and the *Parrott*, the other destroyer that had been sent from Constantinople, did most of the escort work.

Mytilene and Chios were terribly overcrowded. Jennings and Powell had a second challenge—moving the refugees off these two islands to less crowded locations, either other Greek islands or the mainland of Greece. "Shortage of water increases the suffering of the refugees many of whom have fallen ill," Jaquith said in another cable. "Sick women are nursing sick babies and the whole island is become a breeding ground for pestilence."

The span of the evacuation continued to widen. On October 12, Admiral Nicholson informed Powell that there were as many as seventeen thousand refugees at Adalia, on the southernmost coast of Turkey, opposite Cyprus. The Turks had refused Nicholson permission to bring in a British merchant ship to embark them. Powell sent word to Jennings, who sent Greek ships, which traveled under American escort to the town.

In the second week of October, Powell sought and received another deadline extension to retrieve refugees that had gathered in villages back from the coast. In some places, his officers found that refugees were gone, already sent into the interior. At about the same time, in the second week of October, Jennings, whose fame was now spreading through the region, made a trip to Athens to confer with the new government on locations for distributing the refugees. (Aid workers and the Greek government had begun calling him "Commodore Jennings.") The situation was appalling in its breadth and lack of resources, and essentially he and Powell were the main armatures in the evacuation and redistribution of many hundreds of thousands of refugees.

At Mytilene, Jennings constituted another and bigger relief committee to provide food and medical care on the islands. It included Near East Relief, the YMCA, and the American Women's Hospitals, Dr. Lovejoy's organization. In Athens, the government promised Jennings its cooperation and passed along pleas for help from refugees at other locations along the Turkish coast. Jennings asked for more Greek ships and received them, and then he coordinated the wider evacuation through Powell in Smyrna.

It soon was obvious that the refugee situation in Asia Minor was a monumental humanitarian crisis. It reached from Syria in the south (refugees having fled to Aleppo) to the farthest ports of the Black Sea in the north and east—hundreds of thousands of sick and starving people from villages and farms deep inside Anatolia were moving toward the nearest seacoast, filling towns and cities and barren beaches. People trekked over the mountains of northern Turkey, possessions on their backs, a little bit of food in their pockets or sacks. Soon, many would be caught in the mountains' early snowstorms. Food was scarce everywhere. Ten thousand refugees were subsisting on roots on the island of Marmara, where typhoid had broken out. Typhoid was claiming lives in nearly all the areas where the refugees were packed together.

President Harding convened a meeting of relief agencies at the White House in October to initiate a public fund-raising drive to help the refugees. Near East Relief and the American Red Cross took the lead, and the American public responded generously. By the end of October, the Red Cross was feeding a half-million refugees in Greece. Belatedly, at the month's end, Bristol asked for twelve additional destroyers and a supply ship.

In November, Turkish authorities distributed notices in the Black Sea regions and deep in the Anatolian interior that Christians would be allowed to leave until November 30. The invitation to depart was a warning to depart. Moving over rough terrain and with only the possessions they could carry, sometimes through snow, 250,000 people began moving toward Trebizond, Sinope, Inebolu, and all along the Black Sea coast.

The evacuation of Black Sea ports presented a more difficult problem—the Turks would not allow Greek ships through the Bosporus. So, Jennings, who remained at the center of the massive forced ejection of the Christian population of the subcontinent, arranged for the Greek government to lease British-flagged merchant ships. They began the long process of removing Greeks and Armenians from the seven-hundred-mile coast of the Black Sea.

There was yet another enormous problem. The return of eastern Thrace to Turkey had triggered the flight of hundreds of thousands of Greek farmers from that region. Much of Thrace was marshland, and the peasants were departing in a time of heavy rains. At Rodosto, in Thrace, Jaquith reported, "Infants are dying in their mothers' arms. In the confusion children separated from parents wander crying through the streets and hysterical mothers in turn search for them."

Hemingway watched the peasants departing Thrace and was moved to produce his most memorable journalism: "ADRIANOPLE—In a never-ending staggering march, the Christian population of Eastern Thrace is jamming the roads towards Macedonia. The main column, crossing the Maritza River at Adrianople is twenty miles long. Twenty miles of carts drawn by cows, bullocks and muddy-flanked water buffalo, with exhausted staggering men, women and children, with blankets over their heads, walking blindly along in the rain beside their worldly goods."

The tidal wave of refugees overwhelmed Greece. By the end of the year, it had received more than a million people, increasing its population by a fifth. The million was in addition to the hundreds of thousands that had arrived before the defeat of the Greek army. Greece was broke and without resources to absorb, feed, and clothe the refugees. One hundred and ten thousand refugees were camped in Salonika, doubling the city's population. In Athens, people were stashed wherever there was space, in fields of tents, among the city's classical ruins, even in the boxes of the Royal Opera House. In refugee camps, people were dying at the rate of one thousand per day.

A refugee ship from Samsun arrived in Piraeus with two thousand people on board, seventeen hundred of them infected with typhus, smallpox, or cholera. Even two of the three doctors on board were seriously ill.

Greece buckled under the strain and announced in January 1923 that it could take no more refugees. For a while, the door was closed, but the Greeks and Armenians of Asia Minor continued their trek to the Turkish ports. The flow gorged Constantinople with sick, hungry, and ill-clothed peasants. The Selimyeh Barracks in Scutari groaned with disease-ridden refugees, and the backup of refugees in ships and in the cities created enormous problems of sanitation and disease.* The conditions were appalling, and growing worse. At Constantinople, refugees were placed in stables intended for animals.

"Many died on their journey to the sea, many more in the filthy and crowded ships," reported Dr. Post in Constantinople. "Most of them are

---

* The Selmiyeh Barracks was the place where Florence Nightingale, the founder of the modern nursing, had made her reputation during the Crimean War.

insufficiently clothed and lying either on the bare ground or on thin pallets or quilting or sacking. On one such quilt there were seven people, all ill with typhus or dysentery. Two days later there were only three left; two days later only one; and the last time I was there, this last unfortunate had just passed. . . . As one after the other died, their bodies were carried jostling through the crowd to the dead cart, which then moved on until it was full; then it jogged its way through the streets of Scutari to the edge of the town where the bodies were dumped unceremoniously into a long pit."

Powell had remained at Smyrna until late October with the *Edsall*, then returned to Constantinople. At the urging of his crew, the ship returned with orphaned refugee children, the last to be taken from Smyrna. The officers and men of the *Edsall* paid for a house in Stamboul to provide a home for the children, and they allotted a part of their paychecks twice a month to pay for food and a teacher at the orphanage. Each morning, the orphanage's teacher and children said a salute to the American flag.

Jennings had become a central figure in the international relief effort by then and moved between Athens, the Greek islands, Smyrna, and Constantinople. He established his headquarters in Athens, and Admiral Bristol stationed a destroyer at Piraeus so that Jennings could maintain radio contact with destroyers continuing the evacuation. Many Greeks had the impression that Jennings was acting on behalf of the United States government. He was not; the official relief agencies were the American Red Cross and Near East Relief, but Jennings's energy and initiative often outran the official organizations. In December, following a report in the *New York Times*, one of Bristol's aides called Jennings to the embassy to explain to him that he did not have the authority to promise American naval escorts to chartered merchant ships entering the Black Sea. It was a gentle reprimand. Bristol by then understood Jennings's standing.

After the Aegean evacuations were mostly complete, Jennings had turned his attention to the Black Sea ports, where tens of thousands awaited ships. Again, he collected Greek ships and he found ways to charter others, including British-flagged merchant ships. Bristol quietly resisted providing naval support to the Black Sea evacuation. By the late fall of 1922, the League of Nations was involved, and its high commissioner for refugees, the world-famous Norwegian explorer Fridtjof Nansen, traveled to Constantinople to coordinate with Bristol. Bristol's natural antagonisms surfaced, and he took an immediate dislike to Nansen.* Faced with a mounting crisis, Bristol turned again to Halsey Powell and sent him and the *Edsall* to the Black Sea to watch over the movement of refugee transports. Powell and Jennings were reunited in the rescue mission, and together they evacuated many more tens of thousands of refugees.

The situation was reminiscent of Smyrna: "Nearly all are women," an American officer wrote of the refugees in Trebizond. "They are in rags and evidently do not know where to go while waiting for transportation. . . . Many have sold their belongings in order to leave. In the meantime, they are subjected to taxation and confiscations so that soon they will be unable to pay their way out."

The first refugee ship that entered the Black Sea was the British-registered SS *Gabriella*, which Jennings had arranged for Greece to charter at its expense. At the last minute, the ship's captain had refused to make the trip because some of the crew was Greek and he feared trouble on arriving in Turkish ports. Jennings found Russian sailors to replace the Greeks, and the ship sailed for Samsun on December 9 with Jennings aboard. Powell met the ship in Samsun and assisted in its loading. And so it went as before in Smyrna—despite the diplomatic complications and hidden antipathy inside the American embassy, Jennings and Powell continued to rescue cargo after cargo of helpless and frightened people.

In May 1923, as the exodus slowed, the navy transferred Halsey Powell back to the United States, to a desk job as an intelligence officer in Washington, though he soon would be back at sea. Asa Jennings remained in the Near East, continuing his relief work. "I have wondered since many, many times," Jennings said afterward, "how I lived through

---

* Nansen was award the Nobel Peace Prize for his work with refugees after World War I.

those days. I guess it was because God knew I so much needed strength that He gave it to me. I can account for it in no other way." Jennings departed for New York in July, but not before hitching a ride on a navy destroyer that was steaming to Palestine. He went ashore and found his way to Jerusalem.

AFTERWORD

Greece awarded Asa Jennings its highest military and civilian awards, and in the years that followed, he returned to Turkey and embarked on a new project, the American Friends of Turkey, an organization whose mission was to create child-care clinics, sports clubs, and libraries in Turkey. It attracted financial support from American businessmen and put him in Bristol's favor, but it faltered during the Depression and ceased operating. An American policy of engagement with the Turkish Republic divided the missionary community, many of whose members saw the Turkish Republic as a bloody regime that ought to be shunned by the United States. Jennings was not among them, and he developed a close relationship with Turkish officials, including Kemal. It also brought him together with Mark Bristol, who was among the strongest advocates of American engagement with the Republic of Turkey. In 1933, on a visit to Washington to confer with Turkish authorities and after having spent the night as a guest of the Bristols, Jennings was stricken while walking near the White House and died on the way to the hospital. His weak heart had finally stopped working. Widowed, Amy made her home in Winter Park, Florida, until her death in 1970. Asa's oldest son, Asa Will, became a lawyer and handled legal work for the Turkish government.

After returning to Washington, Halsey Powell was transferred to Peking as a naval attaché and then assigned to command the USS *Pittsburgh*. He drew admirers in all his postings for his quiet and reliable competence. In 1936, President Franklin Roosevelt approved his nomination to the rank of rear admiral, but days before the promotion was granted, Powell died of a heart attack in Washington at age fifty-three.

He had continued to list Kentucky as his home address. He is buried in Arlington National Cemetery. In 1943, the U.S. Navy launched the USS *Halsey Powell,* a destroyer. The ship and its men served with distinction during World War II.

Mark Bristol served in Turkey until 1927. He was then sent to China to take command of the Asiatic Fleet. After two years, he returned to Washington and retired in 1932, serving as chairman of the Navy Board. He died at age seventy-one in 1939. The navy named two destroyers for Bristol during World War II. Bristol is remembered fondly in Turkey. Helen Bristol, ever the industrious woman, opened a business selling baked hams from her home in Washington. She died in 1945.

Dr. Hatcherian and his family traveled on board the refugee ship to Mytilene. The family stayed there for seven months, during which time Dr. Hatcherian provided medical care to other refugees. In April 1923, the Hatcherians moved to Salonika, and Dr. Hatcherian became direc-tor of the Armenian hospital there. His granddaughter, Dora Sakayan, who brought his diary to the world through its publication, was born in Salonika. In the 1950s, the Hatcherians moved to Buenos Aires, where Dr. Hatcherian died in 1952.

Theodora Gravou and her sisters also went to Salonika but were soon taken to Athens. Theodora was placed as a servant in a home in Athens, and her two sisters were put into the Amalion Orphanage. Theodora eventually married George Kontos, also from the Smyrna region, and together they raised a family in an apartment in a Piraeus neighborhood with many other Anatolian refugees until their deaths. Her daughter, Eleni, eighty-four, was still living in the apartment in 2012.

Mustapha Kemal married Latife Hanum in 1923, but the marriage lasted only two years. He became Turkey's first president and served from 1923 to 1938, introducing sweeping reforms to nearly all aspects of Turk-ish society. He sought to modernize and secularize the country, greatly reducing the role of Islam in the affairs of government. He took the name Atatürk, "Father of the Turks" and transformed the nation in countless ways and set it on a path of independence and national pride. He died in 1938. He remains a hero in Turkey.

Arthur J. Hepburn rose to the rank of admiral and served as chief of

Naval Intelligence and commander in chief of the fleet. In the 1930s, with the prospect of war looming for the United States, President Roosevelt gave Hepburn the job of reviewing American defenses. When World War II came, he served as chairman of the Navy Board. He died in 1964 in a Washington nursing home.

IN JANUARY 1923, Greece and Turkey agreed to an exchange of populations—Christians would be required to leave Turkey, and Muslims would be required to leave Greece. It was an internationally sanctioned forced transfer of people. The agreement carved out minor exceptions for Greeks in Constantinople and Muslims in western Thrace. About one and a half million Greeks departed Turkey, and about a half million Muslims left Greece. Later in 1923, the Allies and Turkey signed the Treaty of Lausanne, which officially ended World War I. It also affirmed the existence of a new nation, the Republic of Turkey.

The United States and Turkey negotiated a separate treaty of amity and commerce in 1923. Powerful opposition to the treaty arose in the United States among religious leaders and prominent Americans such as Henry Morgenthau. Despite a State Department campaign with Dulles at the point to win the treaty's approval, the Senate defeated the treaty. A new president, Calvin Coolidge, decided not to resubmit the treaty and established diplomatic relations with Turkey by executive authority. In 1929, with Herbert Hoover as president, a new version of the treaty was submitted, and the Senate accepted it. In the years that followed, Turkey and the United States developed a close relationship, and following World War II, Turkey joined the North Atlantic Treaty Organization and became a key strategic ally of the United States on the Soviet Union's southwestern flank.

The regard with which the United States is now held in the Middle East is beyond the scope of this book. It is of course a long and complicated story. Suffice it to say that the United States became more deeply immersed in the region's politics and feuds as it sought to ensure its access to the region's oil.

The Turkish government continues to reject the term "genocide" as a description of what happened to the Armenians, Greeks, and Assyrians, though its position has softened in recent years. It now acknowledges that many people died as a result of the deportations. In speaking of the Armenian deaths, President Obama, mindful of the potential damage to US-Turkish relations, has avoided use of the word *genocide*. He has referred instead to *Metz Eghern*, the Armenian phrase for the Great Catastrophe.

Today, Christians are mostly absent from Anatolia. Smyrna was rebuilt as Izmir in the 1950s. It is a gleaming glass and concrete city of four million people. Cafés and restaurants line the Quay, but very few if any of the well-dressed patrons on the harborfront know the story of what happened there in September 1922.

ACKNOWLEDGMENTS

I first encountered the story of Smyrna thirty-five years ago in Marjorie Housepian's important book, *The Smyrna Affair*. Asa Jennings made a brief appearance in her story, and it set me wondering about this man who seemed a forgotten hero. I only got around to seriously researching his achievement in 2010. The work took me to Turkey and Greece five times. I walked the Izmir Quay with an old map in search of the few buildings that were not destroyed by the fire and flipped through pages of old newspapers at the Izmir Municipal Archives. I also traveled to Theodora Gravou's village, dipped my hands in the Sakaria River, climbed to the top of Kocetepe, and walked the battlefield at Dumlupinar with the guidance of a friendly and helpful Turkish army officer. In Greece, I spent days at the Asia Minor Research Center in Athens, met descendants of Smyrna survivors, and combed the backstreets of Piraeus to find Theodora's daughter. In the United States, I traveled to Asa Jennings's home and pastorates in upstate New York and dug deep into the rich files of the Library of Congress, the National Archives, and the YMCA archives. Along the way, countless people helped me in my work. This book would not have been possible without them.

Among the many people who guided me along the way are these: Roger Jennings, Asa's grandson, who shared family papers and photos, patiently answered innumerable questions, and took me to Asa's birthplace; George Poulimenos and Achillias Chatziconstantinou, two Athenians who have done deep and original research into the cityscape of old Smyrna and repeatedly answered my questions about the streets, buildings, and families of Smyrna; Professor Sevda Alankus, who warmly welcomed me to Izmir and connected me to the city's historians and translated documents and book passages that would otherwise have been inaccessible to me; Professor Ahmet Can Ozcan, whose good humor and knowledge of the city and region was both a delight and a gift; and David and Miriam Levi, who guided me through Izmir and explained its Jewish past.

Nancy Horton, the daughter of George Horton, gave me many afternoons in her Voula apartment as we talked of her father and Smyrna. Sadly, the grandson of Captain Theophanides, Ioannis Theophanides (himself a retired admiral), passed away during the book's preparation. Always generous and gentlemanly, Admiral Theophanides spent many hours with me and provided useful documents. Professor Thanos Veremis of the Hellenic Foundation for European & Foreign Policy in Athens helped me understand the rise of nationalism in the Balkans and Turkey. Professor Nikos Leandros and his wife, Maria, invited to stay in their home in Athens as I pursued my research, and Professor Nikos Bakounakis and his wife, Maria, also welcomed me in their home and provided guidance and encouragement. Kika Kyriakakou helped with translation and many other tasks in Athens, as did Katerina Voutsina, who led our search for Theodora's daughter. Others who helped with translation, from Greek, Turkish, and French, were Petros Kasfikis, Adamantia Pattakou, Gökser Gökçay, Serkan Savk, and Rejean Lebel. Professors Robert Shenk and Paul Halpern offered expert research guidance, and Professor Shenk read the manuscript for errors. (If there are any, they are mine, not his.) Others who provided invaluable guidance were Professors Simon Payaslian, Pelin Boke, Jonathan Winkler, Halil Berktay, Michail Psalidopoulos, Michaelis Meismaris, Klaus Kreiser, Hakan Özoðlu, Elizabeth Prodromou, Alexandros Kyrou, the Reverend Robert Hill, and Erik Goldstein.

Among the early and helpful readers of the manuscript were David Kallas, Elizabeth and Nigel Savage, Adam Ureneck, Dan Mariaschin, Michael D'Antonio, and Irving Rimer.

Librarians and archivists often went to great lengths to help me. First among them is Vita Paladino of the Howard Gotleib Archival Research Center at Boston University. Also: the staff at the Asia Minor Research Center; Valerie S. Ellis at the Mobile Public Library; Jeffrey Monseau at

Springfield College; Rhoda Bilansky at BU's Mugar Library, who tracked down many rare books for me; the staffs at the Izmir Muncipal Archives, the Nea Smyrni Library in Athens, and the Gennadius Library at The American School for Classical Studies in Athens; Amanda Pike at the Mudd Manuscipt Library at Princeton University; Jamie Serran, Archivist at the Yarmouth County Museum & Archives, Nova Scotia; Stratis Karamanis and Efthalia Tourli of the Refugees of Asia Minor Museum in Skala Loutron, a tiny village on Lesbos inhabitated by surivivors of the Smyrna fire and their descendants; Robert Hitchings, formerly of the Norfolk Public Library, and Lynn Sullivan of the Omaha Public Library. Also: Theresa Roy, Kirsten Carter, and Rodney Ross at the National Archives, and Rosemary Hanes at the Library of Congress; Barbara Price of the Gloucester County Historical Society; Candace Bundgard of the Natchez Historical Society; Heather Home, Queen's University Archives; Nat Wilson, Carleton College Library; Christopher Carter, Amistad Research Center; Nancy Adgent of the Rockefeller Archive Center; Robert Smith, Navy Memorial Library; Mary M. O'Brien, archivist at Syracuse University Archives; David D'Onofrio of the U.S. Naval Academy; and Ryan Bean of the Kautz Family Archives.

I must single out Amalie Preston of Harrodsburg, Kentucky, for her persistence in tracking down the papers of Halsey Powell. They added immeasurably to my understanding of the man.

I would like to thank also for their valuable assistance and support: Elias Papadopoulos, Ray Alcala, William Skocpol, John Makrides, Maria Ilou, Joe Nocera, Lee Tstinis, Ümit Kurt, Evgen Titov, Julie Norman, Tom Mullins, Steve and Ann Marie Pitkin, Rev. Carl E. Getz, Rev. James E. Barnes II, Jonathan Powell, Giorgos Dimitrakopoulos, Rifat Bali, Don Kehn Jr., Chrysovalentis Stamelos, and Katerina Titova for her prayers and lighted candles. I fear that I have left off someone important from this list: I apologize for the oversight in advance.

I had the assistance of hardworking graduate students over the long course of the research: Chen Shen; Emma Dong; Shang Jing Li; Kasha Patel; Siutan Wong, Gabriella Kashtelian; Siu Tan Wong; and Sara Bost. I want to also thank Boston University, Dean Tom Fiedler, and colleagues Mitchell Zuckoff, Richard Lehr, and Bob Zelnick for their support. Hilary Redmon, my editor, saw the story's potential from the beginning and made valuable suggestions along the way. I also want to thank Emma Janaskie and Laurie McGee for their skills and careful attention to the book's production. The support of my brother, Paul, never flags, and Irene, my wife, has been patient and supportive beyond measure. This book is dedicated to her. Finally, I must thank Jill Kneerim, my agent. Her wisdom, encouragement, steadiness, and skill were crucial in turning an aspiration into a book.

NOTES

ABBREVIATIONS

ABCFM   American Board of Commissioners for Foreign Missions
AKJP   Asa Jennings Papers
ARC   Amistad Research Center
ARI   American Research Institute (Istanbul)
ASMP   Aaron Stanton Merrill Papers
BWD   Bristol War Diary
CLP   Caleb Lawrence Papers
GHP   George Horton Papers
KFYA   Kautz Family YMCA Archives
MLB   Mark Bristol Papers
NA   National Archives
NER   Near East Relief
NPRC   National Personnel Records Center
RAC   Rockefeller Archive Center
STANAV American High Commissioner in Constantinople

PROLOGUE

1 *Smyrna was burning* Details of the fire and the evacuation from Arthur J.
Hepburn, "Smyrna Disaster; Report On," Sept. 25, 1922. Record Group
45, Naval Records Collection, NA. There are several American and British eyewitness accounts of the first night of fire. Among the most vivid
are the dispatch by Ward Price in the *London Daily Mail*, September 16,
1922, and "Smyrna and After, Part III," *Naval Review*, publication of the
Naval Society, London, Vol. 1, 1924. A moving description of the fire,
based on primary sources, appears in Philip Mansel, *Levant: Splendour*

and Catastrophe on the Mediterranean (London: John Murray, 2010), 215, 216.

1 *It would also serve as* The Ottoman Empire did not officially end until 1923 with the signing of the Treaty of Lausanne, which brought a formal end to World War I and affirmed Allied recognition of the Republic of Turkey, but the military victories that led to the occupation of Smyrna made it clear that the future of Turkey was with the Turkish nationalists under the aegis of the Grand National Assembly and its leader, Mustapha Kemal. The defeat of the army of Greece and occupation of Smyrna was the event that clarified the country's future.

4 *Hepburn, a veteran officer* Hepburn's conflict with Horton is described in Hepburn, "Smyrna Disaster," 20, and Aaron S. Merrill Diary, Sept. 11, 1922, "Diaries of Lieutenant A. S. Merrill," Box 7, Folder 62, Louis Round Wilson Special Collections Library, University of North Carolina, Chapel Hill.

5 *There was also one American* Asa Kent Jennings, "Report for Mrs. Emmons Blaine of Work Accomplished at Smyrna, Turkey," March 1, 1928, Asa K. Jennings File, 1922–1928, KFYA.

6 *Several hours earlier, Jennings* "Mrs. Jennings Relates Tale of Horrors," *Syracuse Journal,* Oct. 27, 1922.

6 *Before it burned itself out* Vice Consul Maynard Barnes to State Dept., Nov. 22, 1922, NA 767.68/463.

CHAPTER 1: END OF AN EMPIRE

9 *Decades after* For a discussion of Raphael Lemkin's work on the genocide of the Greeks, see Leonard Jacobs's "Genocide of Others: Ralph Leminkin, the Genocide of the Greeks, the Holocaust and the Present Moment," in Tessa Hofmann, Matthias Bjørnlund, and Vasileios Meichanetsidis, *The Genocide of the Ottoman Greeks—Studies on the State-Sponsored Campaign of Extermination of the Christians of Asia Minor, 1912–1922 and Its Aftermath: History, Law, Memory* (New York: Aristide D. Caratzas, 2011). Also, Samantha Power, *A Problem from Hell: America in the Age of Genocide* (New York: Basic Books, 2002), 17–30, 40–35.

9 *"The aim of war is not . . ."* Adolf Hitler's "Obersalzburg Speech," August 22, 1939, Modern History Sourcebook, Fordham University, http://www.fordham.edu/halsall/mod/hitler-obersalzberg.asp. The Nazi fascination

with Turkish nationalism, Mustapha Kemal, and the slaughter of the Armenians is examined in Stefan Ihrig's *Ataturk in the Nazi Imagination* (Cambridge, MA: Harvard University Press, 2014).

9 *The Armenians, an ancient people* The Armenian genocide has been described and discussed by scholars in numerous works including these: Power, *A Problem from Hell*; Richard G. Hovannisian, ed., *The Armenian Genocide: History, Politics, Ethics* (New Brunswick: Transaction Books, 1986); Richard G. Hovannisian, ed., *Remembrance and Denial: The Case of the Armenian Genocide* (Detroit, MI: Wayne State University, 1998); Taner Akçam, *A Shameful Act: The Armenian Genocide and the Question of Turkish Responsibility* (New York: Metropolitan, 2006); Taner Akçam, *From Empire to Republic: Turkish Nationalism and the Armenian Genocide* (London: Zed, 2004); Vahakn N. Dadrian, "The Documentation of the World War I Armenian Massacres in the Proceedings of the Turkish Military Tribunal," *International Journal of Middle East Studies* 23, no. 4 (Nov. 1991); Mark Levene, "Why Is the Twentieth Century the Century of Genocide?" *Journal of World History* 11, no. 2 (Fall 2000); Andrew Bell-Fialkoff, "Brief History of Ethnic Cleansing," *Foreign Affairs* 72 (Summer 1993).

9 *The deportations and executions* Tessa Hofmann, "The Massacres and Deportations of the Greek Population on the Ottoman Empire (1912–1923)," in Hofmann et al., *Genocide of the Ottoman Greeks*, 35–108; Michelle Tusan, *Smyrna's Ashes: Humanitarianism, Genocide and the Birth of the Middle East* (Oakland, CA: University of California Press, 2012), 145, 207.

10 *Up until the early twentieth century* A scholarly and sympathetic history of the late Ottoman Empire can be found in Bernard Lewis, *The Emergence of Modern Turkey* (London: Oxford University Press, 1961).

11 *In secret, and beginning with the Treaty of London* The Treaty of London in 1915 was signed between the Entente Powers (Britain, France, and Russia) and Italy to bring Italy into the war against Germany and Austria-Hungary. Italy was promised the Dodecanese Islands, parts of southern Turkey, and other lands. The Sykes-Picot Agreement between Britain and France (with Russian assent) divided the Arab lands of the Ottoman Empire between Britain and France and assigned Constantinople and eastern sections of Anatolia to Russia. In 1915, the British of-

fered Greece territory in western Anatolia (Smyrna) to gain its entrance into the war. See Michael Llewellyn Smith, *Ionian Vision: Greece in Asia Minor, 1919–1922* (New York: St. Martin's Press, 1973), 35; and Laurence Evans, *United States Policy and the Partition of Turkey, 1914–1924* (Baltimore: Johns Hopkins, 1965), 49–87.

11 *After the war ended* Evans, *United States Policy,* 89–107.

12 *It was unclear how Wilson's vision* Simon Payaslian, *United States Policy toward the Armenian Question and the Armenian Genocide* (New York: Palgrave Macmillan, 2005), 135–136.

12 *Four months into the Paris talks* Smith, *Ionian Vision,* 68–88.

13 *The Greeks and the Turks were old enemies* Alexis Heraclides, "The Essence of the Greek-Turkish Rivalry: National Narrative and Identity," *Hellenic Observatory Papers on Greece and Southeast Europe, London School of Economics,* 2011; David Brewer, *Greece, the Hidden Centuries: Turkish Rule from the Fall of Constantinople to Greek Independence* (London: I. B. Tauris, 2010).

14 *Poorly disciplined and led* Victoria Solomonidis, "Greece in Asia Minor: The Greek Administration of the Vilayet of Aidin, 1919–1922." Ph.D. diss., University of London, 1984, 55.

14 *So hostile was* "Smyrna and After, Part I," *Naval Review,* publication of the Naval Society, London, vol. XI, no. 3, 1923. For an explanation of clashing nationalisms: Resat Kasaba, *Greek and Turkish Nationalism in Formation: Western Anatolia 1919–1922,* Mediterranean Program Series, European University Institute.

14 *The stiff Allied-imposed armistice* Halide Edib, *The Turkish Ordeal* (Westport, CT: Hyperion Press, 1928), see especially Part I, "In Istamboul."

14 *"Remember Smyrna"* Robert Dunn, *World Alive: A Personal Story* (New York: Crown Publishers, 1956).

14 *Quietly, the United States* Evans, *United States Policy,* 236–268.

14 *The Europeans went ahead* Evans, *United States Policy,* 269–290.

15 *"Two thirds of the Greek deportees . . ."* Major F. D. Yowell, Near East Relief. See letter to Consul Jesse P. Jackson, at Aleppo, April 5, 1922, NA 867.4016/454. Also, supplementary report to the secretary of state, received July 14, 1922. NA 867.3016/575. John Clayton, "Deportations in Asia Minor," unpublished report for the *Chicago Tribune,* sent as a cable by Jesse Jackson, American consul in Aleppo, to State Department, July

25, 1922. NA867.4016/618. "Over the mountains south of Harput winds a long road from Diarbekir to Nissibin and the desert. It is a road to Calvary. Along its course, mile after mile are strewn the graves where sleep thousands of Greek exiles. Graves that were first barely scratched in the snow; graves which often contain only the bones from which the vultures have feasted."

16 *Soon, Greece's only real ally, Britain* There are numerous turns in the story of Greece's military campaign in Asia Minor. Venizelos, whose presence at the Paris peace talks had opened the way for the Greek army's landing at Smyrna, had come to power as prime minister in Greece in 1910. Under his leadership, and through the Balkan Wars of 1912 and 1913, Greece greatly expanded its territory. But with the coming of World War I, a split opened between Greece's King Constantine and Venizelos over Greece's role in the big war. Venizelos sought to join the Entente Powers, but the king tilted toward Germany and neutrality. The king dismissed Venizelos, who ultimately formed a provisional government in Salonika with the backing of Britain and France, and Constantine was forced to abdicate in favor of his son Alexander. After the war, Greece remained bitterly divided between the supporters of Venizelos and the monarchy. In 1920, while Greece was engaged in its war with Turkish nationalists in Asia Minor, young King Alexander died from the bite of a pet monkey, triggering a political crisis that led to elections and the shocking defeat of Venizelos. Then, in a moment of self-destructive pique, Greek voters recalled Constantine to Athens as king, creating a backlash among the Allies who despised him for his pro-German attitude before World War I. With Greece's military fortunes flagging in Turkey, the return of Constantine alienated Britain, which already was having second thoughts about Greece's ability to prevail in the war. Lloyd George continued to make stirring speeches in favor of Greece right up to the very end, and even after the end, but he was unable to deliver the men or materiel that would have made a difference in the outcome. This is covered masterfully in Smith's *Ionian Vision*. For an inside view of the destructive military ramifications of the Greek political shift, see the book by Prince Andrew of Greece, *Towards Disaster—The Greek Army in Asia Minor in 1921* (London: John Murray, 1930). Prince Andrew was Constantine's brother, and he fought with the Greek army

at the Battle of Sakaria. He was father to the current Prince Phillip, husband to Queen Elizabeth II. See also: "Morale of the Greek Army," G-2 Report, STANAV, Sept. 11, 1922, No. 517. MLB.

16 *Greece prepared for a unilateral withdrawal* Solomonides, 103.

CHAPTER 2: AN INNOCENT ARRIVES

18 *In mid-August 1922* Jennings's biographical details come from a variety of sources: personnel records of the YMCA at KFYA; correspondence of his wife, Amy Jennings, AKJP; Syracuse University Archives; a biographical file including the correspondence of colleagues assembled by MGM Pictures for the making of a short movie about Jennings in the 1940s, which is now in the possession of Turner Properties, Atlanta, Georgia; the records of the Trenton (NY) United Methodist Church; and the archives of the Northern New York Conference of the United Methodist Church.

19 *Jennings's assignment in Smyrna* Asa Jennings to Darius Davis, April 8, 1923. KFYA.

19 *The YMCA director in Smyrna* E. O. Jacob was running the Smyrna YMCA. Jennings had been sent on a short-term contract; Jacob made it clear in a confidential report to higher-ups that he wanted a different person who would work on a longer-term contract. "Administrative Report, Smyrna Young Men's Christian Association," July 1922. KFYA.

19 *"Jennings has a most attractive personality"* Darius. A. Davis to E. O. Jacob, March 29, 1922. KFYA.

19 *"I do not despair . . ."* Asa Jennings to his son Asa, June 26, 1924, AJKP.

21 *Jennings, then twenty-seven years old* The fullest description of Jennings's medical history appears in a letter written Nov. 25, 1942, by his wife, Amy, to William Schneider of St. Louis, Missouri, who had inquired admiringly about Jennings's achievements. KFYA.

22 *The names along the Quay* The basis for street descriptions throughout the book is the *Plan de Smyrne*, prepared as an insurance map by Ernest Bon in 1913.

22 *In the nineteenth and early twentieth centuries* A rich source of information about Smyrna is *A Survey of Some Social Conditions in Smyrna, Asia Minor, May 1921*, a manuscript brought to publication in 2009 by Rıfat N Bali (Istanbul: Libra Kitapçılık Ve Yayıncılık).

Smyrna was a frequent stop for tourists traveling through the Near East in the nineteenth and early twentieth centuries and numerous letters and travel guides describe the city: John Cam Hobhouse Broughton, *Travels in Albania and Other Provinces of Turkey in 1809 & 1810* (London: Murray, 1858); *Guide to Greece, the Archipelago, Constantinople, the Coasts of Asia Minor, Crete and Cyprus, with Thirteen Maps and Thirty-three Plans* (London: Macmillan, 1908); *Handbook for Travellers in Turkey in Asia: Including Constantinople, the Bosphorus, Plain of Troy, Isles of Cyprus, Rhodes, &c., Smyrna, Ephesus, and the Routes to Persia, Bagdad, Moosool, &c.* (London: J. Murray, 1878); *Guide to Greece, the Archipelago, Constantinople, the Coasts of Asia Minor* (Macmillan & Co.); Jerome Alfred Hart, *A Levantine Log-book* (New York: Longmans, Green, 1905); Bilge Criss, *American Turkish Encounters: Politics and Culture, 1830–1989* (Newcastle upon Tyne: Cambridge Scholars, 2011); Mansel, *Levant: Splendour.*

24 *The city was also a principal source of Turkish tobacco* An encyclopedic description of the American tobacco business at the time appears in the record of the Hearings Before the Committee on Finance, United States Senate, Sixty-seventh Congress, First Session, on the Proposed Tariff Act of 1921 (H. R. 7456) 1922: American Valuation. 67th Cong., 1st sess. S. Doc. H. R. 7456. Vol. 7. (Washington, DC: U.S. Government Printing Office, 1922). See also Allan M. Brandt, *The Cigarette Century: The Rise, Fall, and Deadly Persistence of the Product That Defined America* (New York: Basic, 2007); Howard Cox, *The Global Cigarette: Origins and Evolution of British American Tobacco, 1880–1945* (New York: Oxford University Press, 2000).

24 *Smyrna was home to the Oriental Carpet* Antony Wynn, *Three Camels to Smyrna: Times of War and Peace in Turkey, Persia, India, Afghanistan & Nepal, 1907–1986: The Story of the Oriental Carpet Manufacturers Company* (London: Hali, 2008).

25 *The servant staffs* For a portrait of the families and lives of Levantine families in Smyrna, see Giles Milton, *Paradise Lost Smyrna 1922* (New York: Basic Books, 2010). Also, Mansel, *Levant: Splendour.*

25 *A Greek soldier, evoking the city's* The phrase comes from the memoir of Corporal Stamatis Hadjiyannis, an Ottoman Greek whose family was ejected from Asia Minor in the years immediately before World War

I. He enlisted in the Greek army, fought on the Bulgarian front, and after the war ended, traveled with his unit from Salonika to Smyrna in 1919. The memoir is in the possession of his grandson, George Poulemenos, coauthor of *A Lexicon of Smyrneika, Izmir Rumcasi Sozlugus*, Tarih Vakfi Yurt Kitaplari (2012). A memoir excerpt can be read at http://levantineheritage.com.

25 *The first two missionaries* Hilton Obenzinger, "Holy Land Narrative and American Covenant: Levi Parsons, Pliny Fisk and the Palestine Mission," *Religion & Literature* 35, no. 2/3 (2003): 241–267.

26 *Pliny and Fisk were the vanguard* There are many compelling memoirs by American missionaries who served in Turkey during the nineteenth and early twentieth centuries. They include Grace H. Knapp, Grisell M. McLaren, and Myrtle O. Shane, *The Tragedy of Bitlis* (New York: Fleming H. Revell Company, 1919); Bertha B. Morley, *Marsovan 1915: The Diaries of Bertha B. Morley*, ed. Hilmar Kaiser (Ann Arbor, MI: Gomidas Institute, 2000); William Wheelock Peet and Louise Jenison Peet, *No Less Honor* (Chattanooga, TN: Priv. Print., 1939); Cyrus Hamlin, *My Life and Times* (Boston: Congregational Sunday School and Publishing Co.,1831); and Joseph Kingsbury Greene, *Leavening the Levant* (Boston: Pilgrim Press, 1916).

27 *Ernest Otto Jacob, who* In a letter to his brother C. V. Hibbard, associate general secretary for the International Committee of YMCA, Darrel O. Hibbard, who worked for the YMCA in Athens, discusses Jacob's difficult nature and indicates that Jacob had conflicts with other YMCA members in Smyrna and his previous assignment. "He has quarreled with every man he has had sent to Smyrna. Jennings the last one seems to have been too much for him according to all reports." Oct. 8, 1922. KFYA.

CHAPTER 3: THE BEGINNING OF THE END

29 *On the morning of August 26, 1922* This chapter and the subsequent chapter on Kemal are deeply indebted to the two major biographies in English of Mustapha Kemal: Patrick Balfour Kinross, *Atatürk: A Biography of Mustafa Kemal, Father of Modern Turkey* (New York: Quill/Morrow, 1992); and Andrew Mango, *Atatürk: The Biography of the Founder of Modern Turkey* (Woodstock, NY: Overlook, 2000). Also see Hanns

Froembgen, *Kemal Ataturk; a Biography.* Translated by Kenneth Kirkness (New York: Hillman-Curl, 1937). Also, Smith in *Ionian Vision* on the Greek response to the attacks.

30 *Among the poets* Mango, *Atatürk,* 37.

30 *"well-trained superior waiter"* Robert Steed Dunn, *World Alive: A Personal Story* (New York: Crown, 1956).

31 *Only weeks earlier, British officers* Caffrey to State Dept., July 22, 1922. NA 767.68/313. "Fighting Qualities of Greek Troops," Intelligence Report, STANAV, Oct 2, 1920, No. 190. MLB.

32 *Nowhere had his courage* Kinross, *Atatürk,* 87–112; Mango, *Atatürk,* 156–158.

34 *"Greeks and Turks alike fought . . ."* The passage is taken from H. C. Armstrong, *Gray Wolf, Mustafa Kemal: An Intimate Study of a Dictator* (New York: Minton, Balch & Co., 1933). Courtenay was a British officer serving in Turkey.

34 *The Greeks had one friend* See Smith's *Ionian Vision,* "Winter Disenchantment" chapter. See also I. A. Rose, *Conservatism and Foreign Policy during the Lloyd George Coalition, 1918–1922* (London: Frank Cass, 1999), 228–234.

Lloyd George in the House of Commons, August 4, 1922 (Hansard Vol 157): "It is remarkable that she (Greece) has been able to accomplish what she has. She has maintained an army, and a large army. I am told there are men who have not been home to see their families for 12 years in Greece—peasants drawn from the soil—and they are prepared still to go on for the liberation of the men of their race. They have made financial sacrifices which are almost incredible. . . . A people who have done that are worthy of consideration at the hands of any country, and therefore I earnestly trust that, whatever happen, we shall see that the Christian populations of Asia Minor are adequately protected against a repetition of such horrible incidents as have disgraced the annals of that land." See also: "The result of Mr. Lloyd George's Speech on the Near East Question," G-2 Report, STANAV, August 25, 1922. "The speech . . . was received by all Greeks as a positive assurance of strong British support for their cause . . ." Then in October, Lloyd George in the House of Commons: "I am not going into the question of who was responsible in Smyrna. I am not going to discuss whether the Greeks provoked the Turks or the Turks the Greeks. It is enough for me to call attention to the fact that since 1914 the Turks, according to official testimony we have received have slaughtered in cold blood a million and a half of Armenians, men, women and children, and five hundred thousand Greeks without any provocation at all."

CHAPTER 4: GEORGE HORTON, POET-CONSUL

36 *At the end of August* George Horton, *The Blight of Asia: An Account of the Systematic Extermination of Christian Populations by Mohammedans and of the Culpability of Certain Great Powers; with a True Story of the Burning of Smyrna* (Indianapolis: Bobbs-Merrill, 1926), 117.

36 *He had pulled men* V. G. Balabanian to Horton, July 25, 1919: "Your happy return to Smyrna gives us the opportunity of expressing our best thanks for your paternal protection in favor of five of our comrades who were condemned to death by the court martial of Smyrna in July 1915 without any plausible accusation against them." The letter is quoted in Nancy Horton's unfinished biography of GH. GHP.

38 *"The three big kinema . . ."* "Smyrna's Last Days. A Manchester Man's Experiences," *Manchester Guardian*, Sept. 9, 1922, as quoted in Lysimachos Oeconomos, *The Martyrdom of Smyrna and Eastern Christendom: A File of Overwhelming Evidence, Denouncing the Misdeeds of the Turks in Asia Minor and Showing Their Responsibility for the Horrors of Smyrna* (London: G. Allen & Unwin, 1922).

38 *The first, on August 30* Horton to State Department, August 30, 1922. NA 767.68/265.

38 *"My opinion is that the situation . . ."* Horton to State Dept. NA 767.68/276.

39 *Horton had been a consul* Geoge Horton, *Recollections Grave and Gay* (Indianapolis: Bobbs-Merrill, 1927).

39 *Horton's first aspiration* The details of Horton's early life come from an unpublished biography of him by his daughter Nancy Horton, as well as an unpublished memoir, collected in the GHP now at Georgetown University. (In my review of the materials, they were held by Miss Horton's attorney at his office in Washington, D.C.)

41 *Two years earlier, a group* Mango, *Atatürk*, 76–77.

42 *Horton watched* Horton, *Blight of Asia*, 27–40.

42 *Nearly thirty thousand Armenian and Assyrian Christians* Merrill D.

Peterson, *"Starving Armenians": America and the Armenian Genocide, 1915–1930 and After* (Charlottesville: University of Virginia Press, 2004), 28–29; "Brooklyn Man Saw Missionaries Shot," *New York Times*, May 2, 1909.

43 *By September 3, it had taken* Utkan Kocatürk, *Atatürk Ve Türkiye Cumhuriyeti Tarihi Kronolojisi: 1918–1938* (Ankara: Türk Tarih Kurumu, 1983).

43 *The Asia Minor Defense League* Smith, *Ionian Vision*, 238, 239; Solomonidis, "Greece in Asia Minor," 229; Also, testimony in a trial in 1923 in which tobacco companies sought payment for losses. Rev. Dobbs Testimony, Day 8 49-53 (Trial summary), *Smyrna Conflagration, 13th–16th September, 1922: In the High Court of Justice, King's Bench Division, and Court of Appeal: American Tobacco Company Incorporated v. Guardian Assurance Company Ltd., and Socieìteì Anonyme Des Tabacs D'Orient Et D'Outre Mer v. Alliance Assurance Company Ltd. . . . 1- December . . . 1924 and 22nd April to 1st May, 1925* (London: Printed by Wyman, Privately Printed) and Prince Andrew, *Towards Disaster*, ff.

43 *He also encouraged his friend* Interviews with Vassily Skoulakis at his home in Athens, August 2011. Born in Smyrna, Mr. Skoulakis was a friend and an employee of Onassis (traffic director of Olympic Airlines) and traveled with him on his return to Smyrna. Nicholas Gage, *Greek Fire: The Story of Maria Callas and Aristotle Onassis* (New York: Knopf, 2000), 114–128.

44 *He wrote letters on consulate stationery* Interviews with Nancy Horton at her home in Athens, August 2011.

44 *He tried without success* "Barry Domvile His Diary," Sept. 4, 1922, Royal Maritime Museum, Greenwich.

CHAPTER 5: GARABED HATCHERIAN

45 *Garabed Hatcherian lived* Dr. Hatcherian's diary stands alone as a sustained and detailed narrative of events in Smyrna by a resident of the city. Its importance as an insight into lives of Smyrniots before and after the fire would be difficult to exaggerate. The area that had been occupied by his neighborhood, as described in the diary, is now contained within the Izmir fairgrounds.

CHAPTER 6: ADMIRAL BRISTOL, AMERICAN POTENTATE

48 *In Constantinople, Rear Admiral Mark Bristol* Bristol kept a "War Diary," a daily record of his activities. The diary is collected in the Mark Lambert Bristol Papers at the Library of Congress.

48 *The city was crowded, noisy* The description of Constantinople draws on several sources including the sociological study of the city by Clarence R. Johnson, *Constantinople To-day or, The Pathfinder Survey of Constantinople: A Study in Oriental Social Life* (New York: Macmillan, 1922). John Dos Passos provided a vivid description his travel book, *Orient Express* (New York and London: Harper & Bros., 1927). Dos Passos's book was based on his trip to the Balkans, Turkey, the Caucasus, and the Middle East during the latter half of 1921. "Out of Turkish Coffee Cups," the first six sections of "Constant' July 1921," appeared in the *New York Tribune*, October 2, 1921. Robert Shenk, ed., *Playships of the World: The Naval Diaries of Admiral Dan Gallery, 1920–1924* (Columbia: University of South Carolina Press, 2008), ff. *The Russian Refugees*, Constantinople Scrapbooks, 1921–1923, Charles Claflin Davis Digital Collection, Harvard Law School, Cambridge, MA.

50 *"The Bosporus," wrote a navy intelligence officer . . ."* Robert Dunn, *World Alive; a Personal Story* (New York: Crown Publishers, 1956).

50 *A British tailor custom-made* Bristol to Sansom & Bromley, Plymouth, England, April 23, 1919. MLB.

50 *His first caller on Saturday* BWD, Sept. 2, 1922.

50 *In Bristol's mind, Greeks* Bristol's dismissive attitude toward the local peoples and his antipathy especially toward the Greeks, Armenians, and Jews has been well established. "The Greek is about the worst race in the Near East." Bristol letter to Admiral W. S. Sims, May 19, 1919, MLB, as quoted in Housepian. "The Armenians are a race like the Jews—they have little or no national spirit and poor moral character." Bristol to Sims, May 18, 1919, as quoted in Hovannisian, *Armenian Genocide in Perspective*, 105. "If you shake them up in a bag you wouldn't know which one would come up first but the Turk is the best of the lot." Hovannisian, *Armenian Genocide*, 105. H.H. Topakyan, former Persian consul, quoted in the *New York Times* Sept. 17, 1922: ". . . I came in contact with Rear Admiral Mark Bristol, who, not suspecting my Armenian origin, but sup-

posed me to be a Persian, deliberately told me once: 'I hate the Greeks, I hate the Armenians, I hate the Jews. The Turks are fine fellows.'" Peter Michsel Buzanski, *Admiral Mark L. Bristol and Turkish-American Relations, 1919–1922.* Ph.D. diss., University of California, 1960, 116: ". . . the Greeks failed where ever they tried to rule other people but the evidence seemed to indicate that the Greeks could not even rule themselves."

51 *Bristol was sure that the British* "Intelligence Report." STANAV, August 21, 1922, File105-100, MLB. "From two reliable sources it was learned that Sir Basil Zaharoff has bought the controlling interest in the Ionian Bank Limited. . . . Zahaoff intends also to establish a bank of issue at Smyrna with the object of financing the new government."

52 *Even before arriving* Buzanski, *Admiral Mark L. Bristol,* 27, 24–50. Also, Bristol to Lyman April 28, 1919, MLB: "I am practically holding down the ambassador's job but without the name."

52 *"Anyway Irving is . . ."* Bristol to Helen Bristol, Jan. 5, 1919, MLB. Bristol had called in chits . . . Bristol to Knapp, August 26, 1919, MLB; Buzanski, *Admiral Mark L. Bristol,* 36.

53 *He consolidated his authority* "Personnel in Cilicia," Memorandum to Detachment Commander, USS *Sands* (243), Jan. 18, 1922, MLB.

54 A *lot of Bristol's intelligence* Buzanski, *Admiral Mark L. Bristol,* 41. H. S. Knapp, vice admiral of U.S. Naval Forces operating in European Waters to Bristol, June 4, 1919, MLB: "The style of the (intelligence) report is, in places, rather flippant. . . . there are two or three very improper expressions in the report that have probably already caught your eye. . . . I am sure you will agree with me that such expressions are unofficerlike and highly improper." In his June 25 response to Knapp, Bristol, whose fitness report was then being prepared by his navy superiors, distanced himself from his favorite intelligence officer. The report, he wrote, "got by me . . . I feel that your criticism is quite justified and I am glad to say that I had already taken steps to prevent these things from happening again."

54 *Dunn had a reputation* Buzanski, *Admiral Mark L. Bristol,* 41.

54 *She accompanied him* Bristol to Horton October 16, 1919, MLB; Horton back to Bristol, December 11, 1919, GHP.

54 *"The Armenians present were discussing your party"* Horton letter to Bristol, Dec. 11, 1919, GHP.

54 *Helen Bristol threw herself* Robert Shenk, *America's Black Sea Fleet: The U.S. Navy amidst War and Revolution, 1919–1923* (Annapolis, MD: Naval Institute Press, 2012), 77, 83–84, 161.

55 *"A nasty pair . . ."* Domvile Diary, July 2, 1922.

55 *Helen Bristol was the daughter* Biographical details on Helen Bristol are drawn from her correspondence, which is included in MLB; also from the *Mobile Register*, "R. Moore Is dead; End Very Sudden," June 30, 1916; "Personal and General," Aug. 27, 1901; "Mobile Woman Is Given Recognition As First Lady in Constantinople," November (date illegible) 1920. "Funeral of Judge Bailey Thomas Is Held at Athens," Aug. 5, 1901, *Atlanta Constitution*. Thomas W. Reed, "William Bailey Thomas," *History of the University of Georgia 1866–1874*, Hargrett Rare Book and Manuscript Library, University of Georgia.

55 *Bristol's career was not without* Philip Anorans, Bureau of Navigation, to Bristol July 15, 1912, MLB; Bristol to Vice Admiral Adolphus, Sept. 3, 1912. MLB.

56 *He also got into a dispute* George Van Deurs, *Wings for the Fleet: A Narrative of Naval Aviation's Early Development, 1910–1916* (Annapolis: U.S. Naval Institute, 1966), 147, ff.: "Mark Bristol was an ambitious officer, who was awaiting orders after having been court-martialed for grounding his ship in a fog off the China coast. He had no aeronautical experience, no desire to fly and no curiosity about planes, but he was known as a good administrator, and he wanted a job that would enhance his service reputation." Also: Ryan D. Waddel, "United States Navy Fleet Problems and the Development of Carrier Aviation, 1929–1933." Master's thesis, Texas A&M University, August 2005, 10.

56 *The rancor he stirred at Pensacola* Dunn to Bristol, Dec. 20, 1922. MLB.

56 *In 1916, after working* "Bristol, Mark," NPRC.

57 *Only days before, Bristol* "Intelligence Report," 103–100, August 10, 1922. STANAV. MLB.

57 *At the same time, Bristol* Bristol to State, August 28, 1922. MLB.

58 *"The afternoon was . . ."* BWD, Sept. 2 1922.

CHAPTER 7: WASHINGTON RESPONDS

60 *The message had moved* Carl H. Butman, "Secret Lines of Radio Communication," *Radio World* 2 (1922): 18.

60 *It had rained furiously* "Sox Advance at Tribe's Expense" and "City Emerges from Wrack of 40 Year Record Storm," *Washington Post*, Sept. 3, 1922.

61 *Allen Dulles, a promising* James Srodes, *Allen Dulles: Master of Spies* (Washington, DC: Regnery, 1999), 116–133.

61 *Phillips was a lean* William Phillips, *Ventures in Diplomacy* (Boston: Beacon Press, 1953); "William Phillips, Former Ambassador, Dies at 89," *New York Times*, Feb. 24, 1968.

61 *"Too many of his evenings"* Phillips, *Ventures in Diplomacy*, 115.

62 *The U.S. embassy in* Sheldon Whitehouse to State Dept, August 23, 1922. NA 767.61/258.

62 *". . . I respectfully request,"* Horton to State, Sept 2. NA 761.68/274.

62 *The two men stood poles apart* Their differences appear throughout their correspondence. See, e.g., Horton to State Dept., April 18, 1921, regarding Horton's disagreement with Bristol over Aristides Stergiades. NA 868.48/74. Also, Marjorie Housepian Dobkin, "George Horton and Mark L. Bristol: Opposing Forces in U.S. Foreign Policy, 1919–1922," *Bulletin for the Centre for Asia Minor Studies* (4) (1983).

63 *In May, a public debate had broken* Robert A. Hohner, *Prohibition and Politics: The Life of Bishop James Cannon, Jr.* (Columbia: University of South Carolina Press, 1999), 139–141.

63 *Also, in June, the British* "American to Join European Powers in Turkish Inquiry," *New York Times*, June 3, 1922.

63 *He was happy to defer* Harding to Hughes, May 20, 1922, 867.4016/ 498 The entire string of correspondence is instructive: United States Department of State, *Papers Relating to the Foreign Relations of the United States, 1922*, 919–983. http://digital.library.wisc.edu/1711.dl/FRUS.

64 *In 1922, America was having* George Otis Smith, "Where the World Gets Its Oil but Where Will Our Children Get It When American Wells Cease to Flow?" *National Geographic* 37.2 (1920): 181–202. Also see "The World's Oil Supply," *New York Times*, Jan. 7, 1920.

65 *In 1900, there were hardly* For a history of popular automobiles on the period, see "Ford Model T History and the Early Years of the Ford Motor Company." History of the Ford Model T, Henry Ford and Ford Motor Company Background, History and Facts, http://www.modelt.ca/background.html. "Chevrolet's Classic—1920 Chevrolet FB-50 Touring." Classic

Cars for Sale, Collector Car News and Auction Coverage, http://www. hemmings.com/hcc/stories/2005/08/01/hmn_feature12.html.

65 *In the first decade* For this history of the oil industry, I am deeply indebted to Daniel Yergin's masterwork, *The Prize: The Epic Quest for Oil, Money, & Power* (New York: Free Press, 2009).

66 *He sent it along to the White House* Phillips to Harding, Sept. 5, 1922. NA 167.68/276

67 *Before becoming president,* For the basic outline of Harding's life and his administration, see John Dean, *Warren Harding* as well as *The Harding Affair: Love and Espionage during the Great War.* (New York: Palgrave Macmillan, 2009).

67 *Harding's response to Phillips's note* Harding to Phillips, Sept. 5, 1922. NA 767,68/274.

67 *As these White House messages were sent* Horton to State, Sept 4. NA 767.68/27.

68 *"It seems to me it would be wiser . . ."* Phillips to Harding, Sept. 5, 1922. NA 767.68/276.

68 *Yet another cable came in from Horton,* Horton to State Dept, Sept. 5, 1922. GHP.

68 *Amid this flurry of cables* Phillips to Acting Navy Secretary Roosevelt, Sept. 5, 1922. NA 767.68/274.

68 *The twenty-foot-wide hallways* Details on the interior space of the building provided by Kristen Fusselle, fine arts specialist, General Services Administration in an interview with the author.

69 *Roosevelt immediately cabled Bristol* Roosevelt to Bristol, Sept 5, 1922. MLB.

69 *Finally, Phillips responded to Horton* Phillips to Horton, NA 767.68/274.

69 *"Department is not inclined to do more . . ."* Phillips to Bristol, Sept. 5, 1922. MLB.

CHAPTER 8: JENNINGS'S SUGGESTION

70 *The Jenningses had been settled* Jennings to Darius. Davis. April 8, 1923. KFYA.

71 *Most of his neighbors* Sara Jacob to D. Davis, Sept. 14, 1922, KFYA. Annie Gordon to Mrs. Lamson, Sept. 14, 1922. GHP.

72 *The house that Jennings* Various sources describe Paradise and the col-

lege setting: MacLachlan, 124; the memoirs of three members of the Caleb Lawrence family, Helen, his wife; Dorothy Lawrence Smith, his daughter, and Arthur, his son. The first two can be read at Levantine. com and the third, "Barefoot Boy from Turkey," is in CLP.

73 *He had spent his boyhood* Asa Kent Jennings, Boyhood Diary, AJKP.

73 *Asa Jennings had brought something else* Amy Jennings to Schneider; "Interview with Amy Jennings," *Orlando (Fla.) Sunday Sentinel-Star,* Jan. 11, 1953, KFYA; Author's interview with Roger Jennings, Queensbury, NY, May 7, 2011.

74 *Early in 1918, while he was* AKJ's YMCA history in Europe comes from his file at KFYA and Springfield (Mass.) College Archives. About the YMCA in Europe, see YMCA *Yearbook 1920,* 64–77; and "The YMCA in Czechoslovakia," *The Sphere,* 1 (1920), 34–43.

75 *In Paradise, Jennings had* E.O. Jacob, "Jacob's Ladder." Unpublished memoir, KFYA.

77 *Don't you know?* D. A. Davis to Henrietta Harrison, October 16, 1951. KFYA.

78 *The reports included a forceful* A description of the scene in Smyrna as the Greek army retreated appears in Smith, *Ionian Vision,* 284–311; Also, Dobbs, Insurance Testimony Summary, Day 8 49–53.

79 *Still, there was also a lot of loose talk* Horton to State, Sept. 4, 1920. NA 767.68/274.

79 *There was also the troubling* British Admiral de Brock summarized British actions at Smyrna from Sept. 3 to Sept. 23, 1922, for the Admiralty in a long cable on October 2, 1922. ADM 137/1779. It appears in full in Paul G. Halpern, *The Mediterranean Fleet, 1919–1929* (Burlington, VT: Ashgate for the Navy Records Society, 2011), 376–383. In addition to providing key cables and correspondence of the period, Halpern offers insightful commentary and context.

80 *Horton had slept hardly at all* For a description of the first meetings of the American volunteers: Horton, *Blight of Asia,* 123–125; Caleb Lawrence, "The Smyrna Disaster Relief Committee of the American Red Cross," Report to Foster Stearns, May 30, 1923. NA Correspondence of the American Embassy, Constantinople, Class 848, Part 2, Vol. 20. Getchell to Barton, Oct. 12, 1923. GHP. Jennings to Davis; Annie Gordon letter.

80 *Among the missionary group* The American Girls' School was officially the American Intercollegiate Institute. The Missionary Board, formally, was the American Board of Commissioners for Foreign Missions, based in Boston.

82 *It was a humiliation the Young Turks* Hofmann et al., *Genocide of the Ottoman Greeks*, 42; Lewis, *Emergence of Modern Turkey*, 224. Also see Mark Mazower, *Salonica, City of Ghosts: Christians, Muslims, and Jews, 1430–1950* (New York: Alfred A. Knopf, 2005), 275; Mango, *Atatürk*, 115.

82 *In the region outside Smyrna*, Horton to State Dept., April 18, 1921, including attached report on Greek reconstruction. NA 868.48/74; Horton, *Blight of Asia*, 41–45. Also, Mansel, *Levant: Splendour*, 186.

82 *The sultan and his Islamic government* Lewis, *Emergence of Modern Turkey*, 31; C. Ernest Dawn, "From Ottomanism to Arabism: The Origin of an Ideology," *The Review of Politics* 23, no. 3 (July 1961): 380.

83 *The Ottoman government unleashed* Horton, *Blight of Asia*, 42; Payaslian, *United States Policy*, 66.

84 *"The unfortunate men had been tied . . ."* Horton to State March 12, 1917. NA 867.00/739

84 *A massacre against Ottoman Greeks* Hofmann et al., *Genocide of the Ottoman Greeks*, P52; Horton, *Blight of Asia*, 46–51; Matthias BJornlund, "Danish Sources on the Destruction of the Ottoman Greeks, 1914–1916," in Hofmann et al., *Genocide of the Ottoman Greeks*, 152.

84 *Turkish terror drove nearly two hundred thousand* Edward Hale Bierstadt, *The Great Betrayal: A Survey of the Near East Problem* (New York: R. M. McBride & Co., 1924), 52–68. Also see Charles P. Howland, "Greece and Her Refugees." *Foreign Affairs* (July 1926).

84 *"From what all these trustworthy people"* Horton is quoted in Jay Winter, ed., *America and the Armenian Genocide of 1915* (New York: Cambridge University Press, 2003), 179.

84 *The accounts of Armenians being* Peter Balakian, *The Burning Tigris: The Armenian Genocide and America's Response* (New York: HarperCollins, 2003), 38. Also see Peterson, *"Starving Armenians"* 28–50; Payaslian, *United States Policy*, 60; J. Coffey, "Service Diary," 32, 33, Imperial War Museum, London: "As we left at 6 am the country round the pillage was a peculiar and motley sight strewn with the sleeping and semi-awakened bodies of some 1000 Armenian refugees who, after 14 days weary march,

were enjoying a brief rest before completing the journey to Hamda. It was strange and pitiful sight—heaven itself compared with what was to follow."

85 *Its Ottoman governor, or* vali Giles Milton, *Paradise Lost: Smyrna 1922* (New York: Basic Books, 2010),15, 86, 87.

85 *The United States did not declare war* Payaslian, *United States Policy*, 130; Joseph L. Grabill, *Protestant Diplomacy and the Near East: Missionary Influence on American Policy, 1810–1927* (Minneapolis: University of Minnesota Press, 1971), 92.

85 *Horton also maintained friendly* Ilimdar Zade Edham, Sahlebdji Zade Midhat, and fourteen others to State Department, July 30, 1920 (1339 Turkish date on letter), included in Nancy Horton's unfinished biography of George Horton, GHP. "Since the appointment of His Excellency, George Horton as Consul-General of the United States in Smyrna, His Excellency has won the heart of the whole Turkish nation by the sympathy and good will which His Excellency has always shown every Turkish man."

86 *Horton was also discouraged* Horton to (no first name) Carroll, Oct. 1, 1919. GHP.

87 *Back in Paradise, the roads* "Mrs. Jennings Relates Tale of Horrors," *Syracuse (NY) Herald*, Oct. 27, 1922; Amy Jennings's Diary; Sara Jacob to Davis: Alexander MacLachlan, "A Potpourri of Sidelights and Shadows from Turkey," Queen's University Archives, Queen's University, Kingston, Ontario, Canada, 123, 124.

87 *By now, Smyrna harbor contained* Halpern, *Mediterranean Fleet*, 376–383.

87 *"We the undersigned fully endorse . . ."* American Chamber of Commerce, International College, et al., at Smyrna to State Department, Sept. 6, 1922. MLB.

88 *"This telegram from Smyrna . . ."* Harry G. Dwight, administrative employee in Near Eastern section of the department, to Dulles, perhaps reflecting the view of his boss, Sept. 6, 1922. MLB.

88 *Professor Lawrence was a natural* Background on Lawrence derived from the memoirs of his wife Helen, granddaughter Dorothy, and grandson Arthur and from various letters and commendations, CLP, Levantine Heritage.com.

89 *As chairman of the Smyrna Relief,* Caleb Lawrence, "Smyrna Disaster

Relief Committee," *Bulletin of the Constantinople Branch of the Red Cross*, No. 17. June 1923.

90 *Later in the day, still not* Horton to Bristol, Sept. 6, 1922. MLB.

91 *A British observer offered* "A Manchester Man's Experiences," *Manchester Guardian*, Sept. 28, 1922. Quoted in Oeconomos, *Martyrdom*.

CHAPTER 9: THEODORA

92 The substance of this narrative comes from an interview in the collection of the Asia Minor Research Center, Athens, supplemented with information obtained through a trip to the village in June 2012; also, Professor Thalia Pandiri.

93 *A Greek already had been hanged* Interviews with residents remembering the history. June 13, 2012.

94 *It was a small church, built with green stone* "Churches of Smyrna," LevantineHeritage.com.

CHAPTER 10: AN AMERICAN DESTROYER ARRIVES

95 *Admiral Bristol spent Sunday* Bristol, War Diary, Sept. 3, 1922.

96 *Bristol had grown up on a small farm* Information about Bristol's family in Glassboro comes from the Gloucester County Historical Society based on the family's real estate transactions in the Gloucester County Office of Deeds and the 1880 Federal Agricultural Census of the County. Bristol's record at the Naval Academy is noted in his conduct record, the Annual Register of the United States Naval Academy and the Academy's alumni jacket, excerpts of which were provided the Naval Academy. See also: "Ferrell, Thomas Merrill," Biographical Directory of the U.S. Congress, http://bioguide.congress.gov/biosearch/.

96 *While he was definitely not* For an analysis of the family backgrounds of Naval Academy cadets, see Peter Karsten, *The Naval Aristocracy: The Golden Age of Annapolis and the Emergence of Modern American Navalism* (New York: Free Press, 1972).

97 *One such man, though not so young* Dunn tells his own story in his memoir *World Alive: A Personal Story* (New York: Crown Publishers, 1956). See also Richard G. Hovannisian, *The Republic of Armenia, Vol. II: From Versailles to London, 1919–1920* (Berkeley, Los Angeles, Lon-

don: University. of California Press, 1982). For another point of view on Dunn, see Heath W. Lowry, "Richard G. Hovannisian on Lieutenant Robert Steed Dunn," *Journal of Ottoman Studies* V (1985): 209–252. (Formerly the Atatürk Professor of Ottoman & Modern Turkish Studies at Princeton University, Lowry is a controversial figure who asserts the Armenians were not victims of a Turkish genocide.)

98 *His first order of business* BWD, Sept. 5, 1920.

99 *Bristol had complete confidence* Aaron Merrill, Family and Personal Correspondence, ASMP.

99 *Small and light, young Merrill* "Aaron S. Merrill," *Lucky Bag* (the Naval Academy yearbook), U.S. Naval Academy, 1912.

99 *The letters also showed* Merrill to his mother, March 16, 1920 and March 5, 1920, Family and Personal Papers, ASMP.

99 *By September 5, word* "Intelligence Report," 103, Sept. 2, 199, STANAV. MLB.

100 *Two hours before the Litchfield* BWD, Sept 5, 1922.

100 *John Dos Passos was among those* Shenk, *Black Sea Fleet*, 98.

100 *Ernest Hemingway would be* BWD, Oct. 4, 1922.

100 *Brown had replaced the previous* Shenk, *Black Sea Fleet*, 13.

100 *Dapper with a pencil-thin mustache* Constantine Brown, *The Coming of the Whirlwind* (Chicago: Regnery, 1964),147–149.

100 *Clayton had gained notoriety* History of the Chicago Tribune; Published in Commemoration of Its Seventy-fifth Birthday, June Tenth, Nineteen Hundred and Twenty-two (Chicago: Chicago Tribune, 1922), 72. See also Emma Goldman, *Living My Life*, Vol. 2 (New York: Dover Publications, 1970).

100 *Bristol had worked hard* Shenk, *Black Sea Fleet*, 117–119. Incredibly, after the State Department received a copy of Clayton's unpublished story from the consul in Aleppo, Bristol took the position that the report was accurate but it was misleading because it put blame for deportations on the Turks: "The moral responsibility for the present situation of the Christian minorities in Turkey rests largely upon the Allies, although it has been possible up to the present to shift this responsibility to the shoulders of the Turks." Bristol to State Department, August 29, 1922. NA 867.4016/632.

101 *Bristol was a student of the new field* Bristol to Frank Polk, Dec. 4, 1919, NR Record Group 45, as quoted in Housepian. "You know I am a pitiless publicity man . . . "

101 *The* Litchfield *departed Constantinople* Merrill, Personal Diary, Sept. 5, 1922. ASMP.

101 *Like all American destroyers* Donald M. Kehn, A *Blue Sea of Blood: Deciphering the Mysterious Fate of the USS Edsall* (Minneapolis: MBI, 2008), 314.

101 *The* Litchfield *was ordered to steam* Logbook, USS *Litchfield*, Sept. 6, 1922. NA; "Report of Operations for Week Ending 10 September 1922," Commander, U.S. Naval Detachment in Turkish Waters. BWD.

101 *Rhodes was a capable* Rhodes NPRC file contains numerous documents that reference his personal problems including drunkenness. See, e.g., "Report of Medical Survey," John B. Rhodes, Nov. 17, 1921. "From the history of this officer's conduct, he was suffering from Neurasthenia, brought on by family troubles and the effects of excessive indulgence in alcohol."

103 *By September 5, the northern detachment* Smith, *Ionian Vision*, 298–299.

103 *The* Litchfield *came into the mouth* "Ship's Diary," USS *Litchfield*, Sept. 6, 1922. ASMP.

104 *British officers, working with* Halpern, *Mediterranean Fleet*, 376–383.

104 *The* Litchfield's *launch was* Unless otherwise noted, this and subsequent references to the actions and observations of Merrill are taken from his diary, Sept. 6–12. Merrill Diaries, ASMP.

105 *At the consulate, they found* Alexkos Karagheorghiades to Nancy Horton, March 9, 1962. "After seizure of the city by the irregulars (Turkish troops), he (Horton) attempted by every possible means to save the women and children not protected by American citizenship from certain death. This he did by raising American flags on Greek fishing and other boats. His first concern was to notify the inhabitants of the various sections of the city to assemble at the placed Punta. Constantly, and insofar as was possible, he watched over us and aided us in the boarding the ships which carried us to freedom." The letter is quoted in Nancy Horton's unfinished biography of GH.

105 *By Wednesday, September 6* Smith, *Ionian Vision*, 297, 298; Kocatürk, *Atatürk Ve Türkiye*.

107 *Merrill was proud* Merrill mentions his translation skills in his letters and diary. Merrill's Personal and Family Papers, ASMP.

108 *Meanwhile, Contantine Brown, who had obtained* Brown, *Coming of the Whirlwind*, 152. The question arises whether the Greek commander actually said this, or whether Brown put these words in his mouth after he had heard of Hadjianestis's reputation from others. Brown was not an entirely reliable correspondent and his memoir is boastful. Nonetheless, the allegation was widespread.

109 *He was fifty-eight and reputed* Smith, 272–277, 324.

109 *Knauss, a fellow Pennsylvanian* "Knauss, Harrison E." *Lucky Bag*, 1907, U.S. Naval Academy. Knauss, H.E. file, NPRC.

110 *"Old wrinkled women, lying . . ."* "Smyrna and After, Part I," *Naval Review*, The Naval Society, London, 1923, Vol. 3, 358, 555.

110 *the Americans' relief committee* E. O. Jacob to Darius Davis, Sept. 18, 1922. KFYA.

111 *Jennings's assignment required* Amy Jennings to William Schneider.

113 *The Greek general yielded* Jennings to D. Davis.

114 *His boss, Jacob, now back* Sara Jacobs to D. Davis.

114 *Providentially, while making his rounds* Jennings to D. Davis.

115 *On Thursday, September 7, the British* Halpern, *Mediterranean Fleet*, 376–383

116 *Knauss judged the situation* H. E. Knauss, "Ship's Diary," USS *Simpson*. Sept. 6–18, 1922. MLB.

116 *A departing Greek merchant had* Merrill Diary, Sept. 7, 1922. ASMP; Brown, *Coming of the Whirlwind*, 152.

117 *Lawrence put a young instructor* "Heroes in Smyrna" *Missionary Herald*, Nov. 1922, 917.

117 *The Greek reinforcements* Merrill to Bristol, Sept. 6, 1922. MLB.

118 *Around midnight, George Horton boarded the* Litchfield Hepburn, "Smyrna Disaster," 34.

118 *Afterward, he had lunch with* Merrill Diary, Sept. 7, 1922. ASMP.

119 *"The Greek troops passed to the rear singly . . ."* Knauss, "Simpson Diary," Sept. 7, 1922. MLB.

120 *"I have just returned from . . ."* London *Daily Telegram*, Sept. 10, 1922, quoted in Oeconomos, *Martyrdom*. A similar story by Clayton appeared in the *Chicago Tribune*, Sept. 8, 1922.

CHAPTER 11: THE VIEW FROM NIF

122 Again, I'm indebted to Mango and Kinross on the details of Kemal's life. For a chronology of the Turkish advance, see also Kocatürk, *Atatürk Ve* 124.

124 *The inheritors of a fierce martial culture* Lewis, *Emergence of Modern Turkey*, 13–17, including this: "For six centuries the Ottomans were almost constantly at war with the Christian West, first in the attempt—mainly successful—to impose Islamic rule on a large part of Europe, then in the long-drawn-out rearguard action to halt or delay the relentless counterattack of the West. This centuries-long struggle, with its origins in the very roots of Turkish Islam, could not fail to affect the whole structure of Turkish society and institutions."

125 *Three men of the Young Turks movement* Lewis, *Emergence of Modern Turkey*, 225–227.

125 *"Their passion for Turkifying the nation . . ."* Henry Morgenthau, *Ambassador Morgenthau's Story: A Personal Account of the Armenian Genocide* (New York: Cosimo, 2008), 200.

126 *"We've eaten shit . . ."* Mango, *Atatürk*, 185.

127 *He had given the Greek army forty-eight hours* "Smyrna and the Dardanelles," *Naval Review* 23, no. 3 (1935): 468.

127 *The day before, at Salihli* Kocatürk, *Atatürk Ve Türkiye*.

127 *Nonetheless, he agreed* Kinross, *Atatürk*, 363.

CHAPTER 12: BACK IN CONSTANTINOPLE

128 *On Wednesday September 6* BWD, Sept. 6, 1922.

128 *The group was bound by work* Buzanski, *Admiral Mark L. Bristol*, 114, 179.

128 *Peet had instigated the campaign* Buzanski, *Admiral Mark L. Bristol*, 182; Grabill, *Protestant Diplomacy*, 261. Biographical detail on Peet from Personnel Records, American Board of Commissioners for Foreign Missions, American Research Institute in Turkey (Digital Library for International Research). A description of the close connection between Near East Relief and the American Board appears in Peterson, *"Starving Armenians,"* 34, 35.

128 *Jaquith had banged heads* Shenk, *Black Sea Fleet*, 274. Biographical

background on Jaquith appears in "The New Near East," Near East Relief, New York, March 1921, 5. For a description of the way in which Jaquith brought to light the testimony of two Near East Relief workers about Turkish brutality over Bristol's objections, see Shenk, *Black Sea Fleet*, 113–115.

129 *Bristol was openly hostile* In his War Diary, Bristol frequently displayed his animus. See, e.g, BWD, Oct. 4, 1922.

129 *The Near East Relief organization had begun* The astonishing story of Near East Relief is told in James L. Barton, *Story of Near East Relief (1915–1930): An Interpretation* (New York: Macmillan Company, 1930).

129 *In 1916, Near East Relief* Details for this section are drawn from the minutes, reports, and cables of Near East Relief in RAC.

130 *Former ambassador Morgenthau* "Morgenthau Calls for Check on Turks," *New York Times*, Sept. 5, 1922.

130 *Bristol saw responsibility* BWD, Sept. 6, 1922.

131 *"The Greek is about the worst race"* Bristol letter to Admiral W. S. Sims, May 19, 1919, MLB, as quoted in Housepian.

131 *The two men despised each other* Shenk, *Black Sea Fleet*, 44, 45.

131 *A British admiral would call him* On February 10, 1928, Reginald Tyrwhitt, then Commander in Chief China Station, to Roger Keyes (then Mediterranean C.-in-C.) the following: "Then a week at Manila. Very pleasant & quite an entente with the Americans. Adl Bristol was there and on the surface he was v. pleasant but I know him to be a snake in the grass & do not trust him a yard. A nasty bit of work" (citation provided by Professor Paul Halpern).

131 *The British ambassador in Washington* Buzanski, *Admiral Mark L. Bristol*, 188.

131 *The episode ended with a note* Hughes to Bristol, May 4, 1922. NA 124.676/39b.

132 *He cabled the Red Cross* Bristol to State Dept, September 6, 1922. MLB.

132 *The next day, Thursday* BWD, Sept. 7, 1922.

132 *Hamid Bey struck Ernest Hemingway* "Hamid Bey," Ernest Hemingway, *Dateline, Toronto: The Complete Toronto Star Dispatches, 1920–1924*, ed. William White (New York: Charles Scribner's Sons, 1985).

133 *The nationalists, Bristol told* BWD, Sept. 7, 1922.

133 *As a young man, he had been* Biographical detail on Sweeny comes from

Richard Deacon, *One Man's Wars: The Story of Charles Sweeny, Soldier of Fortune* (London: Barker, 1972).

134 *After proposing stories* BWD, Sept. 7, 1922.

134 *Finally on Friday, two days* BWD, Sept. 8, 1922.

134 *As the group was departing* Merrill Diary, Sept. 9, 1922, ASMP.

135 *Prentiss was a peculiar character* Prentiss's reports about Smyrna have helped shape the historical record so it's worth recounting his odd career and unreliability as a witness. He was born in Hokah, Minnesota, in 1874, moved to Missouri as a child, then to Chicago, where he married, had two children, and sold insurance. In 1917, he moved to New Jersey, where he described himself as a consulting engineer. In 1919, Prentiss served as director and publicist of the first iteration of the Council on Foreign Relations, but appears to have had conflicts with its leaders, which led to his departure. In 1920, he was public relations director for the National Surety Co. and about the same time he wrote an article in which he said he was chairman of the United States Clearing House of Foreign Credits, a business he said he started himself. The same year, in an article titled "No Experience Necessary," he advised job seekers to rely on gumption over training to advance their careers and told an incredible personal tale of success. He said he had worked in mines in Missouri and had been indentured as farm hand as a boy before hopping on a "hog train" to Chicago and walking into the city's main department store in his farm clothes and asking to meet its owner, Marshall Field. His persistence so impressed Mr. Field, Prentiss wrote, he got the job and did amazing work, only to get fired six times by lesser executives and rehired by Mr. Field himself, at which point he improved the store's elevator system with such skill he won a project with a major elevator company. He recounts other heroic experiences in business, moved through other jobs, and then said he ended up in Houston, where he redesigned canal piers to reduce the cost of loading cotton. Then, he said, he went off to France as a knife salesman and improved the country's manufacturing methods.

He showed up in Bristol's office in late August 1922 claiming to be an efficiency expert working for Near East Relief. (Near East Relief later distanced itself from him.)

Among Prentiss's most outrageous reports about Smyrna was the story in which he saved an American sailor from a mob and a Greek man from execution after the man's young daughter came to Prentiss saying God had directed her to him. Prentiss was at the heroic center of nearly all the reports he wrote about Smyrna.

He frequently invoked Bristol's name when selling his stories, but even Bristol had his doubts. "In the morning," Bristol noted in his diary, "I received a call from Mr. M. O. Prentiss. He came to discuss with me certain questions that I had instructed my Intelligence Officer Lieutenant Merrill to ask him. I told Lieutenant Merrill to find from Mr. Prentiss just whom he represented out here and to ask him if he had any letters identifying him and his work. Mr. Prentiss said he did not have any letters, that he represented some bankers who were friends of his. . . . I must admit that Mr. Prentiss' further information today did not throw much light on his position out here. He talks very well, he appears very well and yet I cannot quite make him out. He gave me a set of pictures that he had taken down at Smyrna. It is noticeable that he appears very often in these pictures in rather prominent and imposing places."

Even more strangely, on the way back to the United States, Prentiss became enmeshed in a murder in Italy, though he was never charged. He claimed to have been misidentified as the suitor of a wealthy Chicago woman who was vacationing in Italy. Back in Washington, he tried to convince Allen Dulles to support a forum to help win approval of an American treaty with Turkey but Dulles was skeptical, writing in a confidential note, "I have little confidence in Prentiss." Later, Prentiss started a Christmas-card business and stirred up publicity by leading a campaign to ban the word *Xmas*. By 1940, he was widowed and a lodger at the Kenmore Hall Hotel in New York. He died in 1948. His obituary in the *Washington Post* called him an advertising and public relations man.

Also see Mark O. Prentiss, "No Experience Necessary," *System—The Magazine of Business*, March 1920, Vol. 32, A. W. Shaw Co., New York and London, 492; Mark O. Prentiss, "Sophie and Her God," *Good News*, April 1926. "Supplement: For the Young People," *Australasian Pentecostal Studies*, Parramatta NSW 2150, Australia http://webjournals.ac .edu.au/journals/GN/gn-vol17-no4-apr-1926/23-sophie-and-her-god/ "Pessimistic views Not Sanctioned by Eastern Relief," *Schenectady*, N.Y., *Gazette*, Nov. 14, 1922. The following documents relating to Council

on Foreign Relations come from Mudd Manuscript Library at Prince-
ton University: Executive Committee Meeting Minutes, April 8, 1919;
Douglas Dunbar to Frank N. Doubleday, June 25, 1919; Doubleday to
Dunbar, June 26, 1919; Prentiss to Herbert S. Houston, Dec. 30, 1919.
BWD, Oct. 21, 1922; Dulles, Allen, Mark Prentiss Meeting, State Dept.
Memo, NA 711.67/118; "Tells Why He Named Prentiss in Italy Murder:
Claims Mrs. Underhill Spurned Chicagoan," *Chicago Daily Tribune*,
Nov. 19, 1922; "Spelling of 'Xmas' Is Called Irreverent; Clergymen Back
Move to Bar Abbreviation," *New York Times*, Dec. 9, 1926, "Mark O.
Prentiss," *The Washington*, March 23, 1948.

135 *The ship slipped its mooring* "Logbook," USS *Lawrence*, Sept. 8, 1922. NA.

CHAPTER 13: CAPTAIN HEPBURN'S DILEMMA

136 *The USS* Lawrence *entered* Hepburn, "Smyrna Disaster," 2. Unless otherwise noted, subsequent details on Hepburn's actions and observations
are drawn from his report.

137 *Twenty-five years earlier* Hepburn, NPRC.

137 *At the Academy he had* Arthur J. Hepburn," *Lucky Bag*, 1897, U.S. Naval
Academy.

138 *Along with poor eyesight* Hepburn, NPRC.

138 *Ashore, they worked* Merrill Diary, Sept. 9, 1922.

139 *While he waited for* Knauss, "Ship's Diary, USS *Simpson*," Sept. 9, 1922.
MLB.

140 *The men had enlisted* "Muster Roll of the Crew of the USS *Litchfield*,"
June 30, 1922. NA.

140 *As Captain Hepburn worked with his officers* "Smyrna and After, Part
IV," *Naval Review* 2 (1924): 356, 357.

141 *Horton had returned to the consulate* Hepburn, "Smyrna Disaster," 6.

142 *The medical team of Dr. Post* Biographical details on Post from: "Wilfred
Post," Personnel Card, ABCFM, ARI in Turkey; "American Red Cross
Work in Turkey," Levant Trade Review, American Chamber of Com-
merce, June 1915; "Want Method to Erase Brand of Inhuman Turks,"
Evening Independent, St. Petersburg, Fla. Dec. 9, 1919; Morgenthau
to Sec. of State, Oct. 22, 1915. NA 867.4016/ 213; Bio on Agnes Evon:
Mabel Smith, "American Nurse in Beirut," *American Journal of Nursing*
28, no. 2 (February 1928); Bio on Sara Corning: "Sara Corning," Person-

nel Card, ABCFM, ARI in Turkey; Sara Corning file, Yarmouth County Museum & Archives. The team's work is told in Agnes Evon's "Seven Days in Smyrna: The Greatest Indictment of Modern Civilization," *McClure's Magazine* 55, no. 7 (Sept. 1923).

143 *After the meeting, at about* Horton to Sec. of State, August 9, 1920. NA 125.8731.18. The letter describes consulate offices and furnishings.

144 *"Swarthy hard-bitten men"* Smyrna and After II, 742.

144 *The soldiers were dressed* Horton, *Blight of Asia*. Also see "Smyrna and After, Part II," *Naval Review* 4 (1923): 741.

144 *Their entry into the city* "Smyrna and After, Part II," 740.

146 *Davis was at one of the city's* Claflin Davis to Bristol, Nov. 8, 1922, with enclosure. Bristol put a series of questions to seven eyewitnesses at Smyrna. The respondents filed written responses. NA 867.48/1452.

149 *"The only man I had ever seen"* Merrill Diary, Sept. 9, 1922, ASMP.

150 *Knauss witnessed the violence* Knauss, Sept. 9, 1922. MLB.

153 *As he did all of this,* Brock to Admiralty and Admiralty to Brock, Sept. 11, 1922, in Halpern, *Mediterranean Fleet*, 346, 347: "High Commissioner has been authorized to transmit to you full text of Foreign Office telegram of today's date restating general policy of Government, main point of which is that Kemalist Army shall not be permitted at any point or under any circumstances to cross from Asia Minor into Europe."

154 *At Paradise, about a thousand* Amy Jennings gave her account in a diary published the following month. "Horrors of Smyrna, Latest Terrors of the East Revealed in Diary of Brave American Woman Who Witnessed Turks' Unspeakable Atrocities," *The Evening World*, Oct. 24, 1922. KFYA. See also Sara Jacob letter; and MacLachlan Diary.

156 *Davis, the Red Cross chief of the relief committee* C. C. Davis to Bristol.

158 *He was shaken by* Jennings to D. Davis.

158 *"No one can ever describe . . ."* Jennings to D. Davis.

159 *Jaquith reported back* STANAV to NER New York, Sept. 12, 1922. MLB.

159 *The* Times *of London, which* "The Massacres at Smyrna," *Times*, Sept. 18, 1922, quoted in Oeconomos, *Martyrdom*.

160 *The* Morning Post *in London* "Christian Refugees," *Morning Post*, Sept. 11, 1922, quotedin Oeconomos, *Martyrdom*.

161 *Reporter John Clayton saw the execution* London *Daily Telegram*, Sept. 14, 1922, quoted in Oeconomos, *Martyrdom*.

161 *"We watched our . . ."* Leyla Neyzi, "Remembering Smyrna/Izmir: Shared History, Shared Trauma." *History and Memory* Special Issue: Remembering and Forgetting on Europe's Southern Periphery 20, no. 2 (October 1, 2008): 123.

162 *Afterward, he returned* Kinross, *Atatürk*, 367.

163 *The British consul came* William Ferguson (Paradise resident), Transcript of Interview, 1965. AKJP.

163 *Amy Jennings, at home* Amy Jennings Diary.

163 *The violence at Paradise* "Smyrna and After, Part IV, V," *Naval Review*, The Naval Society, London, 1924, Vol. 2, 355–361.

163 *"A Turkish soldier appeared in the street"* Smyrna and After IV, 359.

165 *In his message to Bristol* Hepburn to Bristol, Sept. 12, 1922. MLB.

165 *After their arrival the previous day* Evon, "Seven Days in Smyrna."

167 *"No one could imagine without seeing"* Merrill Diary Sept. 1, 1922, ASMP.

CHAPTER 14: GARABED HATCHERIAN

168 Events in this chapter are drawn from Dr. Hatcherian's diary.

CHAPTER 15: NOUREDDIN PASHA

171 *The city's new military commander* Mango, *Atatürk*, 329, 330, 551.

171 *In November 1914, soon after* Nicholas Gardner, "Charles Townshend's Advance on Baghdad: The British Offensive in Mesopotamia, September–November 1915," *War in History* 20, no. 2 (April 2013): 182–200; S. A. Cohen, "The Genesis of the British Campaign in Mesopotamia, 1914," *Middle Eastern Studies* 12, no. 2 (May 1976).

172 *Throughout the period* Hofmann et al., *Genocide of the Ottoman Greeks*, 97; Shenk, *Black Sea Fleet*, 95.

172 *One of his first orders of business* There are several sources on the death of Chrysostomos. See especially Rene Puaux, *La Mort de Smyrne*, Edition De La Revue Des Balkans, Paris, 1922; Horton, *Blight of Asia*, 136.

173 *A British naval officer described him* "Smyrna and After, Part I," 568–572.

173 *"On the last occasion"* Smyrna and After Naval Review, 564.

174 *On Monday, September 11, Captain Hepburn* The story of Hepburn's activities continues in his report.

175 *The Marsovan incident was well known* "On Behalf of the Armenians," House Resolution 244, United States House of Representatives, March 7, 1922.

178 *As for the women,* "Smyrna and After, Part IV, V," *Naval Review,* 364.

178 *"I afterwards learned"* Charles Dobson, "The Smyrna Holocaust," an appendix to "The Tragedy of the Christian Near East," by Lysimachos Oeconomos, The Anglo-Hellenic League, 1923. London.

178 *"The Turks had taken a girl of fifteen"* Knauss, Simpson Ship Diary, Sept. 11, 1922.

178 *Cabling Bristol, Hepburn reported* Hepburn to Bristol, Sept. 12, 1922. MLB.

180 *The bakeries remained* C. D. Davis to Bristol.

180 *"They were, I think"* Agnes Evon, "Seven Days in Smyrna," *McClure's Magazine,* Sept. 1923.Vo. 55, No. 7.

180 *Jaquith cabled Near East Relief* STANAV to State Department, Sept. 11, 1922. MLB.

181 *Then there came an odd* "Smyrna and After, IV," 364.

181 *What, Lamb wondered* "Smyrna and After IV," *Naval Review,* 364. "Then the bombshell came later in the day. The Turkish authorities announced that they could not be responsible for the nationals after Tuesday night."

181 *Throughout the previous week* "Conditions in Smyrna," Horton to State Dept., Sept. 20, 1922. NA 767.68/241.

181 *"The apprehension of fear-ridden"* London *Daily Telegram,* Sept. 13, 1922, as quoted in Oeconomos.

183 *On the previous day* MacLachlan memoir.

186 *"On my round at 5 A.M."* Simpson Diary, Knauss, Sept. 12,1922.

186 *"I could see that"* Simpson Diary, Knauss, Sept. 12, 1922.

187 *"On Tuesday, a visit . . ."* "Smyrna and After, Part V," 364.

187 *"In the early hours of the twelfth"* Simpson Diary, Knauss, Sept. 12, 1922.

CHAPTER 16 FIRE BREAKS OUT

191 *On Wednesday morning* The wind is mentioned in many accounts, including in Hepburn's report.

192 *"Few patrols were in evidence"* Hepburn, 23.

195 *"The whole harbor was strewn"* Arthur Duckworth (aboard HMS *Iron Duke*) letter to his parents, Sept 13, 1922. IWM.

195 *"You can say order has been completely restored"* London Daily Telegraph
Sept. 15, 1922 as quoted in Oeconomos.

195 *Jennings had spent the night* Jennings to Emmons.

196 *People ascended to high places* Testimony from the Insurance Trial.

198 *Jennings drove his family* Amy Jennings Diary.

199 *"As long as I live I shall . . ."* R. W. Abernathy, "The Great Rescue," collected in Basil Mathews, *The Spirit of the Game* (George H. Doran Co.,
1926).

200 *Minnie Mills was the school's directo*r Biographical background on Minnie Mills from Personnel Card, ABCFM, ARI. Accounts of the fire and
rescue appear in Evon, "Seven Days in Smyrna"; "Miss Mills Blames
Turks for the Fire," *New York Times*, Sept. 27, 1922; Bertha Morley,
"The Smyrna Disaster," *The New Armenia* 14, no. 6 (Nov.–Dec. 1922):
90; "The Burning of Our Girls' School at Smyrna," *Life and Light for
Women*, Boston, Nov. 1922, 381; "Smyrna," *The Orient* (newsletter),
Bible House, Constantinople, Nov. 1922, Vol. IX, No. 10, 88; "Our Consul Praises Americans," *New York Times*, Sept. 21, 1922; Testimony of Sister Mabel Maria Kalfa, "Report of Insurance Trial," 65, 66; "The Angel
of Discord at Smyrna," *Literary Digest*, October 7, 1922, 52, 53.

201 *At about 4 P.M., navy ensign* "Thomas Ackley Gaylord," *Lucky Bag*, U.S.
Naval Academy, 1920.

202 *Miss Christie, born* "Jean Ogilvie Christie," Ancestry.com.

204 *He had decided to stay* Jennings to Emmons.

206 *The facts about the fire* "Report of Insurance Trial," ff.

207 *The lawyer for the insurance* "Report of Insurance Trial," 67–70.

211 *As it happened, the sailors* "Omaha Sailor Witness of Turk Slaughter at
Smyrna," *Omaha World Herald*, Oct. 15, 1922.

212 *And there was yet another macabre element* Melville Chater, "History's
Greatest Trek," *National Geographic*, Nov. 1925 (Vol. 48).

213 *"The sea front is a seething mass"* Duckworth, Sept. 13, 1922, IWM.

213 *Horton was still missing* The story of Horton's intercession on behalf of
the doctor was told by the doctor's daughter, Ida Argyropulos, and included her unpublished biography, GHP.

214 *"The tens of thousands of terrified"* Hepburn, 27.

215 *"as we headed for the harbor entrance"* Simpson Ship Diary, Knauss,
Sept. 13, 1922.

215 *In Athens, Clayton filed a story* "60,000 Greeks, Armenians Are Home-less," *Chicago Tribune*, Sept. 15, 1922; "Fire and Massacre in City of Smryna," *London Daily Telegraph*, Sept. 16, 1922, latter quoted in Oeconomos, *Martyrdom*.

CHAPTER 17: "ALL BOATS OVER"

216 *Hepburn stood on the wood-plank* Details on Hepburn experience continues from his report.

217 *In places, the people were so tightly packed* "Mr. Roy Treloar's Story," *London Daily Telegraph*, Sept. 20, 1922: "I could see the unfortunate wretches, thirteen or fourteen deep, swaying in the sweltering heat"; "Last Days of Smyrna," *Times of London*, Sept. 19, 1922: "As the fire drove them towards the sea, they crowded the whole sea front." Both quoted in Oeconomos, *Martyrdom*.

218 *What he didn't know* "Report of Trial," 25. "Col. Mouharren Bey, agreed that a cordon of Turkish troops had been placed at the Point on the night of the fire. The object of the cordon was to keep the people concentrated where they were. There was a second cordon at the other end of the Quay near the Custom House, and the effect was to prevent the refugees from the fire escaping out the town in either direction."

218 *"I sat up all last night . . ."* Lieutenant Arthur Duckworth to his parents, Sept. 13, 14, 1922. Papers of Arthur Duckworth, IWW.

218 *Davis saw Turkish soldiers* C. C. Davis to Bristol.

219 *Hepburn only had to consider* Shenk, *Black Sea Fleet*, 102, 103. On Houston's "meticulous" character as an officer, see Clark G. Reynolds, *On the Warpath in the Pacific: Admiral Jocko Clark and the Fast Carriers* (Annapolis, MD: Naval Institute Press, 2005), 48.

220 *He nursed ambitions* Lee A. Craig, "Public Sector Pensions in the United States." http://eh.net/encyclopedia/public-sector-pensions-in-the-united-states/.

221 *Miss Evon and Miss Corning* Evon, "Seven Days in Smyrna."

221 *"The spectacle was magnificently . . ."* "Smyrna," September 1922. Private Papers of C. J. Howes, Doc. 2286, IWM. Howes was a chief petty officer aboard the HMS *Diligence*.

221 *The only reporter left* Ward Price's dramatic description of the fire appeared in the *Daily Mail*, September 16, 1922, under the headline "Two

Miles of Fire, Houses Burn Like Furious Torches." Until the fire, Price's reporting generally minimized the killing in Smyrna. His account of the first night of the blaze stands as perhaps its most vivid description. Price went on to cover Germany in the 1930s and developed a close relationship with Hitler.

221 *Another British observer* T. W. Bunter, Memoir, Private Papers of T. W. Bunter, Doc. 1444, IWM. Bunter was aboard the HMHS *Maine* at Smyrna.

223 *But he was not without his critics* Domvile Diary, Sept. 5, 1922. "And (Brock) hesitates until it is v. difficult to be patient with the poor man. He is generally right, too, in the end, but still he is very trying."

223 *Only the day before,* Domvile Diary, Sept. 13, 1922.

223 *Nonetheless, circumstances pointed* Brock to Admiralty, Sept. 11, 1922, quoted in Halpern, *Mediterranean Fleet:* ". . . Kemalists should be informed that failing satisfactory guarantees that they will make no attempt to land in Gallipoli all floating transport will be destroyed."

224 *Domvile was present* Domvile Diary, Sept. 14, 1922.

224 *In minutes, British boats* Several accounts capture the speed and energy with which the British set to the rescue including Hepburn's report. See also Domvile Diary and Howes.

225 *Lieutenant Commander C. H. Drage* "The 1914–1933 Diaries of Cmdr. C. H. Drage, RN," IWM, 143–148.

227 *"One of the saddest cases . . ."* Howes.

228 *As Hepburn met with the relief* Powell, "Ship's Diary," Sept. 14, 1922.

CHAPTER 18: MORNING AFTER

229 *The sun rose Thursday* "Smyrna and After, Part III," 157, 472.

230 *Agnes Evon, defying* Evon, "Seven Days in Smyrna."

230 *As it happened, Miss Morley* Hepburn, "Smyrna Disaster."

231 *"It appeared to me now . . ."* Hepburn, "Smyrna Disaster," 31.

232 *The gap between Jennings* Jacob to D. Davis. While Jacob provides details on many aspects of the committee's work, Jennings's work is passed over in his summary to his superior.

233 *"We gathered in here . . ."* Jennings to D. Davis.

233 *Jaquith told Hepburn* Hepburn, "Smyrna Disaster," 32.

234 *The captain of the* Winona Hepburn, "Smyrna Disaster," 32.

234 *Jaquith radioed a message* Jacquith to STANAV, Sept. 14, 1922. MLB.

234 *The condition and treatment* Jaquith to STANAV, Sept. 14, 1922. MLB.

235 *Walking on the Quay* Vice Consul Maynard Barnes to State Dept, Nov. 22, 1922. NA 767.68/463

235 *Merrill also went ashore* Merrill Diary, Sept. 14, 1922, ASMP.

235 *Soon the entire carpet-warehouse* "Smyrna and After, Part III," 164.

235 *At about 9 P.M., Barnes* Hepburn, "Smyrna Disaster," 33; Horton, *Blight of Asia,* 164. Horton quotes an American YMCA official, who would have been Jacob since he and Jennings were the only two left in the city.

236 *"Number of refugees . . ."* Hepburn to Bristol, Sept. 15, 1922. MLB.

CHAPTER 19: GARABED HATCHERIAN

237 Events in this chapter are drawn from Dr. Hatcherian's diary.

CHAPTER 20: OIL, WAR, AND THE PROTECTION OF MINORITIES

241 *The serious pursuit of oil* For background on the birth of the Near East oil drilling, I have relied on Yergin. Also, Sourkabi, Rasoul, "Centennary of the First Oil Well in the Mideast," *GeoXpro* 5, no. 5, 2008; *Multinational Oil Corporations and U.S. Foreign Policy—Together with Individual Views, to the Committee on Foreign Relations, United States Senate, by the Sub-committee on Multinational Corporations.* Report (Washington, D.C.: US Government Printing Office, 1975); William Stivers, "International Politics and Iraqi Oil, 1918–1928: A Study in Anglo-American Diplomacy," *Business History Review* 55, no. 4 (1981): 517; Gerald D. Nash, *United States Oil Policy, 1890–1964: Business and Government in Twentieth Century*; George Otis Smith, "Where the World Gets Its Oil but Where Will Our Children Get It When American Wells Cease to Flow?" *National Geographic,* February 1920, 181–220; Henry Woodhouse, "American Oil Claims in Turkey," *Current History* 15 (1922): 953–959.

244 *On the day the concession* For a masterful study of the topic, see Margaret Macmillan, *War That Ended Peace: The Road to 1914* (Toronto: Penguin Books Canada, 2014).

245 *"The Allies had floated . . ."* "Floated to Victory," *New York Times,* Nov. 23, 1918.

245 *Oil had twice* Erik Dahl, "Naval Innovation: From Coal to Oil," *Joint Force Quarterly,* Winter 2000–2001.

246 *Secretary Hughes suggested* "Multinational Oil Corporations," Senate Report.

247 *Idealism was out* America's transformation in the years following World War I is subject of William Leuchtenburg's classic *The Perils of Prosperity, 1914–32* (Chicago: University of Chicago Press, 1958). "But prosperity held perils of its own. It invested enormous political and social power in a business class with little tradition of social leadership. It placed economic pre-eminence in the hands of the one country in the world least prepared to guide world trade. It made money the measure of man."

CHAPTER 21: BRISTOL'S RESISTANCE

248 *When he was denied* Bristol to AMNAVPAR (navy delegation in Paris), June 10, 1920. MLB. The likely recipient of the memorandum was Admiral William Benson, chief of Naval Operations, though the ultimate recipient would be the president and secretary of the navy. "I most earnestly request reconsideration by the President and the approval of the Secretary of the Navy."

250 *The hotel was a masterpiece* "Night at the Museum Hotel," *Daily Mail*, Oct. 3, 2010.

250 *"They had been supported"* BWD Sept. 8, 1922

251 *One of the noncommissioned officers* "Louis Crocker, Navy veteran, remembers," *New London Day*, Sept. 8, 1981.

251 *Even Harding* Philip Perlmutter, *Legacy of Hate: A Short History of Ethnic, Religious, and Racial Prejudice in America* (Armonk, NY: M. E. Sharpe, 1999), 167.

252 *The memorandum* BWD, Sept. 7, 1922.

252 *Bristol waited three days* Bristol to Sec. of State, Sept. 9, 1922. MLB. For a sense of the spin: "Smyrna situation most alarming. Greek troops in panic and pouring into city. . . . Repeated threats by Greek officers to burn town. Nazili already burned."

252 *The next day, September* Bristol to Sec. of State. Sept. 10, 1922. MLB. "Smyrna occupied by Mustapha Kemal. Constantinople comparatively tranquil . . ."

252 *On the following day, September 11*, Dr. Peet was back in Bristol's office at the embassy with Jeannie Jillson, BWD, Sept. 8, 1922. MLB.

253 *On approaching Mudania* Addoms to Bristol, "Mudania Diary," Sept. 11, 1922. MLB.

253 *The British destroyer had taken* One of the Greek soldiers was Corporal Stamatis Hadjiyannis. (See note above, "Bride of Ionia.") He left an unpublished memoir, which is in the possession of his grandson George Poulemenos. It reads, in part: ". . . we started swimming towards the French warship, which was about one hundred to one hundred and fifty meters away. We had swum more than two and a half kilometers, and our strength began to diminish. Especially mine, as I was not a good swimmer, . . .

"We arrived at the French warship, where we were welcomed. They threw lifejackets with ropes to help us on board, since there was no stairway. I hadn't the strength to hold the weight of my own body, and the lifejacket was constantly slipping from my hands! The French sailor on the warship, realizing that I was unable to hold on to the lifejacket, hung from the parapet of the warship, perhaps having someone holding him, and grabbed me. Fortunately the sailor had the strength to hold me and get me off the sea, and finally raise me to the warship. When I set my foot on the warship, tears came to my eyes for my misery. I tried not to cry, not wanting to exhibit my frailness."

254 *Back at the embassy* BWD, Sept. 12, 1922.

255 *Afterward, Bristol had lunch* BWD, Sept. 12, 1922.

255 *The* Lawrence *arrived after* BWD, Sept. 12, 1922.

256 *Bristol wrote:* Bristol to State Dept., Sept. 13, 1922. MLB.

256 *Three days earlier, a cable* STANAV to USS Lawrence for Jaquith, Sept. 10, 1922. MLB.

CHAPTER 22: HALSEY POWELL

259 *In 1904, when he graduated* "Halsey Powell," *Lucky Bag,* 1904, U.S. Naval Academy.

259 *As a boy, Halsey* I am indebted to Amalie Preston of the Harrodsburg (Kentucky) Historical Society for this description of the Powell plantation. Ms. Preston proved to be an indefatigable researcher on my behalf and tracked down Powell's personal correspondence, which had remained with the Powell family.

260 *"This my hope and prayer . . ."* E. W. Halsey to Margaret Halsey, August 31, 1883. Harrodsburg Historical Society.

260 *At seventeen, he went off* Faculty Minutes, Sept. 26, 1899, Vol. 3, Special Collections, Centre College, Danville, Kentucky.

260 *In his first fifteen years* "Powell, Halsey," NPRC.

262 *On August 3, Powell's* "Powell, Halsey," NPRC.

262 *Then, with new orders* "Powell, Halsey," NPRC. Intelligence and Technological Archives, U.S. Naval War College, Newport, Rhode Island.

262 *In April, Halsey sent* Halsey Powell to his mother, April 28, 1920. Harrodsburg Historical Society.

263 *In August 1922, Powell* Powell, "Ship's Diary," USS *Edsall*. August, 1922. MLB.

265 *By his own account* BWD, Sept. 10, 1922.

265 *After getting Hepburn's* Powell, "Ship's Diary," Sept. 13, 1922. Except as otherwise noted, this and subsequent information regarding Powell and the *Edsall* in this chapter come from the *Edsall*'s ship's diary in September 1922. MLB.

265 *"Prentiss requests following . . ."* Edsall to STANAV, Sept. 14, 1922. MLB.

266 *Prentiss's first story appeared* "Relief Man Tells Tragedy," *New York Times*, Sept. 18, 1922.

266 *Powell, Morris, and the Greek* For the interior design of the *Edsall*, see Library of Selected Images, Naval Historical Center, Dept. of the Navy. http://www.history.navy.mil/photos/images/s-file/s584045.jpg.

268 *The day before Powell's* Hepburn, "Smyrna Disaster," 34–39.

269 *Over the previous several days*, Smith, 316, 317.

271 *Turkish residents had taken* Melville Chater, "History's Greatest Trek," *National Geographic*, Nov. 1925 (Vol. 48), Photos.

271 *For years afterward* Neyzi, "Remembering Smyrna/Izmir," 123.

271 *Throughout the day*, Merrill Diary, Sept. 16, 17, 1922. ASMP.

273 *On the way back, Prentiss* "Smyrna Now Faces Plague, Famine," *New York Times*, Sept. 20, 1922.

274 *The British in particular* Thomas Woodrooffe, *Naval Odyssey* (New York: Sheridan House, 1938), 109. Brock praised Powell to Bristol. Brock to Bristol, Oct. 16, 1922, NPRC. Admiral Nicholson also praised him to Bristol in a personal meeting. BWD, Oct. 21, 1922.

274 *In a few days, the* Times Harvey to State Dept., Bristol. Sept. 22, 1922. MLB.

275 *All the big tobacco companies* A comprehensive explanation of the American tobacco industry's reliance on Turkish tobacco emerges in the testimony and exhibits contained in the record of U.S. Senate Hearings on a foreign tobacco tariff. "Tariff: Schedule 6 Tobacco and Manufacturers Of," Hearing Before the Committee on Finance, Dec. 7, 1921.

275 *The American companies* "Standard Commercial Corporation History," Funding Universe, http://www.fundinguniverse.com/company-histories/standard-commercial-corporation-history/.

276 *A Standard Commercial manager,* Powell, "Ship's Diary," Sept. 17, 1922. MLB.

276 *The American Tobacco Co.* Testimony of Jehu E. Archbell, Report of Trial, 38–55.

276 *Some of the big warehouses* Powell, "Ship's Diary," Sept. 17, 1922.

277 *Several days after the fire* The story of Onassis as a boy in Smyrna is told in Nicholas Gage, *Greek Fire: The Story of Maria Callas and Aristotle Onassis* (New York: Knopf, 2000), 115–128. Additional detail comes from Skoulakis interview.

278 *Powell had met with these* The location and use of the Spartali mansion as the U.S. consulate comes from the research of George Poulemenos and Achilleas Chatziconstantinou.

278 *By September 17, Jennings* Jennings to D. Davis.

278 *"I must say the Navy . . ."* Jennings to D. Davis.

279 *A favorite character in Greek* "Main Characters in Greek Shadow Theater," Spathario Museum, Maroussi, Greece. http://www.karagiozis-museum.gr/en/figoures//.

279 *The mansions along the Quay* Kyriakos Tsangridis, *From Utopia to Topos: The City of Smyrna* (Athens: Leader Books, 2001). Also: "Dwelling House, Smyrna, 1904," floor plan provided by George Poulemenos.

281 *The fire had destroyed* Descriptions of the city in the days following the fire appear in C. C. Davis to Bristol; Jaquith to Bristol, Oct. 6, 1922. NA 867.48/1452.

281 *John Clayton, back in the city* "Plague Piles Up Death in Smyrna Ruins," *Chicago Tribune,* Sept. 17, 1922.

282 *"The worst sight I have seen"* E.O. Jacob to Darius Davis, Smyrna Diary, Part 2, (Date illegible) KFYA.

283 *He also had the annoying* BWD, Oct. 23, 1922.

284 *Mr. Carathina had returned to Turkey* "Vallejoan to Seek Family and Fortune," *Oakland Tribune*, March 29, 1920.

285 *Lord Curzon immediately cabled* Curzon to Geddes, and hand-delivered to Dulles at State Dept., Sept. 22, 1922. NA 868.48.156.

CHAPTER 23: THEODORA

286 The substance of this narrative comes from an interview with Theodora Kontou in the collection of the Asia Minor Research Center, Athens, and *The Exodus*. Athens: The Asia Minor Research Center, 1980.

287 *In peace let us pray to the Lord*. Language of the Greek Orthodox Liturgy is drawn from "Divine Liturgy of St. Basil the Great," Greek Orthodox Church of America. http://www.goarch.org/chapel/liturgical_texts.

CHAPTER 24: DAYS OF DESPAIR

290 *As the suffering worsened* Unless otherwise noted, Powell's observations and experiences here and in subsequent places in this chapter come from the "Ship's Diary" of the USS *Edsall*.

290 *Lieutenant Commander Knauss had helped* Knauss, "Ship's Diary," Sept. 17, 1922. MLB.

291 *"From the military bakeries . . ."* Jacob to D. Davis.

291 *Dr. Post (who had returned from Salonika)* Charles Claflin Davis to Bristol.

291 *A local doctor, Dr. Margoulis*, "Turkey," *The Reform Advocate: America's Jewish Journal* 42 (Oct. 14, 1911). A news item reports that the Sultan honored Dr. Margoulis for his services in the city.

291 *In some cases, the French*. Demetrius Psalidopoulos, "My Memories of the First Days of the Catastrophe," a privately printed monograph in the possession of Prof. Michail Psalidopoulos, Athens. Mr. Psalidopoulos escaped Smyrna on a French ship, "Phrygia." Also: Peter James Spanos, *Fear and Survival*, Cape Elizabeth, Maine: Privately printed, 1989. Theodore Bartoli to Secretary of State, Dec. 5, 1922. NA 867.016/77. Pathé newsreels distributed in the U.S. at the time also show Italian ships boarding refugees. Library of Congress.

292 *Some of the Allied ships swept the searchlights* Woodrooffe, *Naval Odyssey*, 117.

292 *"The strange thing was . . ."* Ernest Hemingway, "On the Quai at Smyrna," a short story in the collection *In Our Time* (New York: Boni & Liveright, 1925).

292 *Hemingway actually never* Michael Reynolds, *Hemingway: The Final Years* (New York: W. W. Norton, 1999).

292 *While he was* Hemingway, *Dateline, Toronto*.

293 *On September 19, a dirty and ill-kept* "Movement of Vessels at Smyrna, Turkey," included in *Edsall's* Diary, Sept. 19–21, 1922; Woodrooffe, *Naval Odyssey*, 110.

293 *The Near East Relief also* STANAV to Edsall, Sept. 20, 1922. MLB.

294 *"We therefore became more . . ."* Jennings to D. Davis.

294 *Several days earlier,* Hepburn, "Smyrna Disaster," 37.

294 *But additional sightings* Powell, "Ship's Diary."

295 *While running the American hospital.* Jay Winter (ed.), *America and the Armenian Genocide of 1915*, Cambridge University Press, 2004, 193. Raymond Kevorkian, *The Aremenian Genocide: A Complete History*, I. B. Tauris, 2011, 581.

295 *The Young Turk government* Hovannisian, Power, *A Problem from Hell*; Peterson, "Starving Armenians," ff.

295 *The typical method was for soldiers or police* to round up Armenians in the cities, towns, and villages Peterson, *"Starving Armenians:" America and the Armenian Genocide, 1915–1930*, 32,33, ff.

295 *Italian consulate remembered* James Bryce, *The Treatment of Armenians in the Ottoman Empire 1915-1916*, G.P. Putnam's Sons, London, 1916. 290–92.

295 *"The passing of gangs . . ."* Peterson, "Starving Armenians," 34.

296 *In May of 1922,* Yowell to Jackson.

296 *"It seems almost impossible . . ."* Jacob to D. Davis.

297 *Most were driven toward Magnesia* Many Greeks were reportedly killed in the march at a particular deep canyon (Buyuk Dere) along the Magnesia Road. Ioannis D. Kostikdakis, an Ottoman Greek from Kata Panogia, who survived, wrote, "As we arrived at the entrance of the gorge, a stifling stench hampered our breathing. . . . Thousands of corpses, men, women, children, swollen from decay, filled the endless ravine."

See "The Grand Trek to the Ravine of Death," *Kato Panagia Bulletin*, No. 11, September 1957. In an interview collected by the Asia Minor Research Center in its book, *Exodus*, Anastassis Haranis, an Ottoman Greek from a village near Phocaea, said, "In Bunarbassi [near Smyrna], after they had stolen everything from us, they delivered us to new guards. During the night they led us through the ravine of Sypilos (a mountain near Magnesia), where they searched us again and took all our money. Turkish men and women came to the road while we passed, and they kept saying to our guards: 'If we give you two Turkish lira, will you give us one Giaur (infidel)?' The guards ruthlessly gave over the people, and these [the villagers] killed them." A description of the ravine appears in Elias Venezis's novel/memoir *The Number 31328*, his story of being held as a work prisoner by the Turks. (He refers to the ravine as "Kirtik-Dere," which probably was its real name, since "Buyuk-Dere" actually means "Great Ravine.") "One morning they took us, some sixty slaves, for a small chore. It's a small distance out of Magnesia. Next to the track of the railroad ends a long ravine passing through Sipylus mountain. It's called Kirtik-Dere. In this ravine we reckoned that some forty thousand Christians were killed, from Smyrna and from Magnesia, male and female. In the early days of the disaster. The bodies decomposed during the winter, and the water coming down the gorge from above pushed the skeletons downwards. So they reached the road, the tracks."

297 *"Turks were proceeding with . . ."* Knauss, "Ship's Diary," Sept. 18, 1922.

297 *Jacob also witnessed* Jacob to D. Davis.

CHAPTER 25: "WE ARE CELEBRATING SMYRNA"

299 *Mustapha Kemal fell in love* Kinross, Mango, and Edib tell the story of Latife Hanum and Kemal more or less consistently, and I have drawn from each of them here. Turkish journalist Ipek Calislar, in her book *Madame Atatürk* (Saqi Publishing, 2013), tells a somewhat different story with a more modest turn. Calislar provides copious detail on Latife's family.

299 *He had established his* Edib, *Turkish Ordeal*, 384.

302 *"With a rose in her hair"* Translation assistance from Cigdem Aslan.

303 *On September 12, he* moved Edib, *Turkish Ordeal*, 385.

304 *He possessed, as a confidant said, an instinct for the harem.* Mango, 410.

304 *There was one sexual relationship* Mango, *Atatürk*, 388.

305 *On September 19, Latife put* together Edib, *Turkish Ordeal,* 386–389.

306 *Kemal continued to drink* Edib, *Turkish Ordeal,* 338, 389; Mango, *Atatürk,* 352; Kinross, *Atatürk,* 374, 375.

CHAPTER 26: JENNINGS AND THE HAND OF GOD

307 *It is difficult to know precisely* Jennings to D. Davis.

308 *He stood alone* D. Davis to Harrison.

309 A *tramp steamer* "Citta di Torino," Coasters and Other Ships Revived, 7Seas Vessels.com http://7seasvessels.com/citta-di-torino-1898-imo-0000000/.

310 *Elated, Jennings went* Jennings to D. Davis.

311 *"It was heartbreaking"* Abernathy, The Great Rescue, 7, KFYA.

311 *To make matters worse,* Powell, "Ship's Diary," Sept. 20, 1922.

311 *Powell told Jennings* Powell, "Ship's Diary," Sept. 20, 1922.

311 *Jennings and the* Constantinopoli Powell, "Ship's Diary," Sept. 21, 1922.

311 *"I could scarcely..."* Abernathy, "The Great Rescue," 6; Jennings to D. Davis.

312 *"There in that cabin . . ."* Abernathy, "The Great Rescue," 6.

312 *He was Ernesto Aliotti* http://levantineheritage.com/aliotti.htm. Thanks also to the Aliotti family for photos, background.

313 *It was a picturesque port* Jennings to D. Davis.

314 *At about 6* P.M. Powell, "Ship's Diary," Sept. 22, 1922.

315 *On the way back* Powell, "Ship's Diary," Sept. 22, 1922.

316 *On the same day,* Powell, "Ship's Diary," Sept. 22, 1922.

316 *Davis responded with* Powell, "Ship's Diary," Sept. 22, 1922. C. C. Davis to Bristol.

316 *In a cable, either late* Bristol to State Dept. (repeating Powell's message), Sept. 22, 1922. MLB.

317 *Late on the same day, under State Department pressure* Stanav (Bristol) to Edsall Sept. 20, 1922, MLB.

317 *The next afternoon, September 22* Powell, "Ship's Diary," Sept. 22, 1922.

317 *"Your commission is informed . . ."* Powell, "Ship's Diary," Sept. 22, 1922.

318 *The* Litchfield *arrived back* Powell, "Ship's Diary," Sept. 22, 1922.

CHAPTER 27: GARABED HATCHERIAN

319 Events in this chapter are drawn from Dr. Hatcherian's diary. Dr. Hatcherian's age is a matter of consequence throughout this section of

his diary. The nationalist army was arresting Christian men of military age, between eighteen and forty-five. So the error in Dr. Hatcherian's document, making him one year younger than his actual forty-six, was a possible matter of life or death.

324 *". . . Congratulations! You are going . . ."* Agia Sophia is the ancient seat of the Orthodox Church in Constantinople. It had been converted into a mosque.

CHAPTER 28: WASHINGTON FEELS THE PRESSURE

325 *On Friday, September 15* Bristol, Sept. 15, 1922. MLB.

325 *Immediately upon receiving* Bristol to State Dept., Sept. 18, 1922. MLB.

325 *Prentiss's reports of Turkish* "Smyrna in Ruins, Probably 2,000 Dead," *New York Times*, Sept. 16, 1922.

326 *The presiding bishop* "Fear for 300 Girls in Smyrna College," *New York Times*, Sept. 17, 1922.

326 *Henry Morgenthau and Oscar* "The Turkish Victory. New World Peril," *Times of London*, Sept. 12, 1922; "Calls on Lodge to Join England Against Turks," *New York Times*, Sept. 18, 1229; Oscar Strauss to President Harding, Telegram, Sept. 19, 1922. NA 767.68/361.

326 *The American Federation of Churches* Dulles to Phillips, Memorandum with Attachment, Sept. 25, 1922. NA 767.68/350.

326 *The conflict between religious* Hohner, *Prohibition and Politics*, 140.

327 *As Smyrna spiraled toward* Hohner, *Prohibition and Politics*, 139, 140.

328 *"Frankly," he had written* Harding to Hughes, July 24, 1922. NA 867.4016/607.

328 *The State Department had received* Caffrey to State Dept., Sept. 19, 1922. NA 868.48/207.

328 *ambassador to Britain, George Harvey* Harvey to State Dept., Sept. 15, 1922. NA 868.48.

328 *On September 15, Phillips sent* Phillips to Hughes, Sept. 18, 1922. NA 767.68333.

329 *"I have received,"* Bristol to State Dept., Sept. 13, 1922. MLB.

329 *He left the false impression* Bristol to State Dept., Sept. 20, 1922. ". . . having received information that refugees could be evacuated from Smyrna I directed our destroyers to assist in ever way possible."

330 *Bristol's first thought on* Bristol Diary, Sept. 19, 1922. MLB.

331 *Constantinople at the moment* "The Situation in Constantinople," Memorandum, Merrill to Bristol, Sept. 22, 1922. MLB.

331 *On the fifteenth, the same day,* 1922. Bristol Diary, Sept. 15, 16. MLB.

332 *By September 17, Sunday, Hepburn* Bristol Diary, Sept. 17, 1922. MLB.

332 *As Phillips in Washington* "Washington Prepares; But Has Received No Reply from Bristol on Plan for International Action," *New York Times,* Sept. 17, 1922.

332 *The Allied consuls in Smyrna* Allied High Commissioners Smyrna to Allied High Commissioners Constantinople (copy of cable), Sept. 19, 1922. MLB.

332 *Bristol finally responded* Bristol to State Dept., Sept 19, 1922. MLB.

333 *Phillips responded to Bristol* Phillips to Bristol, Sept. 19, 1922. MLB.

333 *Then Phillips sent Bristol* Phillips to Bristol Sept. 23, 1922. MLB.

333 *In the middle of this* Bristol to State Dept., Sept. 17, 1922; Edward Bell to Dulles, Dulles to Bell Sept. 19, 1922. NA 767.68/328.

333 *Bell was more than* David Kahn, "Edward Bell and His Zimmermann Telegram Memoranda," *Intelligence and National Security* 14, no. 3 (Autumn 1999).

334 *Finally on the nineteenth,* BWD, Sept. 19, 1922.

334 *Interestingly, British Admiral De Robeck* Halpern, *Mediterranean Fleet,* 315.

335 *The next day, Bristol* Bristol to State Dept., Sept. 20, 1922. MLB.

335 *On September 21, Phillips* Phillips to Bristol, Sept. 21, 1922. MLB.

335 *In the morning of the next day,* Bristol to State Dept., Sept. 21, 1922. MLB.

335 *As this diplomatic cat-and-mouse* BWD, Sept. 21, 1922. MLB.

336 *The next day, September 22* BWD, Sept. 2, 1922. MLB.

336 *In the meantime, Bristol* Bristol to State Dept., Sept. 22, 1922. MLB.

337 *On September 23,* State Dept. to Bristol, Sept. 23, 1922. MLB.

337 *Heizer had served* Hovannisian, *Remembrance and Denial,* 51, 52. Raymond Kevorkian, *The Armenian Genocide: A Complete History* (London: I. B. Taurus, 2011), 480.

CHAPTER 29: JENNINGS NEGOTIATES WITH A PRIME MINISTER

338 *Jennings had been as eager* Jennings to D. Davis.

338 *Powell agreed, and he* Jennings to D. Davis.

339 *"In accordance with orders"* Rhodes to Jennings, Sept. 22, 1922, MLB.

339 *To a person unfamiliar* Jennings's description of his meeting with Frangos is contained in his letter to D. Darius.

340 *The* Litchfield *arrived* Jennings to D. Davis.

340 *As Jennings had feared* Jennings to D. Davis.

340 *In its former life,* Henry Morgenthau, *Ambassador Morgenthau's Story,* 17.

341 *In the week after* Author interview with the late Admiral Ioannis Theophanides (grandson to the *Kilkis* commander and collector of Greek naval documents and histories) at his home in Athens. August 2011.

341 *Jennings and his committee* Jennings to D. Davis.

343 *Jennings composed a message* The text of the messages contained in this section come from the AKJP.

344 *"In this ultimatum, we showed them"* Jennings to Darius Davis, April 8, 1923

345 *Powell confirmed receipt* Powell, "Ship's Diary," Sept. 23, 1922.

346 *Theophanides immediately summoned* Abernathy, "The Great Rescue," 9.

346 *One of the merchant captains,* Abernathy, "The Great Rescue," 9. (Jennings, in his recollection, says he selected the *Proponidis,* but Powell's records indicate he arrived in the *Ismini.* I have chosen to use *Ismini* because Powell's record was contemporaneous.)

346 *Powell designated the* Lawrence Powell, "Ship's Diary," U.S. Edsall, Sept. 24, 1922; Lawrence to *Kilkis,* AKJP.

346 *"From quite a way out,"* Abernathy, "The Great Rescue," 10.

347 *"As we approached, . . ."* Abernathy, "The Great Rescue," 10.

CHAPTER 30: THE EVACUATION BEGINS

348 *The Greek merchant ships tied* Unless otherwise noted, this and subsequent references to Powell's actions and observations in this chapter come from his ship's diary, Sept. 13 through Sept. 30, 1922. MLB.

348 *The pier was made of rough* A sketch of the pier is saved in the logbook of the *Edsall.*

349 *The Turkish soldiers placed* Woodrooffe, *Naval Odyssey,* 128.

350 *An old woman* Esther Pohl Lovejoy, *Certain Samaritans* (New York: Macmillan Company, 1933), 154.

351 *At one point, a woman became hysterical* Woodrooffe, *Naval Odyssey,* 112.

351 *There was a quarter-acre wedge* Lovejoy, *Certain Samaritans,* 143.

352 *"The din was terrific,"* "Smyrna and the Dardenelles," 474.

352 *The relief committee had been relying* Biographical detail on Lovejoy: "Esther Pohl Lovejoy," Historical Collections & Archives, Oregon Health and Science University; Kimberly Jensen, "Esther Pohl Lovejoy and the Oregon Woman Suffrage Victory of 1912," *Oregon Historical Quarterly* 108, no. 3; "Lovejoy's City Work Shines in New Light," *Portland Tribune*, Oct. 19, 2012.

353 *"In a city with so large . . ."* Lovejoy, *Certain Samaritans*, 159.

353 *After he and the other older* Hatcherian, 38. 39

354 *"Outside the house where . . ."* Hatcherian, 40.

357 *Among the Americans on the pier* "Hasten Evacuation of Smyrna Hordes," *New York Times*, Sept. 27, 1922.

358 *Jennings sent a message* Powell, "Ship's Diary," Sept. 24–27, 1922.

360 *Five days earlier* Woodrooffe, *Naval Odyssey*, 110.

361 *Piraeus ships joined* Jennings to D. Darius.

362 *Going ashore to help* "Smyrna and the Dardanelles," 475.

363 *"One poor old thing sank . . ."* "Smyrna and the Dardanelles," 477.

363 *A British officer who* "Smyrna and the Dardenelles," 475.

364 *"In all the heat,"* Woodrooffe, *Naval Odyssey*, 119.

364 *"As family after family . . ."* Lovejoy, *Certain Samaritans*, 157.

365 *"They would be used . . ."* Woodrooffe, *Naval Odyssey*, 127.

365 *"With great difficulty . . ."* Lovejoy, *Certain Samaritans*, 160.

367 *The sounds of the night* Lovejoy, *Certain Samaritans*, 151.

367 *"A sudden wailing . . ."* Woodrooffe, *Naval Odyssey*, 128

367 *"There was a strange murmur . . ."* Lovejoy, *Certain Samaritans*, 149.

368 *The young men were responding* Lovejoy, *Certain Samaritans*, 166.

368 *While on the Quay* "Smyrna and the Dardanelles," 476.

CHAPTER 31: THE RHODES LETTER RESURFACES

369 *Caffrey did not receive a response* Caffrey to Bristol, Sept. 25, 1922. MLB.

370 *Bristol finally responded* Bristol to Caffrey at Athens, Sept. 25, 1922. MLB; "Bristol Relief Plan Denied in Washington," *New York Times*, Sept. 25, 1922.

370 *A cable Bristol had* Bristol to State Department, Sept. 25, 1922. MLB.

374 *The next day, September 27,* Powell to Bristol, Sept. 27, 1922. MLB.

374 *Later, much later, Bristol would extol Powell's action.*

CHAPTER 32: REVOLUTION

375 *On his return to Mytilene* Jennings to D. Davis.

375 *The revolt had begun* The story of the revolt is drawn largely from a detailed U.S. intelligence report. "The Role of the Greek Navy in the Revolution, G-2 Report," December 1930. MLB.

376 *On landing at Mytilene,* Jennings to D. Davis.

377 *"The island is facing starvation . . ."* Jennings's cable to Powell as quoted in *Edsall's* Ship's Diary, Sept. 26, 1922. MLB.

CHAPTER 33: BRITISH ASSISTANCE

378 *On Wednesday September 27* This and subsequent references to Powell's actions and observations in this chapter come from Powell, "Ship's Diary," USS *Edsall,* Sept. 27–Oct. 1, 1922. MLB.

379 *On Thursday, September 28* "Smyrna and the Dardanelles," 477.

380 *The commanding officer of the* MacLeish Powell, "Ship's Diary," Sept. 28, 1922. MLB.

380 *There were thousands,* Jennings to D. Davis.

380 *Jennings, in consultation* Jennings to D. Davis.

381 *On this day, Prentiss* Powell, "Ship's Diary," USS *Edsall,* Sept. 29, 1922. MLB. Lieutenant (j.g.) E. B. Perry and Prentiss traveled, under Turkish escort, to Alashehir, following in reverse the retreat route of the Greek army and path of the fleeing Ottoman Greek and Armenian refugees. Lieutenant Perry reported back, "All cities except Menem practically destroyed by burning. There are many stories of robbing, looting, rapine, and pillaging by the retreating Greek Army. Saw many wounded and dead Muslims passing through this country. Country absolutely desolate and all shelter and feed has been destroyed." Merrill to Bristol, October 3, 1922. MLB. In addition, Perry sent a report, via Bristol, to the *New York Herald.* "All refugees evacuated Smyrna . . . (Turkish authorities) great desire friendship Americans/wish business relations American born Americans/wonderful opportunity American business." Perry to STANAV, Oct. 3, 1922. MLB.

381 *On the following day,* Powell, "Ship's Diary," USS Edsall, Sept. 30, 1922. MLB.

381 *"Pieces of paper fluttered . . ."* Woodrooffe, *Naval Odyssey,* 130.

CHAPTER 34: AFTER SMYRNA

383 *The evacuation of Smyrna* Chater, "Trek," 568; Bierstadt, *Great Betrayal*, 53–68; Howland, "Greece and Her Refugees," *Foreign Affairs*, July 1926: "At the time of the Greek disaster in Asia Minor 800,000 Greeks fled across the Aegean Sea to the mainland and islands of Greece, most of them destitute, and 200,000 more with their household goods and flocks trekked out of eastern into western Thrace and Macedonia. With the latter arrivals expelled from Constantinople and the 'voluntary' migrants from Bulgaria, Greece has had to receive and to absorb into her national life some 1,400,000 persons, or about 26 percent of her former population of approximately 5,375,000 people."

383 *On that last day of September* This and subsequent passages in this chapter that describe the actions and observations on Powell come from Powell, "Ship's Diary," USS *Edsall*. MLB.

383 *At Vourla, Turkish soldiers marched* Powell, "Ship's Diary," Oct. 7, 1922.

383 *"The usual raping went on . . ."* Lieutenant H. A. Ellis, "Report of Movements," USS *MacLeish*, Sept. 30, 1922. MLB.

384 *On October 2, the* MacLeish "Report of Movements," USS *MacLeish*, Sept. 30, 1922. MLB.

384 *"Thousands more had only . . ."* Jaquith to Near East Relief, Oct. 2, 1922, NER Reports, Rockefeller Archive.

385 *At about the same time,* Jennings to D. Davis.

385 *At Mytilene, Jennings constituted* Jennings to D. Darius.

385 *People trekked over the mountains* Chater, "Trek," 559; "Report of Operations for Week Ending 3," Ship's Diary, Black Sea.

386 *President Harding convened* "Harding Appeals for the Near East," *New York Times*, Oct. 9, 1922.

386 *In November, Turkish authorities* Beirstadt, *Great Betrayal*, 55–59; "Report of Operations," Dec. 17, 1922, BWD.

386 *So, Jennings, who remained* Jennings to D. Davis. See also BWD, e.g., Dec. 22, 1922.

386 *At Rodosto, in Thrace* Jaquith to Near East Relief, Oct. 2, 1922. NER Reports, Rockefeller Archive

386 *"ADRIANOPLE—In a never-ending* Hemingway, *Dateline, Toronto.*

387 *The tidal wave of refugees* Bierstadt, *Great Betrayal*, 188–190, Howland, "Greece and Her Refugees," ff.

387 *A refugee ship from Samsun* Bruce Clark, *Twice a Stranger* (Cambridge: Harvard University Press, 2009), 142.

387 *"Many died on their journey . . ."* Post related his experiences in accounts that were published in many American newspapers. See, e.g., "State of Near East Refugees Held Appalling," *Eugene Daily Guard*, April 28, 1923.

388 *Powell had remained* Bristol Diary, Oct. 21, 1922. MLB.

388 *At the urging of his crew* "The Destroyer's Own Orphanage," *New York Times*, May 20, 1923.

388 *Jennings had become a central* Jennings and the continuing evacuation frequently appear in Bristol's diary and his commanders' ships' diaries from October 1922 through February 1923. See, e.g., Bristol Diary, Nov. 9, 1922: "I received a call from Mr. A. K. Jennings accompanied by Mr. D. J. Van Dommel. I had a very amusing talk with Mr. Jennings and found just a bundle of nerves and energy, as Captain Hepburn and the other officers had told me he was." Also, Dec. 22, 1922. BWD.

388 *In December, following a report* BWD, Dec. 4, 1923.

388 *Bristol quietly resisted* See, e.g., Bristol War Diary, Nov. 22, 1922: "I had a short conference with the staff, giving them in general in a few words the result of my conference with Cannellopoulos (Greek High Commissioner in Constantinople) and directed Hepburn to immediately send a strong dispatch to all our destroyers warning them against appearing in any way to escort or protect Greek ships going to Anatolian ports for refugees."

389 *Bristol's natural antagonisms* See, e.g., BWD, Oct. 7, 1922, MLB: "This conversation with Mr. Nansen convinced me more than ever that we are absolute fools to give our money to the League of Nations . . ."

389 *Faced with a mounting crisis* BWD, Nov. 29, 1922.

389 *The situation was reminiscent* "Report of Operations for Week Ending Dec. 3, 1922," BWD.

389 *The first refugee ship* BWD, Dec. 9, 1922.

389 *In May 1923, as the* "Powell, Halsey," NPRC.

389 *"I have wondered since . . ."* Abernathy, "The Great Rescue," 11.

390 *He went ashore* Amy Jennings to Schneider.

AFTERWORD

391 *Greece awarded Asa Jennings* "Headed Relief Work at Smyrna," *New York Times*, Jan. 28, 1933; Refat Bali, *The Saga of a Friendship: Asa Kent Jennings and the American Friends of Turkey* (Istanbul: Libra Publishing, 2009).

391 *An American policy of engagement* The debate over the proper relationship of the United States to the Republic of Turkey was bitter in the 1920s. An insight into the division comes in the correspondence of Ralph Harlow, one of the missionary teachers at International College. Harlow was outraged about Turkish brutality and spoke out after returning to the United States. His colleague and friend, Cass Reed, remained at the college and criticized Harlow for his outspokenness and called for his resignation. Others were dragged into the dispute, which mirrored the larger debate in the country. Harlow's papers are collected at the Amistad Research Center at Tulane University. See, e.g., Harlow to Cass Reed, Dec. 27, 1922.

391 *In 1933, on a visit* "Asa Jennings Dies on Charity Mission," *Washington Post*, Jan. 28, 1933.

391 *After returning to Washington,* "Powell, Halsey," NPRC.

392 *Mark Bristol served in* "Bristol, Mark," NPRC.

392 *Helen Bristol, ever the industrious* "Mrs. Bristol's famous hams," Photo and Description, Mobile Public Library.

392 *Dr. Hatcherian and his family* This information comes from Dr. Hatcherian's diary as well as the introduction and afterward by his granddaughter, Dora Sakayan.

392 *Theodora Gravou and her sisters* Information on Theodora and her sisters comes from the Amalion Orphanage in Athens as well as the author's interview (through a translator) with her daughter, Eleni, age eighty-four, in Piraeus in August 2012.

392 *Mustapha Kemal married* "Mustapha Kemal Divorced from Wife, G-2 Report," Constantinople, August 20, 1925. MLB. (It is a surprisingly detailed document that includes descriptions of the disputes in the marriage.)

392 *Arthur J. Hepburn rose to* "Hepburn, Arthur J.," NPRC.

393 *In January 1923, Greece and Turkey* "Lausanne Peace Treaty VI. Con-

vention Concerning the Exchange of Greek and Turkish Populations Signed at Lausanne, January 30, 1923," copy at Ministry of Foreign Affairs, Republic of Turkey. http://www.mfa.gov.tr/lausanne-peace-treaty.

393 *The United States and Turkey* "Hughes Gives Summary of Treaty," *New York Times*, August 7, 1923.

394 *The Turkish government continues* "Turkish PM offers condolences over 1915 Armenian massacre," *The Guardian*, April 23, 2014.

394 *In speaking of the Armenian deaths* "Obama Marks Genocide Without Saying the Word," *New York Times*, April 24, 2010.

SELECTED BIBLIOGRAPHY

PUBLISHED AND UNPUBLISHED PRIMARY SOURCES

U.S. National Archives

Record Group 59: General Records of State Department

Record Group 38: Office of the Chief of Naval Operations

Record Group 45: Naval Records Collection of the Office of Naval Records

Record Group 24: Records of Bureau of Naval Personnel

Record Group 165: Military Intelligence Division

Mark Lambert Bristol Papers, Library of Congress. (Contains Bristol's War Diary, "BWD.")

United States Department of State / Papers relating to the Foreign Relations of the United States, 1922: Greece and Turkey

National Personnel Records Center, St. Louis, Missouri

Asa K. Jennings Papers, Held by Roger Jennings, Queensbury, N.Y.

George Horton Papers, Georgetown University

Caleb Lawrence Papers, Held by Michael Smith, Orlando, Florida

Theophanides Family Collection, Athens

Gennadius Library, American School of Classical Studies, Athens

Harvard Law School Library. Charles Claflin Davis. Papers, 1917–1923

Houghton Library. Harvard College. American Board of Commissioners for Foreign Missions Archives

Asia Minor Research Centre, Athens

Kautz Family YMCA Archives, University of Minnesota

Izmir Municipal Archives, Izmir, Turkey

Halsey Powell Papers, Harrodsburg Historical Society, Harrodsburg, Kentucky

Gloucester County Historical Society, New Jersey

C. H. Drage Diaries, Imperial War Museum, London

Barry Domvile Diaries, Royal Maritime Museum, Greenwich

Refugees of Asia Minor Museum, Skala Loutron, Lesbos, Greece

Papers of the Council on Foreign Relations, Mudd Library, Princeton University

Aaron Stanton Merrill Papers, 1912–1950, Louis Round Wilson Special Collections, University of North Carolina, Chapel Hill, N.C.

Imperial War Museum, London

Letters Between President Cowling and Dana Getchell. Gould Library, Carleton College

Sara Corning Papers, Yarmouth County Museum & Archives, Yarmouth, Nova Scotia

INTERVIEWS

Nancy Horton, Athens. August 2011; December 2012

Ionannis Theophanides, Athens. August 2011, 2012; December 2012

Vasilly Skoulakis, Athens, August 2011

Eleni Kontou (Theordora's daughter), Piraeus, August 2012

BOOKS

Akçam, Taner. *From Empire to Republic: Turkish Nationalism and the Armenian Genocide.* London: Zed Books, 2004.

——. *A Shameful Act: The Armenian Genocide and the Question of Turkish Responsibility.* New York: Metropolitan Books, 2006.

Andrew, Prince (of Greece). *Towards Disaster; the Greek Army in Asia Minor in 1921.* Translated by Alice (consort of Prince Andrew of Greece). London: J. Murray, 1930.

Armstrong, H. C. Gray Wolf, *Mustafa Kemal: An Intimate Study of a Dictator.* New York: Minton, Balch &, 1933.

Augustinos, Gerasimos. *The Greeks of Asia Minor: Confession, Community, and Ethnicity in the Nineteenth Century.* Kent, OH: Kent State University Press, 1992.

Balakian, Peter. *The Burning Tigris: The Armenian Genocide and America's Response.* New York: HarperCollins, 2003.

Bali, Rıfat N. *A Survey of Some Social Conditions in Smyrna, Asia Minor, May 1921.* Istanbul: Libra Kitapçılık Ve Yayıncılık, 2009.

Barton, James L. *Story of Near East Relief (1915–1930): An Interpretation.* New York: Macmillan Company, 1930.

Beyru, Rauf. *19. Yüzyılda İzmir'de Yaşam.* Beyoğlu, İstanbul: Literatür, 2000.

Bierstadt, Edward Hale. *The Great Betrayal; a Survey of the Near East Problem.* New York: R. M. McBride & Co., 1924.

Bole, Robert D., and Edward H. Walton. *The Glassboro Story, 1779–1964.* York, PA: Maple Press, 1964.

The Book of Discipline of the United Methodist Church. Nashville, TN: United Methodist Publishing House, 2004.

Bradford, Ernle Dusgate Selby. *Mediterranean: Portrait of a Sea.* New York: Harcourt Brace Jovanovich, 1971.

Bradford, James C. *Admirals of the New Steel Navy: Makers of the American Naval Tradition, 1880–1930.* Annapolis, MD: Naval Institute Press, 1990.

Brandt, Allan M. *The Cigarette Century: The Rise, Fall, and Deadly Persistence of the Product That Defined America.* New York: Basic Books, 2007.

Brewer, David. *Greece, the Hidden Centuries: Turkish Rule from the Fall of Constantinople to Greek Independence.* London: I.B. Tauris, 2010.

Brown, Constantine. *The Coming of the Whirlwind.* Chicago: Regnery, 1964.

Bucerius, Sandra M., and Michael H. Tonry. *The Oxford Handbook of Ethnicity, Crime, and Immigration.* Oxford: Oxford University Press, 2013.

Çalılar, Ipek. *Madam Atatürk: The First Lady of Modern Turkey.* London: Saqi, 2013.

Carpenter, Teresa. *The Miss Stone Affair: America's First Modern Hostage Crisis.* New York: Simon & Schuster, 2003.

Cassimatis, Louis P. *American Influence in Greece, 1917–1929.* Kent, OH: Kent State University Press, 1988.

Churchill, Winston. *The World Crisis.* New York: Scribner, 1931.

Clark, Bruce. *Twice a Stranger: The Mass Expulsions That Forged Modern Greece and Turkey.* Cambridge, MA: Harvard University Press, 2006.

Cox, Howard. *The Global Cigarette: Origins and Evolution of British American Tobacco, 1880–1945.* New York: Oxford University Press, 2000.

Criss, Bilge. *American Turkish Encounters: Politics and Culture, 1830–1989.* Newcastle upon Tyne: Cambridge Scholars, 2011.

Davenport, Guiles. *Zaharoff, High Priest of War.* Boston: Lothrop, Lee and Shepard, 1934.

Dawn, C. Ernest. *From Ottomanism to Arabism: Essays on the Origins of Arab Nationalism.* Urbana: University of Illinois Press, 1973.

Deacon, Richard. *One Man's Wars: The Story of Charles Sweeny, Soldier of Fortune.* London: Barker, 1972.

Dean, John W., and Arthur M. Schlesinger Jr. *Warren G. Harding: The American Presidents Series: The 29th President, 1921–1923.* 1st ed. New York: Times Books, 2004.

DeNovo, John A. *American Interests and Policies in the Middle East, 1900–1939.* Minneapolis: University of Minnesota Press, 1963.

Deurs, George Van. *Wings for the Fleet; a Narrative of Naval Aviation's Early Development, 1910–1916.* Annapolis: U.S. Naval Institute, 1966.

Dobkin, Marjorie Housepian. *Smyrna 1922: The Destruction of a City.* London: Faber, 1972.

Domvile, Barry. *By and Large.* London: Hutchinson, 1936.

Dos Passos, John. *Orient Express.* New York and London: Harper & Bros., 1927.

Dunn, Robert. *World Alive: A Personal Story.* New York: Crown Publishers, 1956.

Eddy, David Brewer. *What Next in Turkey; Glimpses of the American Board's Work in the Near East.* Boston, MA: American Board, 1913.

Edib, Halide. *The Turkish Ordeal: Being the Further Memoirs of Halidè Edib.* New York: Century, 1928.

Engdahl, William. *A Century of War: Anglo-American Oil Politics and the New World Order.* London: Pluto Press, 2004.

Evans, Laurence. *United States Policy and the Partition of Turkey, 1914–1924.* Baltimore: Johns Hopkins Press, 1965.

The Exodus. Athens: The Asia Minor Research Centre, 1980. Published in Greek, the two volumes contain interviews conducted with Asia Minor survivors. In addition to containing testimony about the Greek-Turkish War and its aftermath, the interviews provide information about customs and daily life in Asia Minor.

Fensham, Florence Amanda, Mary I. Lyman, and H. B. Humphrey. *A Modern Crusade in the Turkish Empire.* Chicago: Woman's Board of Missions of the Interior, 1908.

Friedman, Isaiah. *British Miscalculations: The Rise of Muslim Nationalism, 1918–1925.* New Brunswick (N.J.): Transaction Publishers, 2012.

Froembgen, Hanns. *Kemal Ataturk; a Biography.* Translated by Kenneth Kirkness. New York: Hillman-Curl, 1937.

Gage, Nicholas. *Greek Fire: The Story of Maria Callas and Aristotle Onassis.* New York: Knopf, 2000.

Gingeras, Ryan. *Sorrowful Shores: Violence, Ethnicity, and the End of the Ottoman Empire, 1912–1923.* Oxford: Oxford University Press, 2009.

Goldman, Emma. *Living My Life.* Vol. 2. New York: Dover Publications, 1970.

Gondicas, Dimitri, and Charles Philip Issawi. *Ottoman Greeks in the Age of Nationalism: Politics, Economy, and Society in the Nineteenth Century.* Princeton, NJ: Darwin Press, 1999.

Gordon, Leland James. *American Relations with Turkey, 1830–1930: An Economic Interpretation.* Philadelphia: University of Pennsylvania Press, 1932.

Grabill, Joseph L. Protestant Diplomacy and the Near East: Missionary Influence on American Policy, 1810–1927. Minneapolis: University of Minnesota Press, 1971.

Greene, Joseph Kingsbury. *Leavening the Levant.* Boston: Pilgrim Press, 1916.

Guide to Greece, the Archipelago, Constantinople, the Coasts of Asia Minor, Crete and Cyprus; with Thirteen Maps and Thirty-three Plans. London: Macmillan and Co., 1908.

Halo, Thea. *Not Even My Name: From a Death March in Turkey to a New Home in America, a Young Girl's True Story of Genocide and Survival.* New York: Picador USA, 2000.

Halpern, Paul G. *The Mediterranean Fleet, 1919–1929.* Burlington, VT: Ashgate for the Navy Records Society, 2011.

Handbook for Travellers in Turkey in Asia: Including Constantinople, the Bosphorus, Plain of Troy, Isles of Cyprus, Rhodes, &c., Smyrna, Ephesus, and the Routes to Persia, Bagdad, Moosool, &c.: With General Hints for Travellers in Turkey, Vocabularies &c. London: J. Murray, 1878.

Harris, George and Criss, *Nur Bilge. Studies in Ataturk's Turkey.* Leiden: Brill, 2009.

Hart, Jerome Alfred. *A Levantine Log-book.* New York: Longmans, Green, and Co., 1905.

Hartunian, Abraham H. *Neither to Laugh Nor to Weep: A Memoir of the Armenian Genocide.* Boston: Beacon Press, 1968.

Hatzidimitriou, Constantine G. *American Accounts Documenting the De-*

struction of Smyrna by the Kemalist Turkish Forces: September 1922. New York: Aristide D. Caratzas, Melissa International, 2005.

Hemingway, Ernest. *Dateline, Toronto: The Complete Toronto Star Dispatches, 1920–1924*. Edited by William White. New York: Charles Scribner's Sons, 1985.

———. *In Our Time*. New York: Boni & Liveright, 1925.

Heraclides, Alexis. *The Essence of the Greek-Turkish Rivalry: National Narrative and Identity*. London: London School of Economics and Political Science, Hellenic Observatory, 2011.

Herrin, Judith. *Byzantium: The Surprising Life of a Medieval Empire*. Princeton: Princeton University Press, 2007.

History of the Chicago Tribune; Published in Commemoration of Its Seventy-fifth Birthday, June Tenth, Nineteen Hundred and Twenty-two. Chicago: Chicago Tribune, 1922.

History of the Y.M.C.A. in the Le Mans Area. Portland, OR: Arcady Press and Mail Advertising, 1920.

Hobhouse, John Cam. *Travels in Albania, and Other Provinces of Turkey in 1809 & 1810*. London: J. Murray, 1855.

Hofmann, Tessa, Matthias Bjørnlund, and Vasileios Meichanetsidis. *The Genocide of the Ottoman Greeks: Studies on the State-Sponsored Campaign of Extermination of the Christians of Asia Minor, 1912–1922 and Its Aftermath: History, Law, Memory*. New York: Aristide D. Caratzas, 2011.

Hohner, Robert A. *Prohibition and Politics: The Life of Bishop James Cannon, Jr*. Columbia: University of South Carolina Press, 1999.

Horton, George. *The Blight of Asia: An Account of the Systematic Extermination of Christian Populations by Mohammedans and of the Culpability of Certain Great Powers; with a True Story of the Burning of Smyrna*. Indianapolis: Bobbs-Merrill, 1926.

———. *Like Another Helen, A Fair Insurgent*. London: Ward, Lock, 1906.

———. *Recollections Grave and Gay: The Story of a Mediterranean Consul*. Indianapolis: Bobbs-Merrill, 1927.

Hovannisian, Richard G., ed. *The Armenian Genocide in Perspective*. New Brunswick. N.J.: Transaction Books, 1986.

———. *Remembrance and Denial: The Case of the Armenian Genocide*. Detroit: Wayne State University Press, 1998.

Ihrig, Stefan. *Atatürk in the Nazi Imagination*. Cambridge: Harvard University Press, 2014.

Jakle, John A., and Keith A. Sculle. *The Gas Station in America*. Baltimore: Johns Hopkins University Press, 1994.

Jenkins, Roy. *The Chancellors*. London: Macmillan, 1998.

Johnson, Clarence Richard. *Constantinople To-day' Or, The Pathfinder Survey of Constantinople: A Study in Oriental Social Life*. New York: Macmillan, 1922.

Johnson, E. Polk. *A History of Kentucky and Kentuckians: The Leaders and Representative Men in Commerce, Industry and Modern Activities*. Chicago: Lewis Pub., 1912.

Karsten, Peter. *The Naval Aristocracy: The Golden Age of Annapolis and the Emergence of Modern American Navalism*. New York: Free Press, 1972.

Kehn, Donald M. *A Blue Sea of Blood: Deciphering the Mysterious Fate of the USS Edsall*. Minneapolis: MBI, 2008.

Kennedy, Paul M. *The Realities behind Diplomacy: Background Influences on British External Policy, 1865–1980*. London: Allen & Unwin in Association with Fontana Books, 1981.

Kinross, Patrick Balfour. *Atatürk: A Biography of Mustafa Kemal, Father of Modern Turkey*. New York: Quill/Morrow, 1992.

Kinzer, Stephen. *Reset: Iran, Turkey, and America's Future*. New York: Times Books, 2010.

Kitromilides, Paschalis. *Smyrnē: Hē Mētropolē Tou Mikrasiatikou Hellēnismou = Smyrna: Metropolis of the Asia Minor Greeks*. Athēna: Ephesos, 2004.

Knapp, Grace H., Grisell M. McLaren, and Myrtle O. Shane. *The Tragedy of Bitlis*. New York: Fleming H. Revell Company, 1919.

Kocatürk, Utkan. *Atatürk Ve Türkiye Cumhuriyeti Tarihi Kronolojisi: 1918–1938*. Ankara: Türk Tarih Kurumu, 1983.

Kontogiorgi, Elisabeth. *Population Exchange in Greek Macedonia the Rural Settlement of Refugees 1922–1930*. Oxford: Clarendon Press, 2006.

Laurie, Thomas. *Historical Sketch of the Syria Mission*. New York: John A. Gray, 1862.

Leuchtenburg, William E. *The Perils of Prosperity, 1914–32*. Chicago: University of Chicago Press, 1958.

Lewis, Bernard. *The Emergence of Modern Turkey*. London, NY: Oxford University Press, 1961.

Lovejoy, Esther Pohl. *Certain Samaritans*. New York: Macmillan Company, 1933.

Macmillan, Margaret. *War That Ended Peace: The Road to 1914*. Toronto: Penguin Books Canada, 2014.

Mango, Andrew. *Atatürk: The Biography of the Founder of Modern Turkey*. Woodstock, NY: Overlook Press, 2000.

Mansel, Philip. *Levant: Splendour and Catastrophe on the Mediterranean*. New Haven: Yale University Press, 2011.

Mazower, Mark. *Salonica, City of Ghosts: Christians, Muslims, and Jews, 1430–1950*. New York: Alfred A. Knopf, 2005.

McCarthy, Justin. *Death and Exile: The Ethnic Cleansing of Ottoman Muslims, 1821–1922*. Princeton, NJ: Darwin Press, 1995.

Mears, Eliot Grinnell. *Modern Turkey; a Politico-economic Interpretation, 1908–1923 Inclusive, with Selected Chapters by Representative Authorities*. New York: Macmillan, 1924.

Mercer County, Kentucky: History and Biographies. Signal Mountain, TN: Mountain Press, 2005.

Metz, Helen Chapin. *Turkey, a Country Study*. Washington, DC: Federal Research Division, Library of Congress, 1996.

Milton, Giles. *Paradise Lost Smyrna 1922*. New York: Basic Books, 2010.

Morgenthau, Henry. *Ambassador Morgenthau's Story: A Personal Account of the Armenian Genocide*. New York: Cosimo, 2008.

——. *I Was Sent to Athens*. Garden City, NY: Doubleday, Doran &, 1929.

Morley, Bertha B. *Marsovan 1915: The Diaries of Bertha B. Morley*. Edited by Hilmar Kaiser. Ann Arbor, MI: Gomidas Institute, 2000.

Mowat, Charles Loch. *Britain between the Wars, 1918–1940*. Chicago: University of Chicago Press, 1955.

Naimark, Norman M. *Fires of Hatred: Ethnic Cleansing in Twentieth-Century Europe*. Cambridge, MA: Harvard University Press, 2001.

Nash, Gerald D. *United States Oil Policy, 1890–1964; Business and Government in Twentieth Century America*. Pittsburgh, PA: University of Pittsburgh Press, 1968.

Oeconomos, Lysimachos. *The Martyrdom of Smyrna and Eastern Christen-*

dom: *A File of Overwhelming Evidence, Denouncing the Misdeeds of the Turks in Asia Minor and Showing Their Responsibility for the Horrors of Smyrna.* London: G. Allen & Unwin, 1922.

———. *The Tragedy of the Christian Near East.* London: Anglo-Hellenic League, 1923.

Ozakman, Turgut. *Su Cilgin Turkler.* Ankara: Bilgi, 2007.

Papoutsy, Christos. *Ships of Mercy: The True Story of the Rescue of the Greeks: Smyrna, September 1922.* Portsmouth, NH: Peter E. Randall, 2008.

Payaslian, Simon. *United States Policy toward the Armenian Question and the Armenian Genocide.* New York: Palgrave Macmillan, 2005.

Peet, William Wheelock, and Louise Jenison Peet. *No Less Honor.* Chattanooga, TN: Priv. Print., 1939.

Pelt, Mogens. *Tobacco, Arms, and Politics: Greece and Germany from World Crisis to World War, 1929–41.* Copenhagen: Museum Tusculanum Press, University of Copenhagen, 1998.

Perlmutter, Philip. *Legacy of Hate: A Short History of Ethnic, Religious, and Racial Prejudice in America.* Armonk, NY: M. E. Sharpe, 1999.

Peterson, Merrill D. *"Starving Armenians": America and the Armenian Genocide, 1915–1930 and After.* Charlottesville: University of Virginia Press, 2004.

Phillips, William. *Ventures in Diplomacy.* Boston: Beacon Press, 1953.

Porterfield, Amanda. *Mary Lyon and the Mount Holyoke Missionaries.* New York: Oxford University Press, 1997.

Power, Samantha. *A Problem from Hell: America and the Age of Genocide.* New York: Basic Books, 2002.

Reed, Cass Arthur. *Problems of American Education in the Near East.* Cambridge, 1921.

Register of the Department of State. Washington: Govt. Printing Office, 1922.

Reynolds, Clark G. *Famous American Admirals.* New York: Van Nostrand Reinhold, 1978.

———. *On the Warpath in the Pacific: Admiral Jocko Clark and the Fast Carriers.* Annapolis, MD: Naval Institute Press, 2005.

Robenalt, James D. *The Harding Affair: Love and Espionage during the Great War.* New York: Palgrave Macmillan, 2009.

Roeding, George Christian. *The Smyrna Fig at Home and Abroad: A Treatise on Practical Smyrna Fig Culture, Together with an Account of the Introduction of the Wild or Capri Fig, and the Establishment of the Fig Wasp (Blasiophaga Grossorum) in America*. Fresno, CA: Author, 1903.

Rose, I. A. *Conservatism and Foreign Policy during the Lloyd George Coalition, 1918–1922*. London: Frank Cass, 1999.

Sakayan, Dora. *An Armenian Doctor in Turkey: Garabed Hatcherian: My Smyrna Ordeal of 1922*. Montreal: Arod Books, 1997.

Secretary's Fourth Report, Harvard College, Class of 1916. Cambridge, MA: Crimson Printing Company, 1916.

Shenk, Robert. *America's Black Sea Fleet: The U.S. Navy amidst War and Revolution, 1919–1923*. Annapolis, MD: Naval Institute Press, 2012.

———, ed. *Playships of the World: The Naval Diaries of Admiral Dan Gallery, 1920–1924*. Columbia: University of South Carolina Press, 2008.

Singer, Amy, Christoph K. Neumann, and Selçuk Ak°in Somel, eds. *Untold Histories of the Middle East Recovering Voices from the 19th and 20th Centuries*. Abingdon, Oxon: Routledge, 2011.

Smith, Michael Llewellyn. *Ionian Vision: Greece in Asia Minor, 1919–1922*. New York: St. Martin's Press, 1973.

Smyrna Conflagration, 13th–16th September, 1922: In the High Court of Justice, King's Bench Division, and Court of Appeal: American Tobacco Company Incorporated v. Guardian Assurance Company Ltd., and Socieìteì Anonyme Des Tabacs D'Orient Et D'Outre Mer v. Alliance Assurance Company Ltd. . . . 1- December . . . 1924 and 22nd April to 1st May, 1925. London: Printed by Wyman, Privately Printed.

Southon, Arthur Eustace, and R. W. Abernethy. *The Spirit of the Game: A Quest*. Edited by Basil Mathews. London: Hodder and Stoughton, 1926.

Spanos, Peter James. *Fear and Survival*. Cape Elizabeth, Maine: Privately printed, 1989. Spanos, born in Phocaea and present for the fire, told his story to his daughter, Christin Kourapis. He was taken aboard the Winona.

Srodes, James. *Allen Dulles: Master of Spies*. Washington, DC: Regnery, 1999.

Steuer, Kenneth. *Pursuit of an "Unparalleled Opportunity": The American YMCA and Prisoner-of-war Diplomacy among the Central Power Nations during World War I, 1914–1923.* New York: Columbia University Press, 2009.

Taylor, A. J. P. *English History: 1914–1945.* New York: Oxford University Press, 1965.

Totten, Samuel. *Plight and Fate of Women During and Following Genocide.* New Brunswick: Transaction Publishers, 2009.

Trading with the Near East; Present Conditions and Future Prospects. New York, Etc.: Guaranty Trust of New York, 1920.

Tusan, Michelle Elizabeth. *Smyrna's Ashes: Humanitarianism, Genocide, and the Birth of the Middle East.* Oakland, CA: Global, Area, and International Archive, 2012.

Volkan, Vamik D., and Norman Itzkowitz. *The Immortal Atatürk: A Psychobiography.* Chicago: University of Chicago Press, 1984.

Williams, William Appleman. *The Tragedy of American Diplomacy.* New York: Dell, 1962.

Winter, J. M. *America and the Armenian Genocide of 1915.* New York: Cambridge University Press, 2003.

Woodrooffe, Thomas. *Naval Odyssey.* New York: Sheridan House, 1938.

Wrigley, Chris. *Winston Churchill: A Biographical Companion.* Santa Barbara, CA: ABC-CLIO, 2002.

Wynn, Antony. *Three Camels to Smyrna: Times of War and Peace in Turkey, Persia, India, Afghanistan & Nepal, 1907–1986: The Story of the Oriental Carpet Manufacturers Company.* London: Hali, 2008.

Yeğin, Uğur, and Uğur Göktaş. *Evvel Zaman İçinde—I'zmir: Uğur Göktaş, Koleksiyonu'ndan.* İstanbul: İzmir Ticaret Odası, 2009.

Yergin, Daniel. *The Prize: The Epic Quest for Oil, Money, & Power.* New York: Free Press, 2009.

Young Men's Christian Associations. Le Mans Region. *History of the Y.M.C.A. in the Le Mans Area.* Portland, OR: Arcady Press and Mail Advertising, 1920.

ARTICLES AND WEBSITES

Anders, James M. "The Relation of Typhoid Fever to Tuberculosis." *American Journal of the Medical Sciences* 127, no. 5 (1904): 776–86.

"The 'Angel of Discord' at Smyrna." *The Literary Digest,* October 7, 1922, 32–34.

Beers, Henry P. "United States Naval Detachment in Turkish Waters, 1919–24." *Military Affairs* 7, no. 4 (December 1, 1943): 209–20.

Bell-Fialkoff, Andrew. "A Brief History of Ethnic Cleansing." *Foreign Affairs* 72, no. 3 (July 01, 1993): 110–21.

Bolleson, George, "Report on Smyrna," Prepared for the Secretary of War, London, 1856. Collection of the Gennadius Library, The American School of Classical Studies, Athens.

Borio, Gene. "Twentieth Century—The Rise of the Cigarette 1900–1950: Growing Pains." *Tobacco TimeLine.* January 31, 1998.

Bryson, Thomas A. "Admiral Mark L. Bristol, an Open-Door Diplomat in Turkey." *International Journal of Middle East Studies* 5, no. 4 (September 1, 1974): 450–67.

Butman, Carl H. "Secret Lines of Radio Communication." *Radio World* 2 (1922): 18.

Champion, Brian. "Spies (Look) Like Us: The Early Use of Business and Civilian Covers in Covert Operations." *International Journal of Intelligence and Counter Intelligence* 21, no. 3 (2008).

Cohen, S. A. "The Genesis of the British Campaign in Mesopotamia," 1914, *Middle Eastern Studies* 12, no. 2 (May 1976).

Craig, Lee A. "Public Sector Pensions in the United States." EHnet. http://eh.net/encyclopedia/public-sector-pensions-in-the-united-states/.

Dadrian, Vahakn N. "The Documentation of the World War I Armenian Massacres in the Proceedings of the Turkish Military Tribunal." *International Journal of Middle East Studies* 23, no. 4 (1991): 549–76. doi:10.1017/S0020743800023412.

Daniel, Robert L. "The Armenian Question and American-Turkish Relations, 1914–1927." *The Mississippi Valley Historical Review* 46, no. 2 (September 1, 1959): 252–75.

Fuhrmann, Malte. "Down and Out on the Quays of Izmir: 'European' Musicians, Innkeepers, and Prostitutes in the Ottoman Port-cities." *Mediterranean Historical Review* 24, no. 2 (2009): 169–85.

Gardner, Nicholas, "Charles Townshend's Advance on Baghdad: The British Offensive in Mesopotamia, September–November 1915," *War in History* 20, no. 2 (April 2013).

"The Genocide of the Ottoman Greeks: 1914-1923," Center for the Study of Genocide and Human Rights, Rutgers University (Newark), http://www.

ncas.rutgers.edu/center-study-genocide-conflict-resolution-and-human-rights/genocide-ottoman-greeks-1914-1923.

Giannuli, Dimitra. "Greeks or 'Strangers at Home': The Experiences of Ottoman Greek Refugees during Their Exodus to Greece, 1922–1923." *Journal of Modern Greek Studies* 13, no. 2 (1995): 271–87.

Ginio, Eyal. "Book Review." Review of Hervé Georgelin, *La Fin De Smyrne: Du Cosmopolitisme aux nationalismes*, CNRS *Histoire* (Paris: CNRS Editions, 2005), p. 254.

Hellman, Geoffrey T. "Soldier of Fortune." *The New Yorker*, December 21, 1940, 10–11.

Heraclides, Alexis. "The Essence of the Greek-Turkish Rivalry: National Narrative and Identity." The London School of Economics and Political Science. GreeSE Paper No.51, Hellenic Observatory Papers on Greece and Southeast Europe. October 2011. http://eprints.lse.ac.uk/45693/1/GreeSE%20No51.pdf.

"Heros in Symra." *The Missionary Review* 45 (1922): 918.

Hirt, Joe I. "An American Girl Who Gave Herself for the Armenians." *Luther League Review: 1922–1924*, 35–36 (1922): 29.

Hovannisian, Richard G. "Joseph L. Grabill, Protestant Diplomacy and the Near East: Missionary Influence on American Policy, 1810–1927." *International Journal of Middle East Studies* 4, no. 3 (1973): 369–70.

Howland, Charles P. "Greece and Her Refugees." *Foreign Affairs*, July 1926.

Jensen, Kimberly. " 'Neither Head nor Tail to the Campaign': Esther Pohl Lovejoy and the Oregon Woman Suffrage Victory of 1912." *Oregon Historical Quarterly* 108, no. 3 (October 1, 2007): 350–83.

Jensen, Peter Kincaid. "The Greco-Turkish War, 1920–1922." *International Journal of Middle East Studies* 10, no. 4 (1979): 553–65.

Kasaba, Resat. *Greek and Turkish Nationalism in Formation: Western Anatolia 1919–1922*, Robert Schuman Centre for Advanced Studies (RSCAS). European University Institute. Cadmus. November 24, 2003. http://cadmus.eui.eu/handle/1814/1775?show=full.

Kirli, B. Kolluoglu. "Forgetting the Smyrna Fire." *History Workshop Journal* 60, no. 1 (2005): 25–44.

Koglin, Daniel. "Marginality—A Key Concept in Understanding the Resurgence of Rebetiko in Turkey." *Music and Politics* II, no. 1 (2008).

Levene, Mark. "Why Is the Twentieth Century the Century of Genocide?" *Journal of World History* 11, no. 2 (2000): 305–36.

Lippe, John M Vander. "The 'Other' Treaty of Lausanne: The American Public and Official Debate on Turkish–American Relations." *Turkish Yearbook of International Relations* 23 (1993): 65–78.

Lowry, Heath. "Turkish History: On Whose Sources Will It Be Based? A Case Study on the Burning of Izmir." *Journal of Ottoman Studies* IX (1989): 1–27.

Marvin, George. "The Greek Military Debacle." Asia The American Magazine on the Orient (Dec. 1922) 957, 1006.

Neyzi, Leyla. "Remembering Smyrna/Izmir: Shared History, Shared Trauma." *History and Memory* 20, no. 2, Special Issue: *Remembering and Forgetting on Europe's Southern Periphery* (October 1, 2008): 106–27.

Obenzinger, Hilton. "Holy Land Narrative and American Covenant: Levi Parsons, Pliny Fisk and the Palestine Mission." *Religion & Literature* 35, no. 2/3 (July 1, 2003): 241–67.

"Petroleum and Sea Power." American Oil & Gas History. http://aoghs.org/petroleum-in-war/petroleum-and-sea-power/.

Prentiss, Mark O. "No Experience Necessary." *The Magazine of Business* 37 (1920): 494–96.

Reed, Cass A. "After the War in Smyrna." *The Missionary Herald at Home and Abroad* 115 (May 1919): 186–87.

Santiago, M. "Culture Clash: Foreign Oil and Indigenous People in Northern Veracruz, Mexico, 1900–1921." *Journal of American History* 99, no. 1 (June 22, 2012): 62–71. doi:10.1093/jahist/jas114.

Smith, George Otis. "Where the World Gets Its Oil but Where Will Our Children Get It When American Wells Cease to Flow?" *National Geographic Magazine*, February 1920, 181–202.

"Smyrna." *The Orient* 9.10 (1922): 88–94.

"Smyrna and After, Part I," *Naval Review,* Naval Society, London, 1923, Vol. 3, 358.

"Smyrna and After, Part II," *Naval Review,* Naval Society, London, 1923, Vol. 4, 737.

"Smyrna and After, Part III," *Naval Review,* Naval Society, London, 1924, Vol. 1, 157.

"Smyrna and After, Part IV, V," *Naval Review,* Naval Society, London, 1924, Vol. 2, 355.

"Smyrna and the Dardanelles," *Naval Review*, Naval Society, London, 1935, Vol. 3, 467.

"Smyrna Under the Greco-Turkish Terror." Literary Digest, New York. Oct. 28, 1922.

Smyrnelis, Marie-Carmen, ed. Smyrne, La Ville Oubliée? 1830–1930: Mémoires D'un Grand Port Ottoman, Collection Mémoires/Villes (Paris: Éditions Autrement, 2006), p. 252. *International Journal of Middle East Studies* 41, no. 1 (February 2009): 133–36.

Sorkhabi, Rasoul, Ph.D. "The Centenary of the First Oil Well in the Middle East." *GEO ExPro Magazine* Vol. 5, no. 5 (2008).

Stivers, William. "International Politics and Iraqi Oil, 1918–1928: A Study in Anglo-American Diplomacy." *Business History Review* 55, no. 4 (1981): 517.

T.M.J. "With the Greeks in Asia Minor." *Blackwood's Magazine*, September 1922, 292–304.

"Trade of Smyrna," Dipolmatic and Consular Reports—Turkey, Report for the Year 1911–1912, London, 1912. From the collection of the Gennadius Library, The American School of Classical Studies, Athens.

White, Ann. "Counting the Cost of Faith. America's Early Female Missionaries." *Church History* 57, no. 1 (March 1988): 19–30.

Woodhouse, Henry. "American Oil Claims in Turkey." *Current History* 15 (1922): 953–59.

DISSERTATIONS

Buzanski, Peter Michsel. "Admiral Mark L. Bristol and Turkish-American Relations, 1919–1922." Ph.D. diss., University of California, 1960.

Goodman, Robert Carey. "The Role of the Tobacco Trade in Turkish-American Relations, 1923–29." Master's thesis, University of Richmond, 1988. Accessed November 28, 2014. http://scholarship.richmond.edu/cgi/viewcontent.cgi?article=1524&context=masters-theses.

Kenjar, Kevin. "The Ineffable State of Transcendental Ecstasy: Kefi, Rebetiko and Sufi Mysticism," Master's thesis, University of Cincinnati, 2007. Accessed November 28, 2014. http://classics.uc.edu/~campbell/Kenjar/Ecstasy.pdf.

Lenser, Samuel David. "Between the Great Idea and Kemalism: The YMCA at Izmir in the 1920s." Master's thesis, Boise State University, 2010. Ac-

cessed November 27, 2014. http://scholarworks.boisestate.edu/cgi/view
content.cgi?article=1135&context=td.

Shelton, Elizabeth W. "Faith, Freedom, and Flag: The Influence of American Missionaries in Turkey on Foreign Affairs, 1830–1880." Master's
thesis, Georgetown University Washington, DC, 2011. https://repository.
library.georgetown.edu/bitstream/handle/10822/553389/sheltonEliza
beth.pdf?sequence=1.

Solomonidis, Victoria. "Greece in Asia Minor: The Greek Administration of
the Vilayet of Aidin, 1919–1922." Ph.D. diss., University of London, 1984.

Wadle, Ryan David. "'The Fourth Dimension of Naval Tactics': The U.S.
Navy and Public Relations, 1919–1939." Ph.D. diss., Texas A&M University, 2011. http://hdl.handle.net/1969.1/ETD-TAMU-2011-05-9166.

NEWSPAPERS

Chicago Tribune
New York Times
Portland (Oregon) *Tribune*
Times of London
Other British newspapers as quoted in secondary sources.

GOVERNMENT DOCUMENTS AND WEBSITES

Naval Investigation Hearings before the Subcommittee of the Committee on
Naval Affairs, United States Senate, Sixty-sixth Congress, Second Ses-
sion . . . Printed for the Use of the Committee on Naval Affairs. Vol. 2.
Washington: U.S. Government Printing Office, 1921.

U.S. Congress. Senate. Committee on Finance. Hearings Before the Committee on Finance, United States Senate, Sixty-seventh Congress, First
Session, on the Proposed Tariff Act of 1921 (H. R. 7456) . . . 1922: American Valuation. 67th Cong., 1st sess. S. Doc. H. R. 7456. Vol. 7. Washington, D.C.: U.S. Government Printing Office, 1922.

U.S. Congress. Senate. Committee on Foreign Relations. Subcommittee on
Multinational Corporations. Multinational Corporations and United
States Foreign Policy: Hearings, Ninety-third Congress [Ninety-fourth
Congress, Second Session], Part 8. 94th Cong., 2d sess. S. Doc. Wash-
ington, DC: U.S. Government Printing Office, 1975.

U.S. Dept of State Office of the Historian. MILESTONES: 1921–1936.

A former Nieman fellow and editor in residence at Harvard University, LOU URENECK is a professor of journalism at Boston University. He was a deputy managing editor at the *Philadelphia Inquirer* and editor of the *Portland (Maine) Press Herald*. Ureneck's writing has appeared in numerous publications including the *New York Times*, the *International Herald Tribune*, *Boston Globe*, and *Field & Stream*. A former Fulbright Fellow, Ureneck is the author of *Backcast*, which won the National Outdoor Book Award for literary merit, and *Cabin—Two Brothers, a Dream, and Five Acres in Maine*.